Portfolio Practices:

Lessons from Schools,

Districts, and States

Portfolio Practices:

Lessons from Schools,

Districts, and States

Sandra Murphy and Terry Underwood

Christopher-Gordon Publishers
Norwood, Massachusetts

Copyright Acknowledgment

Christopher-Gordon Publishers, Inc.
1502 Providence Highway, Suite #12
Norwood, MA 02062
Tel: 800-934-8322

Printed in the United States of America

10 9 8 7 6 5 4 3 2 1   04 03 02 01 00

Library of Congress Catalog Card Number: 00-102373
ISBN: 1-929024-18-5

For our children,
Christine, John, and Bill Murphy,
and Karen Underwood

Table of Contents

Preface

At all levels of education, and in all disciplines, there has been an explosion of development work in portfolio assessment. In some cases this work has involved creating new approaches; in other circumstances, portfolio development may simply mean a subtle reshaping or a return to old ways. Like chameleons, portfolios seem to take on the characteristics of their surroundings. Because they reflect curricula, and the web of beliefs, goals, and assumptions which undergird education, portfolio programs are less similar than one might expect.

In fact, approaches to portfolio assessment vary widely in ways that may seem quite practical but that in reality are theoretically and educationally important. In some projects, for instance, students are encouraged to choose what their portfolios will contain. In others, teachers assume that responsibility. In some projects, students submit only final versions of work; in others they submit drafts, notes, and other evidence of the processes they engaged in as they produced the work. In some projects, students are asked to reflect on their work, their learning, and/or their processes for producing work. In others, not. All of these basic and practical decisions reflect at some level the priorities we have for children—whether we want them to become life-long, self-regulated learners, whether we want them to be competitive in a global environment, whether we want them to master a body of knowledge or simply to carry on the traditions of our world.

To some extent, these differences may also exist because portfolios are used for different purposes. Within the classroom, portfolios are often used to invite students to analyze and evaluate their own learning, or to serve as evidence for grades. Yet increasingly, portfolios are also being used to satisfy needs beyond the classroom. They are being used for programmatic purposes such as influencing classroom practice—leading the curriculum; for holding schools and teachers accountable; for providing information useful in program evaluation; and for providing evidence useful in making various kinds of decisions with stakes attached for individuals or schools. In these cases, program administrators may be more concerned with the need to obtain particular kinds of information, or with technical adequacy—reliability and generalizability—than they are with the effects of portfolios on learning.

When portfolios move beyond classroom walls, they often serve multiple agendas. In these circumstances portfolio purposes range along a continuum—from those of individual students using portfolios to learn in the classroom and to represent themselves to others, at one end, to government agencies using the information from portfolios to make decisions about policy and the distribution of resources at the other. The perspectives of educators who work in different contexts along this continuum may differ and their agendas may compete. For instance, teachers of writing who see student ownership and learning as the most important elements of portfolio practice may find themselves at odds with those who see a need for controlling portfolio contents for the purpose of responsible measurement or for influencing curricula in the schools. For these reasons, it is all the more important to bring underlying assumptions and goals into the open for discussion and debate.

Our intention in writing this book has been to provide some real-world examples of portfolios that have been used for programmatic purposes and, drawing upon those examples, to create a framework for thinking about educational systems and the roles that portfolios might play in them. In particular, we hope to encourage a broadening of the discourse in the development stages of portfolio projects so that the interests and perspectives of all participants can be better taken into account.

The book contains 10 chapters, in addition to this preface. The first chapter provides definitions for important concepts and a brief historical sketch of the growth of interest in portfolios as an alternative to other forms of assessment. Each of the next 8 chapters provides a practical history of a particular contemporary portfolio program that serves to illustrate a particular set of issues.

Within each of these chapters we follow a similar format, providing information about the context for the portfolio system, the purposes for which it was intended, and the system's design. The description of the context for the system addresses programmatic elements that may influence an assessment's impact such as: 1) the stakes attached (What are the purposes of the assessment? What decisions and consequences are associated with it?); 2) the approach taken to develop the system (e.g. How were design decisions made?); 3) the source of authority and degree of control (Was the assessment locally determined or mandated by a district, state or federal agency? Is participation voluntary, semi-voluntary or mandatory?); and 4) the approaches taken to implement and/or sustain the assessment (e.g. What kinds of support are provided to teachers as they implement the system?).

The description of each system's design is organized by subsections that address key processes in portfolio practice: collection, selection, reflection, and evaluation. Each of these subsections, in turn, addesses important procedural questions that have implications for the impact of the program on student learning (and responsibility for learning), the professionalization of teachers, and the quality of the evidence. For example, questions about procedures for selection raise issues of responsibility and authority (e.g. Who makes the selection, the teacher, or the student?) and instruction (e.g. Are students encouraged to evaluate their work periodically, as part of the day-to-day activities of learning, or only at the end of the process, when the time comes to put the final portfolios together?). Each chapter concludes with a discussion of particular dilemmas of portfolio practice—highlighted issues—and questions for discussion and further inquiry.

The final chapter provides a framework for system designers to employ as a heuristic for developing their own portfolio systems. The framework and accompanying discussion synthesize information from the individual chapters and alert readers to major questions that need to be considered as portfolio systems are designed and implemented.

The framework draws attention to four critical areas of portfolio design, including 1) aspirations for students; 2) views of learning and curriculum; 3) models of reform, assessment and accountability; and 4) the bottom-line concerns of any assessment system: fairness, reliability, and validity. Because the framework addresses issues that are central to all portfolio assessment programs regardless of the particular context in which the program occurs, we think it provides a way to uncover and highlight the different and sometimes competing agendas that various parties bring to discussions about portfolios. We hope as well that the framework will shed light on key decisions about design, development, and implementation that program designers and policymakers must make.

In Chapter 1, "Contrasting Perspectives on Portfolio Assessment," we deal with definitions of terms, and provide a brief historical sketch of the rapid growth in portfolio practice in the last decade. This chapter locates portfolio practices within the recent literature on educational anthropology and examines the influence of this field on current thinking about educational measurement. It also lays out the basic distinctions between standardized tests (which include on-demand writing assessment systems) and portfolios in a way that makes clear how the notion of portfolios has been construed beyond classroom walls.

In Chapter 2, "Mt. Diablo High School: Investigating Teaching," we describe a department-wide portfolio program that illustrates the use of portfolios for instruction and collaborative teacher research. Designed by teachers to provide information about their teaching and to motivate their students as writers, the program evolved and changed over a period of several years. We describe the evolving nature of the teachers' questions and the accompanying changes in portfolio design. The issues that we highlight in this chapter are the impact of assessment on teacher development and professionalism and the use of portfolios for formative assessment and improvement of instruction.

In Chapter 3, "Charles Ruff Middle School: Communicating Standards and Expectations," we describe a portfolio system developed by a group of English teachers at a northern California middle school to accomplish four purposes: 1) to bring some uniformity to instruction across the school's English program; 2) to improve the fairness and validity of the school's report card grades in English; 3) to motivate students to become more deeply engaged in literacy experiences and to self-identify as readers; and 4) to promote in students the capacity for reflective analysis, especially as writers. The issues that we highlight in this chapter are the impact of assessment on instruction and student performance and the impact of interpretive theories of reading on assessment design.

In Chapter 4, "Arts PROPEL: Designing Assessment for Learning, we recap the story of Arts PROPEL," a portfolio system developed in the Pittsburgh Public School District, that successfully merged—in a single program—assessment purposes that are often in conflict: assessment for learning and assessment for accountability. We discuss the implications of a portfolio design—and scoring scheme—that draw attention not only to the products students create, but to the processes and resources they use as they make those products. Drawing upon the work of Pittsburgh teachers and of scholars who have provided insights about the Arts PROPEL experience, we highlight the student-centered view of learning underlying the assessment and discuss the implications of that view for assessment design. We discuss, as well, the vulnerability of reform initiatives in the absence of a stable policy environment

In Chapter 5, "*Chinle: Creating Culturally Responsive Assessment*," we describe an attempt to design a system that could accommodate both the purposes of large-scale assessment—in this case external reporting of student achievement—as well as local, cultural purposes in teaching and learning. Drawing upon earlier accounts by scholars, we describe the effort to address Navajo cultural values and concerns. We also update the Chinle story to consider the impact of other assessment agendas in the state on the original program goals. We highlight issues of equity for ethno-linguistic minority students and tensions between bureaucratic purposes for assessment and local concerns.

In Chapter 6, "Regional School District No. 15: Scaffolding Self-Regulated Learning", we describe one way that teachers and administrators have built a portfolio culture at both classroom and district level. We describe the teachers' use of performance task assessment lists, benchmark models of excellent work, and portfolios to scaffold the development of self-regulated learning. We also describe the educator portfolio system that now complements the student system and that supports improvement of curriculum and instruction in the district. We highlight the planned, long-term pattern of curriculum and staff development that led to the introduction of portfolios and discuss issues of systemic coherence.

In Chapter 7, "Kentucky: Portfolios and Social Justice," we describe and critique the portfolio assessment system developed in Kentucky, a state that undertook an ambitious school reform effort in the early 1990s and that required all fourth, eighth and twelfth grade students to create portfolios. We examine the use of scores for high stakes purposes, the impact of assessment on teachers, and the role of portfolio assessment in a reform initiative that sought to bring equity to students across a school system that had provided inequitable opportunities for many long years.

In Chapter 8, "Vermont: A Worthwhile Burden," we describe the statewide, portfolio-based writing assessment program developed in Vermont and give a user-friendly account of this effort to provide information to the public, to encourage good practice, and to be integrally related to the professional development of educators. We highlight key technical issues raised in earlier publications and update the story of the program's impact on curriculum and instruction. As perhaps the oldest surviving portfolio assessment system in the United States, Vermont offers a number of insights to help new system designers prepare their own systems for durbaility and maximum impact.

In Chapter 9, "The New Standards Project: Assessment for Standards-Based Reform," we describe the development and design of the New Standards Project assessment system. We discuss the implications of standards-based reform for classroom instruction, and we highlight issues surrounding teachers' involvement in large-scale assessment. We discuss contrasting models of accountability and reform and the impact of assessment on curriculum and instruction.

In Chapter 10, "Making Decisions about Assessment," we synthesize issues raised in earlier chapters in order to provide a heuristic for program development—the framework described above. We repeat the framework here: 1) aspirations for students; 2) perspectives on learning and curriculum; 3) approaches to reform and accountability; and 4) methods for establishing fairness, reliability, and validity. Our ordering of these issues is deliberate because we think that debates over technique sidestep too often the more substantive and critical questions pertaining to how students learn, the best ways to teach them, and the impact of assessment programs on curriculum, instruction, and teachers.

In practice, assessment development often proceeds haphazardly. As a result, assessments may not be well anchored in a particular theoretical perspective . Explicit analysis of connections between theory and practice can heighten understanding of the underlying assumptions of assessment practice and prompt decisions tempered by understanding and commitment as opposed to expediency or efficiency—although those considerations must be taken into account. To that end, this publication looks explicitly at the decisions that need to be made in portfolio development and the theoretical positions those decisions represent. Understanding how practice mirrors theory, and vice versa, may be a first step toward the refinement of both and the development of coherent assessment systems.

When a reviewer of an early draft of this book suggested that we include in this Preface some words about how we came to do this work, what method we employed to gather and analyze information, and so forth, we agreed immediately. In fact, we wondered why we hadn't done so in the first place. How ironic that in a book intended to provide a resource for anyone interested in the recent history of the situated assessment of literacy learning, we had not located ourselves in the picture!

Upon reflection, we decided that this oversight was completely understandable. For one thing, both of us have a longstanding commitment to the portfolio movement as teachers, as researchers, and as theorists—so much so that we did not perceive a need to comment on the issue. Sandra's roots in this movement are especially deep and strong. For example, in one of the documents in our files, her handwritten feedback to the design committee can be found on an early draft copy of the first portfolio "pamphlet" written in Vermont circa 1988 when the very first statewide portfolio system was being conceived, evidence of her involvement during a seminal period. She has published several chapters, articles, and a book on portfolios, she has spoken about portfolios in professional conferences across the country, and she has served as a consultant to several of the projects described in this book—all of which has helped shape the very history we report between its covers.

Terry was Sandra's student at the University of California at Davis and completed an award-winning dissertation on portfolio assessment under her direction in the mid-1990s. His work on the design of the California Learning Assessment System (CLAS) beginning in the late 1980s brought him into close contact with budding alternative assessment systems in a number of states during a period of rapid growth and innovation. Both of us were part of the New Standard's Project's earliest effort to create a national portfolio system; both of us have plaques from NCTE on our office walls expressing NCTE's appreciation for our "contributions to the development of portfolios and performance assessments for English/Language Arts 1991-1996."

In many ways, because of our active involvement with portfolios over the years, this book was begun in the 1980s. Sandra began collecting and cataloguing artifacts related to portfolios and to portfolio systems development during this time; her friends and colleagues soon learned about her desire to collect information about portfolios—and started helping her add to the drawers of her filing cabinets in her den at home. Over the years the drawers became filled with newsletter and newspaper articles, drafts from system design work such as the Vermont pamphlet, notes from development and field-trial meetings, professional and scholarly and political documents, field notes from classroom observations and interviews with teachers, and sample portfolios from dozens of projects. Much of the information reported in this work was derived from these files—we selected information from Sandra's collection, analyzed it, reflected on it, organized it, and presented it as the following chapters will reveal.

In addition to this collection of materials, we pursued standard channels of inquiry, including the university library and the Internet. Particularly important to this work were the many individuals—Geof Hewitt of Vermont, Starr Lewis of Kentucky, Sally Hampton and Elizabeth Stage with the New Standard's Project, Jerry Halpern and JoAnne Eresh from Pittsburgh, Don Johnson and Michael Hibbard from Region 15 in Connecticut, Nannette Koesch and Elise Trumbull from Far West Laboratory in San Francisco, Beth Witt from Chinle, Arizona, and Jan Bergamini from Danville, California—who generously shared information with us in the form of written documents and oral interviews. Besides providing us with detailed data, some of these individuals read drafts of the chapters relevant to their experience and knowledge and helped us ensure the factual accuracy of our analysis.

While we have done everything we could to make sure our stories are straight and true, we do not claim that we have presented exhaustive portraits of the systems we explored. What we had suspected about the literature on portfolios, we found to be true: It would be impossible for any individual to read everything that has been written on the topic over the past 10 or 15 years. Consider the case of Kentucky alone. There, the state government and the university system have collaborated since the early 1990s to examine the effects of reform and have documented these developments in an explosion of studies, articles, chapters, digital texts, and the like. Or consider the case of District 15 in Connecticut. There, district administrators and teachers have collaborated in an effort to improve teaching and learning through performance-based assessment for almost 20 years; the amount of internal and external text created over this period would likely engage a researcher for an equal number of years.

The analysis of all of the information we considered was done in accordance with the frame for each chapter which has been described previously. We used the various parts of this frame as categories and examined the information with an eye toward gaining a full and accurate understanding of how each system worked with respect to each category. Sometimes, we could not find written documents that provided sufficient information for particular categories. In those instances we asked our "informants" associated with each portfolio system. Iola Threatt, a volunteer archivist for the Highland Area Historical Society, made an important contribution to this book as well. She spent a good part of a summer reading documents and coding them into the categories with post-it notes, which made the whole process more efficient.

The actual analysis of the data and the writing of the chapters took place in stages. During the first stage we identified the specific set of writing tasks that we knew would have to be done in order to achieve the final product. Next, we assigned one or the other of us primary responsibility for developing text with respect to each task. These assignments were made based largely on which of us had greatest familiarity with the territory in question. For example, Sandra had actually lived and breathed the Mt. Diablo portfolio system for a number of years, while Terry had studied the Charles Ruff system for a year as the basis of his dissertation. Once these decisions were made, we worked in our own separate offices with considerable email and telephone communication and occasional face-to-face sessions.

Once these initial texts were composed, we exchanged them in digital form for purposes of revision. Having had quite a lot of experience in co-authoring pieces, having gained a mutual respect for our complementary writing proclivities, neither of us minded when the other took an ax to our prose, so long as it was done kindly. In almost all instances, we were thankful that one of us had managed to catch problems, and we talked at length about how to solve them. Also during this portion of the writing, we sent versions of texts to those individuals who had been working with the local systems in question; in most cases one of us had lengthy phone conversations with these individuals, poring over the text line by line.

The result is the book you hold in your hands. The original idea for this book came from Sandra, who had watched her filing cabinets fill up over the years and finally decided that somebody ought to put it all together in one place. This volume is our effort to accomplish that task.

1 Portfolio Practices: Lessons from Schools, Districts, and States

Portfolios may seem to have appeared on the educational stage just in the past 15 or so years, but many observers claim that portfolios have had a place, if not a name, in schooling for a long time—perhaps as long as teachers have known about the role of reflection in learning, as long as learners have understood the place of self-assessment in growth (Yancey, 1996). It wouldn't surprise us in the least if Berger (1998) was right when he remarked that "Plato probably carried one to Socrates' classroom."

In a discussion of their own historical impact during the 1980s as early explorers of portfolio assessment at the college level, Elbow and Belanoff (1997) answered the question "Why the portfolio explosion?" by explaining that there never really *was* an explosion:

> We've discovered that many teachers, especially at the elementary level, had been using portfolios in their own quiet ways for years before we did. When we listen at the ubiquitous portfolio conferences, we hear teachers start off, 'Well, in 1965, here's how I did it." We whisper to each other, "We never dreamed of portfolios that long ago!" (p. 22)

Indeed, because documentation of development is central to "portfolio practice" (e.g., Tierney, Carter, & Desai, 1991); because massive physical, cognitive, social, and cultural changes of childhood define this life stage, some portfolio-like practices have probably always been a part of elementary schooling, though not so named.

Elementary school teachers of the distant past may well be the forerunners of modern portfolio practitioners, having plied their craft long before Peter Elbow decided to substitute a portfolio system at Stony Brook for a direct writing assessment strategy (Belanoff & Elbow, 1986). But *portfolio assessment for programmatic purposes* like the system pioneered by Elbow and Belanoff at Stony Brook, by colleagues of Arts PROPEL in Pittsburgh (LeMahieu, Eresh, & Wallace, 1992), and by others seems to be a truly modern—some might say postmodern—phenomenon.

When some unknown, late-20th-century savant yoked together the terms "portfolio" and "assessment," a paradox was born (Underwood, Murphy, & Pearson, 1995) that, despite its inherent tensions, stimulated much assessment activity in classrooms, in schools, in districts, among state education agencies, even at the national level (Calfee & Perfumo, 1996). According to Seger (1992), Dan Kirby commented at the Atlanta NCTE convention in 1990 that the term *"portfolio* transformed into *portfolio assessment* within hours" of its appearance in language arts instruction largely because the times were ripe for a more comprehensive, more powerful assessment strategy that could be used to hold schools accountable (p. 115).

As the fires of accountability raged after their flare-up in the early 1980s, policymakers interested in measuring students' higher-level thinking and problem-solving skills began to ask of portfolios not just that they provide reliable assessment data, but also that portfolios reform the schools (Koretz, Stecher, Klein, & McCaffrey, 1994). Though some researchers and practitioners expressed optimism that portfolios could do both (e.g., LeMahieu, Gitomer, & Eresh, 1995), not everyone was sanguine about the prospects for portfolios in the face of such monumental, possibly contradictory, psychometric and pedagogical challenges.

In this politically charged context, Donald Graves (1992) reminded us that "as educators we are mere infants in the use of portfolios. . . ." He warned us of the danger that "sustained, long-term learning about the possibilities of portfolios . . . may be lost . . . in the rush to mandate their use" (Graves, 1992, p. 1). Subsequent chapters in this book will show that what happened in the years after 1992 can indeed be characterized in some instances as a rush to mandate. As Starr Lewis, director of the Kentucky Writing Program, wrote, "Dennie Wolf exaggerated only slightly when she commented in a presentation at the 1992 NCTE conference in Louisville, 'The teachers in Kentucky woke up one morning to find that it was portfolio day'" (Lewis, 1993, p. 10).

Although accountability issues continue to dominate the discourse of policymakers as we end the decade of the 1990s, political interest in mandating portfolio assessment for large-scale programmatic purposes has clearly diminished. In the 1980s and 1990s much important portfolio assessment activity came about because policy makers in states like Arizona, California, North Carolina, Vermont, Kentucky, and others sought innovations in order to improve schools. By the late 1980s, eleven states planned to develop portfolio assessment systems for writing, many with intentions to go on-line within five years (Aschbacher, 1991). Eight years later, however, although Kentucky and Vermont continue to use portfolio assessment as important components of statewide assessment strategies, many of those states (e.g., Arizona, California, North Carolina) have stopped work on alternative assessment programs and have returned largely to conventional methods, such as multiple choice tests (Calfee & Freedman, 1996).

Portfolio assessment no longer enjoys the same level of political support for large-scale applications that it enjoyed only a few short years ago. Belanoff (1996) may have put her finger on why: "The issue of power, of who has the power to determine forms of assessment, is potentially explosive. Those who currently have it may be threatened by the seeming anarchy of portfolios" (p. 357). On the other hand, despite reports to the contrary (Underwood, 1997), portfolio assessment has decidedly not died, and there has been at least some of the sustained, long-term learning Graves hoped for as evidenced by the emergence of a rich body of literature about portfolios. Those portfolio systems that proliferated during the peak of political interest left behind a legacy which will inform future system designers during the next cycle of interest.

But much of what was done in the 1980s and 1990s remains scattered—in a state of "seeming anarchy," as Belanoff noted. A major purpose of this book is to contextualize in one place the historical events, theoretical antecedents, and conceptual designs of several representative portfolio assessment systems begun in the late 1980s and early 1990s across the K–12 system and across the country. This book provides readers with the opportunity to examine these systems through a common lens and then to synthesize lessons from them which might be applied in local situations.

To begin, we devote the next section of this chapter to a discussion of what portfolios are and how they can become part of assessment for programmatic purposes. We do not mean to define portfolios once and for all. Rather, we want to present a set of conceptual boundaries for you to stretch around the varied examples of portfolio assessment systems described in chapters to come.

Portfolios as a Concept in Educational Anthropology

McCormick (1994) and others have discussed a way of reading called "symptomatic" reading, which offers a useful tool for the discussion of portfolios. A text that is read "symptomatically" is read "for symptoms of the tensions or contradictions of the social formation within which the text was produced" (p. 54) and, therefore, is examined as much for what it does *not* say as for what it says. Further, texts read in this way are also read for what they mean in the reader's historical present: "[T]he questions one asks of the text's history must necessarily come from one's position in the present, [so] the absences one finds are surely [also] determined by the social formation in which the text is being read. . . . " (p. 55). The pedagogical implication from this is as follows: "From this perspective teachers need to ask their students to interrogate all the more carefully the ideological forces that have produced their own readings" (p. 77). We ask you to interrogate both the ideological forces that have produced your current understanding of portfolio as a metaphor *and* the forces which both constrained and permitted the portfolio metaphor to show up in the thinking of people across all of the projects we profile.

The terms people choose to describe what students put inside their portfolios— or to explain what those portfolios even are—often reverberate with symptomatic meaning. Former co-director of the New Standards Project's effort to invent a national portfolio system, Miles Myers (1996), for example, used the term "portfolio *data*" liberally in his chapter on "Sailing Ships" and remarked that "the loss of visible and stable data is an enormous problem in portfolio assessment" (p. 156). Of interest is the fact that Myers was functioning in a historical period when portfolios were being boldly considered as a possible replacement for or supplement to such institutionalized assessments as the ACT or the SAT; a term like "data" captures the tension between reform and the status quo which Myers and his colleagues confronted at every turn.

In contrast, system designers in Kentucky and Vermont who created state writing portfolio systems frequently called the contents of their portfolios "writings" or "pieces" in their discourse (Hewitt, 1995; Kentucky Department of Education, 1999), leaving words like "data" for other voices. In these states at least as much emphasis was placed on portfolios as a tool to reform instruction as was placed on portfolios as measurement devices. Teachers in Kentucky understood "writings" and teachers in Vermont understood "pieces," two words commonly used in classrooms; indeed, when teachers talk about student work, they don't often speak of it as "data," a word associated with research and evaluation, not teaching and learning. This choice of terminology frames the tension between assessment for public accountability purposes and assessment for instructional reform which was an important aspect of the local historical formation in each state. Where the focus is on evaluation, portfolios contain "data." Where the focus is on pedagogy, portfolios contain "writings" or "pieces."

In much of the scholarly and pedagogical literature on portfolios, however, the contents of student portfolios have been referred to as "artifacts," a term somewhere between metaphor and literal descriptor. "Artifact" was an important term used to describe the contents of portfolios in the writings of Donald Graves. In 1992, for example, Graves wrote about the "use of a portfolio [as] a place for literate artifacts" (p. 8) and wondered about what things might limit "how [it is that] significant artifacts . . . are represented in a portfolio" (p. 9). Of great interest, we think, is the way that, reading symptomatically from our social formation, this term explicitly links portfolio assessment to educational anthropology and leaves absent references to fields like, say, cognitive psychology. According to WWWebsters, an "artifact" is "something created by humans usually for a practical purpose; especially an object remaining from a particular period" or "something characteristic of or resulting from a human institution or activity, for example, 'self-consciousness is an artifact of our education system'" (Merriam-Webster, 1999). Through careful examination of artifacts, anthropological researchers can develop explanations as to what purposes, what values and beliefs, what behaviors—what ways of being, living, and doing—people of a given culture shared. A collection of artifacts made by a certain person as in a portfolio could provide the basis for an explanation and understanding of how that person went about transacting with others according to the values, beliefs, and patterns of his/her culture.

It is perhaps no accident that foundational writers about portfolio assessment such as Donald Graves used the term "artifact." This use followed closely on the historical heels of the emergence of a branch of study called "educational anthropology," which had reached maturity in the 1970s and was creating considerable changes in graduate schools of education. In a monograph written to explain how anthropological methods might be applied within educational evaluation, Guba (1978) cited Wilson's (1977) discussion of the rationale for the use of ethnographic research generally in education. In this discussion we find not just the rationale for the use of ethnography Guba wanted us to note, but also a justification for portfolios as collections of artifacts with the potential to illuminate teaching and learning:

> [There are] two sets of reasons underlying the rationale for ethnographic research: (a) Human behavior is complexly influenced by the context in which it occurs. Any research plan which takes the actors out of the naturalistic setting may negate those forces and hence obscure its own understanding. (b) Human behavior often has more meaning than its observable "facts." A researcher seeking to understand behavior must find ways to learn the manifest and latent meanings for participants, and must also understand the behavior from the objective, outside perspective. (Wilson, 1977, as cited in Guba, 1978, p. 21)

As you will see when you read the chapters that follow, most, although not all, of the portfolio systems we profile operated on the basis of the belief that assessment ought to be done in order to develop an understanding of students in their "naturalistic setting." Moreover, most acknowledge that assessment ought to seek an understanding of "meanings for participants" as well as meanings from the "objective, outside perspective."

The emergence of educational anthropology as a systematic and legitimate approach to the understanding of schooling brought with it the notion that schools—

and classrooms—can be thought of as institutions with cultures that are produced and reproduced, constructed and reconstructed, created and recreated, during interactions between institutional participants (i.e., teachers and principals) and local agents (i.e., students) (Eckert, 1989; MacLeod, 1987; Willis, 1978). From this perspective, it is easy to view texts as cultural constructions and, as McCormick (1994) noted, "to recognize that they are produced under specific historical and ideological conditions"; McCormick continued:

> [Thus], reading a text involves not only analyzing the words on the page, but also analyzing the text's relationship to the historical and ideological conditions in which it was produced. To perform such an analysis, one needs to be able to read the text "symptomatically" for . . . the text's "absences," [that is], that which is not explicitly in the text, but which is nonetheless a part of the text's history. (p. 162)

Symptomatic reading of artifacts may be precisely the kind of reading in which ethnographers must engage in order to make sense of insider knowledge from an outsider's point of view—a kind of reading which makes it sensible to talk about "portfolio ethnography" as a synonym of sorts for "portfolio assessment." In any case, the need to situate reviewers for the symptomatic reading of portfolios in light of the situations in which they were created may be an important underlying reason for the emergence of portfolios as a genre of educational assessment.

Advocates of portfolios who want to argue that assessment ought to be situated, thick, and insightful rather than universalistic, thin, and inferential are supported by the work of Brian Street (1984; 1993), an educational anthropologist who developed a theory of literacy which distinguished an "autonomous" model of literacy from an "ideological" model. Street argued that proponents of the autonomous model conceive of literacy in technical terms and view literacy and literacy learning as independent of the social context. Universal and mechanical in nature, literacy is related to mastery of scripts whether alphabetic or otherwise, though the Western bias in most autonomous research privileges alphabetic reading; and once such mastery is accomplished, some argue, the presence of literacy creates changes in mental functioning, cognitive changes which raise literate minds above non-literate minds in their very capacity to think (Goody, 1977). In its strong form, an assumption of the autonomous model is that the mastering of literacy "'fosters' or even 'enforces' the development of 'logic,' the distinction of myth from history, the elaboration of bureaucracy, the shift from 'little communities' to complex cultures, the emergence of 'scientific' thought and institutions and even the growth of democratic political processes" (Street, 1984, p. 44). From this perspective, the term "standardized" in the phrase "standardized tests" could be changed to "autonomous" tests. There is little need to examine situated literacy practices because the foci of interest are the technical skills of literacy, which are in themselves valuable because they broaden and deepen powers of mind and permit civilizations to advance.

Street's ideological model of literacy is based on the notion that different literacies are embedded within ideologies that derive from, and perpetuate, different social practices wherein values lie. Of importance is Street's explanation that the term ideology is not intended "in its old-fashioned Marxist sense of 'false consciousness' and 'simple-minded dogma,' but rather in the sense employed within contemporary anthropology . . . where ideology is the site of tension between authority and power on the one hand and resistance and creativity on the other" (Street, 1993, p. 8). Street also took care to explain that the ideological model does not refute the need for technical skill:

> The ideological model . . . does not attempt to deny technical skill or the cognitive aspects of reading and writing, but rather understands them as they are encapsulated within cultural wholes and within structures of power. In that sense the ideological model subsumes rather than excludes the work undertaken within the autonomous model. (p. 9)

Even in the materials and particular technologies of literacies, however, there is variation across social setting, the source of which is located in authority and power—"the use of manuscripts, print and telescreens; alphabets, ideographs, syllabaries . . . ; slate and chalk, quills and biros, typewriters and word processors; parchment, linen, computer paper" (Street, 1984, p. 97). Dressman (1999) expanded this point by arguing that even the development of a technical skill like phonological awareness among beginning readers is associated with variations across social and cultural factors, in this case the socioeconomic background of students. For good or for ill, social practices in homes rather than psychological processing capabilities in brains may account for differences in phonological awareness. The point is that even technical and physical aspects of literacy are shaped to some extent by sociocultural factors.

Of much greater importance to this discussion is Street's explanation of differences among the "kinds of literacy" that people practice in accordance with different activity systems shaped by differing social, historical, and cultural factors. On a small atoll in the Central Pacific where a population of 350 Nukulaelae Islanders live, for example, Besnier (1993; 1995), who contributed a chapter to Street's edited 1993 volume, found that one practice in particular accounted for most of the written output among the Islanders, namely, the writing of personal letters. Having learned the technology of print literacy during the 1860s when Christian missionaries showed up in their history, the Islanders nonetheless had little need for the kinds of bureaucratic and notarial literacy practices which served the European colonizers in their societies, because the Islanders lived in a subsistence economy based on fishing and coconuts. They did, however, have a great need to communicate with the many friends and relatives who emigrated from Nukulaelae in order to earn money; hence, they developed a complex set of literacy practices for letter writing. If one wanted to understand—indeed, assess—the literacy performances and practices of these Islanders, a methodology for collecting the artifacts of these practices and for examining these artifacts in light of the social and cultural conditions of their production would have to be employed, a methodology that would look more like portfolios than multiple choice tests.

In a similar manner, Camitta (1993) reported the findings of a study of adolescent literacy practices in an alternative high school in Philadelphia where adolescents participated in a network of literacy performances which served them within their own adolescent culture apart from the essay literacy practices that were sanctioned in their classrooms. Camitta (1993) examined a number of "vernacular texts" constructed by these adolescents such as rap, mosaic, patchwork, Dear John letters, and others that emerged to further the social and cultural activities of these young adults under the very noses of teachers who neither knew nor cared that such practices were in use. Again, anyone interested in understanding or assessing these adolescent literacy performances across the various vernacular genres would need a methodology for collecting and examining artifacts together with information describing the social and cultural activities in which those artifacts were embedded.

During the last quarter of the 20th century, educational anthropologists were joined by cognitive anthropologists and social psychologists in reconceptualizing not just *literacy practices* as socially situated rather than autonomous and individual, but *learning and cognitive processes* in general as socially situated (see Cole & Engestrom, 1993, for a historical summary). Just as personal letters from Nukulaelae and patchwork texts from City High in Philadelphia cannot be understood apart from the sociocultural conditions in which they were produced, *learning* to "do literacy" cannot be understood apart from the situation in which the learning occurred. Salomon and Perkins (1998) delineated several features of the social context which they believe must be present for learning to happen:

> The learning entity in question, whether a person trying to skate better or a loose society of individuals trying to get along with one another, must be able to construct a repertoire of new representations or behaviors based on prior experience[;] . . . must have the opportunity to test and select . . . or refine or combine [alternative representations or behaviors;] . . . need[s] feedback of some sort[;] . . . benefits greatly from information sources. . . . The learning entity will also need conditions that sustain motivation and energy. And so on. (p. 3)

A repertoire of alternative representations or behaviors, opportunities to test and select and refine alternative possibilities, feedback, sources of information—all of these elements are part of the sociohistorical context which shapes learning. Given this set of elements, how is it possible to talk about learning apart from the conditions in which it occurs, conditions which can be at least partially represented in portfolios?

Perkins (1993) expanded the borders of the notion by suggesting that it may be impossible to discuss not just *how* one learns, but also *what* one learns and *where* knowledge resides, apart from the situation in which the learning takes place. Perkins gave us the example of a student taking a class in medieval history who created a rich, organized notebook on the topic of 1066. The dominant learning theory of our times, according to Perkins, would locate what this student learned *in his or her head*; assessing what this student learned would take place apart from the notebook. (Perkins did *not* say that the dominant theory would call the notebook irrelevant, for this theory would argue that the act of making the notebook helped the student learn the material more thoroughly and perhaps more deeply, that is, the "writing-to-learn" perspective. Also, the student would be able to use the notebook when writing a term paper.) But one could theorize the situation differently as follows:

> We could take as our unit of analysis not the student without resources in his or her surround—the *person-solo*—but the person plus surround, or *person-plus* for short, in this case the student plus the notebook. We could say that this person-plus system has learned something, and part of what the system has learned resides in the notebook rather than in the mind of the student. (p. 89)

If knowledge can be distributed in the environment as well as in the head, how can it be possible to talk about learning apart from the environment in which it occurred? Portfolios can provide a receptacle for artifacts from the environment.

The notion of "person-plus" provides portfolio theorists with a useful conceptual tool to develop a theoretical rationale for portfolio assessment. As Salomon and Perkins (1998) pointed out, "a focus on the individual in social and cultural solitude" (p. 2) ignores what may be crucial aspects of learning, namely, three-way interactions among the individual, the sociohistorical situation, and cultural artifacts. Such a focus attempts to examine individual learning under conditions that almost never occur in schools—a person with no one to talk with, no access to tools, no access to the "distributed expertise" of teachers and peers (Brown, et al., 1993). At the very least, conceiving of the learning entity as person-plus seems to better match authentic conditions of learning in classrooms.

Viewing the person-plus as the unit of analysis when we are assessing students also requires the rethinking of what we mean by "learning tools." We do not, for example, expect writers to compose without pens or pencils or some sort of utensil— tools available within the sociohistorical situation. We do not expect artists to paint without canvas, brush, and paints, no more than we expect a researcher to determine the p value of a statistic without reference to either a paper or digital chart. Just as the stick to a blind person, these tools are in many respects essential, not simply convenient. The question for the assessment of literacy practices comes down to this: What *other* social tools are essential to composing and comprehension processes beyond those, like the pen or pencil, which have become naturalized and invisible? Social psychologists such as David Perkins have challenged us to explore the full range of technological and human resources and tools which participate in the network of distributed cognition, intelligence, and knowledge that all learners might need access to in order to learn and to engage in productive social practices.

Whether we view the outcome of learning as "knowing" or "doing," the use of person-plus as the unit of analysis suggests that we consider interactions among the individual, the local circumstances of the individual, and the cultural patterns in which the individual is situated anytime we make inferences about student learning or performance. Hatch and Gardner (1993) illustrated this point nicely with a study of preschoolers' behaviors at two centers in a preschool classroom: the sand table and the art table. Differences in behavior were discovered that could be attributed to individual tendencies to enjoy and do well at drawing vs. making things; one child who liked to build did not especially care for art projects. Differences in behavior could likewise be explained by factors residing in local circumstances; experiences at home with a father who happened to be an engineer or a mother who happened to be an artist as well as variance in the affordances of items in the environment (sand, water, buckets, shovels; paints, crayons, scissors) led to changes in behaviors.

Of particular interest in this study was the role that cultural values played in the behavior of preschool children at these tables. Sand products were never signed by their creators, for example, as art products often were; consequently, sand play was much more collaborative and malleable than were art products. Because sand products were valued differently, they were temporary, and the children simply left them without a thought when they had finished their play. Art products, however, were often saved and stuffed in cubbies to be taken home by individuals. This study, of course, raises interesting questions for literacy. Are written products, like art work, individual objects to be saved? Or are they, like sand products, temporary? Or are they more complex, varied according to occasion, genre, audience, purpose? Clearly, the individual reading and writing in social and cultural solitude captures but one small part of what it means to "do literacy."

Lave's (1996) roots in activity theory help us expand the person-plus notion even further by suggesting that rather than examining "particular tools and techniques for learning," learning theorists ought to instead consider "ways of becoming a participant, ways of participating, and ways in which participants and practices change" (p. 157). From this perspective, learning has little to do with gaining knowledge as an individual possession or as a personally owned commodity. Instead, learning is an element of growing into new ways of participation in social practices. Having studied tailors in apprenticeships in Liberia, having considered the learning processes of legal scholars in Egypt, Lave concluded that the telos of learning, that is, the "direction of movement or change of learning," was not the acquisition of knowledge, but a change in social identity:

> The *telos* of tailors' apprenticeship . . . and legal learning . . . was not learning to sew or learning texts, not moving towards more abstract knowledge of the law or . . . special generalization of tailoring knowledge. Instead, the *telos* might be described as becoming a respected, practicing participant among other tailors or lawyers, becoming so imbued with the practice that masters become part of the everyday life of the Alley or the mosque. . . . It seems that the tailors and law participants, as subjects, and the world with which they were engaged, mutually constituted each other. (p. 157)

Lave's perspective on learning focuses on the social activity system in which people do things of increasing complexity, moving the idea of distributed cognition beyond just locating knowledge inside and outside of the mind. In Lave's conception, knowing and learning become doing and practicing and ultimately involve what Lave (1996) terms "identities in practice" (p. 157). Portfolios can offer portraits of such identities.

Within this rich web of ideas surrounding the meaning of literacy and learning, the notion of portfolios spread across all levels of education, becoming more and more complex. Sometimes portfolios were seen as a methodology for assessing literacy as a technology within an autonomous model, and the notion became less and less susceptible to easy definition. Sometimes they were seen as records of identities established in practice. For a time it seemed almost as if the word "portfolio" could be used as an ink-blot test in which one could see whatever s/he decided to see. But the tenor of the field was against the idea of an "anything goes" definition. Indeed, the scholarly literature on portfolios includes entire chapters and articles intended to do no more than provide a clear, comprehensive definition of "portfolio" within a recognizable theoretical framework (Calfee & Freedman, 1996; Farr & Trumbull, 1997; Seger, 1992; Wile & Tierney, 1996). This fact alone suggests that trying to find out what colleagues mean when they use the word is hardly a waste of time.

By now portfolios surely have grown beyond the infancy that Donald Graves (1992) referred to just a few short years ago, but they have hardly reached maturity. Nobody can be completely sure what portfolios will look like when they grow up, but it seems clear that their roots in anthropology and social psychology will ultimately support their growth in directions that promote teaching and learning practices which recognize the situated nature of both literacy and learning.

Portfolios as a Concept in Educational Measurement

Complicating matters still further is the lack of theoretical clarity in the literature, not just on portfolios but on test design in general. Portfolios are one kind of
assessment among an array of possible assessments; but as Snow (1993) noted, much
scholarly work remains to be done to figure out the relationships among this broad
array of possibilities:

> What is still needed . . . is . . . a psychology of test design. This would involve
> the development of a taxonomy—a full elaboration of the facets of real and
> potential test designs . . . —and programs of experimental cognitive and con-
> ative task analysis of test facets in different ability and achievement domains
> to build construct descriptions associated with different test designs. (p. 47)

Certainly, such a taxonomy would be enormously useful here in our efforts to distinguish portfolio assessment from all other kinds of assessment. In the absence of this
taxonomy we will try to situate the notion of portfolios as best we can, realizing that
our readers will need to fill in some gaps on their own and that the field itself will
develop as we gain more and more experience with tests of all sorts.

Though portfolios are relative newcomers to the field of assessment, standardized tests have been around at least since the early 1900s, a century during which we
have become what some have called a "test-oriented culture" (Mitchell, 1992, p. 27–
49). Assessment researchers do make a broad distinction between standardized tests,
the sort of tests most valued in this modern test culture, and other kinds of assessment, a distinction useful to review here in order to isolate the notion of portfolios.
Haney (1984) explained this distinction as follows:

> What is meant by . . . standardized tests? . . . Th[is] term [is] used to mean
> systematic devices for eliciting and recording samplings of individuals'
> knowledge, skills, or attitudes, as represented in problems, questions, or tasks
> posed with such devices. This definition includes instruments commonly rec-
> ognized as aptitude or achievement tests or as norm-referenced or criterion-
> referenced tests, but *excludes . . . things like observation scales and teacher-made
> or classroom tests*. [emphasis added] (p. 598)

What sits at the heart of the design of the standardized test is its uniformity:
Every test-taker faces the same—or demonstrably equivalent—questions, problems,
and tasks and responds according to a uniform protocol. Classroom tests, on the other
hand, may be uniform for all of the students of a particular teacher, but they are not
uniform across a state, district, or even a school. The *method* of data collection in
standardized test design is uniform across test administrations; methods of observation and classroom test-making can vary from classroom to classroom. Note that standardized tests include more design types than the ubiquitous multiple-choice test.
Any method of data collection which poses uniform problems, questions, or tasks to
test-takers regardless of the nature of the response called for—multiple-choice or constructed response—can be classified as a standardized test.

Wixson, Valencia, and Lipson (1994) broadened the distinction made by Haney
in their discussion of three areas of difference between "external" and "internal"
assessments:

1. the content and nature of findings,
2. format and frequency of administration, and
3. measurement characteristics.

According to Wixson, et al. (1994), external tests must be "fair for a wide range of students" and so "would not be tied to any particular textbook, pedagogy, or curriculum" (p. 317). In contrast, internal assessments must be fair only to the students with whom a particular teacher works; they are situation-specific in that they focus on particular students, on the particular content those students were taught, and on the particular pedagogy used by the teacher. External tests are used with large numbers of students and so must be efficient in format and inexpensive in use, two good descriptors of machine-scorable, multiple-choice tests given once or at most twice per year. Internal assessments, in contrast, are used with classroom-size groups of students and can vary even within a classroom in format and frequency of administration.

Finally, external tests usually are designed to take advantage of the statistical characteristics of the normal distribution; that is to say, students can be compared to a norm group based on their location in a distribution. Internal assessments are not so designed: "Teachers certainly do not expect a normal distribution after instruction; instead, they would . . . set performance criteria . . . , teach to those criteria, and then expect a change in performance after instruction and practice" (Wixson, et al., 1994, p. 319).

The paradox of portfolio assessment for programmatic purposes should now be within view. Portfolios differ from standardized tests in that they do not involve Haney's "devices" that pose large groups of students the same curriculum-free, uniform questions, problems, or tasks characteristic of external assessments; in excluding observational checklists and teacher-made tests from the domain of standardized tests, Haney would likely have excluded portfolios as well if they had existed in their current form in 1984. Portfolios are made up of student work done in particular classrooms planned and run according to the professional practices of particular teachers. Indeed, the portfolio strategy is what Wixson, et al. (1994) would call an internal assessment strategy—inefficient, expensive in terms of time and effort, directly tied to local learning goals and objectives.

On the other hand, portfolio assessment systems for programmatic purposes have been implemented as if they were standardized tests with very large groups of students across whole states and even countries *despite the fact that portfolios do not contain student responses to uniform tasks, questions, or problems.* Moreover, portfolio assessment systems have often been used for the same high-stakes reasons standardized tests are used—to hold teachers and students accountable, to inform placement, to certify achievement levels, and the like. Portfolios have been called on to fulfill the same functions that multiple-choice tests have fulfilled for decades—without a psychology of test design (Snow, 1993), without a long tradition rooted in a well-established psychometric theory (Haney, 1984), without a commitment on the part of policy makers (Belanoff, 1996).

After serving for four years as codirector of the New Standards Project's attempt to design a national portfolio system, Miles Myers (1996) summarized the precarious position of portfolios as follows:

> Portfolio assessment often seems to be guided by a conglomeration of psychometric principles from machine-scored tests and personal growth issues from clinical psychology. Portfolios are obviously not just another version of machine-scored tests, and they are not just another private collection of an individual author or reader. Where are we to find the conceptual framework that could productively be applied to portfolios in the new literacy? (p. 151)

Portfolio assessment for programmatic purposes exists within a political and cultural milieu that continues to privilege standardized tests, a milieu that has sustained itself for almost a full century. Given that standardized tests appear to be more fair, more reliable, more efficient, and less expensive, it seems to us to be more than legitimate to ask this question: Why should we bother with portfolio assessment? What's the point? The next section of this chapter will address these questions.

Why Bother with Portfolios?

As theorists have repeatedly pointed out (e.g., Moss, 1994), there is a strong tension between *reliability* (i.e., the stability of scores across measurement events) and *validity* (i.e., the legitimacy of scores as true descriptions of a construct). As reliability increases, it seems, validity decreases, and vice versa. We will see that portfolios have reliability problems which overshadow their virtues as valid measures in the eyes of some. Conversely, standardized multiple-choice tests have high reliability, but serious questions have been raised about their validity as measures of reading and writing (e.g., Bennett & Ward, 1993). Interestingly, though reliability problems have plagued portfolio assessment in the political arena, parallel problems with validity in standardized tests have not detracted from their popular appeal.

Even if a particular standardized test has undergone item analysis and demonstrated acceptable levels of item difficulty and item discrimination, even if this test passed the scrutiny of expert qualitative review, Haney and Scott (1987) argued that validity is still a problem because no one knows for sure how individual children perceive each item until someone takes the time to ask each child:

> These [item analysis] procedures do not necessarily get at the issue of test or item quality from the perspective of individual test-takers. . . . This distinction is important because what . . . a test or item measures—that is, its content validity—depends not on what adult experts or critics *think* [emphasis in original] it measures nor on what item statistics suggest about the item but rather on how individual test-takers perceive and react to the test item. (p. 301)

Haney and Scott (1987) went on to report the results of a study in which they interviewed children to find out how they perceived items and came away with serious concerns about validity claims for standardized tests.

In addition to concerns about the traditional validity claims of standardized tests as measures of learning, recent theorists have developed a broader model of validity that looks beyond the immediate application of the standardized instrument itself to the consequences of its use (Frederickson & Collins, 1989; Messick, 1989a, 1989b, 1994; Moss, 1994). Tests do more than yield achievement scores. They tell us what achievement is. "Through the test," wrote Madaus and Kellaghan (1993), "the teacher, and later the policymaker defined what was expected of students . . . " (p. 6). Frederickson and Collins (1989) coined the term "systemic validity" to refer to this phenomenon: Systemic validity takes into account instructional changes brought about by the use of a test and asks whether such changes are good or bad.

When we explore what scholars and researchers have discovered about the systemic validity of standardized tests in recent years, there is reason for concern. According to Madaus and Kellaghan (1993), standardized tests had little influence on state or federal policymakers from the 1920s to the 1960s. By the 1970s, however, policymakers began to use standardized test data to make high-stakes decisions, and the design and content of these tests began to influence what and how teachers taught.

Highly regarded scholars and professional organizations now agree that state standardized testing programs of the 1970s and 1980s had negative effects on students, teachers, and learning:

> Since about 1970, when standardized tests began to be used for a wider variety of accountability purposes, basic skills test scores have been increasing slightly, while assessments of higher order thinking skills have declined in virtually all subject areas. Officials of the National Assessment of Educational Progress, the National Research Council, and the National Council of Teachers of English and Mathematics, among others, have all attributed this decline in higher order thinking . . . to schools' emphasis on tests of basic skills. They argue that . . . the uses of the tests have corrupted teaching practices. (Darling-Hammond, 1994, p. 16)

Even as we condemn standardized tests for their negative effects on teaching and learning, we must be cautious about attributing any special magic to portfolio assessment systems. If the field solves the problem of reliability in portfolio assessment *by resorting to the strategy of standardizing portfolio contents,* the effectiveness of portfolios will remain in doubt.

In our view, it is critical that portfolio assessment system designers think clearly about the trap of standardization. Indeed, it would be possible to design a system wherein students place weekly spelling tests, sentence diagramming exercises, vocabulary practice sheets, and the like between the covers of their portfolios. Murphy and Grant (1996) discussed (though decidedly did *not* endorse) a commercially prepared "grammar portfolio" system consisting largely of a collection of worksheets. Here is how Spectrum Educational Media described their portfolio system:

> Greatly extends the number of exercises available to supplement the traditional grammar book. Asks students to identify sentence parts, fill in the blanks, distinguish between grammatical elements, and determine how words, phrases, and clauses are used. . . . Fifty reproducible worksheets, answer key. Grades 7–12. (Murphy & Grant, 1996, p. 290)

Camp (1993) provided a helpful perspective on this issue when she described a hypothetical portfolio system design consisting of several student-written compositions drafted over time in response to prompts like those used in on-demand direct writing assessments. Within this hypothetical collection students included one sample composition with evidence of draft review and revision, and students also wrote letters to their portfolio examiners reflecting on their work.

Although this hypothetical portfolio goes well beyond Spectrum Educational Media's 50 reproducible worksheets, Camp found important problems with it, problems related to construct and systemic validity:

> The requirement that students write for a specified audience, especially . . . [during] a timed assessment isolated from real-world context, . . . forc[es] students, in effect, to write for both the specified audience and the audience of teachers who will actually evaluate their work. The requirement that all students write to the same prompt eliminates the . . . shaping of topic that is . . . part of the writing process. The stipulation that students do their best

> brainstorming, drafting, and revision under the constraints of test-like con-
> ditions disallows . . . differences . . . known to characterize students' writing
> processes and eliminates the social interaction that often makes those pro-
> cesses useful. (pp. 195–196)

These hypothetical students would indeed write if they did their work in accordance
with this system design—they would not simply fill in blanks or create lists of words—
but the processes they would use to write their work would be distorted to the degree
that they were inauthentic; that is to say, the processes would not be recognizable as
processes that writers actually employ when writing for real (i.e., non-testing) purposes.

Lucas (1988a; 1988b) addressed the need for students to have sustained classroom opportunities for "authentic" reading and writing in her call for a shift from an
"accountability model" to an "ecological model," ". . . a radical shift [from a] worldview
in which learning is done in the service of evaluation to one in which evaluation is
done in the service of learning; from teaching to the test to testing for teaching" (Lucas,
1988a, p. 2). Lucas identified several phases in the historical development of direct
writing assessment during which there was movement from standardized multiple-
choice tests of editing skills to strategies for holistic scoring of essays to the current
concern with classroom ecology, that is, using assessment designs which promote
rather than diminish learning and achievement. Indeed, neither Spectrum Educational Media's grammar portfolio nor Camp's (1993) depiction of a genre-driven,
on-demand portfolio seems likely to promote learning. The reliance on uniform,
standardized tasks appears to risk the same negative effects on teaching and learning
that we know standardized tests have had over the past decade.

In Camp's scenario the root of the problem grew from the design of the portfolio
system itself. Students were asked to do work in order to fill up a portfolio; they were
not asked to do work for purposes of learning and developing as writers. It seems
likely that portfolio systems—or any assessment system for that matter—which requires students to do uniform tasks specifically for the assessment system runs the
risk of violating principles of systemic and ecological validity. Moreover, there is
empirical evidence to support the deleterious effects of standardization of tasks.
Simmons (1992) studied ten schools involved in non-standardized portfolio assessment projects and found the following:

> Patterns of student performance, preference, and judgment repeatedly dem-
> onstrated that students progress from grade five to grade eight in their abil-
> ity to make the choices that adult writers make, but that such growth is erased
> by high school practices that emphasize testing, rather than the development
> of writing abilities. (p. 105)

Sandra Murphy (1994) has likened portfolios to chameleons; portfolios have a
tendency to take on the colors of their surroundings. The chameleon metaphor fits
nicely with the notion of ecological validity. To understand a portfolio system, then,
the nature of the surroundings—the context in which the portfolio system was designed—are significant considerations. For example, a portfolio system implemented
in an elementary school on a Navajo Indian Reservation in Arizona will differ from a
system implemented in a small state like Vermont. A system implemented in a California middle school where the English teachers are committed to Louise Rosenblatt's
perspective on aesthetic reading will differ from a national system where the ideas of
applied learning theory and school-to-work concerns are paramount.

Seger (1992) made this same point another way when he explained that the portfolio notion is often stretched to encompass whatever issues its makers want it to cover. For example, where a group of teachers seeks to improve its report card by developing a portfolio system, the portfolio notion itself likely encompasses grades, developmental continuums, rubrics, and the like, which articulate standards, values, or criteria to use in making judgments about students. Where a group of teachers seeks to encourage reluctant or resistant students to take ownership of their work, however, the portfolio notion likely does not make heavy use of evaluation schemes, since grading practices tend to locate power—and thereby ownership—in the hands of teachers as institutional authorities.

The chameleon-like nature of portfolios—their flexibility and elasticity—dovetails with a late-20th-century school reform strategy often referred to as the professionalization of teachers. During the early 1900s a model of school reform was developed called "scientific management" (Shannon, 1990) which was supported by the burgeoning development of standardized tests. Schools could be managed and controlled from the outside by scientific managers, who could "teacher-proof" classrooms (Darling-Hammond, 1993). In recent years, as we have learned more and more about the complex nature of teaching and learning, many in the field have adopted the view that professionalizing teaching, that is, giving teachers the right and responsibility to practice in accordance with their own knowledge-based decisions, may prove to be a more productive approach.

Looking Ahead

In the upcoming chapters we will present profiles of eight portfolio assessment systems which were developed in the late 1980s and early 1990s for the purposes of taking student work created in real classrooms beyond those classroom walls for external examination and, in some cases, evaluation with consequences attached. Some of these systems are still functioning much as they were originally designed, some have been changed in significant ways, and some have been put on the shelf until some future date when, we believe, they will either be taken down and used again or taken apart and reassembled in a new design.

All of these systems emerged within an identifiable social and political context, and we go to great lengths in the manner of ethnographers to describe these contexts in enough detail that our readers will be able to link the internal workings of the portfolio systems with those contexts. One lesson from our inquiry is unmistakably clear: Portfolio assessment systems cannot be discussed apart from their contexts— no more than the writings students put in their portfolios can be considered apart from the classrooms in which those writings were created. In order to ensure that we have captured these contexts faithfully, we have asked people who participated either in the design or the implementation of these systems over time to read and respond to the appropriate chapters, and we revised each chapter several times in light of local feedback.

In order to provide support to you as you try to synthesize and see patterns and themes in these portfolio projects, we offer our own attempt in this regard in chapter 10. There, you will find an analysis of the major issues confronted—in one way or another—by designers of all of these systems. We present these issues systematically so that you might consider them in the design of a local system. As a preview of what is to come, we list those themes and patterns here as follows: 1) System designers must be clear about their aspirations for students because portfolios taken beyond classroom walls influence what goes on within those walls; 2) System designers would do well to examine their perspectives on learning and curriculum before they design a portfolio system so that they make certain that their design supports, rather than works against, their perspective on these topics; 3) System designers ought to examine their local approach to reform and accountability and, we believe, take full advantage of the promise of portfolios as a tool in the professionalization of teachers; and 4) System designers must consider carefully how they are going to establish the fairness, reliability, and validity of portfolio data if those data are going to be used to make decisions of consequence. Portfolio assessment is a two-edged sword. The portfolio systems we examined all resulted in at least some improvements in teaching and learning—often great improvements in some areas—but they also raised problems that seem almost unavoidable. Our conclusion is this: Being forewarned is preferable to being surprised. In this spirit we discuss the problems that we perceived in each design and offer some possible solutions, though we do not pretend to have the answers. We do believe, however, that portfolios have grown well beyond their infancy, that their promise has been at least partly fulfilled, and that there is a future for portfolios—even when they are taken beyond classroom walls.

Opportunities for Discussion

1. Teachers across the country by now have become familiar with the term "portfolio assessment" in varying degrees. You may wish to spend some time discussing the experiences and perceptions of colleagues with respect to portfolios as a way to prepare for reading the profiles in the remaining chapters of this book.
2. Validity issues are central to motivations to use portfolios. Discussing local perspectives on reading and writing processes with colleagues would be one way to prepare for examining validity issues that come up in the profiles of projects discussed throughout this book.
3. If you are considering designing a portfolio project, it would be a good idea to talk with colleagues about what you think they should contain. What kinds of literacy artifacts would be most useful and informative to you?

References

Aschbacher, P. (1991). Performance assessment: State activity, interest, and concerns. *Applied Measurement in Education, 4*(4), 275–288.

Belanoff, P. (1996). Portfolios: The good, the bad, and the beautiful. In R. Calfee & P. Perfumo (Eds.). *Writing portfolios in the classroom : Policy and practice,promise and peril* (pp. 349–358). Mahwah, NJ: Lawrence Erlbaum Associates.

Belanoff, P. & Elbow, P. (1986). Using portfolios to increase collaboration and community in a writing program. In P. Connoly & T. Vilardi (Eds.), *New methods in college writing programs* (pp. 28–39). New York: MLA.

Bennett R. & Ward, W. (Eds.) (1993). *Construction versus choice in cognitive measurement: Issues in constructed response, performance testing and portfolio assessment.* Hillsdale, NJ: Lawrence Erlbaum Associates.

Berger, P. (1998). Portfolio folly. *Education Week on the Web* (January 14, 1998). [http://www.edweek.org]

Besnier, N. (1993). Literacy and feelings: The encoding of affect in Nukulaelae letters. In B. Street. (Ed.). *Cross-cultural approaches to literacy*, (pp. 62–86). New York: Cambridge University Press.

Besnier, N. (1995). *Literacy, emotion, and authority: Reading and writing on a Polynesian atoll.* New York: Cambridge University Press.

Brown, A., Ash, A., Rutherford, M., Nakagawa, K., Gordon, A., & Campione, J. (1993). Distributed expertise in the classroom. In G. Salomon (Ed.). *Distributed cognitions: Educational and psychological considerations*, (pp. 188–228). New York: Cambridge University Press.

Calfee, R. & Freedman, S. (1996). Classroom writing portfolios: Old, new, borrowed, blue. In R. Calfee & P. Perfumo (Eds.). *Writing portfolios in the classroom: Policy and practice, promise and peril*, (pp. 3–26). Mahwah, NJ: Lawrence Erlbaum Associates.

Calfee, R. & Perfumo, P. (Eds.) (1996). *Writing portfolios in the classroom: Policy and practice, promise and peril.* Mahwah, New Jersey: Lawrence Erlbaum Associates.

Camitta, M. (1993.) Vernacular writing: Varieties of literacy among Philadelphia high school students. In B. Street (Ed.). *Cross-cultural approaches to literacy*, (pp. 228–246). New York: Cambridge University Press.

Camp, R. (1993). The place of portfolios in our changing views of writing assessment. In R.E. Bennett & W. C. Ward (Eds.), *Construction versus choice in cognitive measurement: Issues in constructed response, performance testing, and portfolio assessment*, (pp. 183–212). Hillsdale, NJ: Lawrence Erlbaum Associates.

Cole, M & Engestrom, Y. (1993). A cultural-historical approach to distributed cognition. In G. Salomon (Ed.). *Distributed cognitions: Educational and psychological considerations*, (1–48). New York: Cambridge University Press.

Darling-Hammond, L. (1993, June). Reframing the school reform agenda: Developing capacity for school transformation. *Phi Delta Kappa*, 753–761.

Darling-Hammond, L. (1994). Setting standards for students: The case for authentic assessment. *The Education Forum, 59*, 14–21.

Dressman, M. (1999). On the use and misuse of research evidence: Decoding two states' reading initiatives. *Reading Research Quarterly 34*(3), 258–285.

Eckert, P. (1989). *Jocks and burn-outs: Social categories and identity in the high school.* New York: Teachers College Press.

Elbow, P. & Belanoff, P. (1997). Reflections on an explosion: Portfolios in the 90s and beyond. In K. Yancey, & I. Weiser (Eds.). *Situating portfolios: Four perspectives*, (pp. 21–33). Logan, Utah: Utah State University Press.

Farr, B. P. & Trumbull, E. (1997). *Assessment alternatives for diverse classrooms.* Norwood, MA: Christopher-Gordon Publishers, Inc.

Frederickson, J. & Collins, A. (1989). A systems approach to educational testing. *Educational Researcher, 18*(9), 27–32.

Goody, J. (1977). *The domestication of the savage mind.* New York: Cambridge University Press.

Graves, D. (1992). Portfolios: Keep a good idea growing. In D. Graves & B. Sunstein (Eds.), *Portfolio Portraits*, (pp. 1–12). Portsmouth, NH: Heinemann.

Guba, E. (1978). *Toward a methodology of naturalistic inquiry in educational evaluation.* Center for the Study of Evaluation, UCLA Graduate School of Education, University of California, Los Angeles.

Haney, W. (1984). Testing reasoning and reasoning about testing. *Review of Educational Research, 54*(4), 597–654.

Haney, W. & Scott, L. (1987). Talking with children about tests: An exploratory study of test item ambiguity. In R. O. Freedle & R.P. Duran (Eds.). *Cognitive and linguistic analysis of test performance.* Vol XXII, (pp. 298–369). Norwood, NJ: Ablex.

Hatch, T., & Gardner, H. (1993). Finding cognition in the classroom: an expanded view of human intelligence. In G. Salomon, (Ed.). *Distributed cognitions: Educational and psychological considerations,* (pp. 164–187). New York: Cambridge University Press.

Hewitt, G. (1995). *A portfolio primer: Teaching, collecting, and assessing student writing.* Portsmouth, NH: Heinemann.

Kentucky Department of Education (1999). *Kentucky writing portfolio: Writing portfolio development teacher's handbook.* Frankfurt, KY.

Koretz, D., Stecher, B., Klein, S., & McCaffrey, D. (1994). *The evolution of a portfolio program: The impact and quality of the Vermont program in its second year (1992–93).* (CSE Technical Report 385). University of California, Los Angeles, National Center for Research on Evaluation, Standards, and Student Testing.

Lave, J. (1996). Teaching, as learning, in practice. *Mind, Culture, and Activity, 3* (3), 149–194.

LeMahieu, P., Eresh, J., & Wallace, R. (1992, December). Using student portfolios for a public accounting. *The School Administrator,* 8–15.

LeMahieu, P., Gitomer, D. & Eresh, J. (1995). Portfolios in large-scale assessment: Difficult but not impossible. *Educational Measurement, 14* (5), 11–28.

Lewis, S. (1993). Kentucky writing portfolios: A history. *Kentucky English Bulletin 43* (1), 9–11.

Lucas, C. (1988a). Toward ecological evaluation: Part one. *The Quarterly of the National Writing Project and the Center for the Study of Writing, 10* (1), 1–3, 12–16.

Lucas, C. (1988b). Toward ecological evaluation: Part two. *The Quarterly of the National Writing Project and the Center for the Study of Writing, 10* (2), 4–10.

MacLeod, J. (1987). *Ain't no makin' it: Leveled aspirations in a low-income neighborhood.* Boulder, Colorado: Westview Press.

Madaus, G. & Kellaghan, T. (1993). Testing as a mechanism of public policy: A brief history and description. *Measurment and Evaluation in Counseling and Development 26,* 6–10.

Merriam-Webster (1999). http://www.merriam-webster.com

Messick, S. (1989a). Meaning and values in test validation: The science and ethics of assessment. *Educational Researcher, 18*(2), 5–11.

Messick, S. (1989b). Validity. In R. L. Linn (Ed.), *Educational measurement* (3rd. ed.), (pp. 13–104). New York: American Council on Education and Macmillan.

Messick, S. (1994). The interplay of evidence and consequences in the validation of performance assessments. *Educational Researcher, 23* (2), 13–23.

McCormick, K. (1994). *The culture of reading and the teaching of English.* New York: Manchester University press.

Mitchell, R. (1992). Assessing writing in California, Arizona, and Maryland. *Testing for learning: How new approaches to evaluation can improve American schools* (pp. 27–49). New York: The Free Press.

Moss, P. (1994). Can there be validity without reliability? *Educational Researcher, 23* (2), 5–12.

Murphy, S. (1994). Portfolios and curriculum reform: Patterns in practice. *Assessing Writing, 1* (2), 175–207.

Murphy, S. & Grant, B. (1996). Portfolio approaches to assessment: Breakthrough or more of the same? In E. White, W. Lutz, & S. Kamusikiri (Eds). *Assessment of writing: Politics, policies, practices* (pp. 284–300). New York: Modern Language Association.

Myers, M (1996). Sailing ships: A framework for portfolios in formative and summative systems. In R. Calfee & P. Perfumo (Eds.). *Writing portfolios in the classroom: Policy and practice, promise and peril* (pp. 149–178). Mahwah, NJ: Lawrence Erlbaum Associates.

Perkins, D. N. (1993). Person-plus: A distributed view of thinking and learning. In G. Salomon, (Ed.). *Distributed cognitions: Educational and psychological considerations,* (pp. 164–187). New York: Cambridge University Press.

Salomon, G., & Perkins, D. N. (1998). Individual and social aspects of learning. In P. D. Pearson & A. Iran-Nejad (Eds.). *Review of Research in Education* (Vol. 23), (pp. 1–24). Washington, D.C.: American Educational Research Association.

Seger, F. (1992). Portfolio definitions: Toward a shared notion. In D. Graves & B. Sunstein (Eds.), *Portfolio portraits* (pp. 114–124). Portsmouth, NH: Heinemann.

Shannon, P. (1990). *The struggle to continue: A history of progressive reading instruction in America.* Portsmouth, NH: Heinemann.

Simmons, J. (1992). Portfolios for large-scale assessment. In D. Graves & B. Sunstein (Eds.), *Portfolio portraits* (pp. 96–113). Portsmouth, NH: Heinemann.

Snow, R. E. (1993). Construct validity and constructed-response tests. In R. E. Bennett and W. C. Ward (Eds.) *Construction versus choice in cognitive measurement: Issues in constructed response, performance testing and portfolio assessment,* (pp. 45–60). Hillsdale, NJ: Lawrence Erlbaum Associates.

Street, B. (1984). *Literacy in Theory and Practice.* New York: Cambridge University Press.

Street, B. (Ed.). (1993). *Cross-cultural approaches to literacy.* New York: Cambridge University Press.

Tierney, R., Carter, M., & Desai, L. (1991). *Portfolio assessment in the reading-writing classroom.* Norwood, MA: Christopher-Gordon Publishers.

Underwood, T. (1997). Portfolios on the precipice. *Assessing Writing 4* (2), 225–234.

Underwood, T., Murphy, S., & Pearson, P. D. (1995). The paradox of portfolios. *Iowa English Bulletin, 43,* 73–86.

Wile, J. & Tierney, R. (1996). Tensions in assessment: The battle over portfolios, curriculum, and control. In R. Calfee & P. Perfumo (Eds.). *Writing portfolios in the classroom: Policy and practice, promise and peril.* Mahwah, NJ: Lawrence Erlbaum Associates.

Willis, P. (1978). *Learning to labor: How working class kids get working class jobs.* New York: Columbia University Press.

Wixson, K., Valencia, S., & Lipson, M. (1994). Issues in literacy assessment: Facing the realities of internal and external assessment. *Journal of Reading Behavior, 26* (3), 315–337.

Yancey, K. (1996). Dialogue, interplay, and discovery: Mapping the role and the rhetoric of reflection in portfolio assessment. In R. Calfee & P. Perfumo (Eds.). *Writing portfolios in the classroom: Policy and practice, promise and peril.* Mahwah, NJ: Lawrence Erlbaum Associates.

2 | Mt. Diablo High School: Investigating Teaching

In the mid and late 1980s and early 1990s, California, like many other states, was in the midst of educational reform. At the time, California's reform goals included integrating reading, writing, speaking, and listening in instruction, empowering students as active meaning makers, and promoting the meaning-centered, literature-based curriculum described in California's *English Language Arts Framework*. Assessment also had a place on the reform agenda, and California was already a lap ahead of other states in the assessment reform race, having moved beyond the five-paragraph theme to develop a direct writing assessment that assessed multiple types of writing. Multiple-choice reading and editing tests were still part of the battery of tests employed by the State to assess students' reading and language skills, but efforts to develop assessment approaches which would better complement and support an integrated view of the language arts—the focus of curricular reforms of the day—were underway.

Eventually, assessment reform efforts at the state level led to the development of a prototype for an assessment that integrated the active processes of reading, talking, listening, and writing. The assessment constituted a radical departure from previous assessment practices, as Fran Clagett points out, since the assessment asked students to make meaning, "rather than to identify 'correct' meanings that test makers have posited" (Claggett, 1991, p. 2). Instead of bubble-marking answers, students created a written response to a reading selection and engaged in a variety of collaborative activities such as group mapping, discussion of the reading selection, pre-writing, drafting, and sharing of first drafts. Surveys of teachers who participated in the field tests indicated widespread support for including such activities in the assessment (Claggett, 1991). Educators recognized the value in creating an assessment that mirrored good instruction.

At that point in California's somewhat checkered assessment history, several special features distinguished the California Assessment Program from the assessment programs in other states:

1. a variety . . . of carefully designed writing types and reading selections
2. assessment of reading and writing as dynamic activities requiring interactions of students with other students, with reading materials, and with the contexts of the reading
3. attention to diverse reading and writing purposes
4. teacher designed and implemented scoring systems

5.   direct teacher-to-teacher reporting as well as a comprehensive annual report to the legislature

6.   teacher-designed instructional materials providing extensive classroom applications

7.   inservice support from teacher/consultants of the California Writing Project and the California Literature Project (Clagett, 1991, p. 13)

During the same time period, efforts were underway to find other ways to move "beyond the bubble"—the CAP theme song during those days of reform. Open to experiments, and pushing toward greater involvement in assessment at the local level, CAP funded a research and development project on portfolio assessment in 1988. The purposes of the project were:

* to develop potential models of portfolio assessment that could inform other local efforts

* to contribute to CAP's work in the development of performance-based/authentic assessments

* to examine the feasibility of portfolio assessment in terms of time, cost, human resources including administrative support, materials, and so on

* to support the notion of locally developed authentic assessments for local circumstances, and

* to examine the kinds of key decisions participants would need to make to design a viable assessment program (Smith & Murphy, 1990)

Complementing the State Department of Education's commitment to integrating assessment with instruction and its Model Curriculum Standards and English Language Arts Framework, the portfolio approach acknowledged current understandings in language learning, that writing is a process occurring over time and in stages, that writing done for one purpose requires skills different from those required for another purpose, and that writing varies with the audience for which it is intended (Smith & Murphy, 1988).

A dozen schools across the state participated in the CAP Portfolio Project at statewide conferences where individual schools shared information about their own experiments with portfolios in instruction and assessment. In addition, two of those schools—Mt. Diablo High School and Jefferson High School—received inservice support and research attention from the project directors. The portfolio system discussed in this chapter was developed at Mt. Diablo High School.

Exemplar System

The selection of Mt. Diablo High School for this portfolio development effort was the outcome of a purposeful selection process. CAP required that the work take place in an urban and a suburban high school, so that different communities in the state would be represented. In addition, the project directors were looking for schools with a high percentage of minority students and representative faculties that included some experts and some novices; schools where there was interest in the teaching of writing and the uses of writing to learn; and schools where there was administrative understanding and support for the project, and where faculty were allowed to volunteer. Mt. Diablo met all of the criteria.

Context for the System

When the portfolio project began, Mt. Diablo High School was a large (1,262 students; 68 teachers), ethnically diverse suburban school located in a lower and lower-middle class suburban neighborhood. Over half of the students were from minority backgrounds: Hispanic, Black, Asian, American Indian, Filipino, or Pacific Islander. The school housed the largest English as a Second Language Program in the school district and offered sheltered classes in the four major content areas. A little more than half of the students planned to go on to college after high school. Fifteen teachers (12 English teachers and 3 student teachers) participated in the project and all were volunteers.

The policy of volunteerism was important to the project directors, because they knew that teachers who volunteer are more likely to demonstrate commitment and a positive attitude. Subscribing to the idea that authentic assessment demanded authentic professionalism, the project directors also believed that teachers who volunteered would be more open to using information from the portfolios—which was sometimes painfully revealing of what did and did not go on in individual classrooms—to improve their teaching, than teachers who were forced to participate.

Teachers are inevitably entangled in educational reform, but how they become involved and the nature of their involvement can vary widely. Educational reform demands highly skilled professionals—teachers who are knowledgeable about learning theory, pedagogy, curriculum, assessment, and child development, who accept responsibility for their students welfare and development, and who plan and evaluate their own work (Darling-Hammond, 1989). Yet many programs aimed at reform fail to engage teachers in the kinds of study, investigation, and experimentation required to undertake the multiple challenges of reform, enrolling them instead in training programs designed only to expand particular sets of pedagogical practices and skills (Little, 1993). Instead of a program to train teachers to conduct assessments, the Mt. Diablo portfolio program was envisioned as an arena for teachers to play informed and active roles as authentic professionals; or as Judith Warren Little puts it, as professionals engaged in "defining the enterprise of education and the work of teaching" (Little, 1993, p. 132).

Certain approaches to assessment may inhibit this kind of professional climate. For example, some scholars argue that prepackaged assessments "frustrate individual initiative and innovation and limit professional prerogative" even when they are explicitly intended to be tools to help the teacher in the classroom (Pearson & Valencia, 1987, p. 1). Other scholars argue that prepackaged and highly standardized assessments lead not to the professionalization of teachers, but rather to their deskilling and deprofessionalization (Darling-Hammond, 1989, 1990; McNeil, 1988). Research indicates that standardized tests, along with workbooks, canned lessons, drills, and other "teacher-proof" instructional packages, including prescriptive portfolios, tend to devalue the professional competence of teachers (Smith, 1991). These kinds of "hand-me-down" materials may restrict opportunities for teachers (and for that matter, students) to demonstrate individual initiative and ingenuity—qualities which are essential in any significant, long-lasting reform effort.

Instead of imposing a prepackaged program, the California Portfolio Project directors invited the English teachers at Mt. Diablo High School to design their own. Moreover, in another departure from traditional procedures, the teachers revised the system each year. Traditional approaches typically provide a norm referenced comparison of student performance, or they measure students' performances against a fixed standard for accountability purposes. In these cases, the assessments usually remain the same from year to year. This system, in contrast, was allowed to grow and change, an approach to assessment development which implicitly recognizes the reciprocity of assessment and curriculum: when one changed, so did the other. When new questions about the curriculum and student performance demanded to be asked, appropriate data had to be gathered to answer them. Thus, teachers defined and redefined the portfolio system in relation to the evolving curriculum and to the teachers' and students' needs.

As Mary Ann Smith said, "the program was not based on 'ready-to-wear' or 'hand-me-down' portfolios" (Personal Communication). It was a program *created* and *recreated* by the teachers and students, not one designed by an expert or agency. Although the teachers achieved consensus about the program's overall purpose and design, the particulars of their agreement were not cast in stone. Specific purposes for portfolio collection changed from year to year.

Purposes for the System

During a series of meetings, the central question—the question from which all other questions about program design flowed—was the purposes of the portfolio. The group grappled with this question and ultimately achieved consensus on the purposes that they wanted to pursue. Although specific purposes changed as the portfolio system evolved, the overall purposes remained the same from 1988 to 1999, the year this manuscript was written. For themselves, the teachers' purpose was to use the portfolios to investigate and rethink their teaching and curriculum. For the students, the teachers hoped to use the portfolios to motivate the students to become engaged in learning.

After working through the process of identifying the purposes they wanted to pursue, the group grappled with questions about the program design such as these (Smith & Murphy, 1988):

1. What kind of information do we want to obtain?
    a. About student writing ability.
    b. About thinking processes and abilities.
    c. About the processes students use to create text.
2. How can we best get that information?
    a. Should the writing tasks be specified? Some? All?
    b. To what extent do we simply want to sample work that is already being done in class? To what extent do we want to use the assessment to articulate what should be done?
    c. What kinds of writing should be required?
    d. What kinds of demands should the writing make on students' skills in thinking, writing, dealing with subject matter?
    e. To what extent and in what ways should the writing exhibit evidence of processes of thinking and writing?
    f. What evidence should be provided of students' engagement with and

    reflection on their writing? What indications of awareness of their own writing process?

3. How should the writing be evaluated?
   a. What kinds of judgments should be made? Yes/No? Pass/Fail? 1 to 4 scale? 1 to 6? Categories for analytical judgment?
   b. Should judgments be made of individual papers? Of the collection as a whole?
   c. Should judgments be made about students' awareness of their writing processes? About their ability to reflect on their writing?
   d. Who should make the judgements and under what circumstances?
   e. How can the reliability of judgments be enhanced?
4. How should the results of evaluation be communicated?
   a. In what form should the results be conveyed to students, to teachers, to parents, to school boards, etc?
   b. How can the results best be used for making decisions in the classroom? About students' readiness to pass through a particular course sequence or to graduate from high school?
5. What provision should be made for revising the assessment after we've had some experience with it?

Although the teachers did not answer all of the questions at once (many were deferred until later), in their first meeting they did agree on basic procedures. One of their agreements was that teachers should make some individual decisions about portfolio practice in the classroom, such as how the portfolios would be organized and coordinated with other classroom procedures, what role they would play in classroom grading practices, how they would be shared with parents, etc. They also developed a time line that they followed each year. After the first hectic weeks of school start-up had passed, the teachers met to discuss the specific purposes and contents of that year's portfolio. During February, they met again for half a day to read student papers and to discuss the criteria they would use in assessing their students' writing. Finally the teachers met during two release days each May to formally review the portfolios. These formal sessions provided support for teachers as they used portfolios to investigate and critically evaluate their teaching and curriculum.

The process of looking closely at the students' work provided the teachers with data for thinking about their teaching and their students' learning—data that had been largely unavailable before. Prior to the portfolio project, the more typical classroom data—stacks of papers written by different students in response to the same assignment—gave the teachers little understanding of the range of ability of individual students, how the quality of their writing varied from one writing genre compared with another, how their writing processes varied from assignment to assignment, or how their abilities changed over time. Nor did those stacks of same-assignment papers reveal what students thought about their work, their views of effective writing, or their processes, abilities, or progress as writers. Portfolios, on the other hand, offered opportunities for the teachers to learn how effectively the same student performed in different writing situations, the extent to which students could gauge - effectiveness in writing, the extent to which students employed effective writing processes, and what students thought of their writing abilities and their progress as writers.

The teachers used information from the portfolios to learn about their students and to inform and reform their teaching. One year, for example, the teachers read at random several three-year portfolio collections, looking in particular at student growth, student reflection, and student attitudes toward using portfolios. Another year, the teachers concentrated on revision. When the teachers analyzed the portfolios at the end of the term, they found little evidence of revision, even though the students had been asked to include examples. Some students simply neglected to provide examples, while others included a second or third draft that was essentially the same in content, recopied, with only surface errors corrected. Few students provided evidence that they had revised their texts in any substantive way. Many of the teachers returned to the classroom the following fall determined to teach revision and to emphasize response. The next spring, when the teachers analyzed the portfolios again, they found that 71 percent contained evidence of response to writing (Murphy & Smith, 1992). Even more interesting, they found that students who received response were using it to revise for content and ideas. Clearly, data from the portfolios had inspired changes in teaching and learning at the school.

The second general purpose of the portfolios, as explained above, was to motivate the students. Like many high school students, Mt. Diablo students appeared to feel relatively little ownership for their work. Dutifully, most of them completed daily assignments, but they showed less motivation and pride in what they had accomplished than the teachers hoped. The teachers at Mt. Diablo were looking for strategies to help the students have meaningful, substantial engagement with their learning. They wanted the students to think of themselves as writers. Portfolios provided a way for the teachers to intensify student efforts, ownership, and experimentation, in short, to encourage personal investment in learning.

System Design

As the preceding section explains, the purposes of this portfolio program were to provide data that would help the teachers improve their teaching and curriculum and to encourage students to see themselves as writers with a personal investment in learning. Designed collectively by the teachers in the English department, the system was revised each year. Begun in 1988 with a single grade level, the portfolio project grew to include grades 9 through 12 over a four-year period.

A basic decision made the first year, one that addressed the teachers' interest in motivating students, was that the teachers would write letters to the students about their writing. Jan Bergamini, the English department chair, explained that at one of the department meetings her colleague Maxine Emerson "looked up from a paper she was reading and said, 'You know, if our first and the most important purpose is to empower and motivate our students as writers, then we are going to have to respond to them. We're going to have to write them a letter or something. We can't just give them a grade" (Bergamini, 1993, p. 147). After much discussion, and a fair amount of debate ("Are you crazy? We'd never have time!") the other teachers agreed. So for 10 years the Mt. Diablo teachers, and any guests, administrators, district personnel, project directors, or student teachers who happened to visit the end-of-year portfolio reading, wrote letters to the Mt. Diablo students about their writing.

Over the years, as the portfolio system evolved the design of the portfolio changed. Although the teachers began with a portfolio model which had very specific requirements to be met by all of the freshman students, ultimately they moved to a model that was open-ended enough to allow latitude in the ways that requirements could be met and that could accommodate a wide variety of evidence of student learning.

Collection

What work was worth collecting?

The first year, the teachers decided to ask students to create a portfolio of specified writing types. Students from all of the ninth grade classes were asked to put the following in their portfolios:

- a paper about a childhood memory
- an opinion paper
- a piece of daily writing from a journal or log
- a piece of descriptive writing
- a "wildcard" (student's own choice)
- one entry that shows process
- an introductory letter

The teachers had three specific purposes which they wanted to accomplish with this design: 1) to empower and motivate their students as writers; 2) to investigate their teaching of writing; and 3) to have the portfolios serve as culminating activity for the students at the end of the semester or year (another approach to motivation). When the students were asked about the program at the end of the year, they made it clear that they wanted more freedom of choice, not less. Some students complained, for example, that except for the "wildcard" slot in the portfolio, there was no "place" in the portfolio for their poetry. The teachers, too, discovered something about the issue of choice when they asked for particular types of writing: if they did not emphasize a particular type of writing in the curriculum, students had little to choose from when it came time to put their final portfolios together. The first year, then, the teachers learned that prescriptive menus put constraints on students' opportunities to make choices about portfolio contents. The menu of required writing types, instead of encouraging students to measure their writing performances against standards or criteria for quality, led students instead in a sometimes frantic search for appropriate forms.

The second year the teachers added new purposes to the ones they had the year before. They wanted 1) to have students recognize and analyze their growth from year to year; 2) to find out whether students revise; 3) to expand the audience of portfolio readers; and 4) to use the portfolios as a tool for ongoing sharing of teaching strategies. Responding to what they had learned the year before, they decided to move away from an emphasis on products to focus instead on processes and on writing strategies. Instead of requiring particular types of writing, students from all of the tenth grade classes were asked to demonstrate their ability to:

- respond to literature
- compare and contrast
- reflect
- state and support and opinion

In addition, students were again asked to include a "wild card" (student's own choice) and an introductory letter. The teachers hoped that emphasizing strategies—as opposed to particular types of writing—would help their students see the portfolios as something more than folders containing individual assignments. Single strategies could be demonstrated, for instance, across several pieces and several strategies could be demonstrated in a single piece. However, when students were asked to write to their English teachers telling how they felt about the portfolios and what they would like to see included, it was clear that students still found the portfolio parameters constraining. Jan Bergamini (1993) described the result this way:

> We learned that categories, types, genres, and labels often stultify students' efforts. They said, "Some of my best writings don't fit into your categories." They said, "Maybe it's just me, but I wasn't happy with the guidelines." They said, "I just can't force my best writing (poetry) into a comparison/contrast category." They said, "Please have fewer literature responses because students often have no response to literature at all." (p. 149)

Because they took their students' comments seriously, in year three the teachers moved even further toward an open-ended design, one that encouraged creativity and which focused on the writer as an individual in the process of development. A particular focus for the year was to see what students knew and could demonstrate about revision. For the most part, students were not asked to write to particular types or topics; rather they were asked to choose and include five of the following six kinds of entries:

- a "personal best"
- a "most imaginative"
- a paper from another discipline
- a paper that shows process and revision
- a piece that shows potential for further work
- a paper that states and supports an opinion
- a reflective letter that focuses on one's self as a writer

In the next year, the design had fewer externally imposed constraints on the student writers in terms of the characteristics of particular pieces. Although students were asked for specific kinds of documentation (an introductory letter, a table of contents, and certain kinds of reflection) substantive decisions about the contents were left up to the students' choice and invention. In this fourth year, the graduation year, a project handout indicated that the teachers wanted to give the students "a sense of completion, pride and celebration," to provide them with "a tangible product" of their four years at the school, to have them "see themselves as writers engaged in writing as a lifelong learning process," to have them "see writing as a tool for personal exploration," and to have them "actively engaged in the process of selecting pieces which show their range as writers." Students were asked to include:

- an introductory letter (a reflection on how the portfolio as a whole mirrors you as an individual, showing your growth and change as a person and as a writer)
- six of your best pieces that show your range as a writer
- reflection on how the six pieces show your range as a writer
- explanation of each piece of writing in the portfolio (assignment, focus of writing)
- table of contents

As long as they demonstrated their competence across a range of different audiences and purposes for writing, students were free to put whatever kinds of writing they chose into the portfolio. The resulting portfolios contained a wide variety of pieces. For example, one senior's portfolio contained the following pieces:

- a "found" poem based on Sophocles' Oedipus Trilogy
- a character journal on Gertrude from Hamlet
- a revision of a myth
- essays on three texts read for independent reading (*When Heaven and Earth Changed Places, Sweet Summer, The Fountainhead*).
- an essay written for the Buck Foundation about the death of her mother as a turning point in the student's life
- an etymology report on the word "rain."
- a saturation report of the career center at the high school
- a University Office of the President's Scholarship essay
- an essay written for the Wa Sung Service Club scholarship on how the student's Chinese ancestry had been both an advantage and a disadvantage in the student's life.
- an afterword/last word reflective essay on self as learner, reader, and writer.

Because the design was open-ended, it accommodated diversity in the ways individuals created their portfolios and in the ways teachers structured their classes.

Who had access to and owned the collections?

Both teachers and students had access in the classrooms to the collections of materials which students gathered over the course of the year. Most teachers provided some sort of storage space in the classroom: a hanging file folder in a filing cabinet or storage box to which students had access during the day. Students were free to take, work on, and replace pieces of writing whenever they wished.

During the last quarter of the year, students worked intensely with the materials they had collected to prepare end-of-year portfolios. After the reading, the students' end-of-year portfolios were stored for the summer. At the beginning of the following year, teacher assistants used the new class lists to sort the portfolios for delivery to the students' new teachers. At the end of four years, the collection of portfolios was turned over to the students during a final "portfolio celebration" held for the graduating seniors. When seniors graduated, they had portfolios that reflected their growth and accomplishments as writers over their four years in high school.

The celebration of senior portfolios was traditionally held on the day before the seniors' last day at Mt. Diablo, during the week set aside for senior finals. Local businesses provided refreshments. The English teachers distributed special invitations and announcements appeared in the daily bulletin. During the celebration, volunteer seniors read from their portfolios. Students typically read pieces such as a reflection on a place, event, or memory other seniors would share, or a particularly effective introductory letter or "afterword"—a brief reflection on a particular piece and the process of its making. After the readings, the English teachers distributed the four-years' worth of portfolios to the seniors.

Selection

When did selection take place?

As we indicate elsewhere, the question of when selection occurs in a portfolio project is complex. In some projects, the selection process is only a formality that occurs at the end of the semester or year. However, when portfolio practice is embedded in day-to-day instruction, the selection process is in some ways continual. At Mt. Diablo, for instance, the process started for many students when they wrote their first paper for the year, and it continued with each subsequent paper during the year. Behind the day-to-day judgments about the quality of their work lay the question: Will this one be good enough for my portfolio?

The teachers at Mt. Diablo found a variety of ways to capitalize on this question in their teaching activities. In addition to providing day-to-day access for students to their working folders, many of them built in classroom time for students to practice making preliminary selections for their portfolios, for instance, to star or mark one or two writing pieces they had in their folder at the end of the quarter which they might wish to include in a final portfolio for the year, and to reflect on their choices. Some teachers asked their students to create "portfolios in progress" each quarter.

At the end of each year, the culmination of the ongoing classroom portfolio process began in earnest. During the week before finals, the students chose entries for their portfolio for that year. Most teachers provided extra class time and arranged for extra time in the computer lab during this period, because invariably there was an end-of-year rush to polish portfolio pieces, to write reflective letters, and to put the finishing touches on the portfolio. For many of the students, this final portfolio preparation was their most intense work of the year. Classes hummed with discussion about portfolio contents: "Should I choose this one?" "I like my poetry the best." "Can I use this one I wrote at home?" "You liked this one; you gave it an A."

As the last comment illustrates, teachers' grades and comments on potential portfolio pieces no doubt played a part in the portfolio selection process. But for the most part, portfolio selection was a time for *students* to exercise judgment about their work.

Who selected artifacts for presentation?

The answer to this question has, in many respects, been answered above: Students made final selections for their portfolios. However, various factors influenced that selection process in interesting ways. No doubt, some students were influenced by the opinions of their teachers, peers, and parents, an influence that is certainly natural, expected, and to be encouraged in classrooms which capitalize in instruction on the idea that literacy is socially constructed. In Jan Bergamini's class, for instance, writing groups were common, built in as regular activities through a succession of drafts, so that students would get regular peer feedback on their writing. Scaffolding for the writing process also included feedback in individual conferences with the teacher. Students were accustomed to hearing others' opinions of their work and to paying attention to those opinions. To be sure, the social nature of literacy learning in the Mt. Diablo classes influenced the selection process.

Another factor that appeared to influence the selection process was the design of the portfolio. The evolution in this particular portfolio program was from a model in which everyone was more or less marching to the same drummer and tune, toward a model which not only accommodated, but privileged individuality and diversity. As we indicated previously, the teachers initially adopted a fairly standardized portfolio design—standardized in the sense that all students were expected to put in particular types of entries. This first year design followed a trend of assessment portfolios in general toward standardization of contents through prescriptive requirements. Valencia and Calfee (1991), commenting on this trend, observe that assessment portfolios are all too often

> . . . standardized, with substantial direction from the teacher, administrator, or district . . . . Artifacts are generally authentic and collected over time, but most entries are predetermined, as are criteria for scoring and evaluating performance. Although there is some room for self-selection and reflection, a substantial core of required activities dominates the portfolio. (p. 337)

In later years, Jan Bergamini, the English department chair, reflected on one of the dilemmas this caused:

> So by those categories [of writing types], it really is structuring your curriculum in a way, if you're talking about a portfolio where you want to give kids as many things to choose from as possible, that's not going to happen, unless you totally say, "O.K., I'm going to teach, you know, three persuasive essays, and three telling stories, and three of this, and three of that." (quoted in Murphy, Bergamini & Rooney, 1998)

Because the teachers didn't teach "three of this, and three of that," but sometimes only "one or two of this, and one or two of that" the highly structured evidence requirements that first year meant that students had few choices to make about their work. Instead of assessing the quality of their work, students were caught up in a scramble to find papers that had particular, predetermined characteristics. If they only had one piece of writing that fit a particular category, they put it in whether they thought it was good or not.

The resulting portfolios gave teachers little information about the choices that their students would have made, had they been able. Nor did they learn much about their students' processes as writers or priorities and goals as learners. The teachers were disappointed in the results. As Jan Bergamini put it:

> We learned that [specifying writing assignments or types] didn't work the first year, and we changed it because I still remember those thin little freshman portfolios, and at the end of the reading, it was sort of like the Peggy Lee song—Is that all there is? (quoted in Murphy, Bergamini & Rooney, 1998)

What the teachers learned during those first years in the project fueled the evolution toward more open-ended portfolio designs. They became convinced that a certain amount of flexibility in the portfolio design itself contributed to the learning potential for students. To learn how to make good decisions about their work, students needed a structure that would allow decision-making.

What was the purpose for selection?

As we say elsewhere, the answer to this question depends upon who is asking. As the project evolved, the teachers developed classroom activities to help their students learn to exercise good judgment about their own work, to monitor their own progress, to learn to set goals for themselves, and to present themselves and their work to others. They designed the portfolios to help them accomplish these goals, for

example, by asking students to make judgments about the relative quality of different pieces of their work (e.g. select "a 'best all around' writing"); to make judgments
about writing that needs improving (e.g. select "a piece that you are not satisfied
with and plan to revise"); and to take initiative as learners (e.g. select "a piece which
shows that you have stretched yourself as a writer"). Portfolio guidelines such as
these invite students to assume an active role in the assessment process and to engage in self-assessment. From the teachers' perspective, then, the selection process
was designed to promote the development of active and engaged learners.

From the students' perspective, the purpose for selection was to create the best
portfolio they could with the material they had available, and in some cases, to improve that portfolio by writing and adding new pieces. It was not unusual to see students working furiously during the last week before the portfolio deadline on a new
piece to round out or improve their collection. To be sure, part of the intensity of their
work stemmed from the impetus of grades. Most teachers at Mt. Diablo treated the
portfolio as a class project and based a percentage (typically 20 to 25 percent) of a
student's grade on its quality. So the students had a practical, immediate incentive—to
get the best possible grade. But other factors influenced the students as well: a desire to
have a good portfolio to show off to their classmates, a desire to make their parents
proud of them, and pride in their work. The students' motivations were complex.

Who was the audience for the presentation?

The students at Mr. Diablo had multiple audiences for their portfolios, some of
them known personally by the students, some of them unknown. A primary audience, of course, was the student's English teacher. During conferences, for example,
the teacher and the student might discuss the students' progress. At other times, teachers and students might negotiate portfolio contents; that is, they might discuss what
work was best to include in the students' end-of-year portfolio. The teacher was also
the person who determined the percentage of credit the portfolio would receive in
relation to other classwork and assigned a grade. Thus the teacher's role was both
coach and evaluator.

Within the walls of their classrooms, other students were an audience. Jan
Bergamini, for example, asked members of writing groups to respond to each other's
portfolios. Parents were sometimes also an audience. One teacher, for example, gave
the students extra credit if they had someone else—a neighbor, a parent or other family member—read and comment on their portfolio. Another teacher invited business
leaders in the community to visit her classroom and "partner-read" with a student.

When the portfolios traveled beyond the classroom, still other persons reviewed
the portfolio contents. At the end-of-year portfolio review, for instance, the teachers
met formally to review and respond to the students' portfolios and to gather evidence about curriculum questions. At these meetings, teachers did not read their
own students' portfolios. Instead, the portfolios were read by one of the visitors to
the portfolio reading or by other teachers. During the first years of the project, the
teachers read the portfolios of a single class, following the freshmen through their
four years of high school. After the first four years, the "external" audience for portfolios prepared in grades 9, 10, and 11 was the English teacher the students would
have the next year. The teachers decided to read only the senior portfolios as a group
during the end-of-year release days.

Over the years, the number of participants in these end-of-year readings increased. Jan Bergamini reports, for example, that during the May 1991 reading, the regular English teachers' ranks were swelled by teachers from other disciplines: science, ESL, and social studies. The Learning Opportunity Program coordinator, the Chapter I coordinator, and a variety of district office people, including the assistant superintendent of secondary education, the assistant superintendent of curriculum, the language arts consultant, and CAP Portfolio Project directors also joined the teachers to read the students' portfolios and to write letters.

Reflection
What opportunities for reflection did the system provide?

Because the portfolios followed the students from year to year, the students had opportunities to reflect on their progress as writers and learners over a two-, then three-, and then four-year, time span. For students—who typically received the same grades year after year—this was an awakening. Looking back, they saw where they had been, and how far they had come. One student wrote: "Over the years my writing has become more descriptive and perceptive. I see not only the surface, but right below the surface as well. I have learned to write for the reader." Another student critiqued his earlier work:

> If my Portfolio was a patchwork quilt with four pieces, one representing each year . . . the piece representing my freshman year would have uneven edges and a few rips at the seams. This is because it was my first year really getting into writing for interest, but [my writing] lacked structure and form. It would be of bright color, to get your attention, but there would be little stuffing inside, because the writing has not a solid substance to it.

A classmate discovered the benefits of revision, "When I looked at last year's writing and this year's writing I see how many more drafts I have. I developed my writings a lot further this year." Another classmate wrote, "I get more to the point more quickly. I also see my major problem of run-a-way sentences decreasing." Reflection gave these students opportunities to become conscious of their growth as writers.

But reflection at Mt. Diablo wasn't just a process of looking back; it happened before, during, and after. The selection practice sessions mentioned earlier encouraged reflection. In addition to choosing one or two pieces as potential portfolio entries, the students' were expected to explain why they selected them, discuss what each piece showed about their abilities as a writer, and consider what they would need to do to make the pieces ready for a final portfolio at the end of the year.

At the end of the year, teachers asked students to reflect on the portfolio as a whole, as well as particular pieces within it. Even this end-of-year process involved more than just looking back, it involved looking forward: One teacher at Mt. Diablo, for example, turned part of his final exam into an occasion for reflection and for reminding students what revision is all about:

> Please do this part of the exam on a separate piece of paper. You may be using this writing for one of your portfolio selections. Please select a paper [from your portfolio] that has the *potential* for expansion and revision. Discuss what you would change and expand. Do not rewrite. You are discussing what you would do *if you did* rewrite the paper. You might think about all the

> details, information, experiences, connections, insights and feelings you ne-
> glected to write about. How would you work this material into the paper?
> Would you cut anything out of the original paper? How would you change
> some of the original sentences? When you are finished with your discussion,
> please staple the response to the original paper.

Looking back and then forward happened at the beginning of the year, too, when teachers asked students to review their previous year's work, assess it, and set one or two goals for the semester.

Although reflection at Mt. Diablo often involved writing, it was not solitary. Rather, it was interactive. Reflective pieces in the students' portfolios had audiences. More-over, in classrooms that are built around interaction, like those at Mt. Diablo, reflec-tion is rarely silent. At any point in time, in such classrooms, there are students talk-ing and writing about their writing and their reading (reflecting on their work), some-times with other students, sometimes with the teacher. These exchanges involve metacognitive work. Thus, we might talk about reflection less as something that stu-dents do individually, and more as something that teachers and students and—and potentially anyone involved in the student's education—do together. Portfolio re-flection, as Roberta Camp (1992) says, is a way to "make learning visible." In turn, this "visible learning" becomes the basis for conversations among teachers (and among students and teachers and parents as well).

Teachers as well as students had opportunities for reflection. Public reflection came in the form of department and grade level discussions of portfolio contents. Memos written by the Department Chair, Jan Bergamini, summarized discussions and re-minded teachers of lessons they had learned. Here are some illustrative excerpts:

> Remember that first set of portfolios in 1988-89 which contained descriptive,
> narrative, opinion, daily writing, and wild card pieces? Listen to the fresh-
> man voices we heard in those introductory student letters, explaining why
> they had selected the pieces in their portfolios. . . . From those first portfolios
> we learned that most students can't figure out the difference between the
> descriptive, narrative, opinion categories we had set. We also learned that
> although we think we are teaching students how to write and develop an
> opinion, their opinion papers were, for the most part, weak and unfocused. . . .

> So, we learned some pretty important things: that we liked and learned from
> sharing our ideas about writing; that students will reflect on their writing if
> given the time and opportunity to do so; that revision elicits good writing,
> but must be guided and taught; and that our students were taking this port-
> folio business seriously.

> Each year we listen to our students tell us what they like to write about, and
> how they write best. They tell us that in the portfolio they want more per-
> sonal choice as to topics and for us to drop categories and types of writing.
> They also want a longer period of time to work in the portfolios. As one
> student wrote, *"Good writing and organization can't be rushed. We need to start
> earlier"* (emphasis in original). They also let us know that in some of our
> classes they are not doing very much writing, so they didn't have much to
> choose from to put in their portfolio: *"It's important to do a lot of writing and to*

save it all. We need to be faced with harder, more challenging assignments" (emphasis in original). Reprinted by permission of Jan Bergamini.

As the comments illustrate, portfolios invite introspection about teaching practice. They also invite discussion.

What kinds of artifacts of reflective activity went into the portfolio?

Although much of the reflection that went on in the Mt. Diablo Project was informal and dialogic, it was also formalized in portfolio practice. One of the entries that teachers asked students to submit was a letter introducing their portfolios—and themselves. In addition to letters, some students submitted brief introductions to each piece they called "forwords." Other students submitted "afterwords"—brief reflections on the process and resulting product.

Student Voices

Students reflected on their work and their progress as learners, but they also reflected on *how* they learned, and on the learning situation itself. For example, consider this excerpt from a reflective letter written by a Filipino senior, (quoted in Bergamini, 1993, and reprinted with permission of the National Writing Project):

> About three years ago, I was the new student. I remember the first time I stepped into an English classroom here in America. It wasn't like the ones I had back in my homeland. There was *talking*. And talking . . . and talking . . .
>
> I felt an interaction going on between teacher and students. It was a bond that seemed so natural to them that it made me feel uneasy, for I never knew such bonding . . . . Out of frustration and disappointment in myself, I turned to writing with a vengiance that I have something to share, too. So in this Senior Portfolio, I have selected six pieces to show everyone that . . . I do have a creative mind in writing . . . looking through the portfolio, I can see that I'm every bit as inclined as my peers . . . .
>
> Sincerely,
> Grace

Notice that Grace (a pseudonym) was challenged by the kinds of verbal interaction that she encountered in this American school and that she turned to writing to participate in "learning by talking."

Some students used the letters to identify favorite pieces, to describe their writing processes, and to explain the kinds of writing they did best. Others used their letters to reflect on their progress as writers. Sometimes they were surprised by what they saw:

> Was that really me who wrote those papers?! I can't believe it! My writing style has changed so much within the last year or so! Back then I was so descriptive, with a little humor added to my work to liven things up! But now, I think I'm more serious about what I write and to read it is like a rainy Sunday morning with no electricity at all while your friends are out. In other words, it's BORING.
>
> I now see why Mr. Cotton and Ms. Garamendi encourage me to write. I am good. Well, used to be. After reading my past "literature" and my present, I

promise to you, Ms. Garamendi and myself, I'll change my style of writing until it is both pleasing to one's mind as well as to her/his senses. I will write the best stuff anybody has ever seen! But, I'll start tomorrow. This paper turned out to be boring also. (Murphy & Smith, 1991, p. 37. Copyright © 1991 by Pippin Publishing Corporation. Reprinted with permission. All rights reserved.)

Letters also revealed the criteria students used when making portfolio choices, as the following excerpts show:

Dear Reader:

I picked the poetry paper and my paper on Charles Dickens, because I got A-on them and it was the best stuff I did all year. I picked the paper about Miss Havisham because it was probably my most descriptive paper. I picked the ones on Francis and *To Kill a Mockingbird* because they were the longest of all my other papers.

Dear Reader:

I'll tell you why I like each of these five pieces of writing.

The first one lets the reader feel a part of the atmosphere, time and feelings of the characters. . . .

Forewords orient portfolio readers and give students the opportunity to make comments on the intentions, merits, or features of each piece. For example, student Ron Cabiltes (a pseudonym), provided separate forewords for each of the pieces in his portfolio in which he noted the assignment and the reason for its selection. Here is one:

We were to write an essay about a particular problem Richard Wright had as a child enclosed within his autobiography and relate it to our own life. I chose to include this paper because this was the first time I admitted that discrimination is a part of my life. I never wanted to accept it until now. (Murphy & Smith, 1991, p. 45. Copyright © 1991 by Pippin Publishing Corporation. Reprinted with permission. All rights reserved.)

Afterwords served the same functions, orienting the portfolio readers to particular entries. In afterwords and forewords, some students also evaluated the portfolio entry, or wrote about the process of its creation.

Evaluation

What was the role of evaluation in the system?

On the whole, teachers at Mt. Diablo followed fairly typical assignment and grading procedures, collecting and returning work with feedback and grades marked on finished pieces of writing. Although "finished" pieces of writing had grades affixed to them, students were free to revisit and refashion such pieces when they put their final end-of-year portfolios together. Both preliminary portfolios and final portfolios were incorporated into the classroom grading/evaluation of students. As explained earlier, a common practice among the teachers was to base a percentage of the students' grade on their practice portfolios and/or their final portfolio for the year. In this respect, the portfolios were treated as classroom assignments. Portfolio scores were not considered in the grading process. (For a different approach to grading with portfolios, see the chapter on Charles Ruff Middle School.)

Although the teachers had decided to score the portfolios as part of their inquiry process, they decided not to give the scores to the students. Reasoning that feedback from evaluation in the form of numbers would not be very useful to students in learning, and concerned that low scores might discourage some students, they decided instead to write letters. For example, to a sophomore portfolio writer, one teacher wrote:

> Dear Ron,
>
> Your portfolio is a delight! It showed that you are aware of your reader and you take care of your reader. For example, your presentation of the portfolio worked well: table of contents, introductory letter, short introduction to each piece, dated papers. I found the collection easy to follow and I felt you were guiding me to the features of your writing that pleased and concerned you.
>
> The outstanding feature of your writing for me is the imagery. The way you described your feelings of boredom—"like a rainy Sunday morning with no electricity at all while your friends are out"—is anything but boring! You observe closely, Ron, and often you find the irony in things. For example, in your monologue of a snake, when the snake owner releases the snake in the wild, you observe: "There were no specially prepared foods in the wilderness, unlike the glass home I so loved." Look at the pieces in your portfolio that bored you. I think you'll find, particularly in the sketch of your mother, that the sharp details, metaphors and pictures are missing. Compare those pieces with the ones that pleased you.
>
> How much do you revise your work: I know I have to write several drafts before I'm satisfied. My impression from looking at the drafts you included in your portfolio is that you've made few changes. I'd like to see you dig in next year and tackle revision. For example, the piece on your mother deserves a second or third round. You want to add examples and incidents for statements like, "She stands strong when troubles occur."
>
> I know you can tuck incidents into your pieces. That's just what you did in the Black Boy paper to illustrate your own bout with discrimination. How would that technique have worked in your other responses to literature? It seems a new technique for you, one you didn't use so much last year. I'd say you've progressed and you should take advantage of what you've learned to do so well.
>
> I'm glad to know that you enjoyed all the writing you did for this portfolio, Ron. Yes, I thoroughly enjoyed reading it and I look forward to what comes next. (Murphy & Smith, 1991, p. 47. Copyright © 1991 by Pippin Publishing Corporation. Reprinted with permission. All rights reserved.)

The example illustrates that teachers used the letters as teaching opportunities, to give focused feedback on student writing, to remind students about what they had learned, and to make suggestions about what they might work on next.

To be sure, the letter writing was labor intensive; it would not have been possible without the release time for the teachers covered by the CAP grant, and later by the

District. But the teachers found the process to be valuable. In a memo about the project, Jan Bergamini wrote:

> As teachers we realized how important it was to write personal letters to each student writer. That was in fact, the highlight of that first reading in May 1989. Those letters set up a conversation, a beginning dialogue between teachers and students. And we agreed to continue that throughout the project. (Reprinted with permission by Jan Bergamini.)

The dialogue was not one sided. Some students wrote back:

> I was glad you understood what I was trying to say. I'm not good at putting my feelings down. You're right. I do leave out a lot of information which is what my problem is. Now I know what to work on for next year.

> You grabbed ahold of my good writings and commented on them. I appreciate that you helped me realize conclusions can make or break a story. (Bergamini, 1993, p. 154. Reprinted with permission of the National Writing Project.)

> Finally I feel that I have found someone that understands the important parts of my writings. In my descriptive writings of the little girl you understand the feeling I was trying to get across to the reader. It's exciting to know that I could do this and inspires me to put even more effort into my writing. (Bergamini, 1993, p. 154. Reprinted with permission of the National Writing Project.)

> I have recive your letter today, on my final day. Before I recive this letter, I said to myself, "Oh no, I hope someone who read my portfolio like it." Because this is my first time doing this, and I'm not sure what I write in this is right. When I receive this letter. I was happy that you like it. I think I'm going to imporve my organizing on writing in paragraphs next year. Thank you for take your time to read this. (Murphy & Smith, 1991, p. 55. Copyright © 1991 by Pippin Publishing Corporation. Reprinted with permission. All rights reserved.)

The students' comments reveal that they were eager to establish a writer-to-reader relationship with their evaluators. Letter writing helped them do this.

In general, the teachers' dialogic approach to evaluation was congruent with their approach to teaching writing. The classrooms at Mt. Diablo reflected a "socio-cognitive" perspective on writing. From this perspective, writing is viewed as embedded in social interaction (Dyson, 1990, 1993; Nystrand, 1989; Witte, 1992). The perspective was evident in the Mt. Diablo program in the interactive kinds of activities in which their students were engaged. Scaffolding happened in the teacher-student conferences, in peer conferences, in feedback tied to the intentions and work of individual writers. Their letters to students were just one more conversational turn in an ongoing dialogue about writing that helped them fulfill one of the portfolio purposes: to motivate their students as writers.

For their other purpose—to use the portfolios to rethink their teaching and curriculum—the teachers experimented with different schemes for scoring and/or reviewing the portfolios. The method changed, depending upon the questions they wanted to investigate that year. For instance, as explained earlier, the first year the teachers asked students to submit particular types of writing along with a wildcard entry (a paper of the student's choosing). The particular types were descriptive, opinion, and memory writing (a memory about a childhood event). During a mid-year meeting, after reading samples of their students writing, the teachers developed sets of criteria. The process went something like this: first, teachers were asked to bring in samples of what they considered good writing in each of the categories for everyone to read and discuss. Then, at the mid-year meeting, they talked about the samples and about criteria for effective writing for different purposes. Notice in this fragment of talk from a mid-year meeting that the teachers comment on general features and particular lines in the writing to illustrate what made descriptions effective:

> We got one that's just packed with all different sorts of imagery, and there was one section that was really neat. . . . "In one corner there was dingy water dripping from a crack in the ceiling . . . rusty old pan . . . big bucket with a dead insect . . ." It's picking up on something that is so tiny, that serves as a center that everything else relates to . . . a central image.

> This one creates and carries through the concept of time. It's a central metaphor—everything staying still. [reading] "Miss Havesham's room was like a time capsule. You could see the dust and it probably smelled musty and old. All the clocks were stopped, and everything was always in the same place, even Miss Havesham . . . The room was a piece of the past. Tears clung to the room. Sunlight was never allowed to come in."

> They used the setting to talk about the characters . . . really good writers make the setting say something about more than just what things look like and the kids have evidently picked up on that.

> There was another aspect I think is really important in description—the way you organize what you're describing. It was Jennifer's. And she's describing the tomb of the Capulets. And she starts with [reading] "As the door of the monument opens, you can vaguely distinguish outlines of bodies . . . "

> The focus. It's like a camera.

> Some kids just have a sense of leaping and lingering. And they know when to leap and when to linger.

> And I think it's important in description to get the idea of where the writer is in relation to what's being described.

Later in the year the teachers refined the criteria at department meetings. Three of the categories of the criteria turned out to be fairly generic: voice/personal connection, effective use of language (e.g. rhythm, figurative language, combined and varied sentences, use of comparison, metaphor), and organization/development.

Although the categories were generic, the teachers scored each entry separately. They knew that effective organization and development in one type of writing would be different from effective organization and development in another, and they wanted their scoring system to acknowledge that fact. In addition, the teachers scored each type of writing for features particularly associated with the particular type. For example, when scoring description, the teachers looked for evidence of close observation, imagery, use of the senses, and so forth. When scoring a narrative memory, on the other hand, the teachers looked for the writer's ability to locate the reader in the place and time of the memory, to adopt a retrospective gaze, to relate what was expected and what really happened, and to explain the significance of the memory. Papers were scored on a three-point scale on four dimensions: (Voice, Effective Use of Language, Organization, and Specific Features). The wildcard entries were scored only on the first three dimensions because this category contained diverse types of writing.

After the scoring, the results were analyzed to see whether students fared better at some types of writing than others—a possibility that single sample assessments simply ignore. Table 2.1 shows the statistics for Wilcoxon matched-pair tests conducted to compare performance across three of the categories of entries. For the purposes of these tests, individuals' scores on three of the scoring dimensions (Voice, Effective Use of Language, and Organization) were combined.

Table 2.1
Matched Pair T-Tests for Combined Scores on Memory, Opinion, and Descriptive Writing

Type of Writing	Means	N	SD	T	P
Memory	6.404	193	1.874	4.456	.0000*
Opinion	5.803				
Description	6.192	214	1.883	3.956	.0001*
Opinion	5.682				
Memory	6.377	199	1.881	1.206	.2294
Description	6.216				

alpha = .05

The results of the analysis indicated that the students were least proficient at stating and supporting an opinion. At subsequent meetings, the teachers talked about how they could better support students in their efforts to produce this type of writing.

Although they relied on a conventional psychometric model for their analysis the first year, in subsequent years they experimented with other approaches. In the second year (1989/1990), the teachers decided to score the collection as a whole instead of individual pieces. As anyone who has scored portfolios knows, they knew that some pieces in a student's portfolio would be better than others, some pieces would be better organized than others, and some pieces would be more fully developed than others. So, they adopted an approach to scoring that would take variation into account. They scored each category of criteria according to frequency and consistency, using the following categories: almost always, frequently, sometimes, and never. Again, the categories were fairly generic—development, voice, effective use of language, organization, and the like. But they also added a scoring category for the writer's use of processes such as revision and editing. For this, they kept a tally of revisions that resulted in longer, more fluent or more developed pieces; revisions that consolidated and "tightened" the writing; revisions that reorganized papers for effect; and revisions that simply corrected for mechanical errors. As explained earlier, when the teachers analyzed the portfolios at the end of the term, they found little evidence of revision, and what they did find was most often simply the correction of mechanical errors. By the following year, the picture had changed.

Other schemes for scoring and/or reviewing the portfolios were used in other years. For the sake of brevity, we will not describe them all here. Suffice it to say that the scoring schemes varied according to the questions the teachers had about the students.

How did the system ensure validity and fairness?

During the early years of the project, the teachers and project directors employed traditional techniques for establishing inter-rater reliability. For instance, during the first-year reading described above, 20 percent of the portfolios were given a second reading to obtain inter-rater reliability data. Correlations between first and second readings of each of the scoring dimensions were moderate to strong, ranging from a low of .47 on the dimension of voice in opinion papers to a high of .82 on the dimension of voice in papers about a childhood memory. Typically, values for the Pearson r ranging between .01 and .35 are considered low, while correlations between .35 and .69 are considered moderate. Correlations of more than .70 are considered to be strong rates of agreement.

Although their analysis techniques were sometimes quite traditional, they deviated from standard practice during the readings: they engaged in dialogues about particular portfolios with a colleague, shared particular "gems," discussed particular students and their progress, and periodically engaged in debriefing sessions in which the entire group participated. When considering their procedures, it is important to remember that the Mt. Diablo Project did not have the obligation of developing assessment strategies that could be used for district accountability. Nor were there high stakes attached to the results. Thus, the teachers had less concern about issues associated with a traditional psychometric approach to evaluation.

A central intention of the traditional psychometric approach to evaluation is the control of external variables which might call assessment results into question. Characteristic concerns are achieving reliability (arriving at similar results on similar occasions), obtaining data which can be processed centrally, and producing information which is broadly applicable to large numbers of students and useable by large numbers of test-givers (Cole, 1988). Instead, the portfolio assessment program at Mt. Diablo had many of the characteristics of classroom assessment: it was determined by particular instructional goals, and it was used to make instructional decisions and, in part, its focus was on diagnosis (Cole, 1988; Calfee & Hiebert, 1988). In addition, the assessment was integrated in, not separate from, their instruction. Thus, the aims and procedures of the Mt. Diablo Portfolio Project were substantially different from the aims and procedures of most large-scale assessment programs.

Their procedures were rooted in the assumption that sharing information would result in a more fully developed and common understanding of the standards they were applying during scoring. That is, they employed interpretive approaches to validity (Moss, et al., 1992; Moss, 1996). While psychometric procedures were sometimes employed, they believed that more powerful means for ensuring validity and fairness came from the dialogues between teachers—and between teachers and students—about curriculum, effective teaching, and the qualities of effective writing.

Issues of Impact

The impact of this portfolio system was not demonstrated with the kind of evidence administrators want most—evidence of student improvement in the form of score increases from year to year—because the portfolio design and approach to scoring was not static. As we indicated earlier, it changed from year to year. However, evidence of its impact surfaced in other ways.

As explained earlier, teachers sometimes used quantitative procedures to analyze scores to look for general trends—which kind of writing students did best, which they needed help with, how much they were revising, and so on. This kind of analysis allowed the teachers to look for evidence of change in the following year. The teachers also collected qualitative data. One year, for example, as part of the senior portfolio review, the teachers wrote comments in response to the following questions:

1. How does this student's portfolio demonstrate what we're doing right when it comes to the teaching of writing?
2. What in this student's portfolio shows areas of weakness or need we might want to address as a department. In other words, what do we need to work on in our teaching of writing?

The comments served as fuel for further department discussions about effective teaching practice.

Evidence of impact also surfaced in the evaluative comments of teachers about the portfolio project: one teacher wrote, for example, "The portfolio reading unified the Department. It allowed us to see the kinds writing assignments that elicit high quality work, and by doing that we are revising and planning our curriculum. We are touching base with long range goals and not focusing just on daily routine." Another wrote: "I learned that I didn't spend enough time on revision. In cases where the students worked on revision and were guided through the process of writing, the papers and the portfolios were better." Commenting on what was valuable about the scoring experience, another teacher wrote: "Being able to see the growth and change in a particular student by reviewing written samples [portfolios]. We see a larger picture of our students' accomplishments and needs." Her colleague summed up her own view of the value of classroom portfolio practice this way: "When kids realize that you really value their writing, that you will give them time to reflect on it, and that you will give them time to revise, then it sets up an entirely different community in your classroom. It totally changes how you teach writing."

Reports from teachers in the project also indicated that the nature of department meetings changed. Time was set aside to discuss writing and, as Jan Bergamini (1993), the department chair put it, teachers discussed: "not only what we teach when it comes to writing, but why we teach it the way we teach it" (p. 146). For these teachers, the time to discuss student work was a welcome change from more typical staff development workshops. Instead of being trained to conduct new practices, they were creating and investigating them.

Evidence of impact surfaced in the student's reflections too. Here's what some of them said:

> As a freshman this was just another assignment, kind of a pain in the butt actually, so I didn't really think about it. As a sophomore I knew what it was about so I paid a little bit more attention to the process. I'd begun to mature

and I tried to sound grown up in my writing and as a result it sounds really corny and now it makes me laugh . . . Now my Senior year I feel that I have come full circle in writing. Through the comments of readers I am able to see what I need more or less of.

Until I started this portfolio project, I never even looked at my writing after it was graded. That didn't help me to see what I was ever doing wrong. Reading papers after a while had passed I could easily spot things that I never noticed before.

It used to be that my stories were graded and ended up as charcoal lighter or "three-point" attempts into the wastebasket. But things changed for the better when I enrolled into high school and this "portfolio project" began. I could see my style of writing over the years. I could see what areas of writing I've improved on and what needs working on. When I look into the mirror, alas there stood staring back at me, a writer.

Problems and Potential Solutions

In a memo to the teachers written when the project was entering its fourth year, Jan Bergamini commented on the benefits of the project and alluded to her concern that it could not survive without continued financial support:

> This is our last year to take part in the Portfolio Project we began in 1988. The first three years the State Department of Education through CAP paid for the project. This fourth year, due to the interest and commitment of Myra Redick, Assistant Superintendent, Secondary Education, the Mount Diablo Unified School District is paying for it. When I think back to September 1988, I think about how much we have learned—about our students, about our teaching practices, and about ourselves as an English department. I also know that without the four release days which were built into the project, that learning would not have occurred. (Reprinted with permission by Jan Bergamini.)

At a later date, a district newsletter titled "Good News' carried a story with the following headline: "Inspiring Kids to Write: The funding ends; the project doesn't." The news story went on to explain that although the CAP funding for the project ended in 1991, the Mt. Diablo High School's English Department decided to use staff development days and mentor money to piece together the four release days they needed to plan portfolio work for the year and to read and respond to the senior's collected works.

The excerpts, suggesting "near misses" of discontinuation for lack of funds, illustrate a problem faced by many projects of this kind. If they do not have the continuing support of administrators in "real" terms—release days, financial support, materials, and so forth—they can easily fade away or be superseded by other agendas. At Mt. Diablo, the English teachers were able to scrape together funds to keep the project afloat—one year of district funding, a Bank of America grant of $500, funded applications for mentor positions by English Department teachers to do portfolio work, and in later years, some funding from the local site council. The support was always tenuous. As Jan Bergamini put it, "We could never take it for granted."

In the context of educational reform, the financial instability of the project is disheartening. Scholars say that reform calls for the professionalization of teaching, with an emphasis on practice that is student-centered and knowledge-based as well as a professional model of accountability which can demonstrate that teachers are making knowledge-based decisions (Darling-Hammond, 1989; Holmes Group, 1986; National Board for Professional Teaching Standards, 1994). Scholars also say that "the key to linking assessment with reform is to view it as a social process grounded in:

- conversations about student work as evidence of learning and accomplishment
- the development of a common language for discussing learning, accomplishments, and standards
- the development of shared values and transparent criteria for evaluating student work (Sheingold & Frederiksen, 1995, p. 7).

Unless teachers come to understand the characteristics of exemplary performance, they will make little progress in their attempts to foster it. And, unless teachers have opportunities to engage in conversations about student work, they will have little chance to discover "what good work looks like" or to develop a shared community of values (Sheingold & Frederiksen, 1995, p. 5).

The Mt. Diablo Portfolio Project's on-going problem of financial instability would be easily solved if either the District or the State would set aside monies expressly marked for activities that engage teachers in the periodic and systematic review of student work. The review need not always involve portfolios, but the existence of such an opportunity for funds would open the door to stability for inquiry-based portfolio projects like the one at Mt. Diablo. Such a move would, of course, also involve educating administrators as to the value of activities of this kind.

Alternatively the teachers could reshape the project to make it more compatible with a bureaucratic assessment model. The bureaucratic model, according to Darling-Hammond (1989), seeks evidence that teachers are adhering to standardized policies and procedures for all groups of students. It is possible to provide that kind of evidence with portfolios, particularly if they are standardized. Dollars tend to flow to such models from state and district coffers. However, as Murphy and Camp (1996) remind us, "while the traditional psychometric approach . . . may address certain issues of measurement, it may not serve the best interests of teachers and students, the primary stakeholders in the assessment process, or of teaching and learning, the central purposes of education" (p. 106). A compromise solution might entail keeping one part of the portfolio static—unchanging from year to year—while the rest is allowed to vary according to the needs of the teachers and students. The advantage of such an approach is that it provides a way to gather information about long-term gains or losses.

In any case, there are multiple purposes for assessment, and staff development and the improvement of teaching are two that deserve our serious attention. Valencia and Calfee (1991) advise caution lest we put too much emphasis on assessment:

> For teachers to render judgments that are valid, consistent, and unbiased calls for substantive, concurrent professional development efforts in curriculum, instruction, and assessment. It is naive and dangerous to conceptualize the portfolio movement as simply an assessment effort. To do so will assure frustration, failure, and retreat to the tried and "true" methods of the past. Portfolios offer great promise, but only as they are connected to the broader task of instructional improvement. (p. 343)

It may be time for policy makers to explore ways to promote professional communities that engage in alternative assessment with stable financial resources.

Opportunities for Discussion and Inquiry

1. The Mt. Diablo Project did not have the dual obligation of developing assessment strategies that would be useful in the classroom and that could also be used for district accountability. What difficulties might the project have faced if the district had wanted to use the portfolios for accountability purposes?

2. Initially the Mt. Diablo Unified School District provided financial support in the form of release time for teachers to participate in portfolio readings from the grant. Later the teachers pieced together other sources of funds to support release time for the work. The readings and time set aside for discussion of the project during department meetings helped to keep the teachers involved and interested in the project. What resources are available at your site? What changes and tradeoffs would be necessary at your site?

3. Teachers in this project benefited from their participation in the portfolio project. What advantages might accrue for teachers at your site from opportunities to participate in an inquiry-based project of this kind?

4. The CAP Portfolio Project involved the teachers at Mt. Diablo in the development of the portfolio design. What are the advantages and disadvantages of involving teachers in portfolio development?

5. Elliot Eisner (1985) says, "Evaluation methods should be instrumental to the ends we seek; they should not, as so many of them do now, impede the realization of such ends" (p. 21). In what ways did the Mt. Diablo Portfolio Project support the teachers' aims? In what ways not?

Acknowledgements

We would like to express our appreciation to Jan Bergamini, formerly the English department chair at Mt. Diablo, who gave generously of her time to review earlier versions of this chapter. Her insights were very valuable. We would also like to acknowledge the work of other scholars who have written about the Mt. Diablo Project, in particular, Mary Ann Smith.

References

Bergamini, J. (1993). An English department portfolio program. In M.A. Smith & M. Ylvisaker (Eds.), *Teachers' Voices: Portfolios in the classroom*, (pp. 145–165). University of California, Berkeley, CA: National Writing Project

Calfee, R. C. & Heibert, E. (1988). The teacher's role in using assessment to improve learning. In E. Freeman (Ed.), *Assessment in the service of learning*, (pp. 45–62). Princeton, NJ: Educational Testing Service.

Camp, R. C. (1992). Portfolio reflections in middle and secondary school classrooms. In K. Yaucey (Ed.), *Portfolios in the writing classroom*, Urbana, IL: National Council of Teachers of English.

Claggett, F. (1991). *Reshaping the culture of testing: A new reading and writing assessment in California*, Unpublished manuscript. Sacramento, CA: California Assessment Program.

Cole, N. S. (1988). A realist's appraisal of the prospects for unifying instruction and assessment. In E. Freeman (Ed.), *Assessment in the service of learning*, (pp. 103–117). Princeton, NJ: Educational Testing Service.

Darling-Hammond, L. (1989). Accountability for professional practice. *Teachers College Record, 91*(1), 59–80.

Darling-Hammond, L. (1990). Instructional policy into practice: "The power of the bottom over the top." *Educational Evaluation and Policy Analysis 12*(3), 233–241.

Dyson, A. H. (1990). *The multiple worlds of child writers: A study of friends learning to write*. New York: Teachers College Press.

Dyson, A. H. (1993). *Social worlds of children learning to write*. New York: Teachers College Press.

Eisner, E. (1985). *The educational imagination*. New York, Macmillan Publishing Company.

Holmes Group (1986). *Tomorrow's schools*. East Lansing, MI: Author.

Little, J. W. (1993). Teachers' professional development in a climate of educational reform. *Educational Evaluation and Policy Analysis,15*(2), 129–151.

McNeil, L.M. (1988). Contradictions of control, part 3: Contradictions of reform. *Phi Delta Kappan 69*, 478–485.

Moss, P. (1996). Enlarging the dialogue in educational measurement: Voices from interpretive research traditions. *Educational Researcher, 25* (1): 20–28.

Moss, P., Beck, J. S., Ebbs, C., Matson, B., Muchmore, J., Steele, D., Taylor, C., & Herter, R. (1992, Fall). Portfolios, accountability, and an interpretive approach to validity. *Educational Measurement: Issues and Practice*.

Murphy, S., Bergamini, J., & Rooney, P. (1998). The impact of large-scale portfolio assessment programs on classroom practice: Case studies of the New Standards field-trial portfolio. *Educational Assessment, 4*(4), 297–333.

Murphy, S. & Camp, R. (1996). Toward systemic coherence: A discussion of conflicting perspectives on portfolio assessment. In R. Calfee & P. Perfumo (Eds.) *Writing portfolios in the classroom: Policy and practice, promise and peril*, (pp. 103–148). Lawrence Erlbaum Associates.

Murphy, S., & Smith, M. A. (1990). Talking about portfolios. *The Quarterly of the National Writing Project and the Center for the Study of Writing, 12* (2), 1–3, 24–27.

Murphy, S., & Smith, M. A. (1991). *Writing portfolios: A bridge from teaching to assessment*. Markham, Ontario, Canada: Pippin Publishing Ltd.

Murphy, S., & Smith, M. A. (1992). Looking into portfolios. In K. B. Yancey (Ed.), *Portfolios in the writing classroom*, (pp. 49–61). Urbana, Il: National Council of Teachers of English.

Murphy, S. & Smith, M.A. (1999). Creating a climate for portfolios. In L. Odell & C. Cooper, (Eds.) *Evaluating writing*, (2nd ed.) (pp. 325–343). Urbana, IL: National Council of Teachers of English

National Board for Professional Teaching Standards (1994). *Early adolescence/English language arts standards for National Board certification*. Washington, DC: Author.

Nystrand, M. (1989). A social-interactive model of writing. *Written Communication, 6*, 66–85.

Pearson, P. & Valencia, S. (1987). Assessment, accountability, and professional prerogative. *Research in literacy: Merging perspectives* (pp. 3–16). Thirty-sixth Yearbook of the National Reading Conference. Chicago, IL: National Reading Conference, Inc.

Sheingold, K., & Frederiksen, J. *Linking assessment with reform: Technologies that support conversations about student work.* (Technical report # 94–06). Center for Performance Assessment. Princeton, NJ: Educational Testing Service.

Smith, M.L. (1991). Put to the test: The effects of external testing on teachers. *Educational Researcher, 20* (5), 8–11.

Smith, M.A. & Murphy, S. M. (1988). *Portfolio assessment proposal to the California Assessment Program.* Unpublished manuscript. University of California, Berkeley: California Writing Project

Smith, M.A. & Murphy, S. M. (1990). *California portfolio project: Summary report to the California Assessment Program.* Unpublished manuscript. University of California, Berkeley: California Writing Project

Valencia, S. & Calfee, R. (1991). The development and use of literacy portfolios for students, classes, and teachers. *Applied Measurement in Education, 4*(4), 333–345.

Witte, S. (1992). Context, text, intertext: Toward a constructivist semiotic of writing. *Written Communication, 9,* (2), 237–308.

3 | Charles Ruff Middle School: Communicating Standards and Expectations

Making a distinction between "junior high school" and "middle school" is no easy task. Consider the fact that John Goodlad (1984), in the tables of his classic study of American secondary schooling, categorized schools for grades 6 to 8 as middle schools and those for grades 7 to 8 or 7 to 9 as junior high schools. In his *discussions* of schools, however, Goodlad lumped middle schools and junior high schools into one category. Nancy Atwell (1998), a well-known and respected authority on teaching students "in the middle" how to read and write, called her 7 to 8 grade students both middle school and junior high students—sometimes on the same page.

Although we can't point to a universal middle or junior high grade span, there *is* a core idea to the middle school concept which emerged in the 1960s and is well worth discussion. In fact, the idea of the middle school stands in opposition to the old conception of the junior high school. Rooted in the factory model of schooling governed by "scientific management" (Shannon, 1990), curriculum in the junior high school of earlier years—a jumble of disconnected "subjects" taught in bites of time called "periods," to faceless youth in a rather cold, mechanical way—was ineffective, some might even say harmful, because it did not accommodate the complex and quickly changing emotional, social, and cognitive needs of children making the transition from childhood to adolescence. Reformers of the junior high school believed things had to change, become more personal, more responsive to students. No longer could we, as a society, tolerate Everhart's (1983) description of the inevitable outcomes of the old junior high: "readin', writin', and resistance." Too many students were either dropping out, tuning out, or being pushed out.

There was, in fact, noticeable change in the middle during the 1980s, at least philosophically. The same year that John Goodlad's book, *A Place Called School* (1984) was published, Theodore Sizer published *Horace's Compromise* (1984), both works eloquent testimony to the historically stultifying nature of American secondary schooling, including junior high schooling. Sizer's characterization of the docility inculcated into students through common practices in the middle and advanced grades was more than mildly persuasive. Voices like Goodlad's and Sizer's brought about changes in thinking among policymakers and politicians. In California, for example, the Superintendent's Middle Grades Task Force published a widely circulated report titled *Caught in the Middle* (California State Department of Education, 1987), a report that sent a clear message about the need to reform middle school education. Widely discussed among middle school educators, the report had considerable downstream impact on the conception of the Charles Ruff portfolio assessment system explained in this chapter.

By the mid-1980s Charles Ruff Middle School in northern California was well on its way to becoming a middle school in more than name only, which it had been called since it opened its doors in the late 1960s. Teachers at Ruff wanted it to be a place where young people would risk exploration of their worlds and feel comfortable, safe, and understood—at least a little. They wanted to help students develop their identities not just academically, but socially, morally, ethically, and aesthetically. They wanted to make students not just competent and knowledgeable, but engaged and interested, connected to their school, their community, and their families.

Teachers at Ruff knew that something in schooling had to slow down and make room for more than information in textbooks and test scores. As it was, there seemed to be little room on the academic conveyor belt for anything of substance that a student might bring to school, and the only thing too many students seemed to take from school were Carnegie units for time served, or at most, bits of knowledge that fit bubbles on standardized test answer documents. To make school better for everyone, the teachers believed children needed more opportunities to think for themselves, to explore and examine, to make choices, and to take responsibility for consequences. Above all, they needed to be *paid attention to*.

By the late 1980s and early 1990s, the alternative assessment movement was in full swing and was widely viewed as an important tool in reformers' efforts to make secondary schools more humane and effective. The portfolio system discussed in this chapter emerged in the early 1990s, a few years after Ruff caught the reform bug, in an attempt to better the daily lives of students.

Exemplar System

The portfolio system explained in this chapter was developed in 1993 and implemented in 1994 by a group of English teachers with the support of a State grant. Because information for this chapter was taken from a year-long study which promised anonymity to the school and to the teachers and students, names of participants and places have been changed. There is no Charles Ruff Middle School—that we know of.

Context for the System

Charles Ruff Middle School, an urban school with over 1,600 ethnically diverse, predominantly low-income students, had been very active as a reform site in California long before the English Department developed its portfolio assessment system in 1993. In the mid-1980s, for example, Ruff was among the first schools in the state to transform its school calendar from a traditional one, in which everyone takes the summer off, to a year-round one, in which the school rarely closes. True, the impetus for this change was ambiguous: California school districts at the time were getting full funds from the State to build new schools for their burgeoning populations only if they could show evidence of maximum use of existing facilities. Going year-round was one way to provide that evidence. Nonetheless, there was also considerable belief that the year-round schedule would be better for students.

In the same decade Ruff's English Department was awarded a grant from the State Department of Education to become a demonstration site for California's new English/Language Arts Framework, a document which promised a new era of literature-based English/Language Arts instruction in all of California's schools. Soon after, the school's Mathematics Department, Science Department, and Physical Education

Department were awarded similar grants. Thus, four large departments were poised to transform themselves into model departments, sentinels of reform for the State.

As if four separate demonstration grants totaling almost a quarter of a million dollars each year weren't enough for this reform-minded site, in the early 1990s the whole school was awarded a large schoolwide grant pursuant to California's Senate Bill 1274 (1990) aimed at restructuring the day-to-day organization of the school, and, for a time, change became the only thing you could count on at Ruff. Although grant funds were used largely to finance staff development, technology, common planning time for the teachers, and curriculum and instruction projects, almost all of the departments and their faculty had been long interested in alternative assessment, especially the English, Science, and Mathematics Departments.

Further, the school's involvement in restructuring, coordinated by the California Center for School Restructuring, had brought home the challenge of "examining student work for what matters most," an important slogan of the State's restructuring initiative. Grant recipients were expected to participate in a "protocol"—a highly ritualized public discussion and analysis of student work from the school's classrooms conducted to gain insight into the school's effectiveness—once each year at a State conference. In addition, the English, Science, and Mathematics Departments had each participated in the field trials of a number of alternative assessment development efforts for several years, including field trials of the California Learning Assessment System's innovative but ill-fated reading and writing test known as CLAS. Importantly, the English Department had participated in a year-long portfolio assessment field trial sponsored by the New Standards Project, a consortium of states and departments of education engaged in the development of an alternative assessment system.

The stage was set for the English Department's effort to put together not a collection of isolated portfolio systems from individual teachers' classrooms, but a departmental system that could help unify the curriculum, provide useful data, and mute the problem of students' disengagement in classrooms—a tall order for a collection of manila folders.

Purposes for the System

The portfolio system designed by the Ruff English Department had four ambitious purposes. First, the portfolio system was to be the method by which English faculty could reach and maintain agreements on what the local goals of the curriculum really were. These agreements would also cover how everyone—teachers, students, and parents—would know whether students had actually reached those goals. Prior to the portfolio system, materials that ostensibly governed local goals—the district's curriculum binder with its matrices and lists, the district's adopted anthology with its teachers' manuals and tests, and the State's assessment handbooks which specified how writing should be taught—had been bestowed on the faculty, not agreed to and construed locally by the teachers themselves.

Because nobody had really agreed to implement these materials and nobody ever checked in the classrooms to see whether anyone *was* implementing them, there was wide variation in what went on in English classrooms. Some teachers taught vocabulary words in list form, for example, with memorized definitions and periodic quizzes. Other teachers taught students to use self-collection strategies and worried about whether new vocabulary transferred to student writing. One purpose of the portfolio system was to bring some uniformity to curriculum and instruction across the school's

English program, ideally a uniformity rooted in what the teachers could agree on as "best practices"—or at least uniform goals.

Second, the portfolio system was designed to improve the validity and the fairness of the school's report card grades in English. Like most middle schools, Charles Ruff Middle School used the letter grading system of A through F to report student progress to parents. And like most middle schools, nobody really knew what it meant to say that a student earned an "A" or a "C" in his/her English class. Each teacher had his/her own curriculum and his/her own grading system with its own standards and expectations.

A serious problem of fairness emerges in a system with such idiosyncratic values and goals. For one thing, students do not enjoy equal opportunities to learn. Yet unequal opportunities to learn are not the only disadvantage students face. When standards and expectations differ from teacher to teacher in unpredictable ways, how students are judged with respect to their experiences also varies, advantaging or disadvantaging them according to chance. In sum, both the nature of what counts as performance in the English classroom *and* how that performance is judged fluctuates unfairly. Following on the heels of the problem of fairness is the problem of validity. When values are not communicated to others—not to fellow teachers, not to students, not to administrators, not to parents—nobody knows what constructs anyone else is teaching. In such circumstances, validity is a hit or miss affair. At Ruff, the portfolio system was to provide an antidote—a common set of standards and expectations so that everyone—teachers, students, parents, administrators, and anyone else who cared to investigate—could know precisely what it meant to get a particular grade in a particular English class.

Third, the portfolio system was to drive reading and writing instruction at the school in a particular direction such that students would become more deeply engaged in literacy experiences and would self-identify as readers. An agreement built into the portfolio system from the start was that a primary instructional mission ought to be to teach students to assume the role of a reader of serious literature. If that mission were indeed primary, then the assessment system would have to include a clear definition of it. In the end, the teachers wanted to influence their students' self-perceptions so that students would come to identify themselves as "readers" as opposed to "non-readers" and would thereafter *behave* as such. Building in the expectation that students would become readers went well beyond asking students to comprehend texts accurately and gain new vocabulary—though comprehension and vocabulary were given instructional attention and assessment weight on the portfolio scoring rubric.

What did Ruff readers do? How did they think?

Readers read every day, for one thing, often for long periods of an hour or more according to the portfolio scoring rubric. Readers also set learning goals for themselves as readers, complex goals that took time and required effort to accomplish, important personal goals that promised to sharpen understanding of life and literature. Readers kept records of their work so that they could periodically analyze themselves. Readers selected texts carefully, not haphazardly, to ensure that texts presented appropriate intellectual, emotional, linguistic, rhetorical, or cultural challenges and furthered progress toward a goal.

Readers were persistent. Instead of abandoning carefully chosen texts when difficulties arose, readers applied strategies that permitted them to clarify and extend and understand. To acquire strategies and to create original ones, readers attended to instruction and then transferred their insights into the arena of self-selected reading. Readers wrote themselves into the books they read and were, in turn, themselves rewritten by those books Above all, readers "dug deeper," that is, they questioned, challenged, proved, explored both the world of the text and their own experiential worlds.

Miall and Kuiken (1995) designed a survey to measure dimensions of orientation toward literary reading that illustrates what the Ruff English teachers meant by digging deeper. For instance, one of the dimensions, "insight," defined an important aspect of digging deeper. Readers interested in gaining insight from text, according to Miall and Kuiken (1995), use the literary text as a guide to the "recognition of previously unrecognized qualities, usually in the reader, but also in the reader's world" (p. 41). The Ruff portfolio teachers agreed that this language described digging deeper, particularly as it related to reality-based thinking. Such reading meant reading the text, but it also meant reading the self, and reading the world.

Interestingly, Miall and Kuiken (1995) distinguished between "a form of absorbing reading that heightens awareness (insight) and a form of absorbing reading that dulls awareness (leisure escape)" (p. 46). Ruff teachers incorporated this distinction in the portfolio scoring rubric under the heading "consistency and challenge," which described A level students as those who select readings that "not only entertain, but also challenge and stretch capabilities." Escaping the world would be an unlikely route to gaining insight into the world.

Miall and Kuiken (1995) identified a second dimension of an orientation to literary reading: "empathy." Defined by these researchers as "projective identification with fictional characters" (p. 41), empathy was seen as an important component of digging deeper by the English teachers at Ruff. They encouraged their students to identify with fictional characters through a variety of whole-class and small-group strategies involving role playing, writing letters to characters, writing letters as characters, and discussing what characters might have been thinking or feeling in selected situations.

As part of an instructional approach aimed at supporting students through the transition from non-reader or leisure-escape reader to literary reader in the habit of digging deeper, the portfolio system required that students establish goals for themselves as readers early each trimester. Although each teacher was free to approach goal setting in his/her own way, the expectation was that all students would articulate their goals for reading at the beginning of the trimester, revisit those goals periodically, and provide evidence in their portfolios of having worked toward achievement of their goals.

The fourth purpose of the Ruff portfolio assessment system was to promote in students the capacity for reflective analysis, especially as writers. To be sure, some *high* school teachers will argue vigorously that even their juniors and seniors cannot reflect with any level of sophistication on their own work products and processes. How could the Ruff teachers expect *middle* school students to do such thinking? Camp (1992) and Howard (1990) describe how we *can* teach students to perform the art of reflective analysis at their own level of sophistication in two ways: (1) by asking students to respond to reflective questions or prompts, and (2) by setting up reflective events in our classrooms involving pieces of writing done over time. The Ruff English teachers extended this line of thinking one step. They concluded that we indeed must nudge and invite with reflective prompts and reflective events, but we must do more—we must *expect* and *assess* the products of reflective analysis.

System Design

As the preceding section explains, this portfolio system was designed to promote four purposes: to bring coherence to the local English/Language Arts curriculum, improve the validity and fairness of grades in English at the school, encourage students to perceive themselves as serious readers of literature written in English and in other languages, and stimulate reflective analysis among students, especially related to their own writings. Designed in 1993 by a small group of English teachers at the site, the system was the subject of a school experiment during the 1994–95 school year and was adopted for departmental use thereafter. The system described here reflects the design originally implemented during the 1994-95 academic year.

Collection

Students collected artifacts in three separate portfolios to illustrate their work in class and at home, one during each of three, twelve-week (trimester) grading periods. Most work completed during a particular trimester could be submitted only in that trimester's portfolio, not in the next trimester's portfolio—not, that is, unless it had been substantially revised, reread, or reworked. The last portfolio of the year was no different from the first in this regard. For example, a student who had written a narrative during the first trimester could not include it in his third-trimester portfolio unless it had been changed during the third trimester in important ways. Some work—for instance, students' text logs—could never be reworked for another trimester's portfolio. Text logs were a chronicle of the students' reading activities over a particular twelve-week period. One exception to this rule was this: All Ruff students were given an on-demand, holistically scored, open-ended reading exam at the beginning and again at the end of the academic year. Many students included their beginning and ending reading exams in their portfolios, particularly if the end-of-year score was higher than the beginning score, or if students could point out more sophisticated thinking in the end-of-course exam than in the beginning one.

What work was worth collecting?

The subcommittee of English teachers who designed the system prepared a Student Handbook to guide students as they went about the business of collecting artifacts for possible inclusion in the portfolio. After all, not everything could go in the portfolio, and for the most part students were discouraged from collecting digital and/or audio- or video-taped evidence. The actual portfolios which students put together at the end of the grading term and sent off to the library for grading included at most two pieces of writing and only a handful of examples of work done in reading. Nonetheless, the Handbook directed students to save *all* of their work over the course of the trimester so that pieces of work could be selected for each of the following categories:

- Best Piece of Writing
- Text Log
- Shared Reading
- Free Choice

Best Piece of Writing. Students had to collect all of the visible—and some of the invisible—work that they did during the process of composing their "best piece of writing." This meant that they had to save preliminary doodles and drawings, they had to make notes that explained with whom they had conferenced and what the outcome of the conference was, and they had to save all of their drafts (if they re-drafted or used a word processor) and their "sloppy copies" if they made changes directly on a paper draft. Because no one could be sure which piece of writing s/he worked on during the trimester would ultimately turn out to be the "best piece," students had to learn to save their work for each writing project they did. Because the regular classroom teachers were giving students discursive feedback but not letter grades on their writings, students could not look to their teachers' grades on individual essays to help them choose their "best." The idea was that students would learn to be responsible for collecting evidence of their own work processes and products if the task of collecting was truly "their own"—and if they were held accountable.

Text Log. Early in each grading period, students were required to self-select several titles of books they planned to read over the trimester. Students set learning goals for themselves as readers and conferenced with their teachers during the first few weeks; from these negotiations the list of titles emerged. Then, as students read, responded to, and analyzed the books they had chosen both at home and in their classrooms, they were required to keep daily records in their text logs. They captured simple historical data in their logs, such as when and how much they read. They also wrote discursive entries which explained how they responded to the previous day's reading, how they processed the text, or anything else important about the reading—anything, that is, except a plot summary. Students were encouraged to write about their engagement with the text, the strategies they used to process the text, and their reflections on the text. They were directly instructed not to summarize or retell.

Shared Reading. The Ruff English teachers taught in a district that had developed a district-wide list of works of "core literature" in accordance with the California English/Language Arts Framework, the reform document of the mid-1980s. As a consequence, the teachers were expected to teach certain novels in seventh and eighth grade. Before the teachers developed their portfolio system, the bulk of their instruction focused on these novels and on teaching students to write particular genres of essays as mandated by the State's holistic writing assessment. After the teachers developed their portfolio assessment system with its emphasis on self-selected reading, they realized that the by-now familiar core literature approach had to change somewhat to accommodate students' own textual choices.

Rather than abandon all core literature, however, the teachers agreed to scale back the number of titles they would teach. They also decided to develop and share lessons using shorter text segments—short stories, essays, and poems—which could be taught in one or a few class periods. The teachers wanted to give students direct instruction in reading strategies that students could try out in a social setting—a shared reading—and then transfer to the reading of their own books. The idea was to teach students something about "good" literature in a context where transference to self-selected literature was the real value. The teachers expected students to collect artifacts from their shared reading experiences over the course of the trimester and then use the collection as a resource when it came time to put together the portfolio for grading purposes.

Free Choice. The Free Choice entry in the portfolio was included to provide students with the broadest possible opportunity to submit evidence of their having accomplished a particular outcome. This entry could hold a second "best writing," if a student had done two good pieces and couldn't decide which to submit. It could hold a piece of work done in response to shared reading, if a student had a similar problem with that entry. Or it could hold a single journal entry, a certain telling quickwrite, a napkin with notes scrawled on it—*any artifact* that a student could link to a learning outcome specified on the portfolio scoring rubric. One student might leave this entry up to chance and not think much about it until near the close of the grading period whereupon s/he would make a mad scramble for something to include. Another student might be consciously on the lookout for just the right piece of work all trimester and thereby learn the habit of self-monitoring.

Who had access to and owned the collections?

The students themselves had primary access to the raw collection of artifacts which they gathered over the grading period. Their teachers did not provide them with any special storage space beyond a filing cabinet drawer (one for each period of students) which students could use or not as they pleased, and occasions were rare when students complained that someone had taken a particular piece of work. Teachers did collect and return work as usual in order to give students feedback (recall that they never put letter grades on any piece of work collected, but wrote comments); so the work did leave the hands of students temporarily. Parents and counselors could request the work of particular students in order to make decisions about how to proceed in certain circumstances, but students were responsible for bringing in work— not teachers.

In the classrooms students were often given opportunities to examine their work and the work of their peers in small and large groups. Whether this meant sharing a piece of writing in a writing response group or for a whole-class audience, discussing a book in a literature circle or a bookshare, or talking about in issue raised during shared reading, students were instructed always to tie their work and the work of their peers to the portfolio scoring rubric and to collect evidence (notes) of their participation in the examination. In this respect, students had frequent access to the work of their peers. In fact, participation was a requirement of the course.

When the portfolios left the classrooms at the end of each trimester and were sent to the library for grading, a committee of Ruff English teachers (not the teachers-of-record) had access to the collections. These teachers examined individual portfolios and, using the portfolio scoring rubrics (see Figures 3.1 and 3.2), gave them grades. They also wrote feedback to students which spelled out strengths and weaknesses evident in the portfolio together with suggestions for improvement in a document called "commentary." Then the examination committee sent the collections back to the classrooms where the teachers-of-record handed them back to students and led discussions in which students talked about the grades and feedback they had received on their portfolios. Students were then the owners of the collections and could take them home to do what they liked with them. (During the pilot year, 1994–95, whole class sets of graded student portfolios were kept for analysis as part of the study.)

Figure 3.1
Reading Rubric

GRADES: READING	CONSISTENCY AND CHALLENGE	CONTROL OF PROCESSES	SELF-ASSESSMENT AND REFLECTION	KNOWLEDGE AND WORK PRODUCTS
A	• reading done habitually almost every day, often for long periods of an hour or so • readings not only entertain, but also challenge and stretch capabilities • reads widely; experiments with new authors and forms	• rereads and revises interpretations • supports views with references to the text • uses a variety of strategies and response types • shows persistence	• sets complex goals for reading and achieves them • applies personal/ public criteria and supports judgments • analyzes own processes thoughtfully	• reads like a writer • creates organized, complete, and effective work products • learns new vocabulary regularly • pays attention to literary and stylistic features of texts • interprets shared readings personally and deeply
B	• reading done habitually almost every day, often for shorter periods of time • readings entertain, not so much challenge and stretch capabilities • less experimentation with new forms, though perhaps tries new authors	• tends to stick with one interpretation • supports views but may need to explain more thoroughly • uses less variety of strategies and response types • sometimes shows persistence; some-times is satisfied when understanding could be improved	• sets complex goals for reading and works to achieve them • applies criteria to texts but with less clear support • analyzes own processes superficially	• creates organized and complete work products • shows some attention to learning new vocabulary • pays less attention to literary and stylistic features of texts • understands shared readings thoroughly
C	• reading done at least once or twice a week, often for brief periods of 10 to 30 minutes • readings mainly for entertainment • little evidence of concern for experimenting with new authors or forms	• interprets readings superficially • only occasional support for own views • relies on one or two strategies and response types • may give up easily or quickly when bored or challenged	• sets simple goals for reading and achieves them • applies criteria to texts mechanically • analyzes own processes with cliches; may use reflective-type terms with little understanding	• creates only superficially polished ones • occasionally shows interest in learning new vocabulary • rarely pays attention to style/literary features • understands shared readings superficially
D	• reading done quite sporadically • resists even readings that entertain • may not finish books	• sketchy interpretations • little if any support for views • relies on one strategy or response type	• sets simple goals and works to achieve them • seems uninterested in own learning and processes	• work products seem sloppy or "slapped together" • little interest in vocabulary development • evidence of exposure to shared readings
E	• little or no evidence of reading	• little evidence that the student interprets reading • little evidence of views	• may set up simple or no goals with little work • doesn't even go through the motions of voicing vague cliches	• few if any work products

Figures 3.2
Writing Rubric

GRADES: WRITING	CONSISTENCY AND CHALLENGE	CONTROL OF PROCESSES	SELF-ASSESSMENT AND REFLECTION	KNOWLEDGE AND WORK PRODUCTS
A	• writes fluently and elaborately for a variety of purposes, both formal and informal • selects personally interesting writing topics that stretch capabilities • experiments with drafts; tries out ideas to see how they look on the page; explains purposes and outcomes of experiments	• uses a variety of writing process tools and strategies • evidence of sophisticated and flexible planning of writing projects • draws on multiple sources to shape ideas • uses drafts to discover ideas, clarify language, and explore alternative possibilities • shows persistence	• sets complex goals for writing and achieves them • applies personal/public criteria to texts written by self and others during both process and product work • is alert to own thought processes during writing events and can recognize learnings	• writes like a reader • creates organized, complete, and effective work products in both content and form • evidence of habitual application of knowledge of conventions in final drafts • evidence of command of a variety of sentence structures; uses sentence structure to enhance the meaning
B	• writes less fluently or elaborately for formal and informal purposes • selects writing topics of personal interest; less concern with challenge • less evidence of experimenting with drafts or less explanation of purposes and outcomes	• uses some process tools and strategies • plans, but less sophistication and flexibility • may overrely on one or more sources • less use of drafts for discovery and clarification • sometimes shows persistence when writing; sometimes is satisfied when piece could be improved	• sets complex goals for writing and works to achieve them • applies criteria to texts but less effectively • is sometimes alert to own thought processes during writing events but only occasionally recognizes new insights and learnings	• creates organized and complete work products in both content and form • shows attention to application of knowledge of conventions in final drafts, but less consistently • evidence of command of sentence structures but with less variety
C	• writes to complete assignments • selects writing topics of personal interest, often concerned with ease • little evidence of purposeful experimentation	• mechanical use of process tools and strategies • plans are routinized and inflexible • usually relies on one source to shape ideas • usually sees drafts as products • usually is satisfied when piece could be improved	• sets simple goals for writing and achieves them • only vaguely applies criteria to texts • is rarely alert to own thought processes during writing and expresses cliches or vague learnings	• creates superficially polished work products • exhibits a basic knowledge of conventions in final drafts • sentence structure is serviceable but usually simple and/or repetitive • final drafts contain occasional surface errors
D	• evidence that writing is attempted • does not develop even topics that are personally interesting	• uses one or two process strategies • may have a vague plan • always sees drafts as products	• sets simple goals and works to achieve them • seems uninterested in own learning but voices vague cliches	• work products are slapped together, • frequent, serious errors in conventions • final drafts look like rough drafts
E	• little evidence of writing • is satisfied with incomplete, unfinished, or no pieces of work	• little or no evidence of process strategies • drafts are not even seen as products	• may set simple or no goals with little work • doesn't even go through the motions of voicing vague cliches	• few if any work products

Selection

The discussion of how artifacts were collected makes clear that the line between collection and selection in this system was not black and white. Students had to think almost constantly about what they might select for their portfolios as they went about their day-to-day business—always with an eye on what work would best fit the criteria of the portfolio scoring rubric. Moreover, although the teachers did not put letter grades on student work, students did get written comments from their teachers, many of which contained evaluative language that colored students' perceptions of the quality of particular pieces of work. Peers also made evaluative comments in many forms, ranging from subtle signals of laughter or rapt attention to overt judgments. Nonetheless, when the time came to put together a portfolio destined for the library, individual students were responsible for making their own choices. The following sections explain in more detail how the selection process worked.

When did selection take place?

As the discussion of collection suggests, the question of when selection occurred is complex. Some students knew the very moment that words were spilling from their pen that the resultant product was going to be so wonderful that it would more than likely make its way into the portfolio. And some students knew that any work they did during a particular period—say, the two-week period after a traumatic event like the loss of a friend—would probably not represent best work and so would not be included. In fact, this aspect of the selection process, perhaps more than any other aspect of the portfolio system design, gave students some measure of control over their work processes.

There was, however, a due date. Students had to make their selections and package their portfolios for presentation by a date near the end of each twelve-week period, and their teachers blocked off most of the final two weeks of the term for portfolio selection and assembly. During these two weeks students worked alone, in small groups, and in conference with their teacher—and in some cases their parents—to review their collections of artifacts and make judgments about the quality of particular artifacts in light of the criteria spelled out on the portfolio scoring rubric. Because their selections determined their entire course grade for the grading period, these two-week sweeps were filled with intense and agonizing work, probably the hardest work of the trimester for most students.

Who selected artifacts for presentation?

The answer to this question has already been given in many respects, but there are some subtle points to explicate. As we have already indicated, students made their own selections. Yet they did so after having been given qualitative and judgmental feedback from peers, teachers, and parents. Thus, the selection process was not without constraints for the students. In an even more profound sense, their selections were constrained because they were made from a collection of work which had in large measure been predetermined for them by their teachers. For example, students might select their "best piece of writing" from among several compositions, but the compositions available for selection could all have been, say, autobiographical compositions—since the teacher had chosen to focus instruction on autobiographical writing for that trimester. However, within the parameters of the curriculum and opportunities for work given by the teacher, students were responsible for making selections.

What was the purpose for selection?

The answer to this question depends upon who is asking. The purpose for selection for the students clearly was to get the highest possible grade on their portfolios. The logic was simple: Collect work, so that you could select the best work, so that you could get the best possible grade, so that you could maximize the rewards that come from good grades (parental and teacher approval, money, development of a good record that could lead to college or to a good job, permission to participate on the basketball team, etc.). Beyond any shadow of a doubt, almost every Ruff English student involved in the portfolio system—even those students who in the past had done very little school work—worked at an uncommon level of intensity during the selection period to put together the best possible portfolio.

The teachers had a more complex purpose for selection. To be sure, they wanted to support their students in making the best possible choices for their portfolios. In some ways, it was not simply the work of the students that went to the library for evaluation. It was the work of the teachers as well—their colleagues were examining and evaluating the fruits of their classrooms. Teachers' reputations were at stake. Moreover, the teachers-of-record were the front line when parents called the school to ask about their child's grades. They were the ones who had to explain to parents why particular portfolios did or did not meet particular standards. Despite these professional and practical matters, the teachers had a deeper instructional purpose in designing the selection principles embedded in their portfolio system. Through giving their students experiences in selection together with direct instruction in the criteria by which portfolios were being evaluated, the teachers aimed to encourage greater engagement, greater awareness of work processes, and ultimately higher levels of learning among their students.

Who was the audience for the presentation?

The audience for the presentation was a volunteer committee of Ruff English teachers who were provided substitute teachers in their own classrooms for three separate, four day periods, one at the conclusion of each trimester, during which they evaluated student portfolios. Although these teachers were not the teachers-of-record, neither were they strangers. Students learned quickly to identify members of the examination committee. Indeed, after the first scoring session of the year, the examination teachers made appearances in the classrooms and fielded questions from students about the general experience of scoring all of the portfolios. The examination teachers were required not just to put a grade on the portfolios. They also had to write signed letters to each student, explaining that student's individual strengths and weaknesses based upon evidence in the portfolio; students therefore had full knowledge of who had graded their portfolio for any given trimester.

The examination committee was the subject of much discussion during day-to-day work in the portfolio classrooms. Often either a teacher or a student could be heard asking a question like "If you were an examination teacher, what would you think about . . . ?" or making a statement like "If I were an examination teacher, I might think that . . . ." In an effort to keep the portfolio system rigorous but humane, the Ruff teachers agreed early on that because references to the examination teachers would be unavoidable in the classrooms, such references should always be dignified and should represent a logical connection between the student work under discussion and the portfolio scoring rubric. No one wanted to paint a portrait of the examination teacher as a monster waiting with red pen poised to destroy the lives and fortunes of adolescents. Instead, every effort was made to help students construct a sense of the examiner audience as being made up of interested, smart, knowledgeable, and dedicated teachers who could be expected to give back helpful advice—not just a mute letter grade.

Reflection

Earlier in this discussion, we said that a major goal of the portfolio assessment system was to promote reflective analysis among students, especially with respect to their writing. While the teachers did emphasize reflection as a central aspect of development as a writer, capacity for self-assessment and reflective analysis were a big part of the scoring guide for reading as well. Generally, students were expected to look back and examine themselves as readers, writers, and learners when they began assembling their portfolios. There were, however, daily and weekly opportunities for reflection built into the system. There had to be, for students knew that their grade was contingent on the quality of their reflection.

What opportunities for reflection did the system provide?

The system required every student to include in his/her portfolio an essay titled "Autobiography of Me as a Reader and Writer," a notion borrowed from the portfolio system developed in the Pittsburgh schools during the late 1980s and early 1990s. An essential guidepost for the examination teachers, the "Autobiography" spelled out the goals the student had set for himself or herself for the grading period. Then it explained what the student had done to accomplish these goals, which goals had been reached, and what the student had learned from the work. Further, it directed the examination teacher to look for specific artifacts as evidence of achievement of particular goals. Once the "Autobiography" had been read and understood, the examination teacher had some sense of the claims made by the student and could evaluate the evidence in light of those claims.

Although students knew that they would write the "Autobiography" near the tenth or eleventh week of class, few of them began work on it before their teacher announced the beginning of the official portfolio assembly phase. In fact, most students didn't start this essay until they were well into the selection process. For many students, the "Autobiography" was the last piece of work finished; some stayed up late the night before deadline completing it.

During the first experience with writing in this particular genre, the teachers gave students a template or outline to follow, consisting of a series of questions like "What were your goals this trimester for reading? for writing?" and "What did you learn about yourself as a writer (or reader) during this trimester?" Many students responded to the questions in order with a paragraph for each question and then recopied their paragraphs to look like an essay. Consequently, many of the early essays read like disjointed responses to a series of questions, a circumstance which caused the examination teachers to wonder whether these students could, after all, be taught reflective analysis.

Later, however, many students moved away from the template, often encouraged to do so by their teacher, because the template or outline appeared not to have served students well in terms of supporting a desirable grade. In fact, the template seemed to have led students to create weak overviews to their portfolios. The examination teachers found themselves better able to read and more confident to judge those portfolios where students had stated their goals and pointed explicitly to evidence; those portfolios in which the learning situation was vague or non-existent were almost impossible to judge.

In addition to this autobiographical writing, students were asked to prepare "entry slips," that is, comments explaining how each entry met the criteria for one of the required entries in their portfolios. Composing these entry slips provided students with another opportunity for reflection. The best writing entry slip, for example, required students to explain their entire writing process for the piece to the examination committee—how they came upon the idea, how they got started, who they used for response, how and why they changed their drafts, and more. This entry slip also required students to point explicitly to artifacts in the portfolio so that the examination teacher could turn right to needed evidence.

Like the autobiographies, the entry slips began the year in the form of templates. In this case, however, there was no pretense at writing an essay. Students were given prepared forms with questions followed by extra long blank spaces for their comments. This practice was borrowed from an early version of the New Standards Project's portfolio system in which entry slips with grading criteria for each entry had been reprinted from the scoring rubric. Again, many students soon rejected the forms and began writing letters to the examination teachers in which students could use persuasive, personal voices.

Another opportunity for reflection that was built into the portfolio system was the text log strategy. Unlike the autobiography and the entry slips, though, the text log system required students to reflect on their reading on a daily basis. Students were given forms divided into five squares, one for each day of the school week, with directions to record the day, date, title of book, time, and pages read. Each of the five squares contained enough blank space for students to write three or four sentences. In those sentences students were to express their thoughts, about what they had read the previous evening (the standing homework assignment was to read for at least thirty minutes). Students were told not to write paraphrases or summaries of the content of their reading. Rather, they were to reflect on its significance or on the reading process itself.

The examination committee had a powerful influence on how text logs were implemented in the classrooms. On one hand, the examination teachers would assign no higher than a C in reading to students whose text logs paraphrased or summarized the story. They needed to see evidence of strategy use, response variations, and the like, in order to warrant judgments of higher grades. On the other hand, the examination teachers could assign a grade no higher than a C in reading to students whose text logs appeared to have been written in isolation from the text—sometimes with connection between a log entry and the content of a text (e.g., "I tried drawing a picture to help me understand the last part of the chapter, and it worked."). To be successful, students had to learn how to paraphrase a bit of reading without seeming to paraphrase, an art with seemingly little utility in real life.

Beyond the autobiographical essays, entry slips, and text logs, the system did not require that students engage in other reflective events. Each in her own way, however, the portfolio teachers all asked their students to participate in reflective events at least weekly, ranging from "Friday Reflections," letters to the teacher written on Fridays, to reflective discussions, conferences, and conversations.

What kinds of artifacts of reflective activity went in the portfolio?

As explained in the preceding section, the system required several artifacts of reflection: a written autobiographical essay, written entry slips, and written text logs. Students did, however, include other artifacts of reflection. Some students, for example, kept reflective notes during the composition of major writing projects, notes which examined writing decisions as they were being made on the fly, and later submitted them as part of their writing project for the trimester. Others scribbled reflective comments in the margins of actual work documents or on post-it notes to give the examination teachers a kind of close up on the work as they graded it. All students were invited to include letters of recommendation from their teacher, their peers, and their parents. Many, though by no means all students included one or more of these letters which tended to be reflective in tone in that they surveyed the student's work over an expanse of time.

Student Voices

The Ruff system, like many other portfolio systems, was designed to create changes in how students participate in learning over a year or more of schooling—not over a short period such as a day, a week, or even a month. To illustrate this intention, we present here excerpts of student reflections from the portfolios of a student, Lori (a pseudonym), who went to school at Ruff for both seventh and eighth grades and kept Ruff-style portfolios throughout this period.

Lori's autobiography written for the Winter, 1997, portfolio scoring period showed that she was beginning to engage in goal-setting activities. Lori wrote the following:

> Dear Evaluation Teacher,
> My reading goal for the second trimester is to explore mysteries and compare them with horror books to see the differences and similarities. I came to select this goal when I saw a mystery movie and I wanted to read the book.

Like middle school students generally and like Ruff students in particular, Lori was no exception in her fascination with horror. Ruff students tended to begin their portfolio experiences either as non-readers or as leisure-escape readers (Underwood, 1999). Lori was in the latter category.

Lori's goal statement reveals a willingness to cross genre boundaries. She had experience with reading books by R. L. Stine and Christopher Pike, and she knew what to expect from them. Moreover, she knew how to use her experiences with Stine and Pike's brand of horror to read other books of the genre written by other authors. The following excerpt from a textlog entry illustrates this point (in this entry Lori was responding to a book titled *Sorority Sister* by Diane Hoh):

> This book is a Nightmare Hall book by Diane Hoh. This author seems familiar to me, but I never remember reading any books written by her, except this one. Nightmare Hall is like how R.L. Stine's books are. Like his are Fear Street and Diane Hoh's are Nightmare Hall. I can't really see why I shouldn't read this book because it seems like a good book and it is a thriller.

This excerpt also shows that Lori resists the message from Ruff portfolio culture that she change her habits and values as a reader: "I can't really see why I shouldn't read this book."

When the Spring, 1997, portfolio scoring period had arrived, Lori revealed that she had taken another small step. In the previous portfolio, she presented evidence of a struggle between familiar and unfamiliar kinds of books, but she also tried to broaden her interest in horror ever so slightly by inching toward a sister genre, mystery. Third trimester, Lori took an even bigger risk:

> Dear Evaluation teacher,
> For the third trimester, I set reading goals that were connected to my writing goals. This way it shows that I am going for complex goals. Also, my reading goal has two parts to it. My reading goal is to explore biographies of singers and other famous people, *and* compare the author's writing style. I came to select this goal when I wanted to explore books that weren't horror or mystery. . . . This stretched me as a reader because I am now completely hooked to another genre that I have never tried before. I took a shot at it, and it turned out that I am enjoying it.

When Lori arrived in the middle of her eighth grade year, her second trimester goals involved reading memoirs by Annie Dillard, Maxine Hong Kingston, and Joan Didion. She wanted to write a memoir; she thought she would do better if she read works by these authors, who had been recommended to her by her examination teacher and by her classroom teacher. The following excerpt from second-trimester text logs illustrates how Lori began crossing boundaries beyond genere boundaries. This entry was written on December 30, 1997, in response to *China Men* by Maxine Hong Kingston:

> I think this part I just read is really interesting because it's about the laws, some of which is related to what I'm learning in history. There's a part about the Constitution and a little about the Fourteenth Amendment saying that it was adopted in 1868 saying naturalized Americans have the same rights as native-born Americans. It also talks about Supreme Court cases where some-one was versing another, testing laws against or what the court ruled . . . When I read about them in here, I think "Hey! What is this? I learned it in history." Wow! This book is not only related to reading, but to history too!!

By the third trimester of eighth grade, Lori seemed to have become fully socialized into the role of the reader as it was spelled out by the portfolio system. Here is what she wrote in her autobiography:

> Through these two years of goal setting, I found that setting goals will help us accomplish what we set for ourselves and we will know what we're do-ing. It'll keep us organized in the present and in the future. And that's why I decided that I would continue to set goals in life and in school even though there's no teacher giving me a goals contract. I know that setting goals is a positive thing and there's no need for someone to tell me to do it, for I am doing this for myself.

(The preceding section titled "Student Voices" was adapted from Underwood, T. *The Portfolio Project: Assessment, Instruction, and Middle School Reform.* Copyright 1999 by the National Council of Teachers of English. Reprinted with permission from Terry Underwood and from the National Council of Teachers of English.)

Evaluation

The Ruff portfolio system relied unabashedly on the traditional grading system. The idea was not to do away with grades and evaluation. Under the portfolio system students still had to earn good grades if they hoped to play basketball, attend dances, make the honor roll, please their parents. They still had to pass their English courses in order to earn sufficient credits to advance to the next grade level. Instead, the idea was to make grades fairer, more understandable, more concrete. If students—and their parents—understood what kinds of academic performances were required for a high grade, teachers believed, then perhaps more students would stretch to accomplish those performances. Moreover, the teachers wanted to bring the evaluation system in better alignment with the real goals of their instruction. If a goal of instruction was to promote daily reading at home, for example, then such reading ought consistently to be a part of the evaluation system. Through alignment of instructional values and evaluative criteria, through a fair and valid application of those criteria, students could better predict the consequences of their actions and make better academic decisions and choices.

What was the role of evaluation in the system?

Evaluation drove the system. Among the very first things students and teachers did together at the beginning of the school year was to review the grading rubrics, one for reading and one for writing (see Figures 3.1 and 3.2). At first, students were overwhelmed by the strange language of the rubric and the unfamiliar expectations. Many were upset that their teacher would not give them grades. Over time, however, as students gained experience in interpreting the rubric and applying it to their own portfolios, as they participated in small-group "translation" sessions where they rephrased the grading criteria into their own talk, they came to understand, if not completely like, the grading criteria—so much so that the teachers changed their minds about rewriting the rubric in "kid-friendly" language. Early on the teachers were frustrated and believed that their students would never grasp the criteria. Later, though, they came to believe that their students' struggles to understand an unwatered-down set of criteria helped them internalize the criteria to a greater depth than otherwise would have been possible.

During the first trimester teachers and students alike used the criteria to guide their work. The teachers invented, modified, and borrowed activities and plans that could provide students with opportunities to do well according to the grading criteria. The students worked hard to match their efforts to the criteria. After the first set of portfolios were returned with letter grades and commentary from the examination committee to the portfolio teachers and students, the teachers analyzed grading patterns, portfolio artifacts, and examination-teacher commentary to determine where they were succeeding and where they needed to improve opportunities for students to do better. Students viewed the commentary as important feedback and factored it into their goal setting work the subsequent grading period.

The academic values of the rubric were relatively simple and were intended primarily to support student growth toward becoming responsible, consistent, and strategic learners, readers, and writers. Almost everyone involved in the system—teachers, parents, and students alike—agreed that there was much good that could come from asking students to set important learning goals, to work consistently toward achieving them, and to develop efficient and effective process strategies along the way. Nonetheless, as they were operationalized in the rubrics and in the work of the examination committee, the values seriously challenged the teachers and the students.

How did the system ensure validity and fairness?

In traditional psychometric terms, validity means the degree to which an evaluation or assessment procedure actually measures what it sets out to measure—construct validity, in other words. There has been an on-going controversy between teachers and test-makers for years on the grounds of validity. For virtually all of the 20th century, for example, English teachers in America have been arguing against the use of multiple-choice tests of editing skills because such tests purportedly measure writing performance but in fact measure only a small part of writing. In short, they are invalid because they don't measure what they say they measure. In the case of the Ruff portfolio system, however, validity meant construct validity plus more. Validity had three dimensions. The first we might think of as instructional validity. Here, the teachers were concerned about how well the system supported and promoted their instructional goals. The second we might think of as construct validity. Here, the teachers were concerned about how well the system supported and promoted what knowledgeable members of the English education community would recognize as legitimate and important reading and writing behaviors. A third component, consequential validity, had to do with the impact of the system on learning and teaching.

Issues of Impact

The Ruff portfolio assessment system had a major impact on instruction during the year it was funded by way of a State grant, an impact which began even before the system was in place. The development of the system's scoring rubrics for reading and for writing, prior to implementation, involved the volunteer portfolio teachers over several months in sustained discussion of their instructional goals and methods. Although the product of these discussions (i.e., the rubric documents) served to guide instructional decision-making throughout the year, the exchange of ideas that occurred during the writing of the rubrics laid a groundwork of common understandings among the teachers which gave them the capacity to collaborate closely as they planned what they would do in their classes with their students. In other words, the language of the rubrics was important as an anchor, but the meaning of this language had been understood through much rich and spirited talk long before words were put on paper.

Moreover, after the teachers began teaching their students using the system, they found that the meaning they had constructed through talk had to be revised in the light of experience. For example, they discovered that teaching students to set goals for themselves was a complicated business, and no one was really sure how to go about it. As the year progressed, goal-setting activities became increasingly more structured and planned. For example, students were asked to develop goal contracts during goal-setting conferences and to have those contracts signed by their parents. The teachers worked together to collect good examples of specific goals to share with their students, and held extended class discussions focused on the worth of particular goals.

In connection with goal setting, they discovered a profound tension between the fixed view of writing genres promoted by the State's writing assessment and the more synthetic, flexible view promoted by the portfolio system. Essentially the State's system, as articulated by the District, spelled out writing goals explicitly for students: Everyone would learn to write an "Autobiographical Incident" essay, for example, or a "Speculation about Cause and Effect" essay. According to the values of the portfolio system, however, students were not to be told what to write; rather, they would set their own writing goals and then receive instructional support in reaching them. This tension was never satisfactorily resolved during the implementation year.

Getting useful feedback to students became an instructional priority. Knowing that the examination committee would take an impartial look at a fairly large body of evidence collected over time, the portfolio teachers learned to make written and verbal comments aimed at fostering change in students' work habits and strategy use over the long run. Comments that began with phrases like "Next time . . ." or "You could have . . ." or "Why don't you try . . ." signaled to students that they needed to look not at their current product, but at their processes. The idea was to support growth in process as a means for achieving product quality, especially important since much of the language of the rubrics focused on process issues.

Interestingly, the portfolio teachers had mixed feelings about the usefulness of the written feedback from the examination committee. Some of the letters back to students following scoring sessions were quite powerful and captured important themes in student portfolios; the portfolio teachers witnessed deep changes in some of their students as a result of this feedback. But some of the letters were superficial, demeaning, and on more than one occasion, what more than one portfolio teacher deemed downright rude. The portfolio teachers began to read each set of comments from the examination teachers and to screen them when necessary—rewrite the commentary, go back to the examination committee member for different commentary, or write a second set of comments to accompany the examination committee's comments. Although there was surprisingly high levels of agreement between the examination teachers and the portfolio teachers on the question of letter grades for portfolios, there were many examples of disagreement on the question of useful feedback.

Student achievement in the portfolio classrooms was examined from a quantitative perspective using locally developed on-demand reading and writing tests. The 200+ students involved in the portfolio project were compared with a cohort of 200+ non-portfolio students at the same site to determine whether any difference could be seen in their achievement. On the direct writing measure, no statistically significant difference was found; that is, the students in the portfolio classrooms demonstrated no more growth as writers than the students in the non-portfolio classrooms demonstrated. On the direct reading measure, however, a statistically significant difference was found in favor of the portfolio students. On this measure of the interpretive reading of literature, the portfolio students demonstrated more growth than non-portfolio students (Underwood, 1998).

Student motivation was also examined using a survey that measured goal orientation. This survey looked at three different types of goal orientation: (a) advancement, wherein students exert effort in academic tasks in order to get a good grade, to move to the next level in the institution, or to ensure greater success later in their careers; (b) learning, wherein students exert effort in order to gain more knowledge, to better understand themselves or their world, or to improve their own capacity to perform; and (c) approval, wherein students exert effort to gain social approval or to avoid disapproval from their teachers and peers.

On this measure there were no differences between portfolio and non-portfolio students on the dimensions of advancement and approval. There was, however, a statistically significant difference on the dimension of learning goal orientation (exerting effort to gain knowledge, understanding, capacity to perform). Portfolio students scored higher on the learning goal orientation measure than did non-portfolio students. This effect was complicated by an interaction between gender and goal orientation. There was no significant difference between females on any of the three dimensions regardless of their placement in portfolio or non-portfolio classrooms. However, there was a significant difference for males, with portfolio males registering significantly higher levels of learning goal orientation than males in the non-portfolio classrooms registered (Underwood, 1998). This finding suggests that systems which promote process-oriented instruction that includes goal-setting, reflective analysis, and impartial evaluation may be more important for males than for females in English classrooms.

Problems and Potential Solutions

The portfolio system at Charles Ruff came into conflict with the State's mandated writing assessment system. The portfolio system asked students to engage in sustained, project-like, process-oriented, self-determined writing experiences. The State system required students to become knowledgeable about fixed genres in order to produce them on demand and de-emphasized writing as a process. Because the State's system carried political authority, the teachers at Ruff had to give it at least as much attention as the kind of writing pedagogy they wanted to implement. Although there is no evidence to suggest that the State's system would produce either superior or inferior results in terms of student achievement in writing, there is some evidence to suggest that students in portfolio classrooms like these, particularly males, maintain equivalent levels of motivation related to advancement and approval yet develop higher levels of learning goal motivation than do students in non-portfolio classrooms.

While this finding is hardly convincing as bottom line evidence in itself, it does suggest that motivational issues related to assessment and instructional methodologies need further examination. A partial solution to the conflict between the State's fixed-genre, product-oriented approach and the portfolio system's synthetic-genre, process-oriented approach lies in continued careful research. For example, research could examine the level of range and versatility writers develop over time in fixed-genre instructional contexts versus synthetic-genre contexts; such studies might tell us whether one approach or the other results in more sophisticated writers able to fulfill their purposes across varied rhetorical situations. Such research is on the horizon given the level of interest in genre studies that has arisen over the past decade (Cope & Kalantzis, 1993; Freedman & Medway, 1994a, 1994b).

The problem of inadequate or less-than-useful feedback from the examination committee could have several solutions. First, the examination teachers in this study were not using the portfolio system in their own classrooms and therefore were not confronted with the daily pressure of generating focused, useful feedback for students that would change their mental habits, attitudes, and processes over the long run. If the examination teachers had also been portfolio teachers, the nature of their feedback might have been different, and students might have found it more useful. Second, all teachers involved in a project such as this might practice writing commentary on student portfolios in a collaborative manner. Clear guidelines with examples of appropriate and useful commentary might be developed. Additionally, teacher research projects focused on discovering the specific kinds of feedback students find most useful could provide empirical data to guide the enterprise.

Opportunities for Discussion and Inquiry

1. The three volunteer portfolio teachers at Ruff spent considerable time talking about their instructional approach and values before they began teaching with their common portfolio system in place. As a consequence, they had rich understandings of their rubrics that would be unavailable to teachers at other schools who had not participated in these discussions. These understandings were clearly important to their capacity to actually use the system. Given this situation, discuss the following questions:

    a. What might have happened to the system if the Ruff teachers had not been able to agree on their values and approach?

    b. If teachers are not able to agree on their values and approach as they go about creating a rubric, what might be done to help them reach agreement?

    c. Given the exporting of the Ruff rubric to another middle school, would it be possible for other teachers not at Ruff to develop the same understandings that the Ruff teachers developed? If so, how could such an understanding be achieved? If not, why not?

2. The portfolio teachers and the examination teachers achieved high levels of inter-rater agreement with respect to letter grades, but they often disagreed with respect to specific feedback written for students. What are the implications for the development of portfolio systems emerging from this finding?

3. This portfolio system appears to have had a positive impact on students' motivation and reading achievement. What features of the system and its implementation might account for this effect? What features might have inhibited this effect? What features of "current traditional" teaching might account for lower levels of motivation and achievement among the non-portfolio students?

4. This portfolio system was tied to the traditional grading system, but it changed the usual relationship between teachers and students in that it transferred the power of the grade to an external committee. How might the system work differently if the regular classroom teacher retained the power of the grade? What other arrangements for issuing grades might be tried?

5. A conflict between the State assessment system and the local portfolio system existed in that each system supported a different writing pedagogy. We have suggested that a potential resolution to this conflict lies in continued research. What other ways might there be to resolve such conflicts?

Acknowledgments

Because the data collected about the Ruff portfolio system was done so under the agreement that the site and its teachers would remain anonymous, we cannot explicitly acknowledge the site principal and teachers who helped us with this chapter. However, they know who they are, and they know that we are grateful.

References

Atwell, N. (1998). *In the middle: New understandings about writing, reading, and learning.* Portsmouth, NH: Boynton/Cook Heinemann.

California State Department of Education (1987). *Caught in the middle.* California Department of Education, 721 Capitol Mall, Fourth Floor, Sacramento, CA 95814.

Camp, R. (1992). Portfolio reflections in middle and secondary school classrooms. In K. B. Yancey, (Ed.) *Portfolios in the writing classroom,* (pp. 61–79). Urbana, Ill.: National Council of Teachers of English.

Cope, B., & Kalantzis, M. (1993). Introduction: How a genre approach to literacy can transform the way writing is taught. In B. Cope & M. Kalantzis (Eds.), *The powers of literacy: A genre approach to teaching writing.* Pittsburgh: University of Pittsburgh Press, (1), 1–21.

Everhart, R. (1983). *Reading, writing, resistance.* Ablex Press.

Freedman, A., & Medway, P. (1994a). Introduction: New views of genre and their implications for education. In A. Freedman and P. Medway (Eds.), *Learning and teaching genre,* (pp. 1–24). Portsmouth, NH: Boynton/Cook.

Freedman, A., & Medway, P. (1994b). Locating genre studies: Antecedents and prospects. In A. Freedman & P. Medway (Eds.), *Genre and the new rhetoric,* (pp. 1–22). Bristol, PA: Taylor & Francis Inc.

Goodlad, J. (1984). *A place called school.* New York: McGraw-Hill.

Howard, K. (1990). Making the portfolio real. *Quarterly for the Center of the Study of Writing and the National Writing Project, 12,* 4–7.

Miall, D., & Kuiken, D. (1995). Aspects of literary response: A new questionnaire. *Research in the Teaching of English, 29* (1), 37–58.

Shannon, P. (1990). Introduction. *The struggle to continue: Progressive reading instruction in the United States* (pp. 1–19). Portsmouth, N.H: Heinemann Books.

Sizer, T. (1984). *Horace's compromise: The dilemma of the American high school.* Boston: Houghton Mifflin.

Underwood, T. (1998). The consequences of portfolio assessment: A case study. *Educational Assessment 5* (3), 147–194.

Underwood, T. (1999). *The portfolio project: Assessment, instruction, and middle school reform.* Urbana, IL: National Council of Teachers of English.

4 Arts PROPEL: Designing Assessment for Learning

During the 1980s and early 1990s, the Pittsburgh Public School District—like many other districts—was changing its writing assessment methods, moving through distinct phases toward increasingly sophisticated approaches (Eresh, 1990). These changes mirrored trends in the field at large with respect to views of writing, of the teaching and learning of writing, and of the teacher's role in writing assessment. In Pittsburgh an increasingly complex perspective on writing and on writing instruction led to a shift from the use of multiple-choice tests to the direct assessment of writing by way of the use of a writing sample and ultimately to experiments with alternative forms of assessment. (For trends in the field at large see Camp, 1993a, 1993b; Lucas, 1988a, 1988b.)

When Pittsburgh used a standardized multiple-choice test of grammar and usage in the early 1980s, the district was using an approach that characterizes knowledge about writing as discrete, hierarchically-arranged components (Camp, 1993a). At the time, the use of multiple-choice tests was widespread in the assessment field at large. But concern had been growing about the pernicious effects on education of indirect, multiple-choice assessments (Haertel & Calfee, 1983; Nystrand & Knapp, 1987). Because they were limited in the range of student skills and knowledge that could be assessed, and because those skills were assessed as separable components, some theoreticians argued that multiple-choice tests led to a narrowed and fragmented curriculum (Corbett & Wilson, 1991; Gitomer, 1993; Resnick & Klopfer, 1989; Wells, 1991). In the writing assessment field in particular, there was a growing consensus that the best way to assess students' writing skills is through the direct assessment of writing (Greenberg, 1992). As Roberta Camp explains, the traditional approach to assessment does not "evoke evidence of the students' ability to engage in complex performances . . ." (Camp, 1993a, p. 184).

When Pittsburgh decided to embrace direct assessment, changing methods to collect an actual sample of writing, their move reflected a growing trend in the educational field at large. By 1984, for example, 22 states conducted direct writing assessments, and 5 more were scheduled to begin conducting direct writing assessments within the next year (Hadley, 1984).

Many educators applauded the move toward direct assessment. They favored the direct collection of an actual writing sample rather than indirect methods because they considered the sample to be essential to the validity of the writing assessment. As Roberta Camp (1993a) explains, "Teachers and researchers in writing and writing instruction have argued that student writers should demonstrate their knowledge and skills not merely by recognizing correctness or error in text, as they do in multiple-choice tests of writing ability, but by engaging in the complex act of creating their own text" (p. 187). The argument was that assessment of a writing sample characterizes writing as a holistic, meaning-making activity requiring the orchestration of diverse skills and strategies, a characterization much more closely related to writing in the real world.

Although it is probably clear that assessing actual writing is preferable to using multiple-choice tests, concern has also been expressed about the limitations of single-sample testing. Research tells us, for instance, that writing done for one purpose requires processes and strategies different from those required for another purpose (Matsuhashi, 1982; Witte, 1988; Witte & Cherry, 1994). Critics of single sample assessment argue that a single sample cannot adequately represent the variety of discourse modes, purposes, and audiences which writing entails (Emig, 1982; Lucas, 1988a, 1988b).

In a third phase, Pittsburgh moved toward an alternative approach to assessment which included long-term projects, reflection, and portfolios. Taking many shapes and names, including "authentic" (Wiggins, 1989); "performance" (Stiggins & Bridgeford, 1985); and "portfolio" (Camp, 1985), alternative forms of assessment have great appeal to those engaged in educational reform. Proponents of reform hope that alternative forms of assessment will encourage teachers to spend more time on activities that cultivate complex understandings (Mitchell, 1992; Simmons & Resnick, 1993); encourage students to become self-directed learners capable of setting their own goals and assessing their own progress (Camp, 1992a; Lamme & Hysmith, 1991; Paulson, Paulson, & Meyer, 1991; Rief, 1990; Tierney, Carter, & Desai, 1991; Wolf, 1989; Zessoules & Gardner, 1991); and give teachers and other professionals more authentic ways to assess and teach students as individuals who have unique needs and patterns of development (Coleman, 1994; Johnston, 1987; Sheingold, Heller, & Paulukonis, 1995; Weinbaum, 1991; Yancey, 1992).

At the time, interest in portfolios was beginning to grow in other areas of the country as well. Reformers found the portfolio approach attractive because portfolios contained multiple examples of student work and could more broadly account for the ways processes and strategies vary as writing tasks vary with purpose, audience, and context. Another attraction was the potential for evidence of students' ability to engage in complex performances and of the processes and strategies they used when they were engaged in them (Camp, 1993a). In addition, in combination with opportunities for reflection, portfolios provided a mechanism for transferring more responsibility to students for their work, including the kinds of goal-setting, record-keeping, and monitoring that characterize the work of independent, self-regulated learners.

In Pittsburgh, the immediate impetus for the shift to long-term projects and portfolios was the project known as Arts PROPEL. A collaborative, multi-year project funded by the Rockefeller Foundation and involving personnel from the Pittsburgh Public Schools, Harvard Project Zero, and the Educational Testing Service, the goal of Arts PROPEL was to develop integrated assessment and instruction in visual arts, music, and imaginative writing. The project was distinctive because it brought together a diverse community of researchers, including skilled arts teachers, practicing artists, developmental psychologists, as well as experienced learning and measurement experts to tackle the problem of how to develop powerful, systematic approaches to assessment that tap qualitative information about students, their standards, and the processes they use to create art.

But information *about* students was not the only, or even the most important goal. For example, in the area of writing, the project brought participants together to talk about two important questions: 'What do we want to learn from the portfolios about students' writing abilities and their development as writers?" and "What do we want students to learn about writing and about themselves as writers?" (Camp, 1992b, p. 253). The result of these discussions, according to Roberta Camp, was that the portfolio was designed primarily to enhance instruction. Teachers were more interested in promoting student learning than in what they could learn about students (Camp, 1992b). In the end, an integrated system was designed that put assessment in the service of learning.

Exemplar System

The name Arts PROPEL stands for "Perception, Production, and Reflection Enhances Learning." Howard Gardner (1992) explains the rationale behind the name:

> The name ARTS PROPEL captures the thinking which underlies our approach. Artistic education ought to feature at least three activities: *Artistic Production*—the creation of art objects and the gaining of facility in "thinking in" particular symbol systems; *Artistic Perception*—the ability to make fine and appropriate discriminations in one's own art works and in art works produced by others, including artistic masters; and *Artistic Reflection*—the capacity to step back from works of art, to think about their purpose, the extent to which and the manner in which they have been achieved, and to clarify the nature of one's own productions and perceptions. (p. 100)

The arts were a particularly "provocative context" for rethinking how to assess student work, as Dennie Palmer Wolf (1988) explains:

> First, in the arts, the ability to find interesting problems is probably at least as important as being able to answer someone else's questions. . . . individuality and invention are at least as essential as mastering technique or knowledge. Second, learning . . . often occurs in very large chunks spread out over a long period of time. Young musicians spend a whole semester coming to a final interpretation of a piece; young painters or printmakers spend months going from thumbnail sketches to finished works. Third, it is essential for young artists—not just their mentors and teachers—to develop a keen sense of standards and critical judgment. (p. 23)

The Arts PROPEL project demonstrated that it is possible to move beyond product-oriented, highly structured, and standardized modes of assessment and further, as will be seen in the sections that follow, that process-oriented portfolios could be used to serve an accountability purpose in the schools. And the portfolios put the student in charge.

Context and Purposes for the System.

As we explained earlier, the Arts PROPEL Project was a collaborative effort of several institutions concerned with arts education in the schools. Not surprisingly, given that the project was the collaborative effort of many individuals, the purposes of the project varied slightly depending upon who defined them. The initial impetus for the project, according to Howard Gardner (1992) of Harvard Project Zero, was the partners' desire to "identify youngsters who possessed intellectual strengths which are not detected by standard scholastic aptitude tests" (p. 100). Eventually, he says, the "desire to pick out 'stars'" gave way to "a wish to develop means of assessing growth and learning in all students" (p. 101). The goal of Arts PROPEL was to create assessments of student learning which were systematic, powerful, and closely tuned to the central elements of artistic development. One of these assessments involved the creation of writing portfolios.

Dennie Palmer Wolf (1989) described the purposes of the Arts PROPEL portfolio somewhat differently, adding the student's role in self-assessment to the mix:

> Central to this work are two aims. The first is to design ways of evaluating student learning that, while providing information to teachers and school systems, will also model personal responsibility in questioning and reflecting on one's own work. The second is to find ways of capturing growth over time so that students can become informed and thoughtful assessors of their own histories as learners. (p. 36)

Similarly, Roberta Camp (1993a) emphasized the portfolio's learning potential, explaining that from her own perspective, and from the perspective of the teachers in the project, the initial purpose of the Arts PROPEL writing portfolios was "to further student learning by providing information directly to students and teachers that is not otherwise available from student writing" (p. 203).

To accommodate that purpose, portfolios were structured around a year-long series of activities in which students learned to look back at their work so that they could set an agenda for what they would like to work on in the future. Students also learned to examine the processes they used, the choices they made, and the purposes they set for themselves in writing (Camp, 1993a). Kathryn Howard reports the district's perspective on the agenda. According to Howard (1990), "the goal of the participating groups is to incorporate new strategies of evaluating student writing, by teachers as well as the students themselves, into district-wide curricula" (p. 4).

System Design

The Arts PROPEL portfolio was built from the inside out. Teachers—who had the conditions of their classrooms and the abilities of their students firmly in mind—developed curricular materials, engaging in a collaborative process that ultimately included multiple individuals, including researchers in developmental psychology, experts in assessment, curriculum supervisors, skilled artists and students (Camp, 1992b). Roberta Camp highlights the active role that students played in the development of classroom activities:

> In important respects, the teachers' students were also part of the collaboration. When they agreed to engage with an activity they did not much like, for example, they asked teachers to indicate to the rest of the research team that they considered the design to be flawed and their work to be less than optimum as a result. (p. 253)

Teachers in turn conveyed that information to researchers.

For example, Bill Perry, a Pittsburgh visual arts teacher reflected on student feedback about "domain projects" (assessment tasks in a particular subject domain) during an interview with Ellen Winner, a researcher at Project Zero:

It is very important that the projects not become recipes. They should be loosely structured so that individual teachers can alter them to fit their own individual style of teaching. . . . If the student has mastered something about design, one can see this, whether it manifests itself in a shape arrangement task like the composition project or in a painting, sculpture, or sketch. There is a cost to having the project clearly structured, as it was this fall. When students wanted to make imaginative changes in the task—for instance, standing the shapes on their edges to make a 3-D structure—I had to stop them. This shut down excitement and led to boredom with the task. To get kids cooking, you need to be able to alter things to fit your particular kids.(Arts PROPEL, 1988. Reprinted by permission of Educational Testing Service, the copyright owner.)

Each activity was tried out, first by a small group of teachers, then by a larger group, and then revised on the basis of the experience (Camp, 1992b). Concepts and accompanying activities were reviewed, and those which failed to meet the project's needs were revised or scrapped.

Students in Arts PROPEL, and later throughout grades 6–12 in the Pittsburgh Public School district, kept writing folders, called "process-folios," to distinguish them from portfolios in the more traditional sense of the term—a collection of best or most representative work (Gardner, 1992). Other assessment systems typically ask students to submit their best work. In contrast, the Arts PROPEL "process-folios" were, as Howard Gardner (1992) explained, "instruments of learning rather than showpieces of final accomplishment" (p. 103).

Collection

What work was worth collecting?

Most portfolios contain a diverse body of work. The range of works in Arts PROPEL portfolios, according to Dennie Wolf (1989), was "deliberately diverse"; a student writer might include "pieces as diverse as journal entries, letters, poems or essays from social studies classes" (p. 37). But Arts PROPEL portfolios contained more. In addition to diverse works, they contained evidence of—and reflections about—the process of creating the works. A student writer, for example, might include "the notes, diagrams, drafts, and final version of a poem" (p. 37). Clearly, the focus of the collection was on learning. As Wolf puts it, teachers in Arts PROPEL asked "students to read their own progress in the 'footprints' of their works. . . ." (p. 37).

Who had access to and owned the collections?

In Pittsburgh, students worked on a daily basis with the materials in their "process-folios," revisiting and revising pieces, comparing pieces of writing, reflecting on the processes they used to create them, and making interim choices about potential portfolio contents. The portfolio process was fully embedded in instruction.

Moreover, perhaps more than any of the other exemplar portfolio systems we have reviewed, the Arts PROPEL portfolio system allowed students to gain some control over the assessment process and to learn to set their own goals and assess their progress toward them. The Arts PROPEL portfolio was designed to encourage students to reflect on pieces of writing that *they* found satisfying or unsatisfying, on their processes for writing, and on their own progress or development over time. In these ways, the Arts PROPEL portfolio encouraged students to take greater responsibility for their own learning.

As Sandra Murphy and Roberta Camp (1996) explain, the development of student ownership is related to the amount of control students have over the contents of the portfolio and over the process of their work:

> The issue of control from the perspective of students has to do with the amount of latitude they have in 1) the conditions for writing and 2) selecting the contents of the portfolio. Giving students decision-making responsibility in these areas gives them opportunities to develop agency, that quality Sizer describes as the "personal style, assurance, and self-control that allow [the individual] to act in both socially acceptable and personally meaningful ways." (p. 113)

The Arts PROPEL guidelines emphasize choice and student ownership. Indeed, they highlight the importance of the students' role in generating the contents of the portfolio and in deciding how their work will be represented to external audiences.

Selection

When the time came to select work for their portfolios, students made selections based on a flexible set of guidelines. Roberta Camp (1993a) describes the Arts PROPEL writing portfolio as containing a minimum of six pieces, four of them selections of writing accompanied by the notes and drafts generated on the way to writing the final piece. The contents included the following:

a. a writing inventory based on questions about the student's past experiences with writing

b. a piece of writing selected by the student as "important," with reflection stimulated by a series of questions addressing criteria for the selection and the experience of writing the piece

c. two pieces of writing, one that the student considers "satisfying" and a second that he or she considers "unsatisfying" with reflection on the qualities of each piece

d. a piece of writing selected to illustrate the student's processes and strategies for writing, accompanied by a description of how the writing was created

e. a "free pick," with a description of the reasons for its selection

f. a final reflection on the pieces in the portfolio and on changes that the student observes in his or her writing over the course of the year (pp. 203–204)

The same piece could be used to satisfy more than one selection. Therefore, the total number of unique pieces could vary. In addition, when the time came to formally evaluate the portfolios, teachers could influence the balance and representativeness of the portfolio by negotiating with students to include an "optional negotiated free pick."

When did selection take place?

As explained earlier, the Arts PROPEL portfolio was designed around a series of experiences aimed at helping students learn about writing and about themselves as writers. Thus in one sense, selection was an ongoing process. Assessment was clearly and thoroughly integrated with instruction and student selection was the "trigger" for assessment:

> Students keep all of their writing in a folder, then engage in activities in which they go into the folder to make selections for the portfolio. Each time they write a major paper, which goes into the folder accompanied by the notes and drafts involved in creating it, students reflect on what they believe to be the paper's strengths and what they find least satisfying in it. Each time they make a selection for the portfolio—approximately five times—they reflect on the selected paper in greater depth, indicating why they selected the piece and what they value in it, as well as something of the processes that went into creating it. Both kinds of reflective activities involve students in evaluation of their own work. (Camp, 1992b, p. 255)

To be sure, some teachers spent more time than others helping students develop understandings about the features of quality in their work and using the selection process to do so (LeMahieu, Gitomer, & Eresh, 1995a). Yet Camp's (1992b) description makes it clear that selection was an ongoing process, not one simply tagged on to the end of the year.

What was the purpose for selection?

Paul LeMahieu, Drew Gitomer and JoAnne Eresh (1995a) explain the purpose of the student selection process was "to engender and support a reflective and self-evaluative capacity . . . " (p. 4). guidelines for student selection clearly support reflection and self-assessment (see Figure 4.1).

Figure 4.1
Cover Sheet for Writing Selection

Please describe the writing assignment.

What do you like best about this piece of writing?

Which of your writing skills or ideas are you least satisfied with in this piece? Why?

Please describe the most significant revision you made while working on this piece of writing?

Thinking about an Important Piece of Your Writing
1. Why did you select this particular piece of writing?
2. What do you see as the special strengths of this work?
3. What was especially important to you when you were writing this piece?
4. What have you learned about writing from your work on this piece?
5. If you could go on working on this piece, what would you do?
6. What kind of writing would you like to do in the future?
7. What did you learn from your writing that surprised you?

Selecting a Satisfying Work
1. Read everything in your writing folder and portfolio.
2. Select a piece of your writing which you would categorize as "satisfying."

cont.

3. Respond to the following questions about your piece:
- Which piece did you select?
- Why do you categorize this piece as "satisfying"? Please give very specific reasons.
- What did you learn about yourself as a writer from your work and reflection on this piece?

Select an Unsatisfying Work
1. Read everything in your writing folder and portfolio.
2. Select a piece of your writing which you would categorize as "unsatisfying."
3. Respond to the following questions about your piece:
- Which piece did you select?
- Why do you categorize this piece as "unsatisfying?" Please give very specific reasons.
- Given the opportunity, how would you revise this piece?

Free Pick
From your folder, choose a piece that you would like to have included in your portfolio. Make the selection carefully, and then answer the questions below.
1. What is the title of the selection? When was the assignment?
2. What date was the piece written?
3. Why would you like to have this piece in your portfolio? Give specific reasons.
   (You may want to revise this piece before you put it in your portfolio.)

How I Have Changed as a Writer
Answer these questions carefully and specifically. You will be asked to use your answers to the questions below to write an essay describing how you have changed as a writer during the course of this year.
1. What do you notice when you look at your earlier work?
2. How do you think your writing has changed?
3. What do you know now that you didn't know before?
4. At what points did you discover something new about writing?
5. How do the changes you see in your writing affect the way you see yourself as a writer?
6. Are there any pieces you have changed your mind about over time — any you liked before but don't like now, or any that you didn't like before but do like now?
7. What made you change your mind about these pieces?
8. In what way do you think your reading has influenced your writing?

_____

Reprinted by permission of Educational Testing Service, the copyright owner.

Who selected artifacts for presentation/inclusion in the portfolio?

Although teachers could influence the balance and representativeness of the portfolio though the "optional negotiated free pick," all of the other portfolio pieces were selected by the student, and none by the teacher alone. Moreover, students had greater control of the selection process than in most other portfolio projects around the country, because there were no specifications of the forms or genres of writing in the portfolio requirements. One student might choose a story for a satisfying piece; another might choose an essay. Project coordinators and teachers in Pittsburgh believed that "it is this selection process that engenders both the understanding of [the student] as a writer and learner and the assumption of [the student's] identity as a writer"(Arts PROPEL handout). Underlying the design of the Arts PROPEL portfolio then, was the belief that learning involves making choices and exercising judgment and that without practicing these skills a student would not learn to write effectively.

When portfolios are used for bureaucratic accountability purposes, the question of who makes selections may be problematic. Some students might be better prepared than others to make perceptive and accurate selections (LeMahieu, Gitomer, & Eresh, 1995a). As Paul LeMahieu and his colleagues explain, from a traditional measurement perspective this might be seen as a source of irrelevant variance. One could argue, however, that information about students' abilities to make accurate choices is relevant to an assessment of their achievement. However, in Pittsburgh, student choice was not at issue. The assessment results in Pittsburgh were aimed at determining program effectiveness, not student achievement, per se. Because a goal of the program was to foster student's abilities to critique their own work, information about the students' selections provided evidence of the program's effectiveness.

Who was the audience for the portfolio?

Without doubt, one of the student's audiences was the assessor. LeMahieu, Gitomer, and Eresh (1995a) explain that "considerable effort was made to explicitly address the issue of selection as well as the purpose of the portfolio with students throughout the year. At a number of points, the purpose . . . was reviewed along with explicit discussion of the evaluative framework and standards of judgment that would be applied" (p. 4). Because only a sample of portfolios were scored, not every student's portfolio was read by an outside audience. But students knew that their portfolios might be reviewed by an external assessor, or for that matter, any number of other outside readers who were interested in Pittsburgh's portfolios.

The teacher was another audience who played an evaluative role. But in Pittsburgh, whether portfolios were graded or not was a decision left to the individual teacher. Teachers in Pittsburgh were aware of the inherent tension between assigning final grades to a collection of work and treating the collection as a reflection of the student as a developing learner (JoAnne Eresh, personal communication). Some teachers awarded points if all elements of the portfolio were present; some used the final reflection as part of a final exam for the course; others didn't assign grades, but required students to formally present their work to other students in the school or to parents.

Parents were a very important audience for students' portfolios. Many teachers found ways to engage parents as "audiences" for their children's work. Kathryn Howard, a teacher at Reizenstein Middle School in Pittsburgh, describes her own rationale for inviting parents to review their children's work:

> In our classroom, students constantly talk about writing. They discuss and establish their own criteria of and standards for good writing. They constantly talk about their own and each other's writing. It seemed natural, then, in this context to create an opportunity for students and their parents to talk about writing as well—to show students what their parents value about writing using conversation and written reflection. (Quoted in Howard & LeMahieu, 1995, p. 394, and reprinted here with permission.)

In the spring of the school year, Howard asked her students to take their writing folders home to be read by their parents. Parents were guided by a review and reflection form that was carefully crafted so as not to steer them toward purely negative responses (see Figure 4.2).

Figure 4.2
Parents' Review and Reflection Form

Student _____

Reader _____

Date _____

    Please read everything in your child's writing folder, including drafts and commentary. Each piece is set up in back-to-front order, from rough draft to final copy. Further, each piece is accompanied by both student and teacher comments on the piece and the writing process. Finally, the folders also include questionnaires where students write about their strengths and weaknesses as writers.

    We believe that the best assessment of student writing begins with the students themselves, but must be broadened to include the widest possible audience. We encourage you to become part of the audience.

    When you have read the folders, please talk to your children about their writing. In addition, please take a few minutes to respond to these questions.

- Which piece of writing tells you the most about your child's writing?
- What does it tell you?
- What do you see as the strengths in your child's writing?
- What do you see as needs to be addressed in your child's growth and development as a writer?
- What suggestions do you have that might aid the class's growth as writers?
- Other comments, suggestions?

Thank you so much for investing this time in your child's writing.

Ms. Howard

K. Howard & P. LeMahieu. Parents as assessors of student writing: Enlarging the community of learners. *Teaching and Change, 2* (4), 392–414, Copyright © 1995 by Sage Publications, Inc. Reprinted by permission of Corwin Press, Inc.

Howard and LeMahieu (1995) report that parents and students seemed willing to participate. In the first year, 30 out of 33 students participated; in subsequent years all students did. They also seemed positive about the experience. Of the 30 participating parents, 24 wrote positive comments about the activity on the response form. No one indicated displeasure. Equally important, Howard and LeMahieu (1995) also observed that parents' initial focus on accomplishment expanded to include appreciation for aspects of the writing process and of growth and development in writing, standards that could only be assessed through reference to a body of work. Thus, the activity served an important function in local accountability by educating parents about current methods of writing instruction.

Reflection
What opportunities for reflection did the system provide?

The cornerstone of the Arts PROPEL project was its emphasis on reflection. Students were encouraged to keep a notebook in their portfolios in which they recorded their reflections, reactions to their work, ideas, and notes on work in process. Some teachers posed questions for students to reply to in their journals. Reflection was threaded throughout instruction in various ways, and on a daily basis. For example, John Davis and Jerome Halpern (1995), teachers at Langley High School in the Pittsburgh schools, describe what reflection looked like in their own classrooms: "We tried to weave reflection into everything we did. Sharing in workshop, developing criteria, setting personal goals, completing cover sheets, and grading conferences were designed to help students focus on the reflective process" (p. 64).

Ongoing reflection was both private and public. That is, it was done individually, but also with others. Sometimes teachers conducted teacher-student conferences. Student "partners" also dialogued with each other about their portfolios. Group reflection occurred during class critique of a work or in a "group conference," when there was no time for individual teacher-student conferences. Some called these conferences "reflective interviews." In group conferences teachers gathered six to eight students at a time and asked students to talk aloud about what they noticed when they reviewed the body of work they had produced. For example, Dennie Palmer Wolf (1988) describes the case of Connie:

> Asked to reflect on her own work in much the same way she might be asked to think about poems by W.B. Yeats or Emily Dickinson, Connie noticed—for the first time—that she had a style, a characteristic signature as a writer. She was able to see how consistently she dealt with the hard facts and everyday ironies of everyday life by making common objects, like mops and chairs, speak. Without this sharpened knowledge of "what she was up to," it is hard to imagine Connie's going on to develop a keen sense for which words, forms, or kinds of figurative language best serve her poems. (p. 28)

Public occasions for reflections such as these gave teachers opportunities to assess how self-aware students were and students opportunities to see their work in a new way (Wolf, 1988).

Whether private or public, reflection was not automatic, however natural it might seem to those who regularly engage in this kind of activity. Some—perhaps most—students who had not had opportunities in their school careers to take stock were reluctant to do so in public. Teachers in Arts PROPEL devised various ways to ease students into it. For instance, in her article "Making the Writing Portfolio Real," Kathryn Howard (1990) affirms the importance of a "warm-up" for reflection:

> For my eighth grade students, thinking of themselves as writers and thinking of writing as a continuing process were at first abstract and foreign concepts. Barriers began to come down, however, as students learned to share their written pieces aloud—with a partner, a small group, or the entire class. (p. 4)

Howard recommends interactive processes such as modeling, collaborating, and questioning, to support reflection.

Roberta Camp (1992a) described ways that Arts PROPEL teachers eased students into reflection, by beginning with reflections on a single piece and moving to reflections on a body of work. Teachers encouraged reflection by asking questions about the writing, the process a student engaged in to produce a particular piece, or the body of work as a whole. As a first step, teachers asked students to reflect on a single piece and then later to select one or two pieces to compare with work done on other occasions. Ultimately, teachers asked students to reflect on a body of work, to consider how they have changed as writers, and to decide on next steps. During this "easing in" process, Arts PROPEL teachers used the reflective questions summarized in Figure 4.3, or their own variations of them.

Figure 4.3
Reflection Questions

Reflecting on Single Pieces of Writing
What do you like best about this piece of writing?
Which of your writing skills or ideas are you least satisfied with in this piece? Why?
Why did you select this particular piece of writing?
What do you see as the special strengths of this work?
What have you learned about writing from your work on this piece?
If you could go on working on this piece, what would you do?
What kind of writing would you like to do in the future?

Reflecting on Processes
Where did you get your idea (or ideas) for this piece?
How did you work on it? Describe the stages the piece went through, when and where you wrote, and roughly how long each stage took.
Did you share your writing with someone else to get their ideas about it? If so, how did this sharing change the way you looked at the piece?
What part of the process was hardest for you? What was easiest?
How did you know that this piece was finished?

Reflecting on Portfolios
What do you notice about your earlier work?
How do you think your writing has changed?
What do you know now that you did not know before?
At what points did you discover something new about writing?
How do the changes you see in your writing affect the way you see yourself as a writer?
Are there pieces you have changed your mind about—that you liked before, but don't like now, or didn't like before but do like now? If so, which ones? What made you change your mind?
In what ways do you think your reading has influenced your writing?
In what ways do these pieces illustrate what you can do as a writer?

These questions were compiled from two sources: Camp (1992a) and Camp (1989). Reprinted by permission of Roberta Camp and Educational Testing Service, the copyright owner.

Students engaged in various kinds of reflection. When they were engaging in more formal, retrospective reflection, their teachers helped them engage in self-evaluation, in finding evidence of growth, in finding evidence of artistic decision making, and in finding evidence of their personal styles or interests (Arts PROPEL, n.d.). For instance, to help students find evidence of growth, teachers engaged students in activities such as the following:

> Order a series of works (minimum of two, more would be better) so that the sequence demonstrates learning. Order the pieces chronologically and discuss the changes and what you think these show that you have learned or discovered about making art. Sometimes you may feel that you have gone backwards instead of forward. If you have a series of works that seem to get "worse"—that is, the later ones are not as clear, strong, or technically proficient as the earlier ones—can you order them chronologically and describe what you were thinking or trying to do and ask why it does not seem to be working? (Arts PROPEL, n.d., p. 5)

As another example, to help students find evidence of their own personal style or interests, teachers engaged students in activities such as the following:

> Choose pieces which are most representative of YOU as an artist at this point in time. What would an outsider, looking at these pieces for the first time, say about the kinds of problems you are dealing with, the kinds of things you are trying to express, the effects you are trying to achieve? (Arts PROPEL, n.d., p. 5)

Teachers were encouraged to adapt activities and reword questions such as these to fit the developmental level of their students.

What kinds of artifacts of reflective activity went in the portfolio?

As explained above, the Arts PROPEL portfolio was fundamentally different from portfolios in the usual sense (a collection of best work). Instead, it was a record of the learning process. Arts PROPEL portfolios contained, therefore, students' written reflections about their goals for a work, notes made along the way as a work progressed, notes about alternatives considered and rejected, and reflections on finished products. Artifacts of reflection appeared in the form of notes and jottings, as well as reactions to more formal questions like those posed in the cover sheet for selection in figure 4.1 above. Since the portfolio guidelines required it, portfolios also contained writing inventories (or a "Portrait of Myself as a Writer" based on the inventories). In preparing the writing inventory, students responded to questions such as the following (Camp, 1992a):

1. What kinds of writing have you done in the past?
2. What do you like to do most in writing?
3. What do you like to do least?
4. Where do you get your ideas for writing?
5. What do you think is important to know about you as a writer?

Finally, the portfolios also contained an essay describing how the student had changed as a writer during the course of the year (see under "Collection" above). Thus, the portfolio requirements not only documented the students' learning processes, they created occasions for students to reflect on those processes and on change over time.

Student Voices

When students created and worked with their portfolios in Arts PROPEL, they had opportunities to look back on their work and to make sense out of what they had learned. For instance, one student in Barbara Ehrlich's dance class described her new understanding of the creative process:

> I was just thinking that I didn't really start to have any goals or even realize I had a way of working until I did this piece. It made me see the value of taking risks—of using my imagination and trying to share it, show it to other people. I mean, you can know that you have an imagination, and you can sit down and think about all of these wild things, but it's incredibly difficult to try and get them across to someone else—to make them understand and feel what you're feeling. And that's what we were trying to learn—just through movement. I think we took a big risk in trying to get something across to people. It was a really hard thing. (Quoted in Zessoules, 1989, and reprinted here by permission of Educational Testing Service, the copyright owner.)

Students also reflected on the processes of their work: where they got their ideas, how they shaped them, and how well their intentions were executed. Anneka Jones an eighth grader in Kathy Howard's class at Reizenstein Middle School quoted in *Portfolio* (1989), reflected on how she created her poem "Rose."

"Rose" by Anneka Jones

A rose is a rose is a rose,

My grandpa used to tell me,

But what untruths has he forshadowed . . .

In my dreary life,

I may be one in a million . . .

And I am One in a million,

He told me that I was nothing but a stupid flower,

Then one day a human being plucked him from his vine,

I laughed and I cried

Till my petals started to drop.

When I was at school, I read a story about a flower. It was written by another kid, someone who I didn't know was a writer, and it really stuck in my mind. It had these lines about being picked and dying. I remember that I started looking up to that person as a writer after that. In the story, the characters were flowers. I had forgotten about it until I had to write an object poem.

You see, everyone writes about erasers or pencils, or things like that. I was sitting there, thinking: "Object, object, object." Then I remembered sitting on my grandmother's couch in Illinois, when she was getting married for a second time. I was sitting among the roses. . . . I got to thinking that neither of my grandfathers was ever alive when I was. So I just started imagining what kinds of things about him that I might remember, if I had a grandfather. I thought of the story I read again.

I really like the line about the untruths. Also the line, "a rose is a rose" is just like the line "You are one in a million." . . . It could have two meanings—like a grain of sand or it could mean you are ONE, the one, the special one. . . . I always think about it going both or either way when I see it. . . .

I was struggling through writing it. Especially the first half. (Someone reading it might guess) I was a girl or a rose. I didn't know what I thought about the ambiguity there. I didn't want to (give it away and) say my name was Rose, because I WAS a rose. I wanted someone reading to know, but I wanted to do it much more gently.

I thought a lot about the ending. I thought maybe I would get plucked from my vine too. . . . Then I thought no, I had to think more inside the poem, as though I was a rose shaking so hard with grief that my petals dropped off. (p. 20) (Reprinted by permission of Educational Testing Service, the copyright owner.)

Students also reflected on what they had learned about their writing and their newfound ability to take advantage of resources for doing it. For example, John Davis and Jerry Halpern (1995) quote Jane, a ninth grade student who had gained a new perspective on taking advantage of prewriting activities and response from peers:

Towards the beginning of my ninth grade year, my writing was unorganized, unclear, repetitive, and full of needless words and exaggeration. Now I see writing that is strong and gets to the point. I have definitely increased the amount of brainstorming and prewriting as well as revision. After always seeing peer response as a useless insult to my writing, I can now look at it as a helpful bit of constructive criticism to improve what I write. . . . (p. 63) (Reprinted by permission of Jerome Halpern and John Davis.)

Writing about student reflection in the Arts PROPEL project, Roberta Camp (1992) reminds us that taken together, portfolios and reflection make visible "much that is ordinarily hidden from student writers and their teachers' including:

What the student believes she has done well in a piece of writing:

The special strength of my thesis [paper] is the way I related the question [the topic for the paper] and the answer to the book. For example in my first paragraph I refer back to ch. 5. That is where I found my main example of my statement. (8th grader, Amy)

What the student values in writing:

It was wild the way I put Beowulf into modern times. (12th grader, Mileak)

I selected the dialogue I wrote about Karen & Stan. The reason I picked this one was because this could be a very real situation. I also liked this dialogue because if it was a real situation this is probably very close to what the conversation would be like. (9th grader, Erin)

The student's own goals and interests—his "agenda"—as a learner and developing writer:

Today I [read] my old work and didn't like it. I decided to rewrite my camping in the woods story. (7th grader, Michael) (p. 13)

This focus on the *students'* perceptions and values fosters their ownership of their writing and at the same time yields information that "both student and teacher use to track and direct the course of learning" (Camp, 1990, p. 14).

In addition to looking forward, to charting the course of future work, portfolios give students opportunities to see where they have been and how far they have come. Reineke Zessoules (1989) explains how portfolios in Arts PROPEL encouraged this kind of reflection by "holding the past still":

The making of portfolios can be a crystallizing experience for both students and teachers simply by its ability to hold the past still . . . To compile a genuine picture of students' learning, one needs a series of "snapshots" that accurately portray students creative processes. . . . Documentation provides hard evidence. It allows teachers and students to see development as it grows, and to point to new understandings, risks, revisions, even to mistakes. (p. 18)

Not all students are fluent writers, who can fully explain how they have learned and how they have improved. But even less able students can enter into dialogues with their teachers about development. The following is a an excerpt from a reflection cited in Camp, 1990. The ninth-grade student who produced the drawing had been working on a series of dialogues:

I feel like my writing formed two hills, like this.

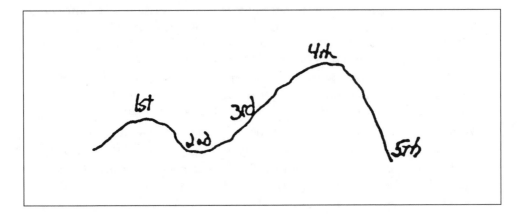

I was writing good, to my standards, then it started lacking what I thought made it good. Then I started climbing again, this time greater than my first one. Finally, my last dialogue was terrible. (Camp, 1990, p. 14. Reprinted with permission by Roberta Camp and the National Writing project.)

As Camp (1990) points out, the student "sees the kinds of peaks and valleys in performance" that challenge scholars and assessment designers alike when they attempt to accurately measure student progress. Although his assessment of his own progress is not fluent, it is a "basis from which he can enter into productive dialogue with his teacher and classmates about the qualities he sees in his writing" (p. 14).

Evaluation

What was the role of evaluation in the system?

A dimensional approach to scoring was adopted in the district. While other kinds of rubrics (holistic, analytic, genre-specific) focus attention on individual pieces of writing within portfolios, the Arts PROPEL framework for evaluation asks the evaluator to look at particular dimensions of learning—accomplishment, processes, and development—across the collection as a whole. The framework is displayed in Figure 4.4.

Figure 4.4
Arts Propel: Portfolio Evaluation Framework

Student writer _____ Grade_____

Teacher _____ School_____
The contents of this student's portfolio demonstrate:
(Please check where appropriate)

	Inadequate		Outstanding	
Accomplishment in writing	____	____	____	____

- meeting worthwhile challenges
- establishing and maintaining purpose
- use of the techniques and choices of the genre
- organization, development, use of detail
- control of conventions, vocabulary, sentence structure
- awareness of the needs of the audience
- use of language, sound, images, tone, voice
- humor, metaphor, playfulness

Use of processes and resources for writing	____	____	____	____

- awareness of strategies and processes for writing
- use of processes: prewriting, drafting, revision
- awareness of features important to writing
- ability to see strengths and opportunities in own writing
- ability to describe what one sees and knows about writing
- use of the classroom social context for writing
- use of available experience and resources
  (one's own, the school's, the community's)

cont.

Development as a writer   ____   ____   ____   ____

- progress from early to late pieces, growth, development
- increased understanding of features and options important to writing
- engagement with writing
- use of writing for different purposes, genres, and audiences
- sense of self as a writer, achievements and purposes as a writer
- evolution of personal criteria and standards for writing
- increased investment in writing tasks

This student's strengths in writing include:

This student's developmental needs as a writer include:

_____

(Educational Testing Service and Fellows of Harvard College, 1993 Figure 4.3, p. 83). This evaluation framework was developed by teachers and administrators in Pittsburgh with the guidance of researchers Roberta Camp and Dennie Wolf. Reprinted by permission of Educational Testing Service, the copyright owner.

As the evaluation framework reveals, Arts PROPEL educators were interested in evaluating outcomes beyond those which could be indicated by a final product or a single sample. While the first dimension "Accomplishment in Writing" refers to the general quality of students' writing, two of the dimensions—use of processes and resources for writing and development as a writer—could be assessed only because the portfolio contained an extensive sampling of student work and reflection. Traditional methods in writing assessment could not be used to gather information about these dimensions of learning.

The second dimension focuses attention on "students' engagement in and application of revision processes and their use of input from other sources (e.g., critiques) to improve and refine their writing" (LeMahieu, Gitomer, & Eresh, 1995b, p. 13). In the Arts PROPEL assessment scheme, students were expected not only to produce effective writing, but to demonstrate that they knew how to execute the processes which can bring it about. Focusing attention on this dimension of learning encouraged students and evaluators alike to reflect on the processes, strategies, and resources that students used and to gauge their effectiveness.

Evidence of the processes that students used was threaded throughout the portfolios. To assess students' use of processes and resources for writing, evaluators looked for notes, outlines or semantic maps as evidence of planning. They compared early drafts with later ones to see whether revision, as the student understood it, meant restructuring or simply recopying. They looked for evidence that the student had responded to feedback from the teacher or from peers about ways to improve their writing—for changes the student may have made in response to comments. In the students' reflective pieces, evaluators looked for evidence that the students were aware of the processes that worked well for them, as well as the practices that impeded their progress. In the students' chronicles of the processes through which individual pieces were created, evaluators looked for evidence that the student had made connections with other resources—the library, books, interactions with teachers and students—in developing their material for writing.

In addition to providing information about outcomes beyond those indicated by a final product, an advantage to the approach adopted in Arts PROPEL is that students are not required to complete identical tasks. When students have some latitude in making decisions about conditions for writing and about selecting the contents for the portfolio, they can be encouraged to assume some responsibility in the assessment process. Exercising control and responsibility encourages the personal development of students. For this reason, many portfolio practitioners highlight the importance of the students' role in generating the contents of the portfolio and in deciding how their work will be represented to external audiences.

The flexibility of this approach also fills an important need in curricular reform (Murphy, 1994, 1997). For decades, formal assessment has relied on assumptions that require uniform methods of test administration and a uniform set of test items (Eisner, 1985). But preoccupation with control and measurement has encouraged assembly line instruction. When curriculum and assessment are standardized, there is little incentive for teachers to adopt individualized forms of teaching or to allow students to explore their own interests. Instead, teachers are more likely to pay particular attention to the content of the test and to the form of the test question, whether it is a multiple-choice question, a short answer, or a genre-based essay, and they shape their instruction accordingly (Corbett and Wilson, 1991; Loofbourrow, 1994). Standardization imparts a sameness to the educational enterprise, a sameness which runs counter to individualism and the development of personal initiative.

Portfolios, in contrast, can be generative. If they are not defined by rigid menus which dictate particular assignments, portfolios leave room for creativity and for students to play some role in the planning of their educational program (Murphy & Smith, 1999). They provide a powerful alternative to prepackaged, bureaucratic kinds of large-scale assessment—the kinds that dictate the curriculum and disempower both teachers and students (Darling-Hammond, 1989). Indeed, the flexibility that portfolios provide, in combination with dimensional approaches to scoring of the kind used in Arts PROPEL, may be their most attractive asset. Rigorous challenges can be presented to all students, but accomplishment can be demonstrated in multiple ways.

How did the system ensure validity and fairness?

A major challenge for student-centered portfolios that are embedded in instruction is to create methods of evaluation that allow for generalization and comparison across classrooms without forfeiting their individuality and the complexity of data that makes the portfolio useful in learning and instruction (Camp, 1993a). The desire for comparability can easily lead to standardization of the required contents and of the conditions for producing them.

Although standardization poses a possible solution because it addresses traditional measurement issues such as reliability, comparability, and generalizability, it introduces a dilemma: Murphy and Camp (1996) explain:

> This trend toward standardization of assessment portfolios . . . reflects honest concern about issues of fairness and a traditional view of the way one goes about arriving at a well-warranted inference in measurement. . . . However, while the traditional psychometic approach employed in external assessment may address certain issues of measurement, it may not serve the best interests of teachers and students, the primary stakeholders in the assessment process, or of teaching and learning, the central purposes of education. (p. 106)

Achieving inter-reader reliability with student-centered portfolios may be difficult because their contents can vary substantially from student to student. However, as explained above, standardization can constrain students' autonomy in ways which may discourage them from engaging with their own learning. Further, the constraints of standardization may weaken the validity of the assessment, particularly in relation to writing done in classrooms where writing is taught as a process occurring over time and in response to personal, social, and intellectual contexts (Camp, 1993b; Moss, 1994; Murphy & Camp, 1996).

Results from this project indicate that it may not be necessary to streamline and standardize collection procedures in order to achieve fair and responsible judgments of student performance. Although Arts PROPEL portfolios include diverse kinds of writing, respectable statistical indicators of consistency in scoring have been achieved (LeMahieu, Gitomer, & Eresh 1995a, 1995b).

As part of their agenda for public accountability, Pittsburgh Public Schools used the evaluation framework above to generate data that could be aggregated and synthesized. As LeMahieu, et al. (1992) explain, the district collected a "large and representative" stratified sample of portfolios that permitted them to describe "performance by grade, school building, and for significant groups of students" (p. 12). Over the course of a week (815 person hours) teachers and curriculum specialists scored 1,250 writing portfolios (approximately 8 percent of the student population in grades 6–12) on the three dimensions in the evaluative framework above (LeMahieu, et al., 1995b). Each portfolio was scored twice, and if raters disagreed by more than a single point on the scale, the portfolio was scored a third time. LeMahieu and his colleagues (1992) report that agreement was "better than 92 percent, with only 7.9 percent of portfolios requiring the third reading for arbitration" (p. 12).

Procedures employed in the Arts PROPEL project and in the district scoring may shed light on the reliability in scoring that was achieved. In preparation for scoring in the district, raters were trained extensively—"for half a day at the beginning of the scoring period" and they were "recalibrated" before each of the morning and afternoon rating sessions (LeMaheiu, et al., 1992, p. 13). Raters reviewed, assessed, and discussed portfolios that illustrated the range of student performance in the sample. The discussions were "designed to lead to a consensus and common understanding about the evaluative scheme—its meaning and its proper application in the judgment of student work" (LeMahieu, et al., p. 13). (For details of the training procedures, see LeMahieu, et al., 1995b.)

Beyond the rigorous preparation for scoring, however, teachers and specialists in the district had many opportunities to develop a shared sense of standards. For example, Roberta Camp (1993a) notes that "[t]he development of the framework for evaluation of the Arts PROPEL portfolios began with documenting the language that teachers used to describe the characteristics of student writing and learning about writing that they observed in sample portfolios" (p. 205). Many teachers participated in discussions about the portfolios and about expectations for what they should contain. They were closely familiar with the work that went into them, and the conditions under which that work was created. In addition, the portfolios were used in annual discussions between teachers and district supervisors about the teaching of writing (Camp, 1992b, p. 205). It is likely that the many discussions teachers had around portfolios, both in the district at large and in standard setting sessions prior to scoring, led to a shared sense of standards.

Drew Gitomer (1993) explains why a shared sense of standards is important in making reliable judgments and comments on the role played by student work in achieving that shared sense:

> The same term can mean very different things to different judges. It is important that a standard setting discussion be directed at achieving a shared understanding of the concepts and issues being assessed. One way to ensure this understanding is to ground the standards in students' work. (p. 251)

Gitomer's analysis of dialogue during an Arts PROPEL assessment conference suggests that just "talking" about student work is not enough though; the quality of the conversation and grounding it in actual work are critically important.

Gitomer (1993) identifies three characteristics of successful dialogues about student work: 1) *specificity* (supporting claims with specific evidence; 2) *search for evidential sources* (a willingness to consider the entire portfolio in making and justifying claims about the student; and 3) *sincere negotiation* ("a working-through to achieve a collective understanding," that is, a genuine effort to listen, respond, and integrate the viewpoints of others) (p. 253). All of these features are apparent in the excerpt from an assessment conference about a student's portfolio in Figure 4.5. In the excerpt teachers, the director of writing, and researchers from Arts PROPEL are looking for evidence in the student's work and reflections in a portfolio to help them understand the student's self-concept as a writer. They also discuss how to design a portfolio so that it will provide a representative portrait of the student.

Roberta Camp (1993b) points out another reason why dialogue about student work was especially important in Arts PROPEL:

> The intention is that the discussions around portfolios will become dialogues informing all parties interested in students' learning about writing; thus, discussions between student and teacher, student and fellow student, student and parent and teacher, teacher and follow teacher, teacher and supervisor are integral to the portfolio program. (p. 205)

In Camp's (1993b) view, such discussions complement a model of accountability "in which all parties in the educational system are mutually responsible for student learning and are responsive to one another's perspectives and concerns" (p. 205).

Figure 4.5

An excerpt from an Assessment Conference Around a Student's Portfolio

Teacher 1	I think she was trying to be different because obviously chronological order would be most logical—but she tried to organize it in a different way.
Teacher 2	I didn't do creative writing. I made them do all the research, all the notes, and then they did the creative writing. They chose either a monologue, dialogue, or short story and kids came up with other ideas. When they were finished they were pleased with the results, and so was I. Someone wrote about George Washington's thoughts on his deathbed, Langston Hughes when he visits his father in Mexico including the background of their relationship. They have to incorporate facts into the creative piece.
Researcher 1	She also says here (there's a really strong thing) about getting control in the sense of not needing a whole lot of help from anyone else and being able to see where she's having problems. Also, she liked having a paper where she could get all her points down and not have to struggle all the time.
Supervisor 1	Well that's part of the "less pressure" of the term paper.
Researcher 2	I really got the sense somehow that she was taking responsibility as a critical reader and particularly in the longer piece about Evaluation of Self as a Writer. I don't even know what I could point out to show her meaning, but she has a good sense of herself as a writer.
Teacher 1	But it's true—she has definitely developed that.
Researcher 1	It's partly in the Evaluation of Self as a Writer. She's very specific about before—"I'm writing about out more realistic issues. I write better and more efficient. I start off with powerful paragraphs, my sentence structure has improved and I can develop my body slowly at this point . . ." She has a sense of process. She has specifics about what she looks at.
Teacher 1	And she understands *why* she's getting better—"I have written more this year, which expanded my success. I didn't have a chance to get lazy."
Researcher 1	It's almost as if you need to read the Portfolio and then look at the folder. Then come back and look at the Evaluation of Self as a Writer—You read it and there's a real person who seems to be saying things that make sense, but you don't have any evidence for it. Then you need to go through all the other pages to see what she did and come back and ask, "What did she say?"

cont.

Note: From Construction versus choice in cognitive Measurement: Issues in constructed response, performance testing, and portfolio assessment, (pp. 252–253), by D. Gitomer, 1993, Hillsdale, NJ: Lawrence Erlbaum Associates, Publishers. Copyright © 1993 by Lawrence Erlbaum Associates. Reprinted with permission.

Supervisor 2	My sense was that from the first page through the tenth page I wasn't sure that anything she said was so—and if I were the next years teacher . . . It wasn't until I read the Dear Senior letter that I thought, yes, this is so. It seemed that the Portfolio had to include something more for me as the teacher receiving this child so I had some sort of substantiation that she really did grow as a writer. It wasn't until I reached that piece (the letter) that I felt she had the control of language that she talked about—She varied the sentence structure, had interesting beginnings. . . .
Teacher 1	And towards the middle, you start to see it.
Supervisor 2	But if I had just seen this documentation at the beginning of the questionnaires...The Evaluation of Self as a Writer helps because I start to see her control of language. But that one really locked it in. I can see what kind of writer I'm receiving when I read that Dear Senior piece. If I had this and the research paper, I wouldn't know her as a writer at all.
Supervisor 1	I want to have the option of teacher-improved solutions.
Teacher 1	I was going to say, "How can you guarantee you're going to get that?"
Supervisor 2	That's what I'm going to argue for then, as each teacher reviews what a student puts in the Portfolio there's a possibility that the teacher can add a piece to the Portfolio.
Teacher 3	Is there another possibility? Every time we talk about having a selection we say the students select, but we always place some kind of parameter—even if it's general such as "most satisfying" or "I like best" it's still a parameter. Do we ever explore just allowing free pick to see if the students will see the gaps and take steps to fill them in? Hopefully that would happen. The teacher would be the fail-safe plan. I wonder if the student could not, given the opportunity, make some kind of selection.
Researcher 1	And the question of whether we need a range of writing just like we need different kinds of writing—when you say Free Pick and filling in the gaps, we need a sense of what's needed to know if they're filling in the gaps.

There are many indications that Pittsburgh's use of portfolios for accountability represented such a model. First, large numbers of teachers and specialists contributed throughout the evolution of the system (LeMahieu, et al., 1995b). Second, the portfolio design and supporting activities were developed out of classroom practices—that is, the portfolio system was built from the inside, not imported from the outside—and over a period of several years. The Arts PROPEL project began in 1987; portfolios were not scored and used for public accounting until the 1991-1992 academic year. Third, the district put an audit system in place that opened the system to public inspection. A committee of representatives from the community ("business leaders, board members, representatives of higher education and local philanthropies . . . superintendents, curriculum specialists, teachers") reviewed the entire process to "provide a bonafide accounting of the performance of the system" (LeMahieu, et al., 1992, p. 14). The charge to the external auditors was: "to inspect the procedures, methods, and logistics of the portfolio assessment to satisfy itself that the results of the application of those assessment procedures would represent a fair, good faith, and critically honest accounting of the performance of the school district" (LeMahieu, et al., 1992). As LeMahieu and his colleagues (1995b) point out, "The whole process enabled various elements of the system to make their accounting in intuitively understandable terms and directly to those to whom they were immediately responsible: teachers to students and their parents; the school to its immediate community, and the district to various publics of concern to it" (p. 27).

Issues of Impact

The Arts PROPEL project was not in place long enough for evidence to be collected about any long-term impact it may have had on student performance—evidence, that is, that came in the form of scores that could be compared from year to year, or that would compare student performance in Arts PROPEL classrooms with students in other kinds of classes. However, evidence of the project's impact surfaced in other ways. Project participants reported that students engaged in periodic reflection became not only more knowledgeable, but more thoughtful about their work (Arts PROPEL, n.d.). Students reflected on the choices and decisions made in creating a work, on alternative ways they could have fashioned it, and the effects of their decisions. They became better able to revise, and also to envision new directions and possibilities. They became interested in experimenting. They began to see links between the problems and tasks they set for themselves and those of other writers and to use those insights as resources in their work.

As explained above, the Arts PROPEL portfolio design allows evaluators to gather information that could not be obtained from a product alone. Although improvement of student products is certainly one aim of any intervention effort, PROPEL teachers looked for other indications of the impact of the project. They looked to the students' experience and their way of thinking about their work. Ellen Winner and Elizabeth Rosenblatt (1989) describe four areas where the project had an impact on students in art classes: reflection, involvement in long-term projects, self-concept, and visual awareness. From their perspective, "changes in final products are not the only, or the most important, places to look for artistic development. . . ." (p. 26).

Winner and Rosenblatt (1989) observed that over the course of the year, as students engaged in reflection, they became "not only more knowledgeable, but also more thoughtful, about the process of art making." Students began to "think about the choices and decisions in creating a work, alternative ways they could have made something, and the effects of the choices made" (p. 22). Winner and Rosenblatt also observed that keeping a portfolio and tracking one's own progress stimulated students to "become involved in the process of carrying out self-initiated projects over a sustained period of time (from a few weeks to an entire semester)" and to "realize the value of working and reworking" (p. 23). Self-concept was also affected by their experiences in the portfolio classroom. Students began "to think of themselves more as novice artists than as students in an art class carrying out the teacher's lesson plan," and they developed "a confidence in their own thinking and appraisals" (p. 24). Finally, because they participated in class critiques and other activities aimed at the analysis of work, students in portfolio classrooms also began to "look more carefully at their own work . . . to look more carefully at the work of fellow students..at art in museums and galleries or other settings . . . " (p. 24). In other words, the sophistication of their perceptions increased.

Ultimately, of course, the goal is to help students produce better work. Production, as the Arts PROPEL acronym implies, was central in PROPEL classrooms. But from a teacher's perspective, assessment of students' processes is at least as important as assessment of their final products. Information about processes provides information that is useful in teaching. And the bottom line was ultimately the student and his or her development as a writer. Central to the PROPEL notion of development was the idea that over time, students would develop personal standards and become more perceptive in their judgments of their work.

Problems and Potential Solutions

In other chapters we have discussed problems that particular systems illustrate and have suggested possible solutions. One problem illustrated by the Arts PROPEL project was its untimely demise. The success of the portfolio project in Pittsburgh makes its demise all the more dismaying. Like many reform initiatives, it required sustained leadership and vision—persons with the power, influence, and vision that matched the vision of the project itself. Unfortunately, the departure of the Superintendent and a shift to school-based management removed key individuals who had sustained the project. At this critical juncture the program was fully developed and poised for expansion throughout the district, but it was not yet firmly entrenched. Resources for the kind of staff development that would have been required to have a widespread impact in the district were not forthcoming. As a result, although some teachers maintained the underlying principles of Arts PROPEL in their classrooms, the portfolio culture envisioned in the project never really became pervasive in the schools. In more recent years, another model of portfolio assessment was adopted—the New Standards model—and the cycle of implementation began once again. Frequent policy changes disrupt the development of coherent educational systems and add to the burden of teachers who are expected to adapt.

The solution to the problem may seem obvious—keep key individuals in place and provide them with the resources they need to do the job. Educational innovations need long-term support and leadership to have any long-standing impact in the schools. But achieving that solution is more difficult than identifying it. Throughout these chapters, there are instances of the vulnerability of reform initiatives to policy changes. Collectively they speak to the need for a stable policy environment.

Apart from the untimely demise of a promising program, we have presented a system in this chapter that illustrates potential *solutions* to several problems that educational systems planning to institute new assessment systems might face. In the section on evaluation above we highlighted Pittsburgh's solution to the standardization dilemma—the perceived need to standardize portfolio contents in order to achieve reliability (Koretz, McCaffrey, Klein, Bell, and Stecher, 1992) versus the danger that standardization may weaken the validity of the assessment, particularly in relation to writing done in classrooms where writing is taught as a process occurring over time and in response to personal, social, and intellectual contexts.

Reliably scoring of collections of work is generally perceived to be more difficult than the scoring of individual student responses to a fixed task, especially if the collections of work contain different assignments. For example, evaluators of the Vermont performance assessment program cited "the tremendous diversity (lack of standardization) of tasks across portfolios" as an explanation for the unacceptably low inter-rater correlations obtained by portfolio raters during the first years of the program's implementation (Koretz, Stecher, Klein, & McCaffrey, 1994, p. 43). Moss (1994) reported that where acceptable inter-rater reliability has not been achieved, field workers have usually tried greater levels of specification of portfolio contents, or a modification of scoring procedures such that work samples are rated one at a time, not as collections, in order to improve reliability in scoring (Nystrand, Cohen, & Dowling, 1993). However, because piece-by-piece scoring focuses attention on the characteristics of a single kind of task, this approach does not tap the unique information available in a *collection* of student work, in particular, information about the student's control of processes and use of resources for reading and writing or the student's ability to evaluate his or her own work (Murphy, 1999). Neither is this approach very useful for capturing information about the breadth of a student's abilities.

Calls to standardize the contents of portfolios are frequently based on a tacit assumption that psychometric procedures cannot change, and that portfolios therefore must be shaped to meet the demands of psychometrics. But work is now being done to create new assessment theory (Frederiksen, Mislevy, & Bejar, 1993; Linn, Baker, & Dunbar, 1990) and new models for assessment (Camp, 1993b; Frederiksen & Collins, 1989). New approaches suggest that an assessment should be compatible with the kind of learning it claims to measure. Rather than fit portfolios to the demands of old psychometric models, then, portfolios might well be seen as providing reasons for devising new methods for obtaining credible judgments about students which would enhance learning and contribute to the health of the educational system as a whole (Murphy & Camp, 1996). As Sandra Murphy and Roberta Camp (1996) suggest, "it is likely . . . that an integrated system . . . will better meet the requirements of emerging conceptions of validity," because scholars are redefining validity to include the consequences of the assessment, in particular, the impact on curriculum and participants (Frederiksen & Collins, 1989; Linn, et al., 1990; Messick, 1989a, 1989b, 1994; Moss, 1992, 1994).

Theory has it that self-assessment is an essential step in learning. For this reason, many teachers ask students to assess their own work and to articulate that assessment in conferences, in introductory essays for portfolios, in explanations for portfolio entries, in reflective essays, and in other assignments. Teachers value these self-assessments for the learning they promote, and for the information they provide about students—about the students' own agendas for learning and about the extent to which students can gauge effectiveness in their writing. External assessors find written self-assessments valuable for many of the same reasons. Like teachers, they value the information which self-assessments provide about students' understandings.

Proponents of assessment reform argue that when portfolios are conceptualized as more than just collections of student work, they encourage the pursuit of personal cognitive learning goals—what Bereiter and Scardamalia (1989) call "intentional learning." They prompt students to look back, to digest and debrief, and to review what happened so that they can set new goals and determine next steps (Camp, 1992a; Johnston, 1983; Zessoules & Gardner, 1991). In fact, a common argument for using portfolios in both instruction and assessment is that they can provide students with opportunities to engage in reflection and formative self-evaluation. For this reason, in many portfolio classrooms the student's participation in reflecting on, and in making decisions about the contents of his or her portfolio, is considered of critical importance (Howard, 1990; Camp, 1992a; Daiker, Sommers & Stygall, 1996; Paulson, et al., 1991). Indeed, within portfolio systems, choice is thought to be central to the construct being assessed: "the ability to reflect on and evaluate one's own writing is seen as a critical component of one's development as a writer" (LeMahieu, et al., 1995a, p. 23).

However, the freedom portfolios can give students to choose how they will present themselves to others, may be perceived as a liability by those who have concerns about technical matters such as interrater agreement in large-scale assessment. Thus, the assets perceived by some participants are themselves sources of tension in portfolio design when perceived by others from another context (Murphy & Camp, 1996). As explained above, one difficulty in creating a system that will accommodate the student's participation in making decisions about the contents of his or her portfolio is that the contents will vary widely from one portfolio to the next. This variability may make it more difficult for judges to obtain acceptable levels of agreement, particularly when the scoring system forbids interaction among judges as was the case in Pittsburgh. (Recall that in the Pittsburgh scheme, judges gave independent ratings and disagreements were moderated by a third "reader.") In such systems, judges are not allowed to negotiate disagreements. To obtain acceptable levels of rater reliability in this kind of system, judges must share the same standards and have finely tuned perceptions of how those standards are realized in student work. In other schemes (such as those employed by dissertation committees) there may be significant amounts of interaction and negotiation among assessors that provide opportunities for clarifying misunderstandings and reaching consensus. But in traditional, independent rating schemes of the kind employed in most assessments for educational accountability, negotiation is not allowed.

Pittsburgh overcame the difficulty associated with the independent rating scheme, that is, the possibility that idiosyncratic standards held by judges and the diversity of portfolio contents might inhibit agreement. Part of the explanation for their success may be that they used a smaller number of more highly trained scorers than has been the case in projects where the consistency of judgments has been more erratic. No doubt, the processes that guided the development of the assessment and the evaluative framework (rubric) also contributed to the reliability of the raters' judgments. Teachers were full partners—and learners—in the development process. In an interview with one of the authors of this chapter, Jerry Halpern, a Pittsburgh teacher, described his participation in the assessment development process as "truly a study group, a staff development and a learning experience. The other partners honored what we teachers felt and thought about student engagement. It was a portfolio process in and of itself" (Halpern, personal communication). As LeMahieu, et al. (1995a) explain, the rubric "was derived from many teachers and administrators repeatedly examining student work and developing a vocabulary that people could use to discuss that work. . . . As this vocabulary evolved and carried a shared meaning among its users, a shorthand version of it was embodied in the rubric" (p. 18). In this way, the process of rubric development contributed to a shared set of meanings.

LeMahieu, et al. (1995a) point out, and it is certainly worth reiterating here, that the sustained and recursive discussions of student work that occurred over several years in the district and in Arts PROPEL may have contributed to the project's success in meeting the traditional psychometic criteria of reliability. They remind us that these kinds of focused discussions form the basis of alternative approaches for arriving at well-warranted conclusions. Pamela Moss (1994) explains the applicability of a hermeneutic approach with respect to generalization across readers:

> A hermeneutic approach to assessment would involve holistic, integrative interpretations of collected performances that seek to understand the whole in the light of its parts, that privilege readers who are most knowledgeable about the context in which the assessment occurs, and that ground those interpretations not only in the textual and contextual evidence available, but also in a rational debate among the community of interpreters. Here, the interpretation might be warranted by criteria like a reader's extensive knowledge of the learning context; multiple and varied sources of evidence; an ethic of disciplined collaborative inquiry that encourages challenges and revisions to initial interpretations; and the transparency of the trail of evidence leading to the interpretations, which allows users to evaluate the conclusions for themselves. (p. 7)

The concept of transparency is important here, because transparency contributes to systemic validity (Messick, 1994). In fact, Sheingold and Frederiksen (1995) claim that a transparent assessment is, by definition, "a system in which values and criteria are openly and widely disseminated and discussed" (p. 6). Transparent assessments, according to Sheingold & Frederiksen, "make students and teachers keenly aware of both the characteristics of outstanding performance that are shared values within the community and the reasons why they are valued" (p. 5). More than mere labels or definitions, transparency demands that participants—students and teachers—learn what those labels and definitions mean in the context of real work.

The development of a shared set of meanings—transparency—was supported by the coherence of the educational system in the district as a whole, including Pittsburgh's approach to assessment development and the institutional supports the district and other project partners provided for teachers to develop a "common language" about the qualities of student work and shared standards. As LeMahieu, et al. (1995a) explain, the Pittsburgh district had pursued a number of ways to support the development of a shared understanding about student writing and the teaching of writing prior to the introduction of the portfolio project itself, including "coordinated and extensive participation in the Pennsylvania Writing Project, district-wide curriculum writing efforts, and other innovative district-wide assessment initiatives" (p. 18). Supervisors in the district made frequent classroom visits and discussed classroom practice in relation to the "important and consensual district goals" that had been adopted. (p. 18)

Institutional supports for the development of shared standards included many opportunities for collegial interchange around the assessment of student work. For example, the Director of Writing had established the practice of conferring with teachers to discuss student learning issues in conjunction with instructional practice while looking at student work (LeMahieu, et al.1995a). Teachers brought three portfolios to these conferences, each representing a different level of student performance. The conference focused on what could be learned from the student writing and what instructional decisions had and/or could be made. Activities of this kind provide an antidote to idiosyncratic standards.

The regular supervisor/teacher conferences also illustrate the coherence of the system as a whole. As LeMahieu, et al. (1995b) explain:

> This reflective process between teacher and supervisor mirrored the process that teachers attempted to create with their students. There is coherence with the assessment at all levels, as the intention of the assessment is not simply to assign grades or evaluations, but to engage in a process of finding out information, creating common understanding among participants, and making information-based decisions that will improve performance in the future. (p 26)

In Pittsburgh there was a shared interpretive framework and continuity between the purposes of the assessment and practices associated with it.

Conditions in schools work against the development of a shared technical culture (Darling-Hammond, 1997; Lortie, 1975). Teachers often work in isolation, without the kind of highly evolved socialization processes that foster shared technical expertise, as do doctors, lawyers, or airline pilots. In other professions, opportunities to learn and personal assistance come from the structured interaction with co-workers. But the "cellular" organization of schools often constrains the amount and kind of interaction among teachers (Lortie, 1975). As Lortie explains it, using the analogy of the cell, isolation in the one-room schoolhouse simply multiplied into many isolated cells as school populations increased. Despite physical proximity to colleagues, teachers in modern schools still mostly work alone, separated for long intervals of time, surrounded by students, and inducted into the profession in a more or less "sink or swim" fashion (Darling-Hammond, 1997; Lortie, 1975; Sarason, 1990). A major cost of isolation is the lack of a common language for talking about teaching and student work. Arts PROPEL and the Pittsburgh Public Schools took a step toward solving that educational problem by engaging teachers in focused discussions of student work. Collaborative assessment of student work can lead to teacher reflection and change (Sheingold, et al., 1994).

Pamela Moss (1994) reminds us that a number of assessment specialists have advised against using the judgments of classroom teachers (Mehrens, 1992; Resnick & Resnick, 1992). Resnick and Resnick (1992) cited in Moss (1994) assert, for example, that teachers should not be involved in grading the performance of their own students:

> A principal requirement of accountability and program evaluation tests is that they permit detached and impartial judgments of students' performance, that is, judgments by individuals other than the students' own teachers, using assessment instruments not of the teachers' devising. . . . The public function of certification would not be met if teachers were to grade the performance of their own students (Resnick & Resnick, 1992, pp. 48–50).

In the context of large-scale programs, some attempt to avoid having teachers score their own students seems warranted. As Moss (1994) explains, from a psychometric perspective, the call for "detached and impartial" high stakes assessment reflects a profound concern for fairness to individual students and protection of stakeholder's interest by providing accurate information" (p. 9).

However, removing teachers from the picture silences the voices of those who are most knowledgeable about the context, an important criterion for credible evidence from the hermeneutic perspective (Moss, 1994). Moreover, if teachers are prevented altogether from participating in assessments, they will fail to reap the professional development benefits that such participation can bring (Sheingold, Heller, & Paulukonis, 1994). Thus, there is a systemic validity consequence to any decision to eliminate classroom teachers from the assessment process as well.

Many educators have raised concerns about the absence of teachers' voices in accountability schemes that affect them and their students (Darling-Hammond & Snyder, 1992; Lieberman, 1992; Lucas, 1988a, 1988b; Murphy 1997) and scholars have voiced concern about the potentially deleterious effects of assessment on teachers (Pearson & Valencia, 1987). If teachers are removed from the picture, there is little chance that the assessment system will have a positive impact on them or the educational system.

An alternative suggested by Lauren Resnick (1996) is that a school faculty could act "corporately, not as individual teachers" (p. 10). After scoring, a sample of a school's portfolios could be sent to another school or a quality control board for rescoring. An auditing procedure of this kind ensures that schools set standards neither too high, nor too low. Another alternative was employed in Pittsburgh. Teachers did not score their own students' portfolios in the final district scoring; they passed them to other teacher-scorers.

In any case, the results of the Pittsburgh scoring suggest that satisfaction of Moss' evidential procedures can also result in the satisfaction of traditional psychometric criteria for reader reliability (LeMahieu, et al., 1995a). Agreement between judges, of course, is not enough. Impartiality demands that teachers also be able to judge students' performance in relation to a set standard. But in a system where standards are shared and transparent, teachers will be consistent in their judgements not only in relation to each other, but in relation to set standards as well. In other words, teachers can be detached and impartial, given the right circumstances, and evidence of that impartiality can be provided via traditional approaches.

The Arts PROPEL project provides other lessons relevant to school reform. There is growing consensus that teaching is intense, complex, and multi-dimensional work. Teachers balance subject matter, lessons, underlying cognitive, social, and affective goals, management of time, materials, and equipment, and all in the context of the needs of the individual students who enter their classrooms. What the teacher does depends upon what the students know. The reverse is also true—what the students do depends on what the teacher knows. From this perspective, teaching consists of interactions that cannot be predetermined given the difference in behavior and experiences of teachers and students. Such a view of teaching and learning precludes the application of predetermined approaches or prescriptive processes (Darling-Hammond, 1997).

To deal with the complexities of teaching, teacher learning needs to be an ongoing process. Teachers have to develop their own understanding of what high standards are and how to go about supporting students' in reaching them. What drives teachers to learn more? Darling-Hammond's (1997) analysis of research indicates that teachers are motivated to learn more when what they are doing is connected to the students they teach, when it is connected to a content area that includes concrete tasks, when it is organized around a problem, supported by teacher collaboration over time, and informed by research. The Arts PROPEL project provided these kinds of opportunities for teachers, at the same time that it worked to improve learning opportunities for students. Thus, as a philosophically coherent system, it showed great promise for solving important problems in teaching and learning. But as Linda

Darling-Hammond (1998) reminds us, solutions to the problems of teaching and learning must be systemic and sustained over time if they are to be successful. Even the most systemically coherent projects are vulnerable to the politics of the moment.

The Arts PROPEL story demonstrates the vulnerability of reform initiatives. But there is reason to hope that the good work that began there continues to have an impact. Policy shifts do not automatically lead to shifts in local practice. For example, a ten-year study by Chrispeels (1997) of policy implementation and change in California suggests that the benefits of stable policy development during the 10 year period studied may have sufficiently prepared the ground for local educators to sustain efforts to develop more effective assessment programs even as the political ground moved beneath their feet. Because teachers were so directly involved in the assessment development, changes in classroom practice that came about during the existence of the Arts PROPEL project may linger. It is likely, however, that the new portfolio system employed in Pittsburgh will change the portfolio culture there in important ways.

Opportunities for Discussion and Inquiry

1. The Pittsburgh Public Schools created a system that nurtured the development of a shared sense of values about writing quality and other important ideas associated with growth in writing such as self-assessment, reflection, and the use of writing processes and resources for writing. What would it take in your own situation to promote shared values? What obstacles would you face? What resources could you draw on?

2. Arts PROPEL's goal was to encourage the development of effortful, strategic, reflective—self-regulated—learners who approach academic tasks with the disposition of an artist. What tensions do you see between this vision of students and educational systems that specify a core set of information that all students should know? What tensions do you see between this vision of students as developing life-long learners and systems that specify minimim criteria for students to meet?

3. What characteristics of curricular and assessment systems support the development of self-regulated learners?

Acknowledgments

We would like to express our appreciation to JoAnne Eresh, formerly the Director of Writing in the Pittsburgh Public Schools, and Jerry Halpern, a teacher in the Pittsburgh Public Schools, for reviewing earlier versions of this chapter. We would also like to thank Roberta Camp, formerly a consultant for Arts PROPEL from the Educational Testing Service, for her support and advice during the writing of the chapter. Roberta Camp is quoted extensively with her permission. We would like to acknowledge the work of these and other scholars who have shared parts of the Arts PROPEL story and whose published work made the writing of this chapter possible, in particular: John Davis, Howard Gardner, Drew Gitomer, Kathryn Howard, Paul LeMahieu, Dennie Wolf, and Rieneke Zessoules.

References

Arts PROPEL. (n. d.). Developing a "portfolio culture" in the artroom under various classroom conditions. Unpublished document. Arts PROPEL, Pittsburgh Public Schools. Author.

Arts PROPEL (1988). Reflections on the composition domain project: An interview with Bill Perry. *Portfolio, 1,* (3), 5–7. Author.

Bereiter, C., & Scardamalia, M. (1989). Intentional learning as a goal of instruction. In L. B. Resnick (Ed.), *Knowing, learning, and instruction: Essays in honor of Robert Glaser* (pp. 361–392). Hillsdale, NJ: Lawrence Erlbaum Associates.

Camp, R. (1985). The writing folder in post-secondary assessment. In P. Evans (Ed.), *Directions and misdirections in English evaluation,* (pp. 91–99). Ottawa, Canada: Canadian Council of Teachers of English.

Camp, R. (1989). Arts PROPEL: Suggestions for creating writing portfolios. Unpublished document. Pittsburgh, PA: Arts PROPEL/Educational Testing Service.

Camp, R. (1990). Thinking together about portfolios. *The Quarterly of the National Writing Project and the Center for the Study of Writing, 12,* 8–14.

Camp, R. (1992a) Portfolio reflections in middle and secondary school classrooms. In K. B. Yancey (Ed.), *Portfolios in the writing classroom,* (pp. 61–79). Urbana, IL: National Council of Teachers of English.

Camp, R. (1992b). Assessment in the context of schools and school change. In H. Marshall (Ed.) *Redefining student learning: Roots of educational change,* (pp. 241–263). Norwood, NJ: Ablex Publishing Corporation.

Camp, R. (1993a). The place of portfolios in our changing views of writing assessment. In R. E. Bennett & W. C. Ward (Eds.), *Construction versus choice in cognitive measurement: Issues in constructed response, performance testing, and portfolio assessment,* (pp. 183–212). Hillsdale, NJ: Lawrence Erlbaum Associates.

Camp, R. (1993b). Changing the model for the direct assessment of writing. In M. Williamson & B. Huot (Eds.), *Validating holistic scoring for writing assessment: Theoretical and empirical foundations,* (pp. 45–79). Cresskill, NJ: Hampton Press, Inc.

Chrispeels, J. H. (1997). Educational policy implementation in a shifting political climate: The California experience. *American Educational Research Journal, 34* (3), 453–481.

Coleman, L. J. (1994). Portfolio assessment: A key to identifying hidden talents and empowering teachers of young children. *Gifted Child Quarterly, 38*(2), 65–69.

Corbett, H. D & Wilson, B. L. (1991). *Testing, reform, and rebellion.* Norwood, NJ: Ablex.

Daiker, D., Sommers, J., & Stygall, G. (1996). The pedagogical implications of a college placement portfolio. In E. White, W. Lutz, & S. Kamusikiri (Eds.), *Assessment of writing: Politics, policies, practices ,* (pp. 257–270). New York: Modern Language Association.

Darling-Hammond, L. (1989). Accountability for professional practice. *Teachers College Record, 91*(1), 59–80.

Darling-Hammond, L. (1997). *The right to learn.* San Francisco: Jossey-Bass Education Series.

Darling-Hammond, L. (1998). Teachers and teaching: Testing policy hypotheses from a national commission report. *Educational Researcher, 27,* 5–15.

Darling-Hammond, L. & Snyder, J. (1992). Reframing accountability: Creating learner-centered schools. In A. Lieberman (Ed.), *The changing contexts of teaching.*

Ninety-first Yearbook of the National Society for the Study of Education. Chicago: University of Chicago Press.

Davis, J. W., & Halpern, J. T. (1995). The portfolio classroom. *The Iowa English Bulletin, 43,* 61–66.

Educational Testing Service and Fellows of Harvard College. (1993). *Arts PROPEL: A handbook for imaginative writing.* Princeton, NJ: Educational Testing Service.

Eisner, E. (1985). *The educational imagination: On the design and evaluation of school programs.* 2nd ed. New York: Macmillan.

Emig, J. (1982, February). Inquiry paradigms and writing. *College Composition and Communication, 33*(1), 64–75.

Eresh, J. (1990, November). *Balancing the pieces: Content, teachers, tests, and administration.* Paper presented at the annual meeting of the Conference for Secondary School English Department Chairpersons, Atlanta, GA.

Frederiksen, J. R., & Collins, A. (1989). A systems approach to educational testing. *Educational Researcher, 18* (9), 27–32.

Frederiksen, N., Mislevy, R., & Bejar, I. (Eds.). (1993). *Test theory for a new generation of tests.* Hillsdale, NJ: Lawrence Erlbaum Associates.

Gardner, H. (1992). Assessment in context: The alternative to standardized testing. In B. Gifford & M. C. O'Connor (Eds.). Changing assessments: Alternative views of aptitude, achievement, and instruction. Norwell, MA: Kluwer Academic Publishers.

Gitomer, D. (1993). Performance assessment and educational measurement. In R. E. Bennett and W. C. Ward (Eds.), *Construction versus choice in cognitive measurement: Issues in constructed response, performance testing, and portfolio assessment,* (p. 241–264). Hillsdale, NJ: Lawrence Erlbaum Associates

Greenberg, K. L. (1992). Validity and reliability issues in the direct assessment of writing. *Writing Program Administration, 16,* (1–2), 7–22.

Hadley, C. (1984, September). Direct writing assessments in the states. *Issuegram,* Education Commission of the States and the California Assessment Project

Haertel, E. H., & Calfee, R. C. (1983). School achievement: Thinking about what to test. *Journal of Educational Measurement, 20,* 119–32.

Howard, K. (1990). Making the writing portfolio real. *The Quarterly of the National Writing Project and the Center for the Study of Writing, 12,* 4–7, 27.

Howard, K. & LeMahieu, P. (1995). Parents as assessors of student writing: Enlarging the community of learners. *Teaching and Change, 2*(4), 392–414.

Johnston, B. (1983). *Assessing English: Helping students to reflect on their work.* Philadelphia: Open Court Press.

Johnston, P. (1987). Teachers as evaluation experts. *The Reading Teacher, 40,* 744–748.

Jones, A. (1989). Rose. *Portfolio* (The Newsletter of Arts PROPEL) 1 (5): 20.

Koretz, D., McCaffrey, L. D. , Klein, S., Bell, R., & Stecher, B. (1992). *The reliability of scores from the 1992 Vermont Portfolio Assessment Program: Interim report.* Los Angeles: National Center for Research on Evaluation, Standards and Student Testing.

Koretz, D., Stecher, B., Klein, S., & McCaffrey, D. (1994). *The evolution of a portfolio program: The impact and quality of the Vermont program in its second year (1992–93).* CSE Technical Report 385. Graduate School of Education, University of California, Los Angeles: National Center for Research on Evaluation, Standards, and Student Testing.

Lamme, L. & Hysmith, C. (1991). One school's adventure into portfolio assessment. *Language Arts, 68,* 629–640.

LeMahieu, P., Eresh, J., & Wallace, R. (1992, December). Using student portfolios for a public accounting. *The School Administrator*, 49 (11), 8–15.

LeMahieu, P., Gitomer, D., & Eresh, J. (1995a). Portfolios beyond the classroom: Data quality and qualities. Center for Performance Assessment. (Technical Report 94–01). Princeton, NJ: Educational Testing Service.

LeMahieu, P., Gitomer, D., & Eresh, J. (1995b). Portfolios in large-scale assessment: Difficult but not impossible. *Educational Measurement*, 14 (5), 11–28.

Lieberman, A. (1992). The meaning of scholarly activity and the building of community. *Educational Researcher*, 21(6), 5–12.

Linn, R. L., Baker, E., & Dunbar, S. B. (1990). Performance-based assessment: Expectations and validation criteria. *Educational Researcher*, 20 (8), 15–21.

Loofbourrow, P. T. (1994). Composition in the context of the CAP: A case study of the interplay between composition assessment and classrooms. *Educational Assessment*, 2: 7–49.

Lortie, D. (1975). *School teacher: A sociological study*. Chicago: University of Chicago Press.

Lucas, C. (1988a). Toward ecological evaluation. *The Quarterly of the National Writing Project and the Center for the Study of Writing*, 10 (1), 1–17.

Lucas, C. (1988b). Toward ecological evaluation: Part II. *The Quarterly of the National Writing Project and the Center for the Study of Writing*, 10 (2): 4–10.

Matsuhashi, A. (1982). Explorations in the real-time production of written discourse. In M. Nystrand (Ed.), *What writers know: The language, process, and structure of written discourse*, (pp. 269–290). New York: Academic Press.

Mehrens, W. A. (1992). Using performance assessment for accountability purposes. *Educational Measurement: Issues and Practice*, 11(1), 3–20.

Messick, S. (1989a). Meaning and values in test validation: The science and ethics of assessment. *Educational Researcher*, 18(2), 5–11.

Messick, S. (1989b). Validity. In R. L. Linn (Ed.), *Educational measurement* (3rd. ed., pp. 13–104). New York: American Council on Education and Macmillan.

Messick, S. (1994). The interplay of evidence and consequences in the validation of performance assessments. *Educational Researcher*, 23, (2), 13–23.

Mitchell, R. (1992). *Testing for learning: How new approaches to evaluation can improve American schools*. New York: Macmillan, Inc.

Moss, P. (1992). Shifting conceptions of validity in educational measurement: Implications for performance assessment. *Review of educational research*, 62(3), 229–258

Moss, P. (1994). Can there be validity without reliability? *Educational Researcher*, 23(2), 5–12.

Murphy, S. (1994). Portfolios and curriculum reform: Patterns in practice. *Assessing Writing*, 1, 175–206.

Murphy, S. (1997). Teachers and students: Reclaiming assessment. In K. Yancey & I. Weiser (Eds.), *Situating portfolios: Four perspectives* (pp. 72–89). Logan, UT: Utah State University Press.

Murphy, S. (1999). Assessing portfolios. In C. Cooper & L. Odell, (Eds.) *Evaluating writing*, 2nd ed. Urbana, IL: National Council of Teachers of English.

Murphy, S. & Camp, R. (1996). Toward systemic coherence: A discussion of conflicting perspectives on portfolio assessment. In R. Calfee & P. Perfumo (Eds.) *Writing portfolios in the classroom: Policy and practice, promise and peril*. Hillsdale, NJ:Lawrence Erlbaum Associates.

Murphy, S. & Smith, M.A. (1999). Creating a climate for portfolios. In L. Odell & C. Cooper, (Eds.) *Evaluating writing*, (2nd ed.) (pp. 325–343). Urbana, IL: National Council of Teachers of English.

Nystrand, M. & Knapp, J. (1987). *Review of selected national tests of writing and reading*. Technical report. Madison, WI: National Center on Effective Secondary Schools, University of Wisconsin-Madison.

Nystrand, M., Cohen, A. S., & Dowling, N. M. (1993). Addressing reliability problems in the portfolio assessment of college writing. *Educational Assessment, 1*(1), 53–70.

Paulson, F. L., Paulson, P., & Meyer, C. A. (1991). What makes a portfolio a portfolio? *Educational Leadership, 48*(5), 60–63.

Pearson, P. D., & Valencia, S. (1987). Assessment, accountability, and professional prerogative. *Research in literacy: Merging perspectives; Thirty-sixth yearbook of the National Reading Conference*. Rochester, New York: National Reading Conference.

Resnick, L. (1996). Performance puzzles: Issues in measuring capabilities and certifying accomplishments. Center for the Study of Evaluation. (Technical Report No. 415). Los Angeles, CA: National Center for Research on Evaluation, Standards, and Student Testing, University of California, Los Angeles.

Resnick, L. B. & Klopfer, K. (1989). *Toward the thinking curriculum: Current cognitive research. 1989 Yearbook of the Association for Supervision and Curriculum Development*. Alexandria, VA: The Association for Supervision and Curriculum Development.

Resnick, L. B. & Resnick, D.P. (1992). Assessing the thinking curriculum: New tools for educational reform. In B. R. Gifford & M. C. O'Connor (Eds.), *Changing assessments: Alternative views of aptitude, achievement and instruction*. Boston: Kluwer Academic Publishers.

Rief, L. (1990). Finding the value in evaluation: Self-assessment in a middle school classroom. *Educational Leadership, 47*(6), 24–29.

Sarason, S. B. (1990). *The predictable failure of educational reform: Can we change course before it's too late?* San Francisco: Jossey Bass.

Sheingold, K., & Frederiksen, J. (1995). *Linking assessment with reform: Technologies that support conversations about student work*. (Technical Report 94–06). Princeton, NJ: Center for Performance Assessment, Educational Testing Service.

Sheingold, K., Heller, J. I. & Paulukonis, S. T. (1995). *Actively seeking evidence: shifts in teacher's thinking and practice through assessment development*. (Technical Report No. 94–04). Princeton NJ: Educational Testing Service.

Simmons, W., & Resnick, L. (1993). Assessment as a catalyst of school reform. *Educational Leadership 50*(5), 11–15.

Stiggins, R. J., & Bridgeford, N. J. (1985). The ecology of classroom assessment. *Journal of Educational Measurement, 22*, 271–286.

Tierney, R. J., Carter, M. A., & Desai, L. E. (1991). *Portfolios in the reading-writing classroom*. Norwood, MA: Christopher Gordon.

Valencia, S. W., & Calfee, R. C. (1991). The development and use of literacy portfolios for students, classes, and teachers. *Applied Measurement in Education, 4*, 333–345.

Weinbaum, K. (1991). Portfolios as a vehicle for student empowerment and teacher change. In P. Belanoff and M. Dickson, (Eds.), *Portfolios: Process and product*, (pp. 206–214). Portsmouth, NH: Boynton/Cook/Heinemann.

Wells, P. (1991). Putting America to the test. *Agenda, 1*, 52–57.

Wiggins, G. (1989). A true test: Toward more authentic and equitable assessment. *Phi Delta Kappan, 70*, 703–713.

Wiggins, G. (1994). The constant danger of sacrificing validity to reliability: making writing assessment serve writers. *Assessing Writing, 1,*129–139.

Winner, E., & Rosenblatt, E. (1989, December). Tracking the effects of the portfolio process: What changes and when? *Portfolio, 1,* (5), 21–26.

Witte, S. (1988, March) *The influence of writing prompts on composing.* Paper presented at the Conference on College Composition and Communication. St. Louis, MO.

Witte, S., & Cherry, R. (1994). Think-aloud protocols, protocol analysis, and research design: An exploration of the influence of writing tasks on writing processes. In P. Smagorinsky, (Ed). *Speaking about writing: Reflections on research methodologies,* (pp. 20–54). Newbury Park, CA: Sage Publications.

Wolf, D. P. (1988). Opening up assessment. *Educational Leadership, 45* (4): 21–26.

Wolf, D. P. (1989). Portfolio assessment: Sampling student work. *Educational Leadership, 46,* 35–39.

Yancey, K. B. (Ed.). (1992). *Portfolios in the writing classroom.* Urbana, IL: National Council of Teachers of English.

Zessoules, R. (1989). The dance marathon: Learning over time. *Portfolio* (The Newsletter of Arts PROPEL) *1* (5), 11, 14–19.

Zessoules, R., & Gardner, H. (1991). Authentic assessment: Beyond the buzzword and into the classroom. In V. Perrone, (Ed.), *Expanding student assessment* (pp. 47–71). Alexandria, VA: Association of Supervision and Curriculum Development.

5 | Chinle: Creating Culturally Responsive Assessment

In the early 1990s, like many other states, Arizona was engaged in assessment reform. A comprehensive accountability program called the Arizona Student Assessment Program (ASAP) had recently been implemented. The Arizona "Essential Skills" had been identified and described, and thematic on-demand performance assessments, including short answers, essays, and other demonstrations of students' achievement, had been designed to monitor student achievement in mathematics, reading, and writing in grades 3, 8, and 12. In addition, districts were required to develop a District Assessment Plan (DAP) for assessing students for mastery of the "essential skills" throughout the grades. For these local assessments, ASAP gave districts the opportunity to choose among several options, including computerized criterion-referenced tests, forms of the ASAP that were not used for statewide assessment, and portfolios.

Chinle, an Arizona public school district located in the heart of the Navajo Reservation, chose portfolios.

Initially, the Chinle portfolio system was designed to bridge state-level and local community concerns. Performance tasks designed by teachers for the portfolios incorporated local Navajo experience, histories, and values. Moreover, portfolios were reviewed with a dual lens: One lens was a rubric tied to culturally responsive and locally developed standards; the other lens consisted of domain-specific rubrics developed by the State. This bicultural focus made the Chinle project one of the most interesting and complex projects attempted anywhere.

Like all of the other portfolio projects profiled in this book, the one at Chinle evolved. In large part that evolution appeared to be the result of external forces, in particular, changes in administrative personnel and in state policies.

Midway through the project, the statewide assessment system (ASAP) was revised. In 1995, Arizona suspended the performance test that had asked students to integrate knowledge across subjects, because state officials "feared the test was not measuring what it was designed to measure" (Olson, 1995). Other critics pointed to the lack of uniformity in local school responses to the mandated state test. When they conducted case studies of instruction in four Arizona schools during ASAP's first two years of implementation, Mary Lee Smith and her colleagues at Arizona State University found little instructional change, except in a suburban school that had already been moving toward the kind of curriculum and instruction the state had advocated (Smith, et al., 1994). Smith and her colleague pointed to the absence of complementary state policies to promote good teaching and learning as one reason for the varying school response to the ASAP mandate. Apart from providing test forms and scoring workshops, the state did little to enhance professional development. Some districts provided support for professional and curriculum development in relation to the tests, but others did not (Smith, et al. 1994).

When the ASAP was jettisoned, districts adapted. Some districts continued to use forms of the ASAP test not eliminated by the state; others came up with their own assessment plans; others used portfolios (Henry, 1994). While districts could test in every grade level on a variety of subjects, they were required to report reading and writing scores to the state in grades 3, 8, and 12. Until a new assessment could be developed, Arizona used the SAT 9 for assessment at all grade levels 2–12.

When the new statewide assessment system was developed, the focus shifted to standards instead of performance tasks. Under the new system, called the Arizona Instrument to Measure Standards (AIMS), the state planned to assess at four levels (grades 3, 5, 8, and 10–12), with high stakes attached to the high school test. Beginning in the spring of tenth grade, students may take the high school test once a semester for a total of five times. Students must pass the AIMS test to receive a high school diploma. The tests were designed to measure proficiency in relation to academic standards, which the state adopted in 1996.

According to education writer Lynn Schnaiberg (1999), the new assessment system was "at the heart of the state's effort to stop social promotion and inject accountability into the public schools" (p. 128). It is worth noting here that the imposition of the statewide tests was an exception to Arizona's usually fierce protection of local control. The tradition of local control was reflected in Arizona's general approach to school accountability, with its practice of publishing report cards on each school that include student test results and its statewide open enrollment policy. But plans for the new statewide system added high stakes.

The design of the new system called for the tenth grade test to determine whether students would receive an academic diploma or a certificate of completion. Students would be required to "pass each of the test's seven components," which "gauge whether they are meeting the state standards in reading, writing, and mathematics" in order to graduate (Schnaiberg, 1999, p. 128). If they failed any part, they could retake the test up to four more times. Although the state did not mandate that students pass the tests in order to move from grade to grade, state officials said that some districts might choose to adopt that policy (Schnaiberg, 1999).

The plan originally called for the Class of 2001 to be the first required to pass the test, but teachers and parents complained that they had not been notified about the new standards in time to revamp the curriculum to prepare students to succeed. Patricia Likens, a spokeswoman for the state Superintendent said, "The concern is not enough schools have adapted their curricula to the standards. In too many instances, the material is stopping at the district curriculum director's desk and not getting to teachers so they can teach it" (cited in Schneiberg, 1999, p. 128). As Liken's comment suggests, the state was putting pressure on districts and schools to reshape their curricula so that students would be prepared to meet the state standards.

Not all Arizona constituents were sure, however, that the new assessment effort would be effectively based on pedagogical concerns. Critics suggested that decisions about what a student needs to demonstrate in order to be certified as proficient would wind up being more political than pedagogical (Schneiberg, 1999). As Gene Gall, the associate dean for research in the education school at Arizona State University in Tempe put the issue, "There's no non-arbitrary place to draw the cutoff score. . . . The score becomes politically manipulated so there's a politically acceptable failure rate. And the real damage is that the focus becomes all on test preparation" (cited in Schneiberg, 1999, p. 128).

At the time this publication was authored, districts were still required to have a district assessment plan and to report on student competency. The AIMS test (a combination of multiple-choice, short answer, true false, and a direct writing assessment) was being phased in. The portfolio system, which began at a single school, had spread to all the elementary schools in the Chinle district.

Exemplar System

In recent decades, research has documented the discontinuity between home and school that exists for children from non-dominant cultures, including, among others, working class and low-income African-American children (Heath, 1983; Taylor & Dorsey-Gaines, 1988), low-income Hawaiian children (Boggs, 1972; Au, 1980; Au & Kawakami, 1994), and Native American children (Phillips, 1972, 1983). In fact, educational practices in American schools often reflect little real understanding of the cultural ways of knowing and learning of students from non-mainstream cultures. Topics in school are often far removed from the experiences of culturally different children; and curricula make few, if any, connections to the histories of their people or their languages (Estrin & Nelson-Barber, 1995). These conditions all too often characterized the relationship between home and school ways of knowing and doing for the Navajo children of Chinle.

Why is this discontinuity a problem? Culturally discordant patterns of discourse can lead to misunderstandings and interfere with learning, and even when teachers and students speak the same language, they may use it in very different ways (Michaels, 1982; Cook-Gumperz & Gumperz, 1986; Delpit, 1988; Villegas, 1991). In some communities, for example, little emphasis is placed on asking children to display information for its own sake. Yet many teachers rely heavily on "test-type" questions, to the disadvantage of minority and working class students (Farr & Trumbull, 1997).

The ways that children are expected to learn in school can be disorientingly incongruent with the ways that students learn at home (Estrin & Nelson-Barber, 1995). For example, learning in Native communities contrasts sharply with the emphasis on verbal instruction in school, capitalizing instead on experience and observation. Students who come from such communities may find school learning less accessible than students who are accustomed to verbal instruction. Similarly, students who have been culturally socialized to learn in informal, cooperative, and collaborative ways may not fare well in classrooms that are highly structured, individualistic, and competitive (Farr & Trumbull 1997).

Further, evidence suggests that when conventional, authoritative, non-native ways of learning are enforced, Native students may resist adopting "school" rules of behavior and retreat to silence (Dumont, 1972; Phillips, 1983). Resistance to acting according to school norms and expectations may also result from peer pressures that discourage academic striving (Ogbu, 1992). In sum, particular instructional styles, negative peer pressures, the absence of contextually relevant materials, and patterns of social organization and interaction in the classroom all appear to contribute to problems that culturally different children experience in school.

Assessment practices in the school exacerbate the situation. Misclassification of students and school policies such as tracking based on the results of biased tests disadvantage minority students (Oakes, 1985; Ogbu, 1978, 1992). Elise Estrin (1993) explains:

> Disproportionate numbers of poor and minority students have long been tracked into low-ability classrooms and special education programs or disproportionately categorized as learning handicapped or language delayed on the basis of norm-referenced tests. . . . And research shows that students placed in low-ability groups rarely, if ever, move into higher-ability groups. The damage to students can be argued to be lifelong, both cognitive and emotional, and even economic—in terms of missed opportunities. (p. 2)

A host of factors that contribute to the inequalities in assessment for children from linguistic and cultural minority groups have been identified, including test design and test use, time pressures, inequality of educational programs, language differences, attitudes toward test-taking, attitudes toward competitiveness, achievement motivation, test-wiseness, and test anxiety (Farr & Trumbull, 1997). We highlight three factors in this discussion, because they are particularly relevant to the efforts of the Chinle district to create a more equitable assessment for Navajo students.

One factor that plays a role in the differential performance of linguistic minority students in both multiple-choice standardized tests and direct writing assessments is time (Garcia, 1988; Mestre, 1984; Rincon, 1979; Hilgers, 1992). Time pressures negatively influence the performance of culturally and linguistically different students on two counts. First, research has demonstrated that reading and responding to test questions are more complicated tasks for students for whom English is a second language or whose dialect is strongly influenced by another language. Second, some communities view time differently and prize reflection over rapid response (Trumbull & Nelson-Barber, 1995).

For example, Farr and Trumbull (1997) report that it is common for Native Americans "to make decisions slowly with the intent of being right the first time" (p.198). Ethnographic research on Navajo children substantiates this cultural interpretation (Longstreet 1978; John 1972). Also, as Werner and Begishe (1968) point out, Anglos and Navajos have different perspectives on performance. Anglos stress performance as a prerequisite for competence, a perspective summed up in the phrase: "If at first you don't succeed, try, try again," (Werner & Begishe, 1968, p. 1, cited in Deyhle, 1987). Navajos stress competence as a prerequisite for performance, an approach summed up in the phrase: "If at first you don't think and think again, don't bother trying" (Werner & Begishe, 1968, p.2). When successful performance on a timed test requires rapid response or guessing, scholars say that Native American students are handicapped (Deyhle, 1987).

Inappropriate test content also creates problems for culturally different children. Cognitive tasks such as reading and remembering are facilitated when students have the necessary schema and cognitive tools (Bransford & Johnson, 1972; Cole & Scribner, 1974). Unfamiliar content on tests for skills such as reading and writing may make cognitive processing more difficult. Extensive research on the influence of schemata supports their importance in cognitive processing. As but one example, Pichert and Anderson (1977) found evidence that a person's schema effects both memory and learning (see also Bransford & Johnson, 1972, and Anderson & Pearson, 1984).

Test-makers, too, have problems with guaranteeing the validity of their tests when content is inappropriate. As Estrin and Nelson-Barber (1995) point out, when "students are asked to respond to entirely unfamiliar content, it is difficult to know what is being assessed" (p. 4). In these cases, the construct validity of the assessment (i.e., the ability of the assessment instrument to assess what it purports to assess) must be questioned. Donna Deyhle (1987) puts the issue this way, "Tests are designed for and validated against the values and lifestyles of the middle class, which in turn discriminates against other socioeconomic groups and nondominant cultural groups" (p. 86). According to Rhodes (1988), this constitutes test bias: "The question of test bias is always valid when dealing with an instrument developed by one culture, primarily for that culture, and yet administered to individuals of another culture" (cited in Farr & Trumbull, 1997).

Bias in the environment of the test itself can also influence the performance of culturally different children. Research evidence indicates that some students from nondominant cultures, Native Americans in particular, begin their schooling with little understanding of the importance of tests in school and what they need to do in order to succeed (Deyhle, 1987). If students do not take tests seriously, the validity of the tests must be questioned. As Estrin and Nelson-Barber (1995) explain, "Formal, on-demand testing is alien to Native ways of demonstrating learning" (p. 4).

In most public schools, testing is used to determine what children have failed to learn, a phenomena echoed in daily instruction in the classroom by teachers who require students to individually answer questions in the presence of their peers. The practice of answering questions or reciting when called upon by the teacher assumes that one will learn by making mistakes in front of others (Phillips, 1972). Yet in Native American cultures, failures to learn are not usually acknowledged publicly. Thus testing, whether of the formal on-demand variety, or the informal on-demand version that happens in many classroom exchanges, can represent a conflict for Navajos between the culture of home and the culture of school. Nevertheless, because it is the major mechanism for defining success or failure in school, assessment cannot be avoided or ignored. To the contrary, it is a challenge that must be addressed. The challenge is to create equitable, culturally responsive assessments.

Because portfolio assessment allows educators to address some of the problems outlined above, it ought not to have surprised anyone that the Chinle Unified District adopted this assessment strategy. For Chinle students time pressures could be eased, since student work in portfolios is most often accomplished during normal instructional activities. Moreover, portfolios could include a range of types of student performance produced under a variety of conditions. In this way, assessments could be aligned with effective instructional practices.

In addition, important Navajo cultural context could be embedded in coursework and in turn in portfolio evidence, aligning the assessment with both the local context and the content of schooling. Finally, unlike most tests, portfolios allow students to show their best work—what they know and can do instead of what they have failed to learn. Koelsch and Trumbull (1996) put the issue this way: "If equity in assessment can be conceived of, in part, as allowing students opportunities to show what they have learned and how they understand it, portfolios (through their processes) may constitute one of the more equitable assessment tools available" (p. 263).

The Chinle Portfolio Project was an attempt to address some of the problems associated with the assessment of ethnolinguistic, nondominant students outlined above and, at the same time, an attempt to link the culture of Navajo students with district and state educational requirements for accountability. The goals of the Chinle educators are challenging. In sum, they are attempting to create "culturally respon-sive education," a model of multicultural education which John Ogbu (1992) describes as an attempt "to enhance minority school learning by including minority cultures in the content of the curriculum and as a medium of instruction" (p. 6).

In the Navajo culture the tendency is to be integrative and to look for connections instead of oppositions (Koelsch, personal communication). "The district's long term goal for schooling," Koelsch and Trumbull (1996) report, "is that Navajo culture and the Navajo way of being walk side by side with non-Native culture. . . ." (p. 265).

Chinle, then, may ultimately be something of a bellwether case for bridging local community concerns with the requirements of a statewide accountability system. That is, conditions seem certainly more promising than when the goals of partici-pants openly conflict. Educators at Chinle, for example, with the support of consult-ants from Far West Educational Laboratory, have taken steps to create connections—an integrated curriculum that addresses district and state standards but which also includes attention to Navajo culture and Navajo languages, and a portfolio assess-ment system that accommodates that curriculum. But to some degree, the jury is still out. Whether a culturally responsive assessment can survive and thrive in the high stakes world of statewide accountability assessment is one of the questions that make Chinle worth watching.

Context for the System

The schools in the area around Chinle focus on a dual mission that attends to basic skills and academic preparation as well as Navajo (DINE) culture. For example, the mission statement for Little Singer Community School says:

> Our mission at Little Singer Community School is, in cooperation with home and parents, to strengthen DINE cultural values, and to assure that each stu-dent will discover, develop, and strengthen their capabilities for use in mean-ingful work and family life. The educational program offers the opportunity for students to learn the basic and critical thinking skills and knowledge about democracy and freedom. Also discover, develop, and strengthen basic and critical thinking skills of each student. (Arizona Department of Education, 1997. Reprinted with permission.)

Similarly, the mission statement for the Chinle Unified District emphasizes the pres-ervation of Navajo culture and language:

> We believe that children are the Navajo Nation's greatest resource. We en-courage and support the maintenance of the Navajo language and promote cultural fluency. Special and unique needs exist in our predominantly Na-vajo student population. These needs require an approach that reinforces tenets, theories, educational values, and philosophies of Navajo culture. (Ari-zona Department of Education, 1997. Reprinted with permission.)

Koelsch and Trumbull (1996) explain that several factors influenced the initial decision by the Chinle district to develop a portfolio system: 1) Native American students had consistently scored more poorly than their mainstream peers on state tests, including the statewide performance assessment; 2) State forms available to districts for use in local assessments were too difficult for Chinle students in grades 4 through 6, perhaps because the topics of the performance assessment were far removed from the experiences of children on the Navajo reservation; and 3) The district had developed culturally responsive curriculum that was inadequately represented in the state's tests and scoring rubrics. Educators in Chinle saw portfolios as a way to "fill in gaps," that is, a way to assess environmental, historical, cultural, and symbolic ways of knowing that were not addressed by state tests, to "link culturally responsive curriculum with state level accountability requirements," and "show others what their students can do" (Koelsch and Trumbull, 1996, p. 262).

The effort to represent Navajo ways of knowing in the portfolio moved the district toward an assessment system that was potentially more culturally responsive and equitable than the forms of the state test that were available for district use. One form of the state test, for example, asked students to pretend that they were designing a tile pattern for a kitchen. Yet many of the students on the reservation lived in dirt floor hogans, or in government housing, where tile design was not an option (Far West Laboratory). The students were more familiar with patterns on a Navajo rug. The example illustrates a dilemma in assessment: how to adequately take the background and experiences of students into account. For the Chinle teachers, portfolios provided a more equitable alternative because they could align the assessment with culturally responsive curriculum presented in the classroom.

Purposes for the System

When it began, the Chinle portfolio project had two primary purposes: 1) "to assess student work against standards and criteria", and 2) to "negotiate meaning in a culturally congruent way" (Koelsch & Trumbull, 1996, p. 264). According to Beth Witt, a teacher in the district, not all entries in the portfolio were formally assessed; the portfolio was used to provide a "snapshot" of student work for the students to see what they had accomplished and for the parents to see as well (Beth Witt, personal communication). Additionally, Chinle educators hoped that new approaches to assessment would "allow teachers to engage students in their own learning process, . . . communicate student achievement to parents, and . . . help teachers to assess student learning" (Far West Laboratory). No doubt the creation of a more equitable assessment was a goal as well.

System Design

As a first step in the early years of the project, members of the Navajo community were consulted and District portfolio standards that reflected shared values of the Navajo community and the school were developed (see Figure 5.1).

The initial portfolio standards were, we believe, particularly noteworthy because they blended community and school contexts. For example, while the standards for Communication and Mathematical Understanding and Power (the only domain-specific standard) reflect typical values in schooling, the Life Skills standard clearly reflects Navajo ways of being and knowing that promote harmony in life, expressed in the phrase: *to walk in beauty* (Koelsch & Trumbull, 1996). This standard also reflects the Navajos' sense of the interconnectedness of all life, as does the standard for Environmental or Cultural Awareness and Responsibility.

Figure 5.1
The Chinle Portfolio Standards

- *Environmental or Cultural Awareness and Responsibility* . Students will develop an awareness of their local and global environment through exploration of the cultures and ecosystems within them. They will be able to identify systems of organization and cause and effect relationships which exist in the world now and historically in order to effect change.
- *Communication* . Students will communicate their academic, social, and affective knowledge and understanding to a variety of audiences and for a variety of purposes.
- *Life Skills. Shá Bike'eh Hozhóón* (a phrase that refers to the principle of walking in beauty throughout one's life): Students will be able to analyze, synthesize, apply, evaluate, and produce knowledge for basic life skills.
- *Mathematical Understanding and Power:* Students will be able to communicate mathematical concepts as they demonstrate their understanding through modeling, identifying, and extending concepts as they learn.

From "Portfolios: Bridging Cultural and Linguistic Worlds." by N. Koelsch and E. Trumbull, 1996. In R. C. Calfee and P. Perfumo (Eds.), Writing Portfolios in the Classroom: Policy and Practice, Promise and Peril. Mahwah, NJ: Lawrence Erlbaum Associates, Publishers, Inc., p. 266. Copyright © 1966 by Lawrence Erlbaum Associates, Inc. Reprinted with permission.

Within the district, student portfolios were scored with two different rubrics, a rubric tied to the standards developed in the Chinle district, and the generic rubrics adopted by the State (see the section on evaluation below). Although the district standards served as an innovative and effective bridge between local and state-level expectations for student learning, assessment of student achievement in relation to the district standards was informal and relatively short-lived. When the statewide system was revised, new statewide standards were adopted by the state Board of Education. The new standards became the basis for curriculum and assessment decisions at both the state and local levels and for the assessment of Chinle portfolios. The assessment of portfolios in relation to the culturally responsive district standards and the generic state rubrics ceased.

The new statewide standards described expectations in language arts (reading and writing) and mathematics. Language arts had two standards (reading and writing) while mathematics had six (Number Sense; Data Analysis and Probability; Patterns, Algebra, and Functions; Geometry; Measurement and Discrete Mathematics; and Mathematical Structure/Logic).

The new standards were accompanied by performance objectives that spell out increasingly rigorous expectations for students as they move through the grade levels (see Figures 5.2 and 5.3). For considerations of length, only the standards and performance objectives for reading and writing are provided here. More elaborated versions of the goals with specific performance objectives for each grade level as well as standards and goals for other areas, including listening and speaking, can be seen on the Arizona Department of Education website.

Both the original Chinle district standards and the new state standards, it should be noted, are stated broadly enough to accommodate diversity in the way they are met within the portfolio system. For example, the old District standard for Communication—"Students will communicate their academic, social, and affective knowledge and understanding to a variety of audiences and for a variety of purposes."—is similar to the new State Standard for Writing in its attention to variety in audience and purpose. Similarly, the new State Standard for Reading leaves content open, focusing instead on strategies to be used with very different kinds of texts. In all of these standards, moreover, content is left open, giving students and teachers room to make choices about topics for writing and subjects for reading.

It is worth noting that the new performance objectives, like the new State standards, leave content open. Apart from a broadly stated emphasis on American and world literature in reading for honors during the high school years, the performance objectives for reading focus on strategies instead of content. And, while the performance objectives for writing specify certain kinds of writing—narrative, creative story, summary, persuasive essay, and analysis of literature—particular topics are not specified.

Flexibility in task content is a critical characteristic of equitable assessment. In order to be equitable for Native Americans, or for that matter, for other groups of culturally different students, "Assessments must incorporate content that reflects local contexts and experiences" (Estrin & Nelson Barber, 1995, p. 5). Material related to students' background and cultural knowledge can be used to assess reading and writing. At the same time, State requirements can be met. Teachers at the Chinle district have found that "tapping local context and local culture can provide a gateway toward mastery of the personal narrative writing skills required by the state" (Far West Laboratory). The idea is to build on the resources that students already have.

In addition to keeping the content of the curriculum flexible, the format of these standards and performance objectives avoids another problem in assessment, one that might have plagued the old ASAP system had it lasted any appreciable amount of time—a *dis*integrating effect on the curriculum. A danger in an assessment system that is organized around particular tasks is that they may be taught only at particular grade levels or by particular teachers, disrupting the "spiraling" of curriculum that helps learners build on previous understandings and experiences when they re-encounter concepts and tasks in increasingly more sophisticated forms.

In the revised assessment system, "spiraling" is built into the performance objectives. Each level builds upon the one before; that is, the objectives at any level include the objectives of the ones before. Students at the proficiency level in language arts, for example, were expected to know and be able to accomplish as well the objectives identified for the levels of readiness, foundations, and essentials. Performance objectives such as these are useful in instruction, because they describe what students are expected to be able to do at different points in their school careers. Finally, because they focus on strategies instead of content, they provide an alternative to prescriptive menus of portfolio contents, for example, reading particular books, or writing about certain subjects in school. To the contrary, very different kinds of assignments might be used to provide evidence that these standards had been met.

Figure 5.2

Performance Objectives for Standard 1: Reading

Standard 1 Reading: Students learn and effectively apply a variety of reading strategies for comprehending, interpreting, and evaluating a wide range of texts including fiction, nonfiction, classic fiction, classic, and contemporary works.

READINESS (Kindergarten)	FOUNDATIONS (Grades 1–3)	ESSENTIALS (Grades 4–8)	PROFICIENCY (Grades 9–12)	DISTINCTION (Honors)
Students know and are able to do the following:	Students know and are able to do the following AND Readiness:	Students know and are able to do the following AND Readiness and Foundations:	Students know and are able to do the following AND Readiness, Foundations, and Essentials:	Students know and are able to do the following AND Readiness, Foundations, Essentials, and Proficiency:
• Identify characters in a story and retell stories in sequence • Predict elements and events in a story • Identify facts in nonfiction material • Use phonetic skills to decode simple words • Comprehend the meaning of simple written selections, using prior knowledge,	• Use phonetic skills to decode words • Use word recognition and decoding strategies such as phonetic skills, context clues, picture clues, word order, prefixes and suffixes to comprehend written selections • Use reading comprehension strategies such as drawing conclusions, summarizing, making predictions, identifying cause and effect, and	• Use structural analysis skills such as identifying root words, prefixes, suffixes and word origins to decode words unfamiliar in print • Use reading strategies such as making inferences and predictions, summarizing, paraphrasing, differentiating fact from opinion, drawing conclusions, and determining the author's purpose and perspective to comprehend written selections	• Apply reading strategies such as extracting, summarizing, clarifying, and interpreting information; predicting events and extending the ideas presented; relating new information to prior knowledge; supporting assertions with evidence; and making useful connections to other topics to comprehend works of literature and documents • Recognize, analyze and evaluate an author's use of literary elements such as	• Analyze complex texts drawn from American and world literature in several historical periods and movements to discern the universality of themes such as the individual's role in society, interdependence, and the interaction between man and nature; and the author's use of literary elements and styles • Use a full range of strategies to judge the reliability, accuracy, effectiveness, and

cont.

Figure 5.2 (cont.)

letter-sound relationships and picture clues	differentiating fiction from nonfiction • Identify facts and the main idea, sequence events, define and differentiate characters, and determine an author's purpose in a range of traditional and contemporary literature • Analyze selections of fiction, nonfiction and poetry for their literary elements such as character, setting, plot, sequence of events and organization of text • Read and comprehend consumer information such as forms, newspaper ads, warning labels and safety pamphlets • Follow a list of directions and evaluate those directions for clarity • Recognize the historical and cultural perspectives of literary selections	• Analyze selections of fiction, nonfiction, and poetry by identifying the plot line (i.e., beginning, conflict, rising action, climax and resolution); distinguishing the main character from minor ones; describing the relationships between and motivations of characters; and making inferences about the events, setting, style, tone, mood and meaning of the selection • Identify the author's purpose, position, bias and strategies in a persuasive selection • Evaluate an instructional manual such as assembly directions or user's guide for clarity and completeness • Compare and contrast the historical and cultural perspectives of literary selections	mood, tone, theme, point of view, diction, dialog and figurative language (e.g., metaphors, allusions, symbolism, similes) in selections of challenging fiction, nonfiction and poetry • Evaluate the author's persuasive techniques in written selections such as editorials, essays, reviews and critiques • Evaluate technical journals or workplace documents for purpose, organizational pattern, clarity, reliability and accuracy, and relevancy of information • Analyze classic and contemporary literature selections, drawn from American and world literature, for the universality of themes such as the individual's role in society, interdependence, and the interaction between man and nature	persuasiveness of literary criticism and analysis, professional and technical journals, and professional-level reading materials • Develop and support a theme or thesis about the craft and significance of a body of literature, both classic and contemporary, from a diverse selection of writers

Arizona Department of Education (1999). Language arts standards. World Wide Web: (http://www.ade.state.az.us). Reprinted with permission of the Arozona Department of Education.

Figure 5.3
Performance Objectives for Standard 2: Writing

Standard 2 Writing: Students effectively use written language for a variety of purposes and with a variety of audiences.

READINESS (Kindergarten)	FOUNDATIONS (Grades 1–3)	ESSENTIALS (Grades 4–8)	PROFICIENCY (Grades 9–12)	DISTINCTION (Honors)
Students know and are able to do the following:	Students know and are able to do the following AND Readiness:	Students know and are able to do the following AND Readiness and Foundations:	Students know and are able to do the following AND Readiness, Foundations and Essentials:	Students know and are able to do the following AND Readiness, Foundations, Essentials and Proficiency:
• Relate a narrative, creative story or other communication by drawing, telling and writing	• Use the writing process, including generating topics, drafting, revising ideas and editing, to complete effectively a variety of writing tasks	• Use correct spelling, punctuation, capitalization, grammar and usage, along with varied sentence structure and paragraph organization, to complete effectively a variety of writing tasks	• Use transitional devices; varied sentence structures; the active voice; parallel structures; supporting details; phrases and clauses; and correct spelling, punctuation, capitalization, grammar and usage to sharpen the focus and clarify the meaning of their writings.	• Expand writing experiences by experimenting with language, form and genres (e.g., poetry, screen plays and public policy documents)
• Spell simple words	• Use correct spelling, punctuation, capitalization, grammar and word usage, and good penmanship to complete effectively a variety of writing tasks	• Write a personal experience narrative or creative story that includes a plot and shows the reader what happens through well-developed characters, setting, dialog, and themes and uses figurative language, descriptive words and phrases	• While a persuasive essay (e.g., editorials, reviews, essays, critiques) that contains effective introductory and summary statements; arranges the arguments effectively; and fully develops the ideas with convincing proof, details, facts, examples and descriptions.	• Reflect the subtleties of language and polished literary style in their writings including the power of imagery and precise word choice, and the use of such literary devices as foreshadowing, flashbacks, metaphors,
• Write the 26 letters of the alphabet	• Write a personal experience narrative or a creative story that has a beginning, middle and end and uses descriptive			

cont.

Figure 5.3 (cont.)

words or phrases to develop ideas and advance the characters, plot and setting. • Gather, organize and accurately, clearly and sequentially report information gained from personal observations and experiences such as science experiments, field trips and classroom visitors • Locate, acknowledge and use several sources to write an informational report in their own words • Write well-organized communications, such as friendly letters, memos and invitations, for a specific audience and with a clear purpose	• Write a summary that presents information clearly and accurately, contains the most significant details and preserves the position of the author • Write an expository essay that contains effective introductory and summary statements and fully develops the ideas with details, facts, examples and descriptions • Write a report that conveys a point of view and develops a topic with appropriate facts, details, examples and descriptions from a variety of cited sources	• Write an analysis of an author's use of literary elements such as character, setting, theme, plot, figurative language and point of view • Craft a cohesive research document that develops a logical argument or thesis; contains comprehensive, supporting information from a variety of credible and cited resources; and conforms to a style manual • Write formal communitcations, such as a résumé, manuals and letters of application, in appropriate formats, for a definite audience and with a clear purpose. • Write a narrative or story that develops complex characters, plot structure, point of view and setting; organizes ideas in meaningful sequence; and includes sensory details and concrete language to advance the story line
		similies, symbolism and idioms • Analyze, synthesize, evaluate and apply principles of formal logic in expository writing tasks

Arizona Department of Education (1999). Language arts standards. World Wide Web: (http://www.ade.state.az.us). Reprinted with permission of the Arozona Department of Education.

Collection

What work was worth collecting?

In the early years of the project, the district standards, the State's Essential Skills, and the State's performance assessment tasks influenced the curriculum and in turn, the work collected in portfolios. To ensure an opportunity to learn, state guidelines specified that students were to have at least three opportunities to perform what was to be assessed in each "cluster" of Essential Skills. Teachers then, had to be sure that their curriculum included a sufficient number of tasks that provided those opportunities. Nanette Koelsh, a Far West Laboratory support provider, created templates to facilitate task development and to foster reliability of tasks across different classrooms (see Figure 5.4). These "task shells" specified the cognitive and structural components of tasks, but left content open. Thus, Chinle teachers could develop their own tasks using the templates, or use tasks developed by others that fit the template parameters.

The teachers used the task shells to guide the development of new tasks or to adapt tasks that had been developed at the state or national level to incorporate Navajo experiences and cultural values. For instance, a video prepared by Far West Laboratory describes how Chinle teachers recommended adapting the "aquarium problem," a mathematics performance assessment created at the state level for fourth graders, to bring the context and setting in line with their students' experience (Far West Laboratory). In this task, students are given a spending limit of $25 to stock a 30 gallon aquarium. A brochure explains the size and cost of the fish and their special needs. As part of the task, students are asked to choose fish for the aquarium, then write letters explaining their choices. Instead of fish, the Chinle teachers suggested that the task focus on stocking a specified grazing area with livestock. Livestock, they said, were more common to the Navajo experience.

These kinds of modifications introduced the Navajo experience but preserved the cognitive requirements of tasks and the educational objectives for which they were designed (Far West Laboratory). It should also be noted that the tasks adapted or developed by the teachers reflected more than just the Navajo perspective. They blended school and community concerns and integrated multiple, high-level skills (Koelsch & Trumbull, 1996, p. 271). For example, the Heritage Task outlined in Figure 5.5 asks students to complete a number of complex activities involving higher-order skills: research (interviews and the analysis of documents) and the coordination and display of information, visually, verbally, and symbolically. Yet the task is also germane to the Navajo students' world, since it asks the student to research his or her family lineage and the structure of his or her clan.

Figure 5.4
Domains of Performance for Chinle Portfolio Tasks

Overview	Task Shell 1	Task Shell 2	Task Shell 3	Task Shell 4
Task shells describe domains of performance across the curriculum	Collecting and representing real data	Investigating the world	Examining, representing, and evaluating information	Creating new models and symbols
Content require-ments of shells	• Make predictions of, generate or collect data to verify • Describe methods and organize data • Interpret data • Evaluate results	• Make connec-tions between academic learning and world • Apply communi-cation techniques or academic concepts to represent current situations • Evaluate application of academic tools and techniques	• Demonstrate knowledge of a subject • Describe significant aspects of a subject • Provide concrete representation of understanding • Evaluate learning	• Generate original models and symbolic forms • Create symbolic representations using aural, written, visual, or other modes • Evaluate models and forms based on tools and goals • Set further goals
Subject matter	Science and mathematics	Writing, mathemat-ics, social studies, health, and science	Reading, science, social studies	Art, writing, social studies, math-ematics, and science
Structural requirements	• Tasks are introduced and discussed in class but completed on a group or individual basis • Tasks include time for revision • Final products may include support materials • Tasks include individual evaluation of final product			
Examples of specific tasks	• Job task • Science fair task • Household survey task	• Position paper task • Hero task • Scale model task • Environmental task	• Voyage of the Mimi • Plant book tasks • Biome tasks • Generic social studies task • Generic reading task	• Fine arts task • Poetry task • Invention task

---

Figure 5.5
Heritage Task

Standards: Communications, Life Skills

Performance Task Domain: Investigating the World

Task Overview: For this task, the student will research his/her family lineage and create a family map, a poem, and an autobiography.

Time: 2-3 weeks.

Re-explanation for Students: To accomplish this task you will need to:

1. Interview relatives about your family.
2. Investigate other documents or sources for information about your family (such as, family records, Navajo tribe, family trees, role numbers, baby books, land use permits).
3. Create your immediate family's map.
4. Design a symbol for your paternal and maternal lineages or nationalities.
5. Extend your research to include larger family.
6. Create extended family map.
7. Create a legend below your map to explain symbols.
8. Write an autobiography of your life from your earliest memory to now. Include information on school and family.
9. Write an original poem about your heritage. Your poem may be bilingual or in the language of your choice.

From Assessment Alternatives for Diverse Classrooms (p. 387), by B. P. Farr and E. Trumbull, 1997. Norwood, MA: Christopher-Gordon Publiishers. Copyright © 1997 West Ed. All rights reserved.

More recently, after the influence of the new AIMS assessment system had been felt at the district level, the new state standards began to drive the development of tasks and the District began to use them to provide evidence of achievement in relation to State standards in reading, writing, and math (Nanette Koelsch, personal communication). While the portfolio collection still has a dual goal—to "show what students know and can do and to integrate Navajo culture"—there is now a heavy emphasis on meeting the new state standards. Portfolio collection "essentials" can be seen in Figure 5.6, along with a summary of suggestions for the fourth, fifth and sixth grades that were provided to teachers for demonstrating performance goals.

Figure 5.6
Portfolio Collection Essentials: Writing and Reading

Goal: Show what students know and can do

Integrate Navajo culture

Standards: Students learn and effectively apply a variety of reading strategies for comprehending, interpreting, and evaluating a wide range of texts including fiction, nonfiction, classic and contemporary works.

Students effectively use written language for a variety of purposes and with a variety of audiences.

Process: Collect samples of work that demonstrate students' achievement of the following at least three times over the course of the year.

Use structural analysis skills such as identifying root words, prefixes, suffixes, and word origins to decode words unfamiliar in print.

Use reading strategies such as making inferences and predictions, summarizing, paraphrasing, differentiating fact from opinion, drawing conclusions, and determining the author's purposes and perspective to comprehend written selections.

4th: examples of paraphrasing, retelling most important ideas, and confirming predictions.

5th: examples of summaries of most important ideas, paraphrasing (retell in own words to a younger audience), confirming predictions based on evidence, differentiating fact from opinion in editorials and articles.

6th: examples of summaries of most important ideas and details, paraphrasing, making inferences based on textual evidence, differentiating fact from opinion in editorials and articles.

Analyze selections of fiction, nonfiction and poetry by identifying the plot line, distinguishing the main character from minor ones, describing the relationships between motivations of characters, making inferences about the events, setting, style, tone, mood and meaning of the selection.

4th: examples of story maps, Venn diagrams comparing characters, treasure hunts

5th: examples of above, character trait maps based on textual evidence, [answers to] short answer questions, generic reading task, reading response logs (students answer questions about setting, plot, character).

6th: examples of above, short essays that address questions about fiction and nonfiction selections.

Use correct spelling, punctuation, capitalization, grammar and usage, along with varied sentence structure and paragraph organization, to effectively complete a variety of writing tasks.

4th–6th

- examples of finished work that reflects the student's level of mastery (not teacher edited and student copied)

Reprinted by permission of the Chinle Unified School District #24.   *cont.*

> • examples of teacher-generated editing exercises that students edit (not worksheets in isolation)
>
> **Write a personal experience narrative or creative story that includes a plot and show the reader what happens through well-developed characters, setting, dialog, and themes; and uses figurative language, descriptive words and phrases.**
>
> 4th–5th: beginning, middle, and end, descriptive details that develop the plot, setting, or characters. 6th: add use of figurative language and dialog.
> • examples of character sketches, story planning, story diagrams
> • examples of finished stories and personal experience narratives
>
> **Write an expository essay that contains effective introductory and summary statements and fully develops the ideas with details, facts, examples, and descriptions.**
>
> 6th–8th. 6th: expository paragraphs (chronological, cause and effect, informative)
> • examples of thesis statements or topic sentences
> • examples of planning (webbing, outlining)
> • examples of finished paragraphs

In 1999, as the list of essentials indicates, portfolios in Chinle contained multiple kinds of evidence for reading strategies and the elements of fiction. In the area of writing, in fourth and fifth grade, portfolios included samples of narrative (plans were underway in the district to expand the types of writing to include persuasive writing in fourth and fifth grade). As Nanette Koelsch, the district's inservice provider explained, sixth grade portfolios contained more evidence of reading strategies at a higher level than they had in the past, as well as expository writing based on personal experience. Students were asked to include a letter to their next year's teacher in the portfolio. Although the letter may have led students to reflect on their likes and dislikes, or what they had learned, reflection was not a portfolio requirement. Some teachers included student reflections on portfolio entries (e.g., I like this piece because . . .) but many teachers did not (Koelsch, personal communication).

Who had access to and owned the collections?

Portfolios were kept in classrooms, but access by students varied from class to class. After scoring, the portfolios were sent to the next year's Chinle elementary school teacher. At the end of sixth grade, the portfolios were sent home to the students' parents, except for the writing portion of the portfolio, which was sent on to the student's English teacher at Chinle Junior High School.

The question of ownership is equally complicated. If ownership is defined as the authority to negotiate portfolio design and to make choices about portfolio contents, it is clear that Chinle students had little. In the classroom, students determined whom, in addition to their teacher, could have access to their portfolios (Koelsch, personal communication). But teachers had the ultimate authority when it came to determining portfolio contents. In turn, the district and the state influenced the teachers' authority. As explained above, in the early years of the project, the task templates guided teachers in determining what materials would best demonstrate the student's achievement of standards. In later years, the state standards drove the development of tasks.

Selection

As the discussion of collection indicates, the line between collection and selection in this system was blurred. Just as District and State standards drove what was collected, they drove what was selected to serve as evidence in the portfolios.

What was the purpose for selection?

The overriding purpose for selection, in both the old system and the new, was to demonstrate mastery. Standards drove the selection process. When the statewide system was revised, detailed performance objectives and criteria also drove the selection process. In Chinle the goal was to select the work that would best fit whatever accountability requirements and criteria were in place at the time.

Who selected artifacts for presentation?

The question of who selected portfolio contents does not have a straightforward, simple answer. Some contents were selected by students, some by teachers. As Nanette Koelsch and Elise Trumbull (1996) explain, students retained authority for portfolio contents when they were "deciding on 'free choice' selections, or writing letters of introduction, reflections on their work, self-assessments, and their own conference comments" (p. 270). Yet teachers had the ultimate authority to decide when a particular task or assessment activity would be included in the students' portfolio. Cognizant of the developmental age of the children, this authority was exercised by most teachers. Although some teachers let students make choices about which pieces of their work would be included, most shaped those choices or simply made them themselves (Koeslch, personal communication).

Although in one sense the teachers dominated the selection process, because they designed the tasks, it would be erroneous to assume that the curriculum was entirely teacher centered. To the contrary, classrooms in the Chinle district were, as Linda Darling-Hammond (1996) advocates, "settings that are both learning-centered—that is, focused on challenging curriculum goals for all students—and learner-centered—that is, attentive to the needs and interests of individual learners." (p. 11). Two of the common features in the practice of teachers who are successful at developing "real understanding of challenging subjects" are particularly relevant to the discussion here:

- They develop engaging tasks that give students meaningful work to do, projects and performances that use the methods of a field of study and represent a whole piece of work within that field: doing historical research, writing and "publishing" a short book, developing a computer simulation or scale model.
- They design these to allow students choices and different entry points into

the work. This helps motivate effort and allows students to build on their strengths and interests as they reach for new and more difficult performances. (Darling-Hammond, 1996, p. 11)

Because the degree to which teachers used the portfolios in instruction varied, portfolio contents—what was selected—also varied. When portfolios went forward to be scored some contained only the contents required for reporting to the state. Others contained a much wider range of materials, a circumstance that may have reflected their use by teachers for classroom instruction and assessment purposes.

When did selection take place?

In classrooms where portfolios are used in instruction, selection is typically a recursive process that occurs throughout the year (see, for example, the description of the English department portfolio system at Charles Ruff Middle School in chapter 3). But in the Chinle district, portfolios were primarily used to provide evidence to the state. Selection typically happened near the end of the year. That is not to say, of course, that portfolios used for accountability can't be used for instruction. Rather, the introduction of the new, more complicated analytic scale for writing, along with all the other changes, may have delayed the development of other elements of the project such as the development of strategies for incorporating the portfolios in instruction (N. Koelsch, personal communication).

Who was the audience for the portfolio?

The ultimate audience for the student's portfolio was the assessor—the person who scored the portfolio. But the portfolios had other audiences as well. One, of course, was the student's teacher who helped prepare the portfolio. During the collection and selection process, teachers no doubt reviewed the evidence in the portfolios in relation to standards. No doubt, they also considered issues such as how well their students were doing and what else they would need to teach to help their students perform well.

Another audience was the teacher who the student would have the next year. At the end of each year, up until sixth grade, portfolios were collected and sent on to the student's new teacher. But although the portfolios were sent, they were not always read. Nanette Koelsch reports that some teachers reviewed the incoming students' portfolios, but that others did not. Clearly, time set aside for reviewing the portfolios and District support for the effort are necessary if teachers are to accomplish this purpose.

Yet another audience was the students' parents. Many teachers used the portfolios in parent conferences. When parents examine children's portfolios, they see real samples of writing and other work which may be more immediately intelligible to them than are traditional forms of assessment information, such as stanines and percentiles. Research conducted in Colorado indicates that third-grade parents consider seeing graded samples of student work to be much more useful in learning about their child's progress than standardized tests (Shepard & Bliem, 1995). From the student's written reflections, and when they are present, from the teacher's written comments on the student's writing, portfolios can give parents a view into classroom instruction and learning and a sense of the interactions that occur in the classroom, as well as insights into the criteria and language used by the teacher for evaluation.

Reflection
What opportunities for reflection did the system provide?

The information about the portfolio scores provided fuel for reflection by the teachers—about how well their curriculum was providing opportunities to learn and about the strengths and weaknesses of students with whom they worked. This kind of reflection was supported through staff development activities. For example, in 1999 at the end of the scoring session, Nanette Koelsch led the teachers in a general discussion about the strengths they saw in the students' portfolios, and what they would need to focus on the following year. Teachers discussed what kinds of topics lent themselves to powerful writing and which didn't. Narratives about field trips, for example, which are very important to the students in this rural area, sometimes led to a disjointed, "we did this, then we did that," kind of development. Other topics generated more powerful and effectively organized writing. In addition, in 1999, teachers looked over the scores of individual traits from the six-point writing scale that had been adopted by the state, to identify general trends. If teachers noticed generally depressed scores on one or more of the traits, they spotlighted that trait as a goal for instruction. Chinle teachers, then, had opportunities to reflect on assessment outcomes and to make use of assessment information.

Student reflection was encouraged, but not required as part of the portfolio system. That is, student reflection and/or self-assessment were not evaluated as evidence for determining mastery. Some teachers asked students to include reflections in their portfolios to show student progress and to share with parents. But asking students to reflect on their work was not a widespread practice (Nanette Koelsch, personal communication). Some of the teachers may have been reluctant to experiment with student reflection because of the age of the students. To be sure, very young students often produce charming, but less than analytical responses (e.g., "I liked the story about my mom because I love my mom."). Other teachers may have been concerned about cultural issues. For instance, the kind of metalanguage valued in dominant, middle-class culture is not necessarily valued in Navajo culture. Students might be reluctant to respond, for example, to a prompt such as "What did you do well?" In Navajo culture, one doesn't write or talk about what one does well, because that would be considered boasting (Nanette Koelsch, personal communication). A future consideration for participants in this project then, might be the question: What is a culturally appropriate form of reflection? To answer such a question, members of the community would need to be consulted, as they were in the development of culturally responsive standards.

What kinds of artifacts of reflective activity went in the portfolio?

A "reflective" letter written by the student accompanied the portfolio when it was forwarded to his or her next year's teacher. The teachers framed this assignment so that "both worlds would matter," by asking students to write about what was important to them out of school and in school. Some teachers also used reflection sheets provided by the district. One, for example, asked students to provide the title of the portfolio activity and to reply to three prompts: "From doing this activity I learned . . ." "I especially liked . . ." and "Next time I do a similar activity for my portfolio I will improve my work by . . ." (Chinle Unified School District, 1996). Some of these reflection sheets found their way into the students' portfolios, but they were

not required, and some teachers did not use them because of the cultural considerations described above (Koelsch, personal communication).

Evaluation

As explained earlier, in the early years of the project student performance was
assessed with a dual lens. Four point generic rubrics in reading, writing, and mathematics were used to report scores to the state. For example, the four-point rubric for
scoring writing appears in Figure 5.7.

Figure 5.7
Generic Writing Rubric: Content (K–12)

A **4** paper will fully address the prompt and will be written in a style appropriate to the
genre being assessed. It will clearly show an appropriate awareness of audience. The
paper will "come alive" by incorporating mood, style and creative expression. It will be
well organized, contain sufficient details, examples, descriptions and insights to engage
the reader. The paper will display a strong beginning, a fully developed middle and end
with an appropriate closure.*

A **3** paper will address the prompt and will be written in an appropriate style. It will likely
be well organized and clearly written but may contain vague or inarticulate language. It
will show a sense of audience but may be missing some details and/or examples, offer
incomplete descriptions and fewer insights into characters and/or topics. The student
may offer a weak or inappropriate beginning, middle or ending.*

A **2** paper does not fully address the prompt which causes it to be rambling and/or
disjointed. There may be little awareness of audience. The paper will demonstrate an
incomplete or inadequate understanding of the appropriate style. Details , facts,
examples, or descriptions may be incomplete. The beginning, middle or ending may be
missing.*

 A **1** paper will indicate that the prompt is barely addressed. Awareness of audience may
be missing. The paper will demonstrate a lack of understanding of the appropriate style.
The general idea may be conveyed, but details, facts, examples or descriptions will be
lacking. The beginning, middle or ending will be missing.*

Assign a **0** if the student failed to attempt the paper, presented writing which is off topic
or answered in an offensive or inappropriate manner.

Assign an N/S (Not Scorable) if the response is illegible or unreadable.

*Poetry does not always have a beginning, middle, or ending. All other sections of the
rubric apply to poetry.

6th Grade Portfolio Sample Tasks & Student Work. January 1996. Reprinted by permission of
Chinle Unified School District #24.

At the time, the state required districts to report the number of students achieving mastery using rubrics of this kind.

However, the generic rubrics were just that—generic. Koelsch & Trumbull, (1996) point out that the generic rubrics did not provide meaningful information for teaching and were not particularly useful in the classroom. Nor did they assess performance in relation to the culturally responsive district standards.

To fill the gap, teachers had developed "culturally responsive" rubrics tied to the district standards that spelled out expectations in detail and served as rubrics for scoring (see Figure 5.8, and Farr & Trumbull, 1997, pp. 304–306). Experiences and values that were important to the Navajo community inform the expectations for students throughout. For example, students who perform at level V (the top level) of the Life Skills standards are expected to be able to "reflect on past experience and apply knowledge to the future . . . relate personal perspective and the perspective of others in the community . . . analyze a social and economic organization in a community . . . demonstrate a complex understanding of cultural narratives and cultural meanings in past and future . . . express personal vision goal beyond self and community . . . show independence and self-direction" (p. 304).

In the early stages of the project, information from scoring with these culturally relevant District rubrics was distributed to the teachers who participated in the project. Although the results were not reported formally to the district, the state, or parents, teachers who scored using the culturally relevant rubrics felt that the experience gave them a richer understanding of their students (Koelsch, personal communication). Information from the generic rubrics, on the other hand, was incorporated into the state's public report on students' achievement.

As explained earlier, when the statewide assessment system was revised, formal portfolio review using the dual lens of the District's culturally relevant standards and the State's generic rubrics ceased. Instead, portfolios were scored by domain: reading, writing, or math. The multiple math standards, concepts, and performance objectives led the district to plan to use a combination of criterion referenced assessment and portfolios to assess student achievement in math. To assess achievement in reading, Nanette Koelsch developed a rubric for use with multiple pieces of evidence, both observed behaviors during oral and silent reading and samples of evidence of reading strategies and elements of literature.

Although multiple pieces of evidence were used to assess achievement in reading and math, only one portfolio entry was scored for the domain of writing in grades four and five, a personal experience narrative or creative story. In grade six an expository essay was added. For scoring, a version of the Oregon six-point analytic trait scoring rubric was used. The Oregon rubric addresses the following aspects of writing:

1. *Ideas and Content*: A top-level paper is "exceptionally clear, focused, and interesting. It holds the reader's attention throughout. Main ideas stand out and are developed by strong support and rich details suitable to audience and purpose."

2. *Organization*: "The organization enhances the central idea(s) and its development. The order and structure are compelling and move the reader through the text easily."

Figure 5.8
Portfolio Assessment

Life Skills: Shá Bik'eh Hózhóón
Students will be able to analyze, synthesize, apply, evaluate and produce knowledge for basic life skills.

I	II	III	IV	V
Student is able to state an opinion. Students is able to identify components of a community. Student is able to list facts but does not make strong connections. Student is able to illustrate meaning by creating a story. Student is able to identify personal goals with guidance. Student is able to illustrate meaning by creating a story. Student is able to identify personal goals with guidance.	Student is able to express personal opinions. Students is able to identify the role of services available within the community, Student is able to relate a process of sequencing. Student has conceptual knowledge of cultural narratives and their cultural meanings. Student is able to identify personal goals and is aware of personal needs.	Student is able to identify and relate with others of the same opinion. Student is able to communicate understanding of his/her role in a family to the community. Student can demonstrate role of cultural narratives and their cultural meanings. Student shows a sense of leadership.	Student is able to present and defend personal beliefs and values. Student is able to to portray personal and community relationships through communication. Student is able to use past events to reflect on current issues. Student is able to integrate cultural meaning with works of imagination through projects. Students is able forecast knowledge of personal goals.	Student is able to reflect on past experience and apply knowledge to the future. Student is able to relate personal perspective and the perspectives of others in the community. Student is able to demonstrate a complex under-standing of cultural narratives and cultural meanings in past and future. Student is able to express personal vision goal beyond self and community. of personal goals. Students is able to show indepen-dence and self-

3. *Voice*: "The writer has chosen a voice appropriate for the topic, purpose, and audience. The writer seems deeply committed to the topic, and there is an exceptional sense of "writing to be read." The writing is expressive, engaging, or sincere."

4. *Word Choice*: "Words convey the intended message in an exceptionally interesting, precise, and natural way. The writer employs a rich, broad range of words which have been carefully chosen and thoughtfully placed for impact."

5. *Sentence Fluency*: "The writing has an effective flow and rhythm. Sentences

show a high degree of craftsmanship, with consistently strong and varied structure that makes expressive oral reading easy and enjoyable."

6. *Conventions*: "The writing demonstrates an exceptionally strong control of standard writing conventions (e.g., punctuation, spelling, capitalization, paragraph breaks, grammar, and usage) and uses them effectively to enhance communication. Errors are so few and so minor that the reader can easily skim right over them unless specifically searching for them." (Category descriptions are quoted from the 1999-2000 Writing Official Scoring Guides. Reprinted by permisson of the Oregon Department of Education.)

Although there are six traits in the Oregon rubric, the Arizona plan required that only four be scored for grades 4–6: ideas/content, organization, sentence fluency, and conventions. Each trait was scored separately. An example of a scoring rubric for one of the traits scored by Arizona can be seen in Figure 5.9. (Reprinted by permisson of the Oregon Department of Education.)

Figure 5.9
Scoring Rubric for Conventions

6	5	4
The writing demonstrates exceptionally strong control of standard writing conventions (e.g., punctuation, spelling, capitalization, paragraph breaks, grammar and usage) and uses them effectively to enhance communication. Errors are so few and so minor that the reader can easily skim right over them unless specifically searching for them. The writing is characterized by	**The writing demonstrates strong control of standard writing conventions (e.g., punctuation, spelling, capitalization, paragraph breaks, grammar and usage) and uses them effectively to enhance communication. Errors are so few and so minor that they do not impede readability. The writing is characterized by**	**The writing demonstrates control of standard writing conventions (e.g., punctuation, spelling, capitalization, paragraph breaks, grammar and usage). Minor errors, while perhaps noticeable, do not impede readability. The writing is characterized by**
• strong control of conventions; manipulation of conventions may occur for stylistic effect.	• strong control of conventions.	• control over conventions used, although a wide range is not demonstrated.
• strong effective use of punctuation that guides the reader through the text.	• effective use of punctuation that guides the reader through the text.	• correct end-of-sentence punctuation; internal punctuation may sometimes be incorrect.
• correct spelling, even of more difficult words.	• correct spelling, even of more difficult words.	• spelling that is usually correct, especially on common words.
• paragraph breaks that reinforce the organizational structure.	• paragraph breaks that reinforce the organizational structure.	• basically sound paragraph breaks that reinforce the organizational structure.
• correct grammar and usage that contribute to clarity and style.	• correct capitalization; errors, if any are minor.	• correct capitalization; errors, if any are minor.
• skill in using a wide range of conventions in a sufficiently long and complex piece.	• correct grammar and usage that contribute to clarity and style.	• occasional lapses in correct grammar and usage; problems are not severe enough to distort meaning or confuse the reader.
• little or no need for editing.	• skill in using a wide range of conventions in a sufficiently long and complex piece.	• moderate need for editing.
	• little need for editing	

cont.

Figure 5.9 (cont.)

3	2	1
The writing demonstrates limited control of standard writing conventions (e.g., punctuation, spelling, capitalization, paragraph breaks, grammar and usage). Errors begin to impede readability. The writing is characterized by	**The writing demonstrates little control of standard writing conventions. Frequent, significant errors impede readability. The writing is characterized by**	**Numerous errors in usage, spelling, capitalization, and punctuation repeatedly distract the reader and make the text difficult to read. In fact, the severity and frequency of errors are so overwhelming that the reader finds it difficult to focus on the message and must reread for meaning. The writing is characterized by**
• some control over basic conventions; the text may be too simple to reveal mastery.	• little control over basic conventions.	• very limited skill in using conventions.
• end-of sentence punctuation that is usually correct; however, internal punctuation contains frequent errors.	• many end-of-sentence punctuation errors; internal punctuation contains frequent errors.	• basic punctuation (including end-of-sentence punctuation) that tends to be omitted, haphazard, or incorrect.
• spelling errors that distract the reader; misspelling of common words occurs.	• spelling errors that frequently distract the reader; misspelling of common words often occurs.	• frequent spelling errors that significantly impair readability.
• paragraphs that sometimes run together or begin at ineffective places.	• paragraphs that often run together or begin in ineffective places.	• paragraph breaks that may be highly irregular or so frequent (every sentence) that they bear no relation to the organization of the text.
• capitalization errors.	• capitalization that is inconsistent or often incorrect.	• capitalization that appears to be random.
• errors in grammar and usage that do not block meaning but do distract the reader.	• errors in grammar and usage that interfere with readability and meaning.	• a need for extensive editing.
• significant need for editing.	• substantial need for editing.	

Reprinted by permission of the Oregon Department of Education. World Wide Web: (http://www.ode.state.or.us).

The assessment system required the District to determine mastery scores and to report percentages of students achieving mastery to the state. In Chinle, a three or higher on the four point reading rubric indicated mastery. On the writing rubric a four or higher on the five point scales indicated mastery.

The decision to assess writing with a single sample is somewhat ironic in the context of a portfolio approach to assessment. One of the advantages of portfolio assessment is that multiple pieces of evidence can be evaluated. Because they contain multiple pieces of evidence, they can be used to gather information about students' accomplishments across a range of different writing experiences. They can also be used to gather information about students' development over time, about the processes students use, and about what they think and value. Clearly, as far as writing is concerned, the Chinle district is not yet taking full advantage of the potential of portfolios. It should also be noted, however, that there is no real need to do so for accountability purposes. The analytic rubrics adopted by the state for assessing writing are not designed to assess how well students succeed in crafting writing for different purposes and audiences; they can be applied to any type, a single sample at a time. In this respect they are not congruent with the emphasis in the state standards on writing for "a variety of purposes and with a variety of audiences." Other sorts of scoring procedures provide more useful information about a student's ability to demonstrate range and versatility in writing (Murphy, 1999).

What was the role of evaluation in the system?

As the previous discussion indicates, the portfolio scores were used primarily for accountability purposes. Plans for public reporting at the state level included the District scores for reading, writing, and math, the Stanford 9 score, and eventually the AIMS score once the new test was in place. However, the portfolio also "counted" in the teacher's grade book. Individual pieces of evidence in the portfolios also showed up in the teacher's grade book, and some teachers treated the portfolio as an assignment, worthy of a grade in and of itself. A student's grades, however, were not dependent on the portfolio scores.

How did the system ensure validity and fairness?

At the local level, well-established procedures were adopted to ensure reliability and fairness in scoring. District samples for writing were selected and scores for the samples were annotated. Scoring anchors and training sets were developed. Portfolio materials were scored twice. One-point discrepancies were not reconciled; the scores were simply added together. However, if there was a two-point discrepancy or a question between mastery and non-mastery, the discrepant scores were reconciled by a third reader. In 1999, the department chair and co-chair at each site were trained for scoring. At the state level, plans were made to monitor any large discrepancies between local scores and state scores.

On another dimension, validity and fairness were promoted by the inclusion of culturally appropriate material in both the curriculum and the portfolio assessment. In this way, the assessment was aligned with both the community and the classroom.

Issues of Impact

Impact on Learning and Teaching

There is no doubt that the Arizona Student Assessment Program had an impact on the Chinle district portfolio program, and in turn on the curriculum itself, through its emphasis on performance tasks. As we explained earlier in this discussion, the Chinle portfolio was, itself, originally a collection of performance tasks, some of which were developed at the state level and adapted, or designed anew to incorporate Navajo experiences and perspectives. But all tasks also had to contain appropriate evidence for the District's report to the State. Further, under the old system the Chinle portfolio was scored with both the statewide generic rubrics and the Districts' culturally responsive rubric. In other words, tasks were designed to provide evidence that the skills reflected in both rubrics had been met.

Knowing the power of assessment to drive curriculum, Lauren and Daniel Resnick (1992) have proposed three principles for use as guidelines for accountability assessments:

1. *You get what you assess.* Educators will teach to tests if the tests matter in their own or their students' lives. . . .
2. *You do not get what you do not assess.* What does not appear on tests tends to disappear from classrooms in time. . . .
3. *Build assessments toward which you want educators to teach.* Assessments must be designed so that when teachers do the natural thing—that is, prepare their students to perform well—they will exercise the kinds of abilities and de-

velop the kinds of skills and knowledge that are the real goals of educational reform. . . . (Resnick & Resnick, 1992, p. 59).

In the case of Chinle it seems that the first of the Resnicks' principles was true: "You get what you assess." What remains to be seen in the Chinle story is whether the second of the Resnicks' principles will also prove true. In time, as the Resnicks point out, material that does not appear on tests tends to disappear from classrooms. That is, another obstacle to assessment reform is the tendency of high-stakes tests to restrict curricular attention to the objectives and content that is tested (Cohen 1987; Darling-Hammond & Wise 1985; Kellaghan, Madaus, & Airasian 1980; Romberg, Zarinnia, & Williams 1989; Smith 1991).

Earlier in the discussion we explained that the old Arizona Student Assessment Program was a task-based system. Arizona's new AIMS system shifts the emphasis from performance tasks scored with generic rubrics to literacy strategies. If the Resnicks' second principle holds true—*You do not get what you do not assess*—one would expect less attention in the curriculum to particular kinds of performance tasks.

A shift of this kind could be seen as a step in the right direction since a preoccupation with particular kinds of tasks can discourage teachers from spiraling the curriculum to help learners build on their previous understandings and experiences. However, a lessening of attention to cultural concerns would be regrettable.

The overview statement describing the new state standards and means for assessing them published by the Arizona Department of Education (1999) makes the concern for the needs of particular populations of students explicit:

> Assessment tasks should reflect those experiences encountered in the home, community, and workplace. Issues concerning assessment of specific populations pose complex questions with no simple solutions. As programs and assessments are developed, these issues must be resolved to enable all students to meet the standards.

Yet at the time of publication, Chinle portfolios were no longer formally scored with the culturally based rubric. As Resnick and Resnick (1992) remind us, "when the stakes are high—when schools' ratings and budgets or teachers' salaries depend on test scores—efforts to improve performance on a particular assessment instrument seem to drive out most other educational concerns" (p. 58).

There is some evidence from Arizona's own schools to justify concern about the potential for the AIMS assessment to "drive out" other educational concerns—in this case, culturally responsive curriculum and assessment. Noble and Smith (1994b) report that in the days before "testing reform," a survey of Arizona schools conducted by researchers at Arizona State University showed that nearly one-third of the elementary school teachers began preparing their students as early as two months before the test schedule (Nolen, Haladyna, & Haas, 1989, cited in Noble & Smith, 1994b). Another study showed that many districts aligned their entire curriculum to the standardized tests and spent an inordinate amount of time preparing for them (Haas, Haladyna, & Nolan, 1989, cited in Noble and Smith, 1994b). There is ample evidence in Arizona and elsewhere that "educators will teach to tests if the tests matter in their own or their students' lives. . . ." (Resnick & Resnick, 1992, p. 59).

The picture is not totally grim, however. Arizona has a strong culture of local independence and site-based control is currently mandated in state statute. Moreover, although statewide competency assessments are made widely public, assessment in Arizona is not tied to rewards for teachers or monies for schools, so the assessment system may have less impact than it would if the stakes were higher (although one could argue that the most common way to place high stakes on tests results is to simply publish them). More recently, the state delayed a requirement that students pass the tenth grade test to graduate until the Class of 2002 after teachers and parents complained that they were not informed about the standards. The state's trend toward local control may also explain why several bills pushing tougher accountability for low-performing districts died in the legislature (Education Week, 1999).

Further, in recent years the Chinle District has been able to hire more Navajo teachers than in the past (Koelsch, personal communication). As Nanette Koelsch explained, "A balanced proportion is what you want, because the Navajo students need to learn Anglo ways. But Navajo teachers can help Anglo teachers understand the Navajo culture" (Koelsch, personal communication). With more Navajo teachers in the District, there may be more attention in the curriculum to cultural concerns. Culturally based standards and curriculum may survive in Chinle, in spite of the fact that they are not formally assessed. As we said earlier, the jury is still out.

Problems and Potential Solutions

The story of the Chinle District's attempt to develop a district portfolio system that would link culturally responsive curriculum with state level accountability requirements reveals several problems and tensions that other assessment systems may share. We will outline them here: 1) an instability of policy at the state level, 2) a tension between the demands of accountability and the issues of ownership and reflection, and 3) a failure to take full advantage of the potential of portfolios in the assessment of writing. In the discussion that follows, we will address each of these issues in turn.

The effort to design, develop, and implement an innovative new system demands time and resources. Yet as reform instruments, assessment mandates typically specify targets or ends, but ignore means (Noble & Smith, 1994a). This has been true in Arizona in the past. For example, Audrey Noble and Mary Lee Smith's study of the impact of ASAP in four elementary schools indicated that some districts lacked resources for staff development to prepare teachers to teach what at that time was the "new" curriculum and that the State paid little attention to this need. A member of the State Department of Education, quoted in Shafer (1994) acknowledged the problem:

> Staff development is kind of a missing piece of ASAP. We know that. It's never been funded, it's never been even put in the new ASAP legislation that came out. . . . the legislature focused on the student, not the teacher (p. 14)

The ASAP story of short time frame and minimal budget appears to have repeated itself during the phasing in of the new AIMS system. Although the switch to the standards-based assessment was certainly an improvement over the commercial, norm-referenced tests used in the interim, all these changes no-doubt required a significant amount of "retooling" at the district level. The new state standards began to drive the development of tasks for the portfolio; in addition, time and effort that might have been devoted to the portfolio project were directed to meeting the requirements of the new mandates (Nanette Koelsch, personal communication). The

District Assessment Plan had to be revised, and teachers had to be introduced to the new rubrics that were tied to the new state standards.

A point we want to emphasize here is that portfolio projects need a stable policy environment and time to become established and to evolve. A stable policy environment around assessment in Arizona did not exist. As one assessment program director in another district said about the state's policies, "Certainly it's important to assess. . . . But we don't want to be dependent on the state, because they do keep changing things" (Henry, 1994).

In Chinle, staff development resources that could have been used to help teachers find new ways to integrate the portfolios in instruction and to pay more attention to the role of reflective analysis in teaching and learning were diverted to meet the demands of the new state system. Thus, the second problem we identified above—the tension between the demands of accountability and attention to the issues of ownership and reflection—is likely to be related to the first—the absence of a stable policy environment.

The lack of attention to reflective analysis might be partly ameliorated by a change in the portfolio design. That is, particular reflective entries written by the students might be required. Many portfolio projects make reflection part of the portfolio requirements in one form or another. In this way, they use portfolios to engage students in reflection, making assessment a learning experience.

This would, however, address the issue at only a surface level. For reflection to have any meaning, it needs to be interwoven throughout the curriculum. When it is integrated with instruction, reflection fosters self-regulated learning. Students exercise self-regulation when they actively participate in their own learning. To actively participate, they need to have opportunities to work on self-selected goals, to learn how to plan, allocate resources, seek help, to learn how to evaluate and to revise their own work (Paris & Ayres, 1995). In short, they need to have both ownership of and responsibility for their work. When we give students opportunities to reflect on their own work and writing processes, they learn to exercise judgment about their own work, monitor their own processes and progress, set goals for themselves, and present themselves and their work to others (Camp, 1992; Murphy and Smith, 1991; Paris & Ayres, 1995; Rief, 1990; Wolf, 1989; Yancey, 1992).

New forms of assessment such as portfolios have great potential for redirecting instruction toward self-assessment, an essential component of learning, but attempts will fail without adequate support and staff development. Teachers need time to try out new strategies, observe what works and what doesn't, and then talk with their colleagues about their discoveries. And, they need ongoing support. As Lorrie Shepard (1995) reminds us, "If teachers are being asked to make fundamental changes in what they teach and how they teach it, then they need sustained support to try out new practices, learn the new theory, and make it their own" (p. 44).

The Chinle Project has yet to take full advantage of the instructional potential of portfolios as a means to help students develop personal criteria for assessing their work and for setting personal goals. But the project faces a special challenge in this regard, if reflection is to become an effective tool for learning. As explained earlier, the kind of metalanguage valued in dominant, middle-class culture is not necessarily valued in Navajo culture. If reflection were to become an appropriate learning strategy for Navajo children in school, members of the Navajo community would need to play active roles in developing appropriate instructional strategies to support it.

The Chinle Project appears to be moving in other ways toward taking advantage of the potential of portfolios. A particularly promising direction is their addition of a second genre of writing to the portfolios in the sixth grade, because it expands the range of writing represented in the portfolio.

In recent decades, research and practice in writing have led to a view of writing as a meaning-making activity requiring the orchestration of diverse skills and strategies in the completion of tasks that vary with purpose, audience, and context (Camp, 1993; Hairston, 1982; Langer & Applebee, 1987; Odell, 1981). Although it is clear that assessing actual writing is preferable to multiple-choice tests, scholars have expressed concern about the limitations of single-sample testing. Critics argue that a single sample cannot adequately represent the variety of discourse modes, purposes, and audiences which writing entails (Emig, 1982; Lucas, 1988a, 1988b). In fact, the concern about single sample testing has been so widespread in the professions that in November 1992, the National Council of Teachers of English (NCTE) passed a Sense of the House Motion (No. 3) expressing opposition to the practice: "Be it resolved that the Council oppose the practice of claiming to measure a student's overall ability at writing by means of a single score on a single piece of writing produced at one sitting, and be it further resolved that the Council work to eliminate this practice."

Because portfolios are collections, we can look at several papers written by the same student, collected over time and in a variety of situations. We can ask students to show us that they can write for different audiences, both public and private, and for varied purposes. We can see how a student performs in different circumstances and in response to different tasks, observing in the process the highs and lows of the student's performances and the scope of the student's work and expertise. For teaching, this kind of information is useful, because it helps us know how to guide students to next steps in their growth as writers. We can learn, for example, which writing strategies or genres a student has under control, and which call for more work and more instructional support. For assessment, this kind of information is valuable because it gives us a fuller, more accurate picture of the student than a single sample ever could.

Opportunities for Discussion and Inquiry

1. The Chinle portfolio project is testing the possibility that assessment systems can be designed to assess student work against statewide standards and performance objectives and to reflect community context and values at the same time. In short, the system was designed to promote equity. What features of portfolios make them a potentially valid, equitable, and valuable form of assessment for students from non-dominant linguistic and cultural groups? Is it possible for assessments to represent both the non-dominant and the dominant culture? What kind of assessment system would make this possible? What attitudes and current structures of schooling would get in the way?

2. In Chinle, the bicultural assessment was built from the ground up. That is, "A second cultural viewpoint was not 'infused' after the fact (Koelsch & Trumbull, 1996, p. 282). What are the advantages and disadvantages of using prepackaged assessments? Why might it be important to involve the local community in curriculum and assessment development?

3. Ensuring fairness for students from non-dominant linguistic and cultural groups

is a complex issue. Among the many criteria that have been suggested by various groups working on the problem are the following:

a. Assessment tasks should reflect the diversity of cultures and experiences of students to be assessed.

b. Assessment tasks should allow for different modes of presentation to reflect different learning styles and different cultures.

c. Assessments should be given in students' primary language when it is the student's language of communication.

d. Students should be given a choice of the language in which they will complete an assessment task except when the purpose is to assess the language ability of the student. (Farr & Trumbull, 1997, p. 221)

What concerns might educators have about each of these criteria? How might those concerns be addressed?

4. The teachers at Chinle were involved in developing tasks for the old ASAP system, in the review of portfolios, and in scoring. What other roles might teachers play in the development and implementation of effective assessment systems? How might their participation enhance the effectiveness of the assessment?

5. The Chinle project evolved at the local level in a context where policy-makers encouraged local communities to develop their own ways to monitor teaching and learning. In this climate a system responsive to both local and statewide concerns was designed. Shortly thereafter, however, policy-makers changed their minds. What kinds of long-term consequences for schools, teachers, and students result from these abrupt policy shifts?

6. Most of the portfolio assessment systems profiled in this book were designed to monitor and support student accomplishment in the performance of academic tasks valued by the dominant mainstream culture. In many states and local communities around the country, however, teachers, parents, and political leaders have been struggling to find ways to honor non-dominant, minority cultural patterns among their children while still helping their children become part of the mainstream. Sometimes there have been clashes between non-dominant and dominant ways of knowing and doing things in classrooms, clashes that some observers believe usually spell subjugation of the non-dominant culture. What are some ways in which portfolio assessment strategies might be useful to support growth in accomplishment of academic performances valued by the mainstream culture while simultaneously honoring non-dominant cultural ways?

Acknowledgments

We would like to express our appreciation to Beth Witt, a teacher in the Chinle district, and to Jan Reed, a principal in the district, for giving generously of their time to review an earlier version of this manuscript. Their suggestions were very helpful. We would also like to express special appreciation to Nanette Koelsch, who generously shared information about the project with us. Koelsch is conducting her doctoral research in the Chinle Public Schools, focusing in particular on the development and implementation of portfolios within a bicultural context. Her help was invaluable. We also would like to thank Elise Trumbull for her insights about the assessment of non-dominant students and the many resources she shared with us.

References

Anderson, R. C., & P. D. Pearson. (1984). A schema-theoretic view of basic processes in reading comprehension. In P. D. Pearson (Ed.), *Handbook of reading research*, New York: Longman.

Arizona Department of Education (1997). Arizona School Report Card. World Wide Web: (http://www.ade.state.az.us).

Arizona Department of Education (1999). Language arts standards: A vision for Arizona's students. World Wide Web: (http://www.ade.state.az.us).

Au, K. (1980). *Theory and method in establishing the cultural congruence of classroom speech events*, Asian Pacific American Education Occasional Papers. (Gov. Doc. # ED1: 310/2:204465). Washingtion, DC: National Association for Asian and Pacific American Education.

Au, K., & Kawakami, A. (1994). Cultural congruence in instruction. In E. Hollins, J. King, & W. Hayman (Eds.), *Teaching diverse populations: Formulating a knowledge base*. Albany: State University of New York Press.

Boggs, S. (1972). The meaning of questions and narratives to Hawaiian children. In C. Cazden, D. Hymes, & V. P. John (Eds.), *Functions of language in the classroom*, (pp. 299–327). New York: Teachers College Press.

Bransford, J. D., & Johnson, M. K. (1972). Contextual prerequisites for understanding. Some investigations of comprehension and recall. *Journal of Verbal Learning and Verbal Behavior, 11*, 717–726.

Camp, R. (1992). Portfolio reflections in middle and secondary school classrooms. In K. B. Yancey (Ed.), *Portfolios in the writing classroom* (pp. 61-79). Urbana, IL: National Council of Teachers of English.

Camp, R. (1993). Changing the model for the direct assessment of writing. In M. Williamson & B. Huot (Eds.). *Validating holistic scoring for writing assessment: Theoretical and empirical foundations*, (pp. 45–79). Cresskill, NJ: Hampton Press, Inc.

Cohen, S. A. (1987). Instructional alignment: Searching for a magic bullet. *Educational Researcher, 16* (8), 16–20.

Cole, M., & Scribner, S. (1974). *Culture and thought*. New York: Wiley.

Cook-Gumperz, J., & Gumperz, J. (Eds.). (1986). *The social construction of literacy* Cambridge, United Kingdom: Cambridge University Press.

Darling-Hammond, L. (1996). The right to learn and the advancement of teaching: Research, policy, and practice for democratic education. *Educational Researcher, 25* (6): 5–18.

Darling-Hammond, L., & Wise, A. E. (1985). Beyond standardization: State standards and school improvement. *The elementary school journal, 85*, 315–336.

Delpit, L. D. (1988). The silenced dialogue: Power and pedagogy in educating other people's children. *Harvard Educational Review, 58* (3), 280–298.

Deyhle, D. (1987). Learning failure: Tests as gatekeepers and the culturally different child. In H. Trueba (Ed.), *Success or failure* (pp. 85–106). Rowley, MA: Newbury House.

Dumont, R. V. Jr. (1972). Learning English and how to be silent: Studies in Sioux and Cherokee classrooms. In C. B. Cazden, D. Hymes, & V. P. John (Eds.), *Functions of language in the classroom*. New York: Teachers College Press.

Education Week on the Web (1999). *Quality counts. 18* (17), 128. (http://www.edweek.org) Author.

Emig, J. (1982). Inquiry paradigms and writing. *College Composition and Communication, 33* (1), 64-75.

Estrin, E. (1993). Alternative assessment: Issues in language, culture, and equity. *Knowledge Brief,* (No. 11). San Francisco: Far West Laboratory.

Estrin, E. & Nelson-Barber, S. (1995). Issues in cross-cultural assessment: American Indian and Alaska native students. *Knowledge Brief,* (No. 12). San Francisco: Far West Laboratory.

Far West Laboratory (n.d.). *Effective assessments: Making use of local context.* An alternative assessment videotape from the Rural School Assistance Program. San Francisco: Far West Laboratory.

Farr, B. P., & Trumbull, E. (1997). *Assessment alternatives for diverse classrooms.* Norwood, MA: Christopher-Gordon Publishers, Inc.

Garcia, G. (1988). *Factors influencing the English reading test performance of Spanish-English bilingual children.* Unpublished doctoral dissertation. University of Illinois at Champaign-Urbana.

Hairston, M. (1982). The winds of change: Thomas Kuhn and the revolution in the teaching of writing. *College Composition and Communication, 33,* 76–88.

Haas, N. S., Haladyna, T. M., & Nolen, S. B. (1989). *Standardized testing in Arizona: Interviews and written comments from teachers and administrators.* (Technical Report No. 89-3). Phoenix: Arizona State University, West Campus.

Heath, S. B. (1983). *Ways with words: Language, life, and work in communities and classrooms.* London: Cambridge University Press.

Henry, B. (1994). Schools fill state's test vacuum in their own ways. *The Arizona Daily Star.*

Hilgers, T. (1992). Improving placement exam equitability, validity, and reliability. Paper presented at the Conference on College Composition and Communication, March. Cincinnati, OH.

John, V. P. (1972). Styles of learning—styles of teaching: Reflections on the education of Navajo children. In C. Cazden, D. Hymes, & V. P. John (Eds.). *Functions of language in the classroom.* New York: Teachers College Press.

Kellaghan, T., Madaus, G. F., & Airasian, P. W. (1980). *The effects of standardized testing.* Dublin/Boston: St. Patrick's College/Boston College.

Koelsch, N., & Trumbull, E. (1996). Portfolios: Bridging cultural and linguistic worlds. In R. C. Calfee & P. Perfumo (Eds.), *Writing portfolios in the classroom: Policy and practice, promise and peril,* (261–284). Mahwah, NJ: Lawrence Erlbaum Associates, Publishers.

Langer, J. A., & Applebee, A. N. (1987). *How writing shapes thinking.* Urbana, IL: National Council of Teachers of English.

Longstreet, E. (1978). *Aspects of ethnicity.* New York: Teachers College Press.

Lucas, C. (1988a). Toward ecological evaluation: Part I. *The Quarterly of the National Writing Project and the Center for the Study of Writing, 10* (1), 1–17.

Lucas, C. (1988b). Toward ecological evaluation: Part II. *The Quarterly of the National Writing Project and the Center for the Study of Writing, 10* (2), 4–10.

Mestre, J. (1984). The problem with problems: Hispanic students and math. *Bilingual Journal, 32,* 15–19.

Michaels, S. (1982). *Sharing time: Children's narrative styles and differential access to literacy.* Unpublished doctoral dissertation. Berkeley, CA: University of California, Berkeley.

Murphy, S. (1999). Assessing portfolios. In C. Cooper & L. Odell (Eds.), *Evaluating writing*, (2nd ed.). (pp. 114–135). Urbana, IL: National Council of Teachers of English.

Murphy, S., & Smith, M. (1991). *Writing portfolios: A bridge from teaching to assessment*. Ontario, Canada: Pippin Publishing Ltd.

Noble, A. J. & Smith, M.L. (1994a). *Old and new beliefs about measurement-driven reform: Build it and they will come*. Unpublished paper. College of Education. Arizona State University, Tempe, AZ.

Noble, A. J., & Smith, M. L. (1994b). *Old and new beliefs about measurement-driven reform: "The more things change, the more they stay the same."* (Technical Report No. 373.) National Center for Research on Evaluation, Standards, and Student testing (CRESST). Los Angeles: University of California, Los Angeles.

Nolen, S. B., Haldyna, T. M., & Haas, N. S. (1989). *A survey of Arizona teachers and school administrators on the uses and effects of standardized achievement testing* (Technical Report No. 89-2). Phoenix: Arizona State University, West Campus.

Oakes, J. (1985). *Keeping track: How schools structure inequality*. New Haven, CN: Yale University Press.

Odell, L. (1981). Defining and assessing competence in writing. In C. Cooper (Ed.), *The nature and measurement of competency in English* (pp. 95–103). Urbana, IL: National Council of Teachers of English.

Ogbu, J. (1978). *Minority education and caste: The American system in cross-cultural perspective*. New York: Academic Press.

Ogbu, J. (1992) Understanding cultural diversity and learning. *Educational Researcher, 21* (8), 5–14.

Olsen, L. (1995, March). The new breed of assessments getting scrutiny. *Education Week on the Web*: (http://www.edweek.org).

Oregon State Department of Education. 1999-2000 Scoring Guides. [http//www.ODE.k12.OR.US]

Paris, S. & Ayres, L. (1995). *Becoming reflective students and teachers with portfolios and authentic assessment*. Washington, DC: American Psychological Association.

Philips, S. U. (1972). Participant structure and communicative competence: Warm Springs children in community and classroom. In C. B. Cazden, D. Hymes, & V. P. John (Eds.), *Functions of language in the classroom*. New York: Teachers College Press.

Philips, S. U. (1983). *The invisible culture: Communication in classroom and community on the Warm Springs Indian Reservation*. New York: Longman.

Pichert, J. W., & Anderson, R. C. (1977). Taking different perspectives on a story. *Journal of Educational Psychology, 69*, 309–315.

Rief, L. (1990). Finding the value in evaluation: Self-assessment in a middle school classroom. *Educational Leadership, 24–29*.

Resnick, L., & Resnick, D. (1992). Assessing the thinking curriculum: New tools for educational reform. In B. Gifford & M. C. O'Connor (Eds.), *Changing assessments: Alternative views of aptitude, achievement and instruction*. Boston: Kluwer Academic Publishers.

Rhodes, R. W. (1988, November). *Standardized testing of minority students: Navajo and Hopi examples*. Paper presented at the Annual Meeting of the National Council of Teachers of English, St. Louis, MO.

Rincon, E. T. (1979). Test speediness, test anxiety, and test performance: A comparison of Mexican American and Anglo American high school juniors. (Doctoral Dissertation, University of Texas at Austin). *Dissertation Abstracts International, 40*, 5772A.

Romberg, T. A., Zarinnia, E.A., & Williams, S. (1989). *The influence of mandated testing on mathematics instruction: Grade 8 teachers' perceptions*. National Center for Research in Mathematical Science Education, University of Wisconsin-Madison.

Shafer, R. (1994, November). State standards and performance assessment in the English language arts. Paper presented at the annual conference of the National Council of Teachers of English, Orlando, Florida.

Schnaiberg, L. (1999). Arizona: The heart of the matter. Editorial Projects in Education. *Education Week on the Web, 18*, (17), 128: (http://www.edweek.org).

Shepard, L. (1989, April). Why we need better assessments. *Educational Leadership*, 4-9.

Shepard, L. (1995). Using assessment to improve learning. *Educational Leadership*, 54 (5), 38–43.

Shepard, L., & Bleim, C. (1995, May). Parents' thinking about standardized tests and performance assessments. *Educational Researcher*, 25–32.

Smith, M. L. (1991, June-July). Put to the test: The effects of external testing on teachers. *Educational Researcher*, 8–11.

Smith, M. L., Noble, A. J., Cabay, M., Heinecke, W., Junker, M. S., & Saffron, Y. (1994). *What happens when the test mandate changes? Results of a multiple case study*. (Technical Report No. 380.) Los Angeles: National Center for Research on Evaluation, Standards and Student Testing (CRESST), University of California, Los Angeles.

Taylor, D. and Dorsey-Gaines, C. (1988). *Growing up literate: Learning from inner-city families*. Portsmouth, NH: Heinemann.

Tierney, R. (April 22, 1974). Coming to grips with alternative assessment. Presentation at the Elementary Education Association Conference, San Francisco, CA.

Trumbull, E., & Nelson-Barber, S. (1995). Issues in cross-cultural assessment: American Indian and Alaska Native students. *Knowledge Brief*, (No. 12), San Francisco: Far West Laboratory.

Villegas, A. M. (1991, September). *Culturally responsive pedagogy for the 1990's and beyond*. Princeton, NJ: Educational Testing Service.

Werner, O., & Begishe, K. (1968). Styles of learning: The evidence from Navajo. Paper presented for conference on styles of learning in American Indian children, Stanford University, Stanford, California (cited in Deyle, 1987).

Wolf, D. P. (1989). Portfolio assessment: Sampling student work. *Educational Leadership, 46*, 35–39.

Yancey, K. B. (Ed.). (1992). *Portfolios in the writing classroom*. Urbana, IL: National Council of Teachers of English.

6

Regional School District No. 15: Scaffolding Self-Regulated Learning

In some cases, portfolios are little more than folders for students' work, mandated by policymakers in an attempt to reform curriculum, and tacked on by teachers at the end of the year, like an appendix at the end of a book. Teachers and students dutifully collect work, save it, but then do little with it. That is to say, in the worst of cases, the portfolios are not integrated in instruction, but isolated from it; nor do they provide information that might be used to measure or improve teaching and learning.

Not so in Connecticut's Pomperaug Regional School District 15. There, portfolios were introduced as the next logical step in a sustained and philosophically coherent process of curricular improvement. In a school culture that was already deeply immersed in performance based learning and assessment, they served administrators, parents, teachers, and students as a window on student growth over time and as a catalyst for students to take responsibility for their work.

In Region 15, the curriculum improvement process was based on the assumption that teachers can be trusted to make sound decisions about curriculum and teaching. Moreover, the approach to management was anything but bureaucratic. In a bureaucratic approach schools are viewed as:

> agents of government to be administered by hierarchical decision-making. Policies are made at the top of the system and handed down to administrators who translate them into rules and procedures. Teachers follow these rules and procedures (class schedules, curriculum guides, textbooks, rules for promotion, and assignment of students, etc.) . . . (Darling-Hammond & Snyder, 1992, p. 16)

Instead, reform in Region 15 was the collaborative work of teachers, site level administrators, and superintendents.

Instead of a "mandate for Monday," the curriculum improvement process leading to the introduction of portfolios extended over 15 years. In contrast to other portfolio projects profiled in this book that came at teachers out of the blue, portfolios were introduced in Region 15 after several years of work with process writing instruction and several more with performance-based learning and assessment strategies.

John Voss, who conducted a study of the change process surrounding the implementation of writing portfolios in the district, wrote that the origin for change was rooted in the movement toward process approaches to the teaching of writing that occurred in the late 1970s and early 1980s (Voss, 1997). In an interview conducted by Voss, teacher Gary Waugh (Grade 10) described the evolution that led to portfolios like this:

The writing portfolio began in earnest with the start of the conferences about ten years ago when we had sessions with students that were evaluative and to begin some form of assessment. . . . They were rubrics or oral standards between you and the student. This was the genesis of the writing portfolio, because you need this kind of interaction, need this kind of evaluation, you need the ownership on the part of the student and the teacher. The fact that we had four classes and that we were able to spend a big piece of our day doing this [helped]. I can remember during certain weeks having 25–30 writing conferences. We documented them at that time. Kids took ownership for their own writing. I took ownership for what had to be done to enhance the writing. From there, it only made sense to look at a long-term evaluative assessment on the part of the teacher and student. What kind of writing worked? What kind of strategies worked? What kinds of conferences worked and transferred into the growth of the kid. . . . The writing portfolio evolved through this process. It began with writing folders and then moved from the folders to the writing portfolio. It started about 1990 for us. My first set of formal portfolios in my teaching was in 1991. (Quoted in Voss, 1997, p. 109 and reprinted here with permission.)

A timeline of steps in the change process covering the period from 1980 to 1995 is outlined in Figure 6.1.

In the years after teachers like Gary acted as "scouts" for portfolio development, the Region 15 educators refined their performance-based learning and portfolio practice, moving steadily toward a portfolio system that supports student responsibility in learning. After several years of widespread and consistent use of portfolios throughout the Region, the district decided to allow individual schools to experiment with their own portfolio designs as long as they encompassed essential elements of portfolio practice set by consensus in 1997:

1. Writing is a foundation for thinking and learning.
2. The portfolio responds to some goal involving writing.
3. This writing is done as part of performance tasks embedded in curricula.
4. Students do analytical self-assessment of their writing. Work habits may also be assessed in this way.
5. Enough samples of student writing and assessment are included to respond to the goal.
6. The student writes some form of self-reflection in which the goal is evaluated.
7. The student's opinions are supported by specific reference to the writing and assessment included in the portfolio.
8. The student sets meaningful goals to improve.
9. The teacher responds to the student's self-reflection and goals in a way that gives the student clear and specific feedback and encouragement. (Pomperaug Regional School District No. 15, 1997. Reprinted with permission by Pomperaug Regional District 15.)

Figure 6.1
Timeline of Region 15 Initiatives—Portfolio Implementation

1994-95 **Full Implementation (Settlers)**

All students in grades 1 through 12 were engaged in creating a portfolio of their writing. In-Service Courses were offered at each school (Beginner and Advanced) to assist teachers with the process. During the summer of 1995, the three manuals were revised.

1993-94 **Expanded Pilot (Pioneers)**

In-Service Course was taught at each school as a "critical mass" of teachers became involved in performance-based assessment and the creation of portfolios. The Region Portfolio Team wrote manuals on the portfolio process at the elementary, middle and high school levels. some models of portfolios were selected to be used as models for each grade level.

1992-93 **Pre-Pilot (Scouts)**

Performance-based learning using assessment lists became more common. Professional development at the school level focused on using performance tasks and assessment lists. The Portfolio Leadership Team planned the model that the Region would use. Other teachers joined in the experimentation.

1991-92 **Research and Experimentation (Scouts)**

The Assistant Superintendent formed the Portfolio Leadership team, composed of volunteer teachers from each school, the English Department Chairperson from the high school, a middle school and an elementary school principal, to learn more about portfolios and formulate a list of criteria for a successful portfolio plan and coordinate analysis and use of data from the Connecticut Mastery Test. Experimentation with portfolios by individual teachers began.

1990-91 **Research and Experimentation (Early Scouts)**

Performance tasks using various forms of writing were beginning to be used across the grade levels and disciplines. Teachers were learning how to use assessment lists and coach students to be more honest and perceptive self-assessors. Teachers attended conferences and workshops to learn about portfolio development and use.

Pre-1990 **Ten +/- Years of Study, Inservice, and Practice in Process Writing**

From 1980 to 1985, improving writing across the curriculum through use of the writing process was a Regionwide goal. Staff members were trained; a Regionwide holistic writing sample was taken in the fall and spring of each year and scored by staff; and an analytical scoring process was developed and implemented.

From *A Teacher's Guide to Performance-Based Learning and Assessment*, K. Michael Hibbard, et al., (1996) p. 237. Alexandria, Virginia: Association for Supervision and Curriculum Development. Reprinted with permission by K. Michael Hibbard.

By 1994, a portfolio system for teachers and administrators complemented and supported the portfolio system for students, enhancing the coherence of the educational system as a whole. For their evaluation, tenured teachers in Region 15 had the option of creating a "collaborative educator's portfolio." The collaborative portfolio linked evaluation with professional development. Working with administrators who acted as coaches, teachers engaged in teacher research projects, reflected on their past work, and set new goals. In other words, in Region 15 there was a portfolio culture for everyone, not just students, and not just teachers.

Exemplar System

Self-regulated learning means that learners are "aware of *what* strategies are available to help them; they understand *how* the strategies operate; they understand *when* they should be applied; and they understand *why* they are necessary" (Paris & Ayres, 1995, p. 30). For example, a self-regulated student writer might decide to develop dialogue in a narrative in order to deepen her reader's sense of immediacy at a crucial turning point in the story—and then actually go forward with the work, using human resources in her writing community to support and sustain improvements in the piece. Self-regulated learners analyze their work processes and products, reflect on their concrete experiences as readers and writers, and set goals for themselves as legitimate participants in their literate culture.

How does this get translated into curriculum?

Scott Paris and Linda Ayres (1995) remind us that when learners "are provided choice, challenge, control, and collaboration in their classrooms, they are motivated intrinsically to learn" (p. 28). Paris and Winograd (1990) also identify self-appraisal and self-management as critical components of self-regulated learning. Indeed, it seems that success as an appraiser and manager of one's self might well be achieved only to the degree that we experience opportunities to do work in a context characterized by choice, challenge, control, and collaboration.

Self-regulated learners need choices, according to Paris and Ayres (1995), because "self-selected goals are governed by curiosity and intrinsic motivation to display one's competence" (p. 27). In contrast, goals announced by the teacher are governed by compliance and often require extrinsic rewards such as grades, tokens, and praise before students will exert effort. It seems clear that narrow assignments and tasks with few options built in do not promote self-regulation since, by definition, they are other-regulated. Thus, choices, while not particularly necessary for cognitive reasons, appear essential for motivational reasons.

Self-regulated learners set goals for themselves that are *challenging* yet also within reach. Aware that levels of challenge are determined in part by how much and what kind of resources are available in the learning environment, we believe that these learners examine not just their own capabilities, but opportunities for support from peers and others, as they decide on goals. Self-regulated learners "have *control* of their own learning" (Paris & Ayres, 1995, p. 28). That is, they know how to use the resources available to them, when to use them and why, and they use them intentionally. And finally, self-regulated learners *collaborate*. Collaboration, say Paris and Ayres, encourages persistence and provides strategic help when necessary.

Portfolios are one way for learners to exercise choice, establish control, meet challenges, and collaborate. Teachers can use portfolios to provide opportunities for students to exercise metacognitive aspects of learning such as monitoring performance and evaluating progress against established criteria and standards. Indeed, much of the literature on portfolios indicates that in the process of creating portfolios, learners practice exercising judgment about their own work, monitoring their own progress, setting goals for themselves, and presenting themselves and their work to others (Camp, 1992; Murphy & Smith, 1991; Rief, 1990; Tierney, Carter & Desai, 1991; Wolf, 1989; Yancey, 1992). In sum, portfolios give learners—students and teachers alike (and in the case of Region 15, administrators as well)—opportunities to assume ownership of assessment, to assess their own work, and to make learning conscious (Howard, 1990; 1993; Rief, 1990).

Context for the System.

In 1999 Region 15 was a mid-sized district that served the towns of Southbury and Middlebury in the wooded hills and valleys of New Haven County in Connecticut. The district had seven schools, including four elementary schools (Pomperaug, Gainfield, Middlebury, and Long Meadow), two middle schools (Rochambeau and Memorial), and one high school (Pomperaug). There were few minority students in the district—in 1997–1998, 130 of the 3,873 students enrolled. The district received no Title I support from the State and Federal government because less than 5 percent of the students qualified for reduced or free lunches. Average class size in 1997–98 ranged from a low of 20.6 in kindergarten to a high of 26.3 in grade 7. The professional staff was highly qualified, with an average of 13.7 years of experience and with 85.3 percent of the staff having a master's degree or above.

System Design

As explained earlier, Region 15 had a dual portfolio system, one for students and one for educators. The latter supported the former. Both were designed to improve student performance. In the case of the student portfolio, that meant using the portfolio to help students learn. In the case of the Educator's Collaborative Portfolio that meant finding better ways to help students learn. An important goal in Region 15 was to improve the "performance maturity" of all students so that they would be "life-long learners." District documents defined performance maturity as the degree to which an individual works independently to:

1. Produce quality work that shows deep understanding of essential concepts within and among disciplines
2. Produce quality work that shows connections between schoolwork and its application to the larger world
3. Use information location, selection, and gathering strategies in appropriate and flexible ways
4. Use problem-solving strategies in appropriate and flexible ways
5. Use productive work habits
6. Use skills of collaboration
7. Use a rich repertoire of skills to produce final products in many formats
8. Communicate to a variety of audiences for a variety of specific purposes

9. Show respect for the personal, intellectual, and property rights of others

10. Self-assess and self-evaluate accurately

11. Make and carry out goals to improve (Pomperaug Regional School District No. 15, n.d. Reprinted with permission by Pomperaug Regional District 15.)

In the sections of this chapter that follow we will describe the student portfolio first and the educator's collaborative portfolio next.

The Student Portfolio

The student portfolio in Region 15 was but one tool in the larger arsenal of performance-based learning and assessment, one of "a set of strategies for the acquisition and application of knowledge, skills, and work habits through the performance of tasks that are meaningful and engaging to students" (Hibbard, et al., 1996). Not a curriculum, performance-based learning and assessment supported curriculum by engaging the student in self-assessment and in interactions with the teacher around the qualities of criteria for good work. For example, in Region 15, teachers regularly used a combination of what they called "assessment lists" (lists of criteria for particular performances) and models of excellent work (benchmarks) to help students learn to assess their work.

Assessment lists were used throughout the performance task process: *before*, to clarify expectations; *during*, as a guide for completing the task; and *after*, as a basis for self-assessment about how well expectations had been met. Teachers gathered models from several sources, including student writing from previous years, state writing benchmarks, Region 15 benchmarks, teacher-constructed models, class-constructed models, and examples from quality literature (Anctil, et al., 1999). Woven throughout the curriculum, assessment lists and models provided the foundation for portfolio practice.

Teachers developed the tasks and assessment lists. Typical steps in their process were to:

- Define what students should know and be able to do
- Create performance tasks that are engaging to students and well connected to content knowledge, process skills, and work habits
- Make assessment lists tailored to student needs and instructional objectives
- Provide several models (benchmarks) of excellent work
- Embed performance tasks in instruction so students can use their content knowledge, process skills, and work habits
- Assess and evaluate student work and plan adaptations in curriculum, instruction, allocation of resources, testing, and assessment (Hibbard et al. 1996, p. 47. Reprinted by permission of Pomperaug Regional District 15.).

Tasks that were particularly engaging to students and that were well connected to the content knowledge, process skills, and work habits of the curriculum could be designated as "anchor" tasks, if other teachers agreed. Anchor tasks were those required by all teachers dealing with a particular curriculum; they provided common experiences for the students. Because students shared the same experience, data from anchor tasks could be used to analyze the performance of groups.

Performance tasks and assessment lists were used at all grade levels to encourage students to assess their work, even during first grade, and typically teachers created a simulated or authentic role for the student to play. For example, in the task authored by Elizabeth Wagner, an educator from Region 15 (see Figure 6. 2), the student assumed the role of an entomologist to draw the stages of the butterfly life cycle, using a graphic organizer (see Figure 6. 3). The thinking skills demonstrated by the successful student, and identified in the district's coding form for this task, were an initial understanding of the life cycle, describing and sequencing, developing an interpretation, making connections, and assuming a critical stance. The work habits measured were the child's organization, accuracy, and use of detail.

Figures 6.2
BUTTERFLY LIFE CYCLE

Background
How good is your memory? Show me the stages of how our hungry caterpillars became beautiful butterflies!

Task
Your task is to draw the four most important stages of a developing butterfly in the right order. Label each stage.

Audience
Your audience is your teacher.

Purpose
Your purpose is to show how much you remember about the four most important stages in the life cycle of a butterfly.

Procedure
1. Use the assessment list for "Butterfly Life Cycle."
2. Draw and color what you remember about each stage in the correct sequence.
3. Label each stage.
4. Complete the assessment list.

Reprinted with permission. Pomperaug Regional School District No. 15.

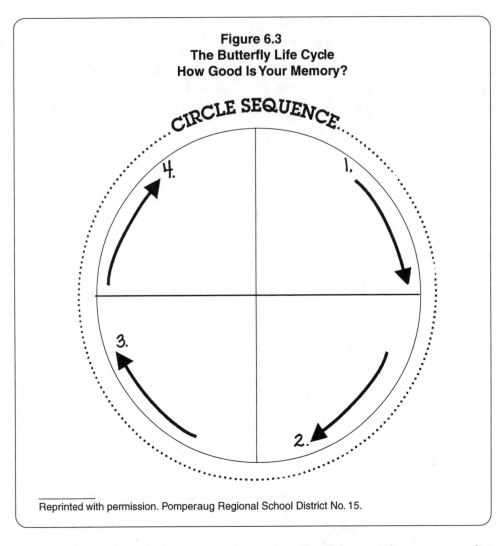

Figure 6.3
The Butterfly Life Cycle
How Good Is Your Memory?

Reprinted with permission. Pomperaug Regional School District No. 15.

Note that in the task description, the child is directed to use the assessment list (see Figure 6.4) to guide his or her work and that the list contains questions for the student to answer: Did I show the four important parts of the life cycle? Did I draw the picture in the correct sequence? Questions such as these are aimed at helping the child apply criteria to his or her work.

The goal was to have the students pause before they began working to reflect on the criteria they would use to judge the quality of their work. Initially, students used lists as in Figure 6. 4, but eventually the student was responsible for determining the criteria for quality. More sophisticated tasks, of course, were provided for students as they matured. For example, the grade 8 task authored by Debbie Patchkofsky for use with *To Kill a Mockingbird* asked students to assume the role of a poet to show how character traits define a theme (see Figure 6. 5). Some assessment lists also included space for teacher feedback on the students' self-assessment, and an indication of credit earned (see Figure 6.6).

Figure 6. 4
Performance Task Assessment List
Butterfly Life Cycle

1. Did I show the four important parts of the life cycle?

| Terrific | OK | Needs Work |

2. Did I draw the picture in the correct sequence?

| Terrific | OK | Needs Work |

3. Did I label each picture?

| Terrific | OK | Needs Work |

4. Is my work neat?

| Terrific | OK | Needs Work |

Figure 6. 5
Taking a Theme to Heart
To Kill a Mockingbird Ballad and Collage Task

Name:_____ Date:_____

Background

Literature touches the eternal: it expresses a truism, something that is true for all people, in all places, in all times. *To Kill a Mockingbird* is certainly a work of literature for Harper Lee illuminates many truths through her use of the theme. As we recently explored in our thesis papers, Lee uses theme to communicate important messages regarding attributes of human nature, such as courage, empathy and prejudice. The themes she deals with touch ALL of our lives in some form: we know a person who is courageous or a person who is a coward, someone who is empathetic or someone who is uncaring. Her themes provide a means for us to personally connect with the novel, thus making it eternal.

Task

Your task is to connect the theme you explored in your thesis essay to your life. You will write a ballad (a narrative poem with an abcb rhyme scheme) describing a person who exhibits the quality (or lack thereof) you wrote about in your theme thesis paper. If you write about courage, write about a courageous person you know—friend, family member, even yourself—or a person who did not act courageously in a time of need. In either case, you should attempt to send a message to your reader regarding this attribute just as Harper Lee did. You will also create a collage that represents both the person you are writing about and the theme you are discussing. Lastly, you will present both your ballad and your collage to this class.

Audience

Your audience is your teacher and classmates.

Purpose

Our attempt to embed a message within our own writing will help us to further appreciate the work of great writers and to hopefully recognize theme more easily in the future. In addition, a personal connection to a piece of literature makes the work more meaningful to us. It will help us to better understand the relevance of the message Lee was sending to us through her work of art.

Procedure

1. Review the attached task assessment list and clarify anything you do not understand.
2. Brainstorm possible candidates to immortalize in your poem.
3. Write a rough draft of your ballad.
4. Engage in peer conferencing exercises with two students and complete the conference sheet.
5. Revise your work considering your peer's feedback and advice.
6. Collect photographs, magazine and newspaper clippings, mementos, clip art, etc., to create your collage.
7. Write the final draft of your ballad on a sheet of poster board and surround it with your collage. Add additional color and graphics if needed to create a superior design.
8. Present your poem and collage to the class. Submit your completed assessment list.
    *   Best Non-Fiction (Expository).
    *   Best Timed Writing (45 minutes, focus on narrative writing).
    *   Favorite piece (could be poetry).
    *   Full processed piece with all materials and drafts attached (can be one of the above).
    *   Optional—two pieces selected (one from beginning & one from end) to show growth.
    *   Each piece should include an entry slip and assessment list.

Reprinted with permission. Pomperaug Regional School District No. 15.

Figure 6. 6
Taking a Theme to Heart
To Kill a Mockingbird Ballad and Collage Task

Name_____ Date_____

	Points Possible	Self	Teacher
Ballad			
1. The ballad describes how the individual displays (or does not display) the attribute of human nature discussed in your thesis essay. It is in narrative form.	30	_____	_____
2. A message is clearly sent to your reader regarding this theme.	15	_____	_____
3. Vivid language, description and detail are used.	15	_____	_____
4. The poem is 50 to 70 lines long.	15	_____	_____
5. The poem is written in quatrains with an acbc rhyme scheme.	15	_____	_____
6. Correct spelling, capitalization, punctuation and sentence structure are used.	10	_____	_____
Collage			
7. The picture and graphics complement the content of the poem. They are clearly related to either the person discussed or the theme represented.	15	_____	_____
8. The layout is attractive, colorful and pleasing to the eye.	15	_____	_____
9. The ballad is neatly written on the poster board, and the entire surface is filled with either words or illustrations.	15	_____	_____
Presentation			
10. A brief background is provided explaining the theme selected and your personal connection to it (who, what, where, when, why, how).	20	_____	_____
11. The tone is serious.	10	_____	_____
12. Appropriate body language is used. Eye contact is made with the audience.	10	_____	_____
13. Volume is appropriate and enunciation is clear.	15	_____	_____
TOTAL POINTS	**200**	_____	_____

Comments: _____

_____

_____

_____

_____

_____

Reprinted with permission. Pomperaug Regional School District No. 15.

The assessment lists addressed common elements, including expected content knowledge and standards, thinking skills, problem solving skills, communication skills, execution or craft skills, and work habits. They brought criteria out into the open for students, so they would know what the teacher expected. They also provided "scaffolding" for students while they self-assessed their work. That is, they supported students as they attempt to identify the strengths and weaknesses in their work—a goal they might not have been able to reach on their own. On the surface, the lists might seem mechanistic and predetermined, but teachers adapted the list concept to make classroom activities both generative and interactive. A variety of these strategies were described in a book authored by Region 15 educators, *Performance-Based Learning and Assessment*. For example, some teachers asked students to brainstorm criteria in small cooperative groups. When done, groups shared their lists with each other. Individual students then use the list created by their group, or the various lists were synthesized into a master list for use by the class as a whole. As explained elsewhere, benchmarks or exemplars of performance also played a role in teachers' attempts to help students develop shared understandings of criteria and standards.

The lists, and other strategies that the teachers used for bringing criteria into the open, served an important function. When the time came for formal assessment, these kinds of strategies contributed to the specialized validity criterion that Frederiksen and Collins (1989) referred to as "transparency." Samuel Messick (1994) explained the concept:

> The concern is that if the assessment itself is to be a worthwhile educational experience . . . then the problems and tasks should be meaningful to the students. That is, not only should students know what is being assessed, but the criteria and standards of what constitutes good performance should be clear to them in terms of both how the performance is to be scored and what steps might be taken or what directions moved in to improve performance . . . (p. 16)

Frederiksen and Collins (1989) contended that when clear performance standards applied in scoring are also applied by teachers in instruction and learning, then assessments may "directly reflect and support the development of the aptitudes and traits they are supposed to measure" (p. 28). In sum, the assessment list concept provided one way to address concerns about systemic validity.

It is also true that as students matured, as they honed their skills and internalized criteria, they became less dependent on teacher-made lists. When students were ready, teachers asked students to make their own lists. In other words, "Scaffolds are temporary. Students do not need them forever. They are adjustable; they can be raised, lowered, or moved depending upon one's goals" (Underwood, Murphy, & Pearson, 1995, p. 76). Eventually, students were able to assess their work on their own. In the meantime, according to educators in Region 15, assessment lists helped them "produce work that was far superior to that produced when they were playing the 'Guess what the teacher wants' game" (Hibbard, et al., 1996, p. 171).

Work generated by performance tasks, and other less formal assignments, along with evidence of self-assessment—assessment lists, reflective letters, entry slips, and the like—eventually found its way into portfolios. As the teachers in Region 15 saw it, self-assessment was the foundation of the portfolio and assessment lists were one way to provide the scaffolding:

> Portfolios help the learner see the "big picture" of their work and see themselves as learners. Performance tasks assessment lists and models (bench-

marks) of excellence are the specific tools that make self-assessment honest. The assessment lists and benchmarks also make perceptive self-reflection and goal setting possible. (Hibbard, et al., 1996, p. 191).

As Hibbard and his colleagues suggested, the portfolio was a natural extension of day-to-day self-assessment.

Purposes for the Portfolio

Teams of teachers in Region 15 created their own guidebooks for portfolio practice, one for elementary and another for secondary. The K–5 team defined a student portfolio as follows:

a purposeful collection of student work that exhibits the student's efforts, progress, and achievements in one or more areas. This progress must include student participation in selecting contents, the criteria for selection, evidence of student self-reflection, and teacher response to that self-reflection.(Anctil, et al., 1999, p. 1)

The definition provided by the secondary team was similar:

A portfolio is a purposeful collection of student performances that exhibits a student's effort, progress, and achievement over a period of time. In Region 15 middle schools, the portfolio is comprised of student-selected works, and it includes both a student's reflection on his or her performances as well as the teacher's reflection on the student's work. (Schultz, Patchofsky, & Van Wagenen, 1999, p. 1).

The teams also identified several ambitious goals for the district's student portfolio system. The K-5 team identified the purposes of the K-5 portfolio as:

to collect student work over time, to review the work and articulate or celebrate progress, to set short term learning goals for future efforts, to use student work in communicating with parents, and to allow students to assume ownership of their learning by requiring them to collect, select, and reflect upon examples of their work. (Anctil, et al., 1999, p.1).

The secondary team identified the purposes of the secondary portfolio as:

- To improve student performance
- To promote the students' skills of self-assessment and goal setting
- To build a sense of ownership and pride of accomplishment in the student
- To build the student's self-esteem and confidence in his or her abilities as a learner
- To present a clear portrait of the students as learners
- To provide a vehicle for communicating a student's progress to the student, parents, and future teachers
- To develop a structure for accomplishing the above that is manageable with a reasonable amount of work for the teacher
- To develop a structure for accomplishing the above that is valued by both the student and current teacher, as well as the teacher receiving the portfolio the next year. (Schultz, et al., 1999, p. 1. Reprinted with permission by Pomperaug Regional District 15.).

Collection

What work was worth collecting?

In order to address the wide range of developmental differences in K–5, somewhat different models for the different grade levels were recommended in the teacher's guide. In addition, it was expected that teachers would adapt the model to fit the needs of their particular classroom (Anctil, et al., 1999). The guidelines for the different elementary schools varied slightly, but they all required portfolio entries that had been taken through the steps with pre-writing materials and drafts attached, as well as timed-writing samples, student self-reflections, individual writing goals, and the teacher's response. A required element of the K-5 portfolio, the teacher's response, was written as a letter to the student. The guidelines for Pomperaug Elementary School are provided in Figure 6.7 as an example.

The guidelines illustrate how scaffolding was adjusted as students matured. Choice, for example, became less constrained as students progressed through the grades. Portfolio entries in grade 2 were "chosen collaboratively by the teacher and student." By grade 3, it was the student who made the choices. Over the years, the following items stayed in the student portfolios: their kindergarten and grade 1 self-portrait and sentence, their grade 1–5 self-reflections, and K–5 teacher responses.

The inclusion of timed writing samples in the portfolios introduced a degree of standardization that seems to contradict the idea that students would learn to monitor and self-regulate their own processes. However, the inclusion of samples produced under varying conditions also illustrates one of the potential advantages for using portfolios: educators can examine how student performance varies in different circumstances (Murphy, 1999). In the real world, people are sometimes required to write under constrained conditions, so the argument could be made that the inclusion of timed samples represented challenges students might face in the years to come. It is likely, however, that the focus on timed-writing samples reflected a pragmatic response to the influence of the statewide test. Students had practice.

At the secondary level, the Region 15 educators began in the early 90s with a fairly open-ended menu of portfolio entries. For example, an early set of portfolio guidelines at the high school required the following entries:

1. *Introduction.* Introduce yourself and your work to your reader(s). Create a sense of who you are and allow the reader(s) to get a feel for the processes that led to the pieces you selected for your portfolio. This is a good time to establish your unique personality through creativity and personal voice. The introduction should help the reader(s) recognize your voice as a writer.

2. *Process piece.* One selection must include all stages of the writing process—pre-writing, graphic organizers, drafting, notes of teacher or peer-writing conferences, revisions, and final draft. This selection should illustrate that learning occurs through the act of writing and revising.

3. *Entry slips.* Each piece of work must include a short introduction which will explain the purpose for writing the selection, the amount of time spent working on it, the changes that were made during the process, the things learned as a result of writing it, and the reasons for including it in the portfolio.

4. *Concluding self-reflection.* This is the most critical piece in the portfolio. . . .

5. *The self-reflection(s) from the previous year(s).* (Johnson, 1995, p. 7. Reprinted with permission by Pomperaug Regional District 15.)

Figure 6.7
Pomperaug Elementary School
Southbury, Connecticut
Outline of Portfolio Contents

Kindergarten
* Fall and Spring self-portrait, name, and sentence (with brief teacher comment)
* The teacher scores the sentence and name only.
* These self-portraits stay in the student's writing portfolio until he/she graduates from high school.
* The teacher must briefly reflect (1 or 2 sentences) on the student's name/sentence growth.

Grade 1
* Individual writing goals, 4 timed writing pieces, 1 fully processed piece, student's self-reflection, and teacher's response.
* Teachers should score sentence and name only on self-portrait.
* The 4 pieces of timed writing are completed without aid or editing by the teacher.
* Students should be allowed up to 45 minutes for each timed writing piece.
* There should be 2 non-fiction (expository) and 2 fiction (narrative) pieces of timed writing.
* Timed writing prompts should be chosen by the classroom teacher, flowing from content curricula or related to real events in the child's life.
* Teachers should consider essential questions when developing timed writing prompts.
* Complete one piece per marking period with 2 in the last marking period.
* Each piece should include an entry slip and assessment list.

Grade 2
* Individual writing goals, 3 timed writing pieces, 1 fully processed piece, student's self-reflection, and teacher's response.
* Writing pieces should be chosen collaboratively by the teacher and student.
* The 3 timed writing pieces (1 fiction & 2 non-fiction) are completed without aid or editing.
* Students should be allowed up to 45 minutes for each timed writing piece.
* Timed writing prompts should be chosen by the classroom teacher, flowing from content curricula or related to real events in a child's life.
* Teachers should consider essential questions when developing timed writing prompts.
* The 1 fully processed piece should have all pre-writing materials and drafts attached. This piece may be fiction or non-fiction.
* Each piece should include an entry slip and assessment list.

Grades 3, 4, and 5
* Individual writing goals, 3-5 writing pieces chosen by the student, student's self-reflection, and teacher's response
* Best Fiction (Narrative or Fantasy).
* Best Non-Fiction (Expository).
* Best Timed Writing (45 minutes, focus on narrative writing).
* Favorite piece (could be poetry).
* Fully processed piece with all materials and drafts attached (can be one of the above).
* Optional—two pieces selected (one from beginning & one from end) to show growth.
* Each piece should include an entry slip and assessment list.

Anctil, et al., p. 17 (1999). *K-5 Writing Portfolios: A Teacher's Guide.* **Reprinted with permission. Pomperaug Regional School District No. 15.**

Although the menu categories were open-ended, in the early stages of portfolio development in the district, writing portfolios were built around analytical assessment of the many different forms of writing that students were producing in language arts and the content areas as part of the performance-based assessment and learning program. For example, assessment lists and rubrics for fiction writing, narrative fiction writing, and expository (non-fiction) writing guided the instruction and assessment of writing in the Region. The portfolios were defined by the particular kinds of writing that were taught and assessed.

John Voss (1997), a principal in the district reported that there was general agreement among the teachers that he interviewed about the portfolio contents:

> one piece of non-fiction, one piece of fiction, a favorite piece which might be one of the first two, a piece that demonstrates the complete writing process, from idea development through final draft, one or more pieces of timed writing, varieties of entry slips which are reflections on each piece of writing, and the overall reflection developed at the end of the year . . . (p. 82)

However, Voss also noted that at the time of his study, teachers were already beginning to question the rigidity of these requirements. One sixth grade teacher, for example "spoke about some leeway in having the writing submitted in the portfolio as being directly related to student and class goals in writing for the year" (p. 83). Another teacher reported that she and her colleagues "were questioning the need for five pieces of writing and the need for fiction, if the student's objective was more in the expository realm" (p. 83).

Voss also reported that at the time of his study, one of the essential elements of the portfolio in Region 15 was its flexibility. Teachers could create variations on the basic portfolio structure "to address the individual and group needs of the students in the particular class" and to create portfolios that "prove[d] both motivating and rewarding to both students and teachers" (Voss, 1997, p. 85). One teacher, for example, used the portfolios in September, in partnership with her students, to set goals for the class as a whole for the year. The goals for the year were posted in the classroom and each writing activity was referenced to the writing goals.

As students became accomplished at reviewing their own progress and needs, teachers reshaped the portfolio requirements so that by 1999 the portfolio "menu" was more driven by the goal-setting process. That is, by 1999 the contents of any student's portfolio were determined in part by the goals that students set for themselves at the beginning of the year and in part by the progress students made toward those goals. For example, students compiling a middle school portfolio reviewed all works written throughout the current year, including works written in classes other than English, to determine "areas of growth and strength as dictated by the individual teacher's reflection criteria" (Schultz, et al., 1999, p. 52.). Particular reflection criteria varied from teacher to teacher, but all focused on improvement and/or accomplishment. For instance, a student's final reflection for the year might focus on best piece in a particular genre, a greatest accomplishment, an improvement in a particular genre, or an improvement made in a goal set at the beginning of the year. Once the students identified areas of improvement and/or accomplishment, they selected three to five essays as evidence.

According to Don Johnson, Chair of the English Department at Pomperaug High School, the way that self-assessment at the high school level was embedded in instruction had also evolved over the years. Initially teachers created extended projects, then asked their students to self-assess their work; later self-assessment was embedded in the task itself (Don Johnson, English Department Chair at Pomperaug High School, personal communication, 1999).

Who had access to and owned the collections?

As explained earlier, choice became a less constrained as students progress through the grades. Ownership appears to follow along. Teacher Karen Ryan explained the changes she saw in her students' perceptions of portfolios:

> The younger kids have a difficult time understanding the expectations. First and second graders see the portfolio as something the teacher keeps. My writing, but the teacher keeps it. Third and fourth graders begin to take more ownership. I would like to have younger students feel that way too, but I am not sure it is easy to do. (Voss, 1997, p. 105.)

Ryan's observation suggests a topic for teacher research. During upper elementary and secondary school, students clearly "own" their portfolios; it would be interesting to explore the kinds of activities that might help first and second graders own them as well.

Selection

When did selection take place?

In Region 15, there were a series of steps in the selection process. On a day to day basis, students were involved in the "selection" process because they worked with performance task assessment lists, or engaged in other more collaborative approaches to the development of criteria to evaluate individual pieces of work. As Hibbard and his colleagues (1996) explained:

> The use of assessment lists and self-assessment throughout the year provides students with much specific information about the quality of their work. This detailed knowledge empowers students to see ways in which the processes and products of their work are improving. (p. 189)

The general process worked something like this: throughout the year, individual samples of work were collected in "working folders." During the year, looking for patterns across assessment lists helped students see patterns in the strengths and weaknesses of their work. Hibbard, et al. (1996) also suggested that written, reflective self-assessments during the year "help[ed] the students become explicit and specific about the patterns of change seen" as they examined work collected over time (p. 189). Teachers at some grade levels also had their students do a mid-year assessment of writing for the portfolio (Voss, 1997).

Near the end of the year, students made final selections for their end-of-year portfolio and wrote reflective self-assessments. At this time, students looked both forward and back. Looking back they reviewed their work for the year; and looking forward, they wrote learning goals for the next. As Hibbard et al. (1996) pointed out, the portfolio process "encourages students to go beyond a piece-by-piece 'assessment' and look critically at themselves as learners, answering the questions 'How am I doing?' and 'Where do I go from here?" (pp. 189–190). This "big picture" look by students made the portfolio a natural adjunct to the piece-by-piece self-assessments conducted on a day-by-day basis in the classroom—the next logical step in an extended and philosophically coherent process.

Who selected artifacts for presentation?

As we have said elsewhere, the question of who selects portfolio contents is often quite complicated. As explained above, the district's selection guidelines suggested that as students matured and moved through the grades, they should be given more authority and responsibility in the selection process. While teachers at the early grades might have been reluctant to allow students full rein, students were rapidly given more authority. For instance, in an interview about portfolio practice at the third grade level, grade 3 teacher Roberta Kugler said, "In the beginning, the portfolio is to share with parents and next year's teacher. . . . Our children choose their own pieces to go on to the fourth grade" (cited in Voss, 1997, p. 101). Teacher JoAnne Wislocki emphasized the role that reflection could play in helping students assume responsibility. Of reflection she said, "It is most important that the student can articulate, where he wants to go, what he wants to do" (quoted in Voss, 1997, p. 95). John Voss (1997) elaborated, "The student's ability to tell his or her own story and make choices is the 'driving force' behind the portfolio. At the end of ninth grade, it is the student who says where he or she belongs" (p. 95).

At Pomperaug High School students selected the work that went into their portfolios, but teachers certainly influenced the process. To put it another way, the process was not "anything goes." Students were not free to build their portfolios from scratch. The teacher-designed "performance tasks" were a given, just as "assignments" were in most classrooms. No doubt, the teacher's feedback on assessment lists, when they were used, also influenced the selection process. Yet selections were not predetermined. Students had the freedom to choose entries from whatever tasks they had accomplished. Moreover, many of the performance tasks allowed latitude for students to use their imaginations and to create products which were uniquely their own. For example, although the performance task described in Figure 6. 5 provided a highly structured description of the expected characteristics of the ballad and collage, the student chose the subject.

What was the purpose for selection?

At least three purposes for selection were mentioned in the literature on Region 15's portfolio: selection to demonstrate growth, selection to inform the next year's teacher, and selection for reflection. Evelyn Skowronski (Grade 3), for example, said that it is important for a portfolio to allow a teacher to "see the growth of the individual student over a period of time. Everyone is unique" (quoted in Voss, 1997, p. 98). Other teachers emphasized the role played by the portfolio in the cycle of learning. Roberta Kugler (Grade 3) for example noted, "Our children choose their own pieces to go on to the fourth grade; yes, they set goals for the next year" (quoted in Voss, 1997, p. 101). Other teachers commented that passing along the portfolios from year to year helped them know their students better. As teacher Debbie Patchkofsky said, "It helps to know each of your students at the beginning of the next year" (quoted in Voss, 1997, p. 107).

Who was the audience for the presentation?

As the last comment illustrates, in Region 15, one audience was the next year's teacher. Parents were also important audiences for both the assessment lists and the students' portfolios. According to teachers and administrators, the assessment lists provided a focus for discussions with the teacher about the student's work, helping parents to understand what students were supposed to do, or why they received a particular grade or rating. When the time came, parents were better able to provide support and guidance for their students. Parents appreciated being kept informed of the teacher's expectations. For example, one parent who wrote to commend the program said: "The assessment sheets and tasks are invaluable. They help parents know exactly what is expected" (quoted in Hibbard, et al., 1996, p. 228). As the Region 15 educators explained, ". . . performance tasks and assessment lists [took] the mystery out of classroom assignments and grades for parents" (Hibbard, et al., 1996, p. 228). Portfolio and benchmarks also played a role in keeping parents informed. As Karen Ryan, Grade 3 teacher explained, benchmarks of student writing and portfolios were helpful in showing parents the degree of improvement in relation to a fixed standard (Voss, 1997).

Portfolios also contributed to ongoing student, teacher, and parent communication about learning. Methods used to involve parents were varied and reflected individual teaching styles. The K-5 team wrote, for example, that some teachers used portfolios in open house presentations. Some teachers sent portfolios home for review. Teachers also began holding student-directed conferences in 1998. All students presented their portfolios (and other work) to their parents in late May. The students created, practiced, and then delivered in the conference a "What? So What? and Now What? presentation. These elements of the Region 15 design, explained in more detail below, engaged students in a cycle of learning; they asked students to identify and set goals, reflect on the progress they had made toward them, and set new goals for future work.

Portfolio guidelines for teachers also included numerous examples of ways to "celebrate learning." For instance, among other things, the first grade "sharing guide" reminded students to "Share your portfolio with your parents." and to "Ask your parents to choose a favorite writing piece." The second grade student-led conference agenda remind students to "Read your favorite story to your parents," and to "Ask your parents to fill out the response form." The third grade parent/student checklist asked parents and students to "Look through the fiction pieces. Read them and discuss your favorite." The fourth grade parent/student checklist reminded students to "Tell your parents what has improved in your writing and what you are going to work on improving next year." Another conference guide asked students to share "Two things I need to improve on, two things I'm proud of, and two goals for next year" (Anctil, et al., 1999).

Secondary teachers also used the portfolios to communicate with parents. Some used them during parent conferences. Other teachers sent the student's portfolio home with an invitation for a parental response. Some teachers also asked the students to write their own progress reports to their parents at mid-quarter. Methods such as the ones described in this section invited parents into the teaching and learning process and involved them in setting and monitoring their children's learning goals.

Reflection
What opportunities for reflection did the system provide?
In the elementary grades, teachers gradually introduced students to reflection.

For example, although the concept of formative assessment was widespread in the Region, the form of this activity varied from school to school and from grade level to grade level (Voss, 1999). Some teachers believed that first and second grade students have a difficult time with self-assessment. As teacher Evelyn Skoronski put it, it is difficult to "get to the world of the little people" (quoted in Voss, 1997, p. 94). By the end of grade 3 however, teachers reported that students were "perfectly able to set simple, yet realistic goals" and they used entry slips with their students. (Voss, 1999, p. 93). At least one grade 3 teacher reported having her students use the full writing process to write the reflective letter at the end of the year. And "by fourth grade," as teacher Liz Elia (Grades 2, 4) said, "students really have a handle on self-assessment. They have been through it for several years and they are older. They can say this is not good, I can make it better. In second grade, just because a piece is in their hand-writing with their name on it, it seems God sent to them because of a lack of matu-rity" (quoted in Voss, 1997, p. 93)

The portfolio guidelines for the secondary team identified the components of a portfolio self-reflection as follows:

What?
- What have my goals been?
- What have I done to accomplish these goals?
- What have I selected to include in my portfolio to show how I have worked towards my goals?
- Specifically, why have I decided to include these particular items in my portfolio?

So What?
- What have I learned about how I learn and work?
- What have I learned about the quality of my work?
- What are my strengths and weaknesses?
- How do the items in my portfolio substantiate the conclusions I have made about my work and me as a worker and learner?

Now What?
- From the analysis I have made of me and my work, what are my goals for improvement?
- What are my specific action plans to accomplish these goals? (Schultz, et al., 1999, p. 9. Reprinted with permission by Pomperaug Regional District 15.)

During the year, teachers at all grade levels provided multiple opportunities for students to practice self-assessment. For example, teachers asked students to write "entry slips" for all pieces of writing that would be placed in their portfolios. Entry slips explained the task, the audience, and the purpose for a particular piece of writing and the reason for placing it in the portfolio. Teachers used a variety of formats to engage students in analyzing their work, asking questions such as the following:
- What is one thing that you think you did well in this work?
- What made that part of the work so good?

- If you could change one thing about the work, what would you change?
- Why would you change this?
- What does this piece show about your writing or your improvement in writing? (Schultz, et al., 1999, pp. 20–28. Reprinted with permission by Pomperaug Regional District 15.)

Here, as in other areas, teachers adapted the idea to fit their needs and preferences. For example, one teacher at the high school developed a practice that falls somewhere between the use of entry slips for each piece of writing and a final reflection. The teacher scaffolded development of the final reflection by having students write a reflective piece after two or three major pieces of writing. When the time came to write a final year-end reflection, the student had the earlier reflection as a resource (Voss, 1997).

As explained earlier, teachers also engaged students in goal setting activities that involved reflection on past work. For example, at the beginning of the year students reviewed the contents of their portfolios from the previous year and decided on one to three goals. After setting goals, they developed a specific action plan for meeting them. Periodically during the year students reviewed their writing folders, looking for evidence in their writing that showed progress toward a particular goal. At that time, students could decide to continue to work on the goals they had set, or if they had made significant progress, to develop new ones.

It is also important to note that in Region 15, teachers routinely responded to students' reflections. Sue Shaw, a Grade 4 teacher cited in (Voss, 1997) commented on the importance of providing teacher response to the reflective piece in the portfolio:

> Neither one can stand alone. Students need to be honest about who they are as writers, (and) where they are going. Set goals. What is successful, what needs improvement? The analytical validation of the student's reflection (by the teacher) is a powerful piece of the portfolio.

Several teachers in the district wrote letters to students, commenting on the students' work and growth as writers. A teacher at the high school created an interesting variation on this practice. He used large post-it notes to write comments about issues that students raised in their reflective essays. The students knew they had the option of removing the notes as the portfolio moved on to the next grade. This sent a message to the student that said, "I value your work and I respect your right to use this comment as you wish"(Voss, 1997, p. 87).

Student Voices

As explained above, in Region 15, students practiced reflection even in the earliest grades, beginning by circling smiley faces, as in the example in Figure 6.4 above, or completing starter sentences, as Samuel did in the example that follows:

> In the beginning of first grade I *rote with no periods. I owso did one sentence in righting. I used more capital ledrs then I was supoest to!*

> Now I *I us talking marks at the right time in my sentences. Now I make a lot more inchorresting sentences.* (cited in Anctil, et al, 1999, p. 92. Reprinted with permission by Pomperaug Regional District 15.)

Perhaps because they had a good deal of experience assessing their own work, by fourth grade they were often able to provide specific examples to support their observations. For instance, in an excerpt from a letter to her next year's teacher, one fourth grade student explained what she had learned during the year, and she illustrated with examples from her work:

> As a writer I have made many improvements. . . . I have . . . improved on my description of objects and places. In my story "The Luck Seed," I described Maine as a beautiful place with tall mountains and deep blue ocean. Now at the end of my 4th grade year I would have described Maine as a breathtakingly beautiful place with tall thundering gray mountains and deep glistening aquamarine oceas sparkling with beauty. This adds to my story and makes it more interesting. I have also improved in my area of details. In my piece, "Clara and Me," which I wrote at the beginning of the year, I described Clara as curious. But in my picture book story, "The First Winter Snow," I described the main character in the story, a snowman, as a perfectly sculpted figure and I wrote that his large foot prints padded into the snow looked like giant polar bear prints. In this way my reader will get a better sense of what things look like in my story and they will feel more involved in the story. I have also improved on writing feelings in my story. In the beginning of the year, in my piece "Clara and Me," I did not add many actions or feelings. In the end of my 4th grade year, in my piece "The First Winter Snow," I wrote that I felt I could fly. I think adding feelings into stories are important. They help to link stories to real life. These are some of the major improvements I have made as a writer.

Her reflection on what she had learned led her to consider what she needed to work on next, and finally, to an action plan for further work.

> Although I have made many improvements as a writer I still need to improve many things about my writing. I still need to improve on organizing my stories. In my last writing piece of the year "The First Winter Snow," I had a long story but it was not divided into paragraphs very well. I think organizing writing pieces will help readers to understand and to get a clearer picture of my story. I also need to improve on the endings of my stories. I often have trouble finishing and balancing details in my stories because I put so much thought into my stories therefore the end of my stories are often overlooked. I am going to improve on balancing my stories with details and writing the end of my stories well. Also I must try to improve my spelling and my puncuation. For example, in my last draft of "The First Winter Snow" I had many spelling errors. In my timed writing I also had many spelling errors. I hope to get much better in this area. Spelling words correctly can improve your presentation of a writing piece. Puncuation is also something I must improve. When I write timed writing or a short essay I often make many puncuation errors, I am going to work on making fewer puncuation errors. I think puncuation is important because it makes your work more presentable and easier to read. These are some things I still need to improve on in my writing.
>
> I have 3 goals in writing for next year. One of my goals is to organize my writing paragraphs. I plan to accomplish this goal by practicing everyday to make my writing interesting, but organized. I will keep that writing in a

small journal and I will bring it everywhere I go. Another goal I have is to balance the details in my story. To do this I will keep a separate journal. Here I will practice balancing my beginning, middle, and end so my story is interesting. My third goal is to work on my spelling and puncuation to accomplish this goal I will take my time to write the words I know correctly. But for the words I cannot spell, I will carry a small pocket dictionary with me. To improve my puncuation I will take my time on writing and when I read I will pay attention to how the story is puncuated. In that way I will learn more. These are my goals and plans in writing for next year. I love to write and it means a lot to me. I am very excited about next year and I hope I will always love to write. (Quoted in Hibbard, et al, 1996, p. 209, and reprinted here with permission by the educators in Pomperaug Regional District 15.)

Reflections such as these, set as they are in the context of goal setting, encouraged students to become active, thoughtful participants in the analysis of their own learning and in the determination of next steps. At the same time, reflections provided teachers with useful information about the students' criteria for good writing and how they applied those criteria in their work.

Region 15 teachers also came to know their students as individuals, with their own preferred writing "rituals," their own goals and intentions, their own preferred topics, their own reasons for feeling proud about what they had accomplished.

Hi my name is Lauren. I love to write because there are so many things to write about. Writing is very important to me because you can always treasure it and look back at it when your older. I like to write about animals and people. I like to write in fiction because you can make things up such as your stuffed animals and even some of your dreams. I also like fiction because I can be creative. I be creative by writing things people may not think of. My ideas come my dreams and what happened to me or someone earlier such as my friends and my family. My favorite place to write is on my porch because it si outdoors and it is very peaceful. The thing that helps me write is my imagination and what we have learned in school like colonial times. My next piece is going to be about a pond. I am proud of my BFG piece because I used a lot of similes "like Blarney is as big as the Empire Sate Building." If you read my peublo home you will see that I used a lot of spicy words. A example is "I feel the white moon is gleaming through the open square door in the roof." I could have said "shiny", but I said "gleaming." That is how I improved as a writer. I will use the 5 senses more and write a variety of sentences some short some long. I will use those goals to help me write next year in forth grade because the goals help me write better. Writing was fun this year!
Lauren   June 16, 1999
(Quoted in Anctil, et al, 1999, p. 99, and reprinted here with permission.)

Evaluation

What was the role of evaluation in the system?

Unlike some other portfolio systems, in which grades are assigned on the basis of portfolio review, there was not much emphasis put on grades in the Region 15 portfolio process. During regular classroom instruction, teachers graded individual pieces of writing when students had taken the pieces to final draft stage. The portfolio was the "final exam" at the high school, but for the most part, the focus of the portfolio was on instruction as opposed to grades.

The team of teachers who wrote guidelines for portfolio practice at the secondary level had this to say about the grading issue:

> Many students and teachers believe that it is important to "count" or grade everything. However, it is neither necessary nor desirable to grade very single piece of writing that the student produces. Students must be trained to understand that they should do their best work regardless of whether or not it "counts." The purpose of portfolio assessment is for the student to take pride in his or her writing **progress**. . . . Ultimately, students need to learn that it is the **process** that is important and not the **grade**. When we communicate that message effectively, they will eventually take pride in what they are doing to improve. They will learn that they can set their own goals and standards, and then work toward those goals by practicing and experimenting with feedback and guidance from their teachers, peers, parents, and mentors. (Schultz, et al., p. 69. Reprinted with permission by Pomperaug Regional District 15.)

That is not to say, of course, that evaluation played no role in the Region 15 student portfolio process. Students got highly detailed feedback about their performance on individual tasks when the work was done. And although the portfolios themselves were not typically "graded," in grades 1–8, they were reviewed. Some teachers made general comments and others wrote a one or two page response looking at the student's self-assessment and commenting on the students' growth over the year (Don Johnson, personal communication).

At the high school level, the portfolio took the place of the final exam, and the final portfolio received a grade on the report card (Don Johnson, personal communication). The focus of the evaluation was different, however, than in many other portfolio projects. Instead of evaluating the quality of the student's work, per se, the teacher looked in the letter of introduction and the entry slips for specific references to selected pieces and for articulate discussion to evaluate the quality and accuracy of the *student's* self-assessment and to formulate the student's grade for the portfolio work. The teacher then coached the student on areas that needed improvement. The approach to evaluation was consistent with the Region's emphasis on life-long learning and the development of self-regulation. While teachers in most other portfolio projects looked at portfolios and asked "How well do you write?" in Region 15 teachers asked "To what degree are you becoming an independent learner?" (Mike Hibbard, personal communication).

How did the system ensure validity and fairness?

George Madaus described high stakes tests as "those whose results are seen—rightly or wrongly—by students, teachers, administrators, parents, or the general public, as being used to make important decisions that can immediately and directly affect them" (Madaus, 1988, p. 87). Among others, high-stakes decisions include "(a) graduation, promotion, or placement of students; (b) the evaluation or rewarding of teachers or administrators; (c) the allocation of resources to schools or school districts; and (d) school system certification." (Madaus, 1988, p. 89). Although portfolios in Region 15 did not carry the high stakes that are sometimes attached to other assessment programs, students, teachers, and parents took them seriously. The stakes were associated with learning. There was concern, then, that the system would be valid and operate fairly.

As Pamela Moss explained, portfolio-based conclusions about student learning can be used in credible ways to communicate with various audiences outside the classroom (Moss, 1992). In fact, a case can be made, she said, "for the enhanced quality of information that includes an integrative interpretation of the achievement and growth reflected in student work, based upon an intimate knowledge of the learning context" (Moss, 1992, p. 14). Drawing upon strategies typically used by interpretive researchers to develop, warrant, and document their conclusions, she developed a rationale for an "interpretive" approach to validity. A key element in this approach was the provision of an "adequate evidentiary warrant" for assertions made. Although Moss' comments were directed at developing a rationale for using portfolios or other forms of alternative assessment in the high stakes world of accountability, we believe they apply equally and, ironically, to the world of student learning. In districts like Region 15, it is students who are involved in producing the "evidentiary warrant." The adequacy of that warrant is assessed by teachers and parents who act as outside or secondary analysts, so to speak, sampling student portfolios and reflections to trace the path of a student's self-evaluation and to validate it—or not—in relation to the evidence provided. Certainly, a strength of the Region 15 program was that it included the student's perspective in the evaluation process.

Another strength of this program was that it made criteria public and discussion of criteria a very public process. In many assessment programs, criteria for evaluation are not public. Feedback for student performance comes in the form of scores or grades, a rather obscure form of feedback, and one that cannot be applied effectively in learning. When feedback comes in the form of scores or grades, students learn that they did poorly or well, perhaps in relation to how other students performed, but not always why. In classrooms where students and teachers work together in assessment, there are no mysteries about criteria for evaluation. Criteria are public for everyone to talk about. Students benefit from knowing expectations.

The Educator's Collaborative Portfolio

An Educator's Collaborative Portfolio was made by a team of individuals working together to create "a purposeful collection of work selected by educators in an attempt to provide insight into a chosen research question" (Van Wagenen, Nelson & Hibbard, 1996 p. 2). While individuals on the team could assume a variety of roles, acting as a critical friend or consultant, or providing technical support, the key role was that of "full partner." Those members who were full partners were each individually responsible for a clearly defined section of the portfolio. Working together with other full partners on the team, they established the study question that the team would address, made a plan for addressing it, and collected materials to include in the portfolio. Full partners agreed to:

- Attend periodic team meetings
- "Bring materials for sharing and discussion"
- "Experiment with the strategies the team decides to investigate"
- Engage in "self-assessment and reflection about his or her own work and the work of the team"

- Make "a portfolio or a section of the team's portfolio"
- Write "a final reflection about his or her work" (Van Wagenen, et al., 1996 p. 8. Reprinted with permission by Pomperang Regional District 15.)

Of importance was the fact that the ending point—the "final" reflection—was often only the beginning. Gathering evidence for the portfolio and reflecting on it often generated more questions.

Administrators in the district supported the ECP program in a variety of ways. They took the lead in encouraging teachers to become involved by providing release time or other resources to the team members They also provided "cognitive coaching"; that is, they helped the team think through key steps in the process by supplying needed information in the form of "professional reading material, strategies, research support, technical assistance in data gathering, feedback on work in progress, etc." (Van Wagenen, et al., 1996, p. 13). Most important, they worked to create "an environment that supported risk-taking, experimentation, and a commitment to improvement" (Van Wagenen, et al., 1996, p. 14). As the evidence we will present later in this chapter illustrates, this teaching portfolio system, embedded as it was in a context of administrative support, played an important role in establishing reflective practice as the norm in Region 15.

Purposes for the System

Although educators in Region 15 had long worked collaboratively to improve student performance, they began to use collaborative portfolios in that effort in 1994 when a Goals 2000 grant enabled the district to partner with other districts to explore methods to improve student performance. Groups of educators from each district selected an area to study, met throughout the year, and completed their first set of portfolios in 1995. In the fall of that year, the program was expanded in the Region. Linda Van Wagenen, a teacher at Memorial Middle School in the Region 15 Public Schools, and her colleagues described the purpose of the collaborative portfolio:

> The Educator's Collaborative Portfolio provides a structure and forum for educators to show how they make decisions that have impact on students. Teachers can show how programs, strategies, and/or technique improve student performance over time. Administrators can demonstrate how decisions are made to provide leadership and management skills that help teachers make decisions to improve student performance according to the priorities of the school and school district. In other words, the Educator's Collaborative Portfolio helps all of us see the pattern of our teaching and its impact on student learning over time. This perspective enables us to make better decisions to improve student performance. (Van Wagenen, et al., 1996, p. 2)

In a manner consistent with Darling-Hammond's (1989) perspective on professional accountability, the Educator's Collaborative Portfolio provided a systematic way to investigate the processes and products that teachers and administrators used to improve the performance of students. Its primary purpose "[was] to give the authors insight about how their work affects student performance" (Van Wagenen, et al., 1996, p. 7). From our outsiders' perspective, the effort makes sense. Fred Farrell, a social studies teacher at Pomperaug High School, quoted in Van Wagenen & Hibbard (1998) explained the rationale behind the development of collaborative portfolios as follows:

The students constantly are asked to assess their work and the work of their peers. Because this [portfolio] is such a valuable teaching tool, it makes sense that we as teachers assess our own teaching methods too. (p. 28)

As Murphy and Camp (1996) explained, "To establish an integrated assessment approach with a healthy relationship to the educational system as a whole, the impact on teachers and their professional development must be carefully addressed" (p.109). Healthy educational systems create situations in which teachers profit directly from their experience in assessment development. In Region 15, teachers' professional development was enhanced by their direct participation in the development of performance-based learning and assessment for students—and by their participation in a portfolio project of their own.

Collection
What work was worth collecting?

Like the goals for student reflection described earlier, three questions organized the Educator's Collaborative Portfolio: 1) "What did you do?" 2) "So what did you learn?" and 3) "Now what are you going to do?" (Van Wagenen, et al., 1996, p. 11). Choices about how to answer these organizing questions were left to the team members. However, a guide for constructing the portfolio suggested the following possibilities:

What
- The research question about the influence of some element of instruction on student performance
- Entry slips and/or an annotated index/table of contexts
- A description of what the educators and/or students did
- The connection between what the educators did and the priorities of their school's improvement plan
- Samples of student work including self-assessment if available
- Photographs of what educators and students did
- Short video clips of what educators and/or students did . . .

So What?
- Completed entry slips
- Reflective analysis of student performance and what influenced its quality
- Student self-reflections about their performance and what influenced its quality
- Letters and other input from parents
- Short video clips that show how educators studied student work and discussed what they learned . . .

Now What?
- Reflective writing about how to adapt curriculum, instruction, allocation of time and other resources, communication with parents, and assessment
- Reflective writing about how the process of the Educators' Collaborative Portfolio served as a professional development experience . . . (Van Wagenen, et al., 1996, pp. 11–12. Reprinted with permission by Pomperaug Regional District 15.)

These guidelines provided for direct links among school improvement plans, teacher research initiatives, and student work so that those with the authority to determine how classrooms operate were continuously confronted with the realities of classroom life.

Who had access to and owned the collections?

As Van Wagenen and her colleagues explained, "Educators who create portfolios have the flexibility of deciding how their portfolios will be used and who will view them" (p.7). However, the educator's sole authority for the portfolio was modified when it was used in evaluation. In Region 15, when the portfolio was used in place of the more typical clinical observation process for teacher evaluation, the educator and administrator agreed to be "joint audiences" for the portfolio (Van Vagenen, et al., 1996). If teachers so chose, the Educators' Collaborative Portfolio could also serve a purpose in a wider teacher-evaluation agenda: practice for preparing the "Site Portfolio," a requirement for National Board Certification (Van Vagenen, et al., 1996, p. 6).

Selection

Who was the audience for the presentation?

Because the primary purpose of the portfolio as a staff development activity was to give the authors insight about how their work affected student performance, the authors of the educators' collaborative portfolio were its first, and most important audience (Van Wagenen, et al., 1996). However, the portfolio could also be viewed by other audiences: other teachers interested in the same research question, beginning teachers, potential employers, administrators, parents, even students. This broad range of audiences who had genuine interest in the work of the teacher invested the teaching portfolios with a mantle of seriousness and legitimacy that symbolized the kind of reflective instructional culture the educators in Region 15 were trying to create.

Reflection

In Region 15, reflection was a central element in the ongoing process of school improvement. The definition of reflection in the portfolio development guidelines clearly linked reflective activity to the *what, so what, now what* questions that guided the development of the portfolio:

> Simply put, reflection is thinking on paper. It is the art of looking back on an event or activity for the purpose of evaluation. During reflection we try to answer the questions "What did I (or my students) do? Why did we do this? What value is there in the activity? What problems emerged during the activity? What did we learn from it? Would we benefit from repeating the activity? Why? Why not? How does this connect with prior learning or activities? What will we do next? (Van Wagenen, et al., 1996, p. 51. Reprinted with permission by Pomperaug Regional District 15.)

This emphasis on "we" might seem curious to those of us who have come to associate portfolios with an "I" in the name of ownership and personal engagement. What seems significant to us about this focus on "us"—educators and students alike—is that it underscores the pervasive role of collaboration across the system.

What kinds of artifacts of reflective activity went in the portfolio?

Several 'possibilities' for artifacts were suggested in the guide for portfolio development, including entry slips, reflective analysis of student performance and what influenced its quality; student self-reflections about their performance and what influenced its quality, reflective writing about how to adapt curriculum, instruction, allocation of time and other resources, communication with parents, and assessment, and/or reflective writing about how the process of the Educators' Collaborative Portfolio served as a professional development experience.

In one case, for example, a teacher who had a personal goal to improve student writing in science submitted samples of a student's work, the student's assessment lists, and the student's reflections on what was helpful to her in completing a task called "Creature Feature." The task asked students to write a scientific explanation of where students think a creature with a particular set of characteristics lived. To complete the task, the student had to use her knowledge about the life functions of animals and how their body structures help or hinder them in meeting those functions within the contexts of specific environments, and to write in a way that convinces other "scientists," of the student's opinion. An excerpt from the student's reflection indicates what she thought was helpful:

> I used a lot more details of information to explain my opinions. The examples of good writing on the plant test you showed us in class helped me to know how to use details and how to use what I already knew such as the similarities between the Creatures and an elephant, an owl, and my dog. Another thing that was really helpful to me was my drawings. I did not think about how the waterweeds would get in the way of the Creature's huge ears until I drew that little picture. I think that drawing helps me get more ideas to write. . . . (Student sample reprinted with permission by Pomperaug Regional District 15.)

The teacher had revised the "Creatures" task to require students to add details and to complete drawings about their ideas. Here are a few of the teacher's comments:

> First of all, my emphasis on using more details really paid off. Most students used at least five accurate supporting details, including details that made connections between the Creature and animals such as camels, elephants, owls, and dogs with which they were familiar. The student whose work I have attached used and explained eight details . . . .

> A strategy I employed to get students to more accurately assess their own work was to require that they find and underline each supporting detail that they used. See the eight pieces of evidence labeled E1, E2, etc., in the student's work attached here . . . .

> Another high point was the students' use of drawings to support their written explanations. Several students, including this one, commented that making the drawings really helped them think more deeply about their explanations . . . .

> However, there are two areas of the students' responses that still frustrate me. One is the students' inability to explain how all . . . the details add up to be more powerful than any individual piece of data. The second is the stu-

dents' inability to use the science vocabulary we have been learning. . . . My discussion of these two areas of relative weaknesses will reveal my goals to make the adaptations necessary to bring these students to a higher level of understanding. (Sample teacher relfection reprinted by permission of Pomperaug Regional District 15.)

Notice how the teacher's analysis of student work helped her plan ways to improve her teaching. Notice also that the student was asked to contribute to the conversation. Taken together they show that reflection can be an effective tool for improving teaching and learning.

In creating an Educator's Collaborative Portfolio, each teacher was encouraged to find his or her own voice, style, and structures. As Van Wagenen and her colleagues explained: "there is no one absolutely correct form of reflection! Some of us feel comfortable using poetry; some like to use pictures, sketches, or drawings; others need the structure of lists; still others are best able to express ourselves in prose" (Van Wagenen, et al., 1996, p. 51).

Evaluation

In Region 15, instead of being observed by their administrators, experienced teachers could choose to use the Educators' Collaborative Portfolio to demonstrate their professional growth. So that portfolios could be used for this purpose, and to encourage self-assessment, each full partner in a team was responsible for a clearly defined section of a collaborative portfolio. When portfolios were completed, an administrator might review the entire portfolio, or if an individual was being evaluated, only the section of it that represented that individual's practice. But the evaluation process itself actually began long before the administrator saw the final portfolio. In fact, it started at the very beginning of the portfolio process.

Most teams that created Educator Collaborative Portfolios also created an "assessment list" for their work. Like the assessment lists they devised for their students, these were used to guide the development of the work and to scaffold self-assessment. While the list might be revised at the mid-year point if team members wanted to shift the focus of their investigation, the teachers were advised not to revise them later in the year. The administrator used the assessment list generated by the team in conducting his or her own evaluation of the team's work, or of the work of an individual teacher if the portfolio was being used as part of the formal teacher-evaluation process. Some administrators also wrote a narrative evaluation.

Issues of Impact

Performance-based assessment had been a part of the landscape in Region 15 for almost 20 years. Although the portfolio assessment systems we have profiled had existed for a shorter duration, their emergence in the Region is itself testament to the impact alternative assessment had among the educators there. Because of the pervasive nature of this work in alternative assessment, it is truly a daunting task to try to examine its effectiveness. We believe it would take the sustained efforts of a team of ethnographers trained in Guba and Lincoln's (1989) Fourth Generation model of educational evaluation to do the job justice. Nonetheless, we will give you a flavor for the kinds of impact the system has had, particularly on teachers.

Impact on Learning and Teaching

At a basic level, the teachers' portfolio system considerably raised the status of the art of asking questions about teaching practices in the eyes of teachers and administrators. Unlike traditional observational or clinical models of teacher evaluation where the focus tends to be on what administrators see during their visits, the focus here was on *what* teachers saw over time—and what *they* learned from what they saw: The focus was on the kinds of questions the teacher asked about his/her classrooms, the approach the teacher took to answering these questions, and the effectiveness of the teacher as a reflective practitioner engaged in making sense of his/her teaching. Linda Van Wagenen and her colleagues (1996) described, for example, one group of teachers who studied the question "How can we improve students' self-assessment skills?" in their first year, then moved on to study "Does improved self-assessment skill result in improvement in student performance in writing?" the next (p. 71). This sort of questioning, which after all gets at a foundational element in learning and leads teachers to think about classroom events throughout the year (not just during the day of the visit), seems to us to hold much more promise of improvement than a question like "Did the teacher manage the class well enough on the day of the visit to achieve a small and defined instructional objective?"

In keeping with the wide-open nature of reflective analysis, individual portfolios varied, of course, according to the research questions asked, and the particular method of organization adopted by the teams and the individuals within the team. One sixth grade teacher, for example, chose to investigate the following question: "How do we use authentic performance assessment to help students learn? As she explained, during the year, she collected a variety of artifacts:

> Items I gathered included: tasks, assessment lists, checkpoint lists, goals and objectives, tests, lesson plans, photos, magazine/newspaper articles, and what I called 'before' and 'after' work. I also gathered student quotes, and I recorded exciting events in the learning process which occurred in our classroom. Often I had students stop and write reflections describing what we did, what happened and what they felt or learned. (Quoted in Van Wagenen, et al., 1996, p. 47).

Organizing her portfolio as the "story" she wanted to tell about her efforts to help students learn, she sorted the artifacts she had collected "into an 'Intro, Body, and Conclusion.'"

Another fifth and eighth grade team, who investigated how to facilitate student self-assessment, selected a somewhat different set of artifacts:

- Photographs of "big and bulky" posters and projects
- Books created by students
- Videos showing fifth graders peer-evaluating their poetry books and eighth graders writing entry slips
- Write-ups of instructional strategies for helping students to acquire and apply self-assessment skills
- Sets of work from three students, "one consistently underrated her work, but improved as the year progressed; one consistently over-rated his work, but responded well to instruction and improved significantly by the end of the year; and [a] third one who was inconsistent in her use of self-assessment and remained inconsistent" (quoted in Van Wagenen, et al., 1996, p. 48).

Teachers wrote about many things, among others, about discoveries they had made:

> Since a writing portfolio is one large year long self-assessment activity, I real-
> ized that I needed to help the students begin to self-assess slowly, step by
> step, before I could ask them to sit down and assess what they had done all
> year." (Van Wagenen, et al., p. 59)

> I discovered that I only needed to do one of the complex self-assessments
> shown in the [ECP] portfolio. After that, I could do simpler and shorter guided
> activities to make the point. For example, I asked students to use two differ-
> ent colored highlighters to locate character and setting details in a short story.
> This strategy enabled students to discover and to really see where their de-
> tails were and where they probably needed to add more.

> Perhaps most exciting for me this year was to discover the power of having
> students self-assess on the rough draft. (Van Wagenen, et al., 1996, p. 59)

About new strategies they had tried:

> I began to use models of excellent writing whenever giving my students an
> assignment. For example, when we started persuasive writing, I showed them
> two models of published letters to the editor that were written by sixth grade
> students. We analyzed the models to see what elements were found in a well-
> written persuasive piece. I then let the students create the assessment list.
> Since they had seen models, they were able to identify elements that should
> be included (Van Wagenen, et al., 1996, p. 59).

About problems they had encountered:

> Some of my first assessment activities were too long or complicated to com-
> plete without much frustration, and I realize now that sixth grade students
> need structure when first beginning to self-assess. (Van Wagenen, et al., 1996,
> p. 61)

About plans for the future:

> Next year I want to examine student motivation as a component of the self-
> assessment/evaluation process. . . . I am beginning to think that we need to
> do more than merely provide tools for student achievement—we also need to
> explore the issue of motivation. Some students have a well-developed inter-
> nal drive for success—they love learning for its own sake. Others are driven
> by external factors—parental expectations, for example. But far too many have
> neither the intrinsic motivation nor the extrinsic motivation to do well. Thus
> to explore ways to use self-assessment/evaluation/regulation to help moti-
> vate students, seems a logical next step (Van Wagenen, et al., 1996, p. 65).

Just as they encouraged students to do, teachers were encouraged to refer specifically to evidence in the portfolios when they wrote reflections, and this evidence provides us with information on the impact of the system. In the following example, the
teacher refers to a newly instituted strategy for self-assessment and a student's reaction:

> Aside from self-assessment using analytical criteria, I also had students ex-
> periment with a variety of rubrics, thereby using a more holistic approach.
> Many students liked this form of self-assessment, particularly for their final
> drafts. Pam, for example, stated that the analytical forms were "important for
> the rough draft when you're making sure you have everything that you need.

> But I like the holistic ones for the final draft when you're really seeing if every-
> thing 'works' together. It's not so important if you have each little thing; it's
> how it all comes out and sounds at the end. . . . This is an area that the Region
> is beginning to explore, so it's interesting that a student stumbled into it. (The
> teacher reflections in the section above are quoted in Van Wagenen, et al., 1996,
> p. 64, and reprinted here with permission of Pomperaug Regional District 15.)

As the examples illustrate, experimentation, reflection, and analysis of the evidence
were used to understand, and thereby improve student performance.

In keeping with their interest in assessment, Region 15 educators gathered a substantial amount of evidence that their long-term systemic change resulted in improved
student performance (Hibbard, et al., 1996). In addition to "internal" measures of
student performance—"spelling tests, essay questions, integrated tasks requiring the
application of content and process skills from several disciplines, and writing portfolios for all students"—Region 15 educators analyzed the results of several "external"
measures of student performance (Hibbard, et al., 1996, p. 262). External measures
included:

- the Iowa Test of Basic Skills, administered in grades three, five, and seven
  (replaced in 1993–94 by the Connecticut Mastery Test, administered in grades
  four, six, and eight)
- the Scholastic Aptitude Test (SAT)
- Advanced Placement Tests in U.S. History, European History, English Literature, English Composition, Biology, Physics, Chemistry, Calculus, Computer
  Science, Studio Drawing, French, and Spanish

Analyses of these measures produced evidence of improvement. While the basic
skills tests could not be used to measure long-term growth, because the same test
was not used consistently during the period of curricular reform, scores for the SAT
and the AP tests increased substantially over the years. Detailed charts can be seen in
Hibbard, et al., 1996. We provide only a brief summary of the increases here. In 1981–
82, average scores for the SAT in Region 15—slightly above 410 on the verbal component and approximately 440 on the math—were well below the state and national
averages. By 1994, average scores had improved to approximately 440 on the verbal
component and approximately 500 on the math. In 1981–82 approximately 65 percent of the students took the SAT, but by 1994–95, 88 percent were taking it. In 1989–
90, 64 percent of the students taking AP tests received score of 3, 4, or 5 (scores of 3 or
better on the 5 point scale are considered excellent). By 1994–95, 85 percent of the
students taking the test received scores of 3 or better. And, as the years passed, more
AP tests were taken: 107 in 1989–90 and 144 in 1994–95.

Other evidence of the impact on students came in the form of observations by
teachers. Some teachers observed, for instance, that students gained a new perspective on their progress by reviewing their portfolios. Teacher Liz Elia (Grades 2, 4) for
example, observed that while first grade students were just learning to write, learning letters, and putting words together, third grade students were already writing
paragraphs: "The progress is tremendous from the beginning to the end of second
grade and the portfolio proves that" (cited in Voss, 1997, p. 105). Other teachers commented that writing reflective letters for the portfolios seemed to have bolstered the
students' ability to talk about their writing; as teacher Roberta Kugler (Grade 3) said:

"They can describe what should be in a piece of writing before I even bring out the assessment list" (cited in Voss, 1997, p. 105). Debbie Patchkofsky (Grades 7, 8) reported that students appeared to have more ownership in the portfolio: "I think the kids appreciate it. They are focusing on what they want to change, (and) how they want to grow as a writer" (cited in Voss, 1997, p. 107).

Still other teachers commented about the impact of the portfolio on their classrooms and teaching. Ninth grade teacher JoAnne Wislocke, for example, summed up the impact of the portfolio process like this:

> It is a great teaching tool. I can take the students at the end of August. They present their portfolio. This is where I have been, this is what I can do. We do not have to go through the awkward period of getting to know one another.

> You can pick up on an individual basis and set goals. Have the students take responsibility. What do you want to learn in writing? That changes the dynamic in the classroom immediately. (cited in Voss, 1997, p. 108)

Problems and Potential Solutions

One of the teaching portfolios presented above indicated that the Region ought to consider the examination of "student motivation as a component of the self-assessment/evaluation process." This teacher was "beginning to think that we need to do more than merely provide tools for student achievement" and that "some students have a well-developed internal drive for success - they love learning for its own sake [while] others are driven by external factors" (Voss, 1997). As Anderman (1997) pointed out, achievement motivation has been an area of neglect among recent educational reformers. Neglect seemed not to be the case in Region 15. In the years after the teacher raised that potential problem, educators in Region 15 moved to address it. The revisions to their portfolio program—revisions that provided guidelines with more running room for students to make choices and that emphasized goal setting and ownership—have great potential for increasing student motivation.

The example illustrates another lesson to be learned from Region 15. Teachers there appeared to feel free to question and criticize the existing system in the spirit of improving it. John Voss' (1997) case study of the change process that was used to introduce and institutionalize writing portfolios in Region 15 confirmed this. Voss pointed out that a key to change lay "with the teachers and their willingness to take risks without fear of failure" (p. 18). As one teacher said, "In this school . . . we know we can give feedback when (the principal) gives us something to try" (cited in Voss, 1997, p. 53). As the example illustrates, Region 15 supported change with an organizational culture that supported constant learning, dialogue and revision during the implementation process" (Voss, 1997, p. 7).

The conceptual framework for the roles teachers played in the change process adopted in Region 15 was based on the analogy of scout, pioneers, and settlers (Voss, 1997). Scouts experimented for one or two years and networked with other teachers who were also experimenting with the innovation as well as teachers at the scout's school. As Voss explained, the assistant superintendent, Michael Hibbard, worked closely with building-level principals and other administrators to encourage these "scout" teachers to take leadership in experimenting and implementing portfolios (see also Figure 6.1 above). In the next phase of change "pioneers" took the newly tried innovations and experimented with them in more classrooms, gathering additional information about what worked and what didn't. Settlers, according to Voss "are the final arbiters of the innovation" (Voss, 1997, p. 9). Typically they were more cautious about change and wanted to see evidence of success (Hibbard, et. al., 1996).

According to Voss (1997), the role that teachers played in the change process was critical, particularly the role played by "scouts" and "pioneers": "it is the teacher in the classroom who has contributed the energy, creativity, risk-taking, and steadfastness that makes change possible" (p. 33). Voss also pointed out that teachers often played the role of "experts" in Region 15, presenting to other teachers in the district. Other evidence that teachers were valued as professionals and evidence of the spirit of collaboration in the district can be found in the references to this chapter. Teachers and/or principals and the assistant superintendent co-authored many of the publications on which this chapter is based.

Voss (1997) reported that there were several other reasons for the success of the change process in Region 15. First, instead of focussing on specific innovations across individual content areas or disciplines, Region 15 focused on an innovation that more broadly impacted all departments of the school—self-assessment. Second, the leadership was quite stable during the development and implementation years, with the assistant superintendent, the principals, the department heads, and many of the teacher leaders present for a significant portion of the time. Third, the Region adopted and maintained an effective balance between top down and bottom-up change strategies, taking advantage of administrative support for top-down change and of the buy-in that happens when change involves a group of teachers who want to improve curriculum and instruction through some initiative of their own.

A key player in this change process was the assistant superintendent, Michael Hibbard. John Voss (1997) reported that teachers see Dr. Hibbard as a person who "generates ideas, then filters them through key people so that they can experiment, model the ideas for others, and gather information about what works and what doesn't" (p. 62). Another teacher described Hibbard as "catalyst for change" from the district office who encouraged him to become a scout for innovations (Voss, 1997, p. 58). Other reports characterize principals in the district as exhibiting the same kind of leadership. No doubt, the leadership in this district was one reason for the success of its process of change.

We believe that the Connecticut design offers a number of solutions to problems we identified in other systems. Many new assessment systems face the issue of teacher engagement and teacher buy-in. Indeed, almost all of the systems we've profiled have, in one way or another, been designed such that improvement in teaching is a major outcome. If teachers do not "buy in" to an innovation, no substantial change will occur. The Region 15 system seems to have solved this problem by developing the collaborative portfolio system in alignment with principles of teacher research. Murphy and Camp (1996), commenting on the powerful interplay between curriculum and assessment, saw a need for an integrated, systemic approach to portfolio assessment that would take into account the impact that assessment necessarily has on curriculum:

> In an integrated approach, assessment is shaped to fit the goals for learning, not the reverse. The goals for education and the views of learning in such a system are reflected in its assessments, and assessment and curriculum are compatible across its different levels. . . . (Murphy & Camp, 1996, pp. 108)

Region 15 was—and still is—a good example of an integrated approach to assessment, and there are many lessons to be learned from this model. The emphasis on self-regulation applied to students and teachers alike, and it was supported by a management approach that fostered a climate in which self-regulation could thrive.

The district was supported by a state that took a similar approach to accountability. Olsen (1999) characterized two broad camps in the approaches that states take to accountability: "Those that think schools and students will improve if they are given enough resources, support, information, and encouragement; and those that think they need a substantial, external push" (p. 8). Connecticut fell into the former camp, putting much of its energy into "honing the skills of its teaching force: drafting new standards for licensure, paying beginning teachers more, and financing a mentoring program for novices" (Olsen, 1999, p. 8). According to Olsen, the state gave grants to districts that showed sustained progress over time and published report cards on every school, but there were no explicit sanctions for schools that failed to make progress. Connecticut's policies, like Region 15, reflected a model of professional accountability.

Opportunities for Discussion and Inquiry

1. The Educator's Collaborative Portfolio described in this chapter was intended to help teachers improve teaching and learning through analysis, reflection, and goal setting. This suggests that teachers need to maintain a critical stance vis a vis their work. But the portfolios were also used for evaluation, a circumstance that invited teachers to show their work in the best light possible. How can teachers demonstrate *growth* as educators instead of just collections of best efforts?

2. In Region 15, change was introduced in a rational fashion—over time, with much support for teachers' professional roles in the process. How would this kind of approach improve the odds for successful introduction of a new approach to instruction and assessment?

3. Over time, the portfolio design in this district evolved from a fairly rigid set of requirements to a fairly flexible set of guidelines aimed at documenting student growth and promoting more student responsibility for learning. What are the advantages of allowing this kind of assessment to evolve? If assessments are intended to provide information for accountability purposes, what are the disadvantages?

Acknowledgments

We would like to express our appreciation to Don Johnson, Chair of the English Department at Pomperaug High School, K. Michael Hibbard, Assistant Superintendent of Pomperaug Regional School District No. 15, and John Voss, a principal in the district, for their help with this manuscript. Region 15 is a district where educators are very happy to share good ideas and information about them with their colleagues and they have much more information than we were able to provide here. Individuals interested in learning more about performance-based learning and assessment and portfolios in Region 15 are encouraged to contact Dr. Hibbard at Pomperaug Regional School District No. 15, 286 Whittemore Road, Middlebury, CT 06762. All materials from district documents are reprinted with permission of Pomperaug Regional School District 15.

References

Anctil, A., DellaRatta, N., Iannone, H., Kloss, J., LaBella, J., Rado, L., Shaw, S. (1999). *K–5 writing portfolios: A teacher's guide.* Middlebury/Southbury, CT: Regional School District 15.

Anderman, E. (1997). Motivation and school reform. In M. Maehr & P. Pintrich (Eds.). *Advances in motivation and achievement* (Volume 10, pp. 303–337). Greenwich, Connecticut: JAI Press, Inc.

Camp, R. (1992). Portfolio reflections in middle and secondary school classrooms. In K. B. Yancey (Ed.), *Portfolios in the writing classroom*, (pp. 61–79). Urbana, IL: National Council of Teachers of English.

Darling-Hammond, L. (1993, June). Reframing the school reform agenda: Developing capacity for school transformation. *Phi Delta Kappan*, 753–761.

Darling-Hammond, L., & Snyder, J. (1992). Reframing accountability: Creating learner-centered schools. In A. Lieberman (Ed.), *The changing contexts of teaching*. Ninety-first yearbook of the National Society for the Study of Education, (pp. 11–36). Chicago, University of Chicago Press.

Frederiksen, J. R., & Collins, A. (1989). A systems approach to educational testing. *Educational Researcher*, 18 (9), 27–32.

Guba, E., & Lincoln, Y. (1989). *Fourth generation evaluation*. Newbury Park: Sage Publications.

Hibbard, K. M., Van Wagenen, L., Lewbel, S., Waterbury-Wyatt, S., Shaw, S., Pelletier, K., Larkins, B., Dooling, J., Elia, E., Palma, S., Maier, J., Johnson, D., Honan, M., Nelson, D., Wislocki, J. (1996). *A teacher's guide to performance-based learning and assessment*. Alexandria, VA: Association for Supervision and Curriculum Development.

Howard, K. (1990). Making the writing portfolio real. *The Quarterly of the National Writing Project and the Center for the Study of Writing*, 12 (2), 4–7, 27.

Howard, K. (1993). Portfolio culture in Pittsburgh. In Randolph Jennings (Ed.), *Fire in the eyes of youth*, (pp. 89–102). St. Paul: Occasional Press.

Johnson, D. (1995). Portfolio assessment: An implementation guide. Unpublished document. English Department, Pomperaug High School, Southbury, CT.

Madaus, G. (1988). The influence of testing on the curriculum. In L. N. Tanner (Ed.), *Critical issues in curriculum: Eighty-seventh yearbook of the National Society for the Study of Education*, (pp. 83–121). Chicago: University of Chicago Press.

Messick, S. (1994). The interplay of evidence and consequences in the validation of performance assessments. *Educational Researcher*, 23, (2), 13–23.

Moss, P. (1992, Fall). Portfolios, accountability, and an interpretive approach to validity. *Educational Measurement: Issues and Practice*, 12–21.

Murphy, S., & Camp, R. (1996). Toward systemic coherence: A discussion of conflicting perspectives on portfolio assessment. In R. Calfee & P. Perfumo (Eds.), *Writing portfolios in the classroom: Policy and practice, promise and peril*, (pp. 103–148). Hillsdale, NJ: Lawrence Erlbaum Associates.

Murphy, S. (1999). Assessing portfolios. In C. Cooper & L. Odell (Eds.), *Evaluating writing*, (2nd ed., pp. 114–136). Urbana, IL: National Council of Teachers of English.

Murphy, S., & Smith, M. (1991). *Writing portfolios: A bridge from teaching to assessment*. Ontario, Canada: Pippin Publishing Ltd.

Olsen, L. (1999). Shining a spotlight on results. *Education week*, 18 (17), 8.

Paris, S., & Ayres, L. (1995). *Becoming reflective students and teachers with portfolios and authentic assessment.* Washington, DC: American Psychological Association.

Paris, S., & Winograd, P. (1990). How metacognition can promote academic learning and instruction. In B. F. Jones & L. Idol (Eds.). *Dimensions of thinking and cognitive instruction.* Hillsdale, NJ: Lawrence Erlbaum Associates.

Pomperaug Regional School District No. 15. (n.d.). *To region 15 educators.* Unpublished handout. Middlebury, CT.

Pomperaug Regional School District No. 15. (1997). Essential elements of the Region 15 portfolio. Unpublished handout. Middlebury, CT.

Rief, L. (1990). Finding the value in evaluation: Self-assessment in a middle-school classroom. *Educational leadership, 47*(6), 24–29.

Schultz, D., Patchkofsky, D., & Van Wagenen, L. (1999). *Region 15 portfolio system: An implementation guide.* Middlebury/Southbury, CT: Regional School District 15.

Tierney, R. J., Carter, M. A., & Desai, L. E. (1991). *Portfolios in the reading-writing classroom.* Norwood, MA: Christopher Gordon.

Underwood, T., Murphy, S., & Pearson, P. D. (1995). The paradox of portfolio assessment. *The Iowa English Bulletin, 43,* 72–86.

Van Wagenen, L., & Hibbard, K. M. (1998). Building teacher portfolios. *Educational Leadership, 55* (5), 26–29.

Van Wagenen, L., Nelson, D. M., & Hibbard, K. M. (1996). *Creating an educator's collaborative portfolio: Documenting classroom strategies to enhance learning.* Southbury/Middlebury, CT: Regional School District 15.

Voss, J. H. (1997, November). *A case study of change in Region 15 public schools: Implementing the use of the writing portfolio to assess student progress, K–12.* Unpublished doctoral dissertation. Sarasota, FL: University of Sarasota.

Wolf, D. P. (1989). Portfolio assessment: Sampling student work. *Educational Leadership, 46,* 35–39.

Yancey, K. B. (Ed.). (1992). *Portfolios in the writing classroom.* Urbana, Il: National Council of Teachers of English.

7 | Kentucky: Portfolios and Social Justice

Like other portfolio assessment projects discussed in this book, the Kentucky writing portfolio system was conceived in the early 1990s as one part of a larger strategy to improve writing instruction for children. But only Vermont's and Kentucky's systems were designed to do so across an entire state. Although the Vermont system served as a model in Kentucky's developmental stages (Callahan, 1997), Kentucky's story is unique. Although Vermont and Kentucky's systems both set out to increase student opportunities to write in a variety of genres for a variety of purposes and audiences, Kentucky's writing portfolio system was made in response to mandatory state legislation, while the Vermont system came about as a strategy to prevent mandatory testing legislation. In this historical difference, perhaps, lay the roots of all of the major differences between the Vermont system and that of Kentucky.

Kentucky's writing portfolio system was part of a conscious design to give Kentucky's children opportunities to learn the higher-order thinking and problem-solving skills they would need to survive in an increasingly complex society (Steffy, 1993)—a society referred to in the Kentucky Department of Education writing portfolio handbook as "the real world" (Kentucky Department of Education, 1999). Along with "performance events" (Jacobs, 1997) and related assessment strategies, the portfolio system was intended to stimulate and monitor "massive . . . school reform" toward "a new statewide curriculum that call[ed] for activity-based instruction and interactive classrooms" (Huot & Williamson, 1997, p. 49).

Indeed, some believed that the effects of reform in Kentucky would echo in other commonwealths and states whose schools presumably were failing to accommodate the future needs of the real world. According to Thomas C. Boysen, Kentucky Commissioner of Education during this period, Kentucky would set an example for other states: "American education has been shooting at baskets that are six feet high. Kentucky has decided to move up to world-class competition and to begin shooting at baskets that are ten feet high" (quoted in Steffy, 1993, p. 42).

The belief that schools needed to change from low-level drill and skill factories (baskets at six feet in an unreal world) into dynamic sites of thinking and inquiry (baskets at ten feet in the real world) had gained a foothold in the 1980s (Goodlad, 1984; Sizer, 1984), and the idea of using tests as a lever of change was widely accepted as well (Honig, 1987). But because many believed that traditional multiple-choice tests narrowed the curriculum and encouraged shooting baskets at six feet (Madaus & Kellaghan 1993), the nature of the tests themselves had to change. Wiggins (1992) had been arguing for some time that test-obsessed policymakers intent on reform ought to at least make sure that the tests they mandated were indeed "worth taking" and therefore worth teaching to. Indeed, Aschbacher's (1991) survey of state assessment activity during this period showed that policymakers across the country were buying Wiggin's argument and trying to make their tests worthwhile.

What sorts of test were worth taking—and teaching to—in Kentucky in the 1990s? Almost nobody would dispute the value of good writing skills in the real world, and the presence of the National Writing Project had been felt in the state. In 1986, the Kentucky legislature had enacted the Kentucky Writing Program, a $4 million per biennium program to improve the teaching of writing across the state. The program funded seven National Writing Project affiliates and numerous grants to schools and districts for projects focused on improving the teaching of writing. Through the NWP affiliates and the school and district grants, many teachers experienced direct writing assessment using holistic scoring (E. Lewis, personal communication, 1999).

By the late 1980s Kentucky teachers had explored the possibility of a statewide holistic writing assessment as a way to promote and improve the teaching of writing (Lewis, 1993; Spalding & Cummins, 1998), and writing program consultants in Kentucky knew all too well what Applebee's (1980) study of writing in classrooms had taught: Most American students were doing very little writing—a few sentences now and then—and on those rare occasions when students were asked to write longer pieces, the first draft was the only expected draft. Members of the Kentucky Writing Program believed that writing in Kentucky's schools meant, at best, essays, reports, or research papers, and wanted to broaden opportunities to write aesthetically, expressively, transactively, and reflectively (Russell, Lewis, & Riggs, 1996, p. 15). Though they were new and untested by way of experience, portfolios had caught the attention of policymakers everywhere, it seemed; and the message was clear that they held the promise of improvement in writing instruction. Given the times, perhaps no one should have been surprised when the Kentucky Department of Education turned to writing portfolios as a test worth taking and teaching to.

But there was surprise—and concern—in Kentucky during 1990 among many of the writing teachers who were associated with the Kentucky Writing Program and the NWP projects. The state's Writing Assessment Committee, a committee of teachers, assessment experts, and administrators from across Kentucky that was convened by Tish Wilson as director of the KWP in 1989, worked until 1991 to field test a series of tasks to serve in a direct writing assessment system. When this Assessment Committee learned about the intention to design a portfolio system, many of them believed that the state ought to continue to develop an on-demand system while gradually—and slowly—developing a portfolio system. The committee went so far as to write a memo to the yet-to-be-named Education Commissioner arguing that Kentucky was not ready for portfolios (Lewis, 1993).

In the Fall of 1991, however, the Kentucky Department of Education under legislative mandate of the Kentucky General Assembly demanded for the first time that the teachers in its public schools, specifically those teachers who taught fourth, eighth, and twelfth grade students, instruct all of their students to assemble writing portfolios. These portfolios would be scored locally, with an external audit procedure built in to guard against inflated scores. The portfolio scores would be combined with other data, never more than 14 percent of the formula (S. Lewis, personal communication, 1999), to determine current and expected levels of school improvement over two-year cycles. Schools that improved could receive monetary rewards. Schools that did not improve sufficiently could be sanctioned in a number of ways.

Exemplar System

The Kentucky writing portfolio assessment system was designed between 1990 and 1991 and implemented across the state during the 1991–92 school year in accordance with legislation. As of this date, the system is still operating largely as it was designed with minor internal modifications (the grade levels during which portfolios are scored have been changed, for example). Kentucky's writing portfolio system was—and still is—part of a reform initiative unprecedented in scope that involved the full array of adult stakeholders in public education—parents and community members, teachers and university professors, scholars and political leaders. Its design and its history are the consequences of political, technical, and professional work on the part of a small army of people over almost a decade. Volumes of research pieces have been written and published about it. We cannot give it the comprehensive treatment it deserves as an exemplar, so we urge our readers to look upon this chapter as necessarily incomplete. However, we have been fortunate enough to get feedback from founding members of the Writing Advisory Committee and other Kentucky Writing Program consultants and have made several revisions based on this feedback to try to present as accurate a portrayal as possible.

Context of the System

In some respects, policymakers in Kentucky during the early 1990s responded in the only way they could. On June 8, 1989, the Kentucky Supreme Court declared the state's public school system unconstitutional. The law suit that had challenged the schools was much like a number of other school finance court cases that had been filed across the country over the past 30 or so years. According to Van Slyke, Tan, and Orland (1994), suits challenging school finance systems, which have historically relied on local property taxes, began in earnest in the 1960s. The suit in Kentucky was filed in 1986 by 66 largely rural school districts in an effort to get equitable and adequate funding. The verdict in the case of Rose v. Council for Better Education, Inc., in 1989, however, required the Kentucky General Assembly to act legislatively as a remedy for the entire state, not just for the 66 rural counties named in the suit.

Importantly, the high court ruling went well beyond typical rulings in past cases in other states, which had directed legislatures to address per pupil expenditures. Kentucky's ruling directed the legislature to consider educational outcomes in its reform plans as well (Foster, 1991; Steffy, 1993). The Court found inequities in school funding policies, concluded that far too many students were getting an inadequate education, and established April 15, 1990, as the deadline for change. By April, the General Assembly was to have created the blueprint for a completely new and equitable system of public schools in which all children would get an adequate education—baskets at ten feet as expected in real world games. As a result, the Kentucky Education Reform Act of 1990 (KERA) was passed (Foster, 1991).

In addition to creating the broad reform plans ordered by the Court, leaders made the unusual, and we think wise, decision early on to create and fund independent review agencies made up of educators and scholars who could examine and report on the effects of reform strategies. In April of 1990, Kentucky's governor issued an executive order requiring that an independent agency be formed to evaluate the effects of KERA. Thus the Kentucky Institute for Education Research was born. Also in 1990, the chancellor of the University of Kentucky called for the development of a university-based agency to stimulate research into questions of reform. This agency was called the Institute on Education Reform. Since 1993, the Institute for Education Research and the Institute on Education Reform have collaborated on an annual publication titled *Review of Research on KERA*, a compilation of empirical studies intended to build cumulatively on findings. According to Pankratz, Lindle, and Petrosko (1999), the early publications of the *Review* focused mainly on issues of implementation and compliance; more recent issues present findings of some potential use in drawing conclusions about the effectiveness of KERA-based reform (see the webpage for the Institute on Education Reform, *http://www.uky.edu/Education/home1.html*, for more information).

By requiring the Department of Education to develop an assessment system capable of monitoring student progress toward higher-order learning goals and objectives, Kentucky legislators hoped to remedy social injustice and to create equality of opportunity. It is one thing, however, to require a Department of Education to develop an effective social tool for solving the problems of poverty; it is quite another to give that Department a little more than a year to get that tool fashioned and implemented. But that is precisely what happened in Kentucky. Despite the short time line, the Kentucky Writing Advisory Committee seized the opportunity to advise on the creation of a portfolio system that would do two things: 1) bring about an increase in opportunities for students to write, and 2) change the focus of classroom writing so that the "teacher-as-examiner" audience would no longer dominate instruction (S. Lewis, personal communication, 1999).

Purposes for the System

Political attempts to use standardized tests as reform levers were common long before Kentucky decided to use its writing portfolio system as a part of an accountability and reform plan (McDonnell, 1994). Airasian (1987) identified four social trends beginning in the 1960s which resulted in this increase in policy-oriented tests mandated and controlled by external agencies seeking to certify student and teacher competency. These four trends are as follows:

1. Movement of the social system into self-consciousness (e.g., the appearance of a number of federal programs aimed at improving the quality of life for various social groups)
2. A growing belief in the malleability of human behavior (e.g., if society can alter its institutions, it can alter its people in basic ways; the institution which touches all people early in life is the school)
3. A press for equity and equality of opportunity (e.g., legislation and social programs aimed at remedying social injustices because of race, gender, handicap, age, and the like)
4. Changes in the structure of the American family (p. 395–400)

American society's growing awareness of both the possibility of amelioration and the depth of social problems led to a conflict between state and local control. Airasian (1987) put it this way: "One consequence [of these four trends] has been a clash between the values advanced to justify increased state control, namely, equality, accountability, and efficiency, and the values of freedom of choice and differentiated treatment, which are embodied in justifications for local control" (p. 400). Clearly, Kentucky's writing portfolio designers were operating in a context where the power of the state to control classroom instruction had been invoked; just as clearly, however, they knew that formulaic writing instruction would not work (S. Lewis, personal communication, 1999) and, therefore, understood the significance of local control in writing instruction. The degree to which they succeeded in finding a balance is a matter for debate.

To exert political control from a distance, the Department created what came to be called the School Accountability Index (Foster, 1991). The state government would use this Index to show Kentucky's citizens, who had experienced a tax increase of over $1 billion as a consequence of KERA, that tax money was being spent effectively (Huot & Williamson, 1997). The state government would also use this Index as a means for doling out reward money and for taking charge of failing schools. An assessment system called the "Kentucky Instructional Results Information System" (KIRIS) was developed to feed evaluative data to the formula which yielded Index scores (Steffy, 1993).

Of importance in this regard is the fact that writing portfolio scores were never factored into the Accountability Index in a proportion greater than 14 percent. Nonetheless, no one had ever linked portfolio assessment and accountability for classroom performance so tightly together before. In fact, the decision to rely on ordinary classroom writing as part of the basis for a public accountability report surprised people beyond the members of the Kentucky Writing Assessment Committee, who had argued that any portfolio system ought to be created slowly. In 1992, the director of planning and policy development for the Vermont Department of Education described his surprise at the developments in Kentucky as follows: "Until now, performance assessment has been nurtured, like tender shoots, in a greenhouse. The work being done by Project Zero and ARTS PROPEL, the imaginative approach to assessment that has emerged in the Pittsburgh Public Schools, the slow and deliberate emergence of mathematics portfolios in California, and the development of science and mathematics assessment in Connecticut have taken place in sheltered environments, out of the public eye and the policy arena—stakes have not been attached to performance" (Brewer, 1992). KERA and KIRIS took these tender shoots out of greenhouses on the east and west coasts and transplanted them in the heat of the sun.

If Kentucky's system represented a "sledgehammer" approach (Darling-Hammond, 1997, p. 241), the well-documented resistance of American schools to change (Sarason, 1990) gives some perspective on why reasonable people in Kentucky might have accepted, albeit uneasily, the role of the Accountability Index in reform. The schools had to change, and so KIRIS had to have meaning in the real world. Beginning in 1991, the idea was to collect standardized tests and related data—portfolio scores together with a range of other data such as attendance, etc.—for fourth, eighth, and twelfth grade students throughout the state over each two-year cycle and then to average those data in order to determine whether particular schools had made progress (Jacobs, 1997). The Department of Education used scores from the 1992 implementation to create the Accountability Index, that is, a scale ranging from 1 to 140 to indicate the overall quality of each school (a score of 100 is considered proficient, 140 is distinguished). It also created goals or expectancies for improvement for each school on a two-year cycle when rewards and punishments would be administered (Steffy, 1993).

What would happen to schools that met their expectancy score? To those that failed? The plan was that schools that were able to demonstrate improvement over the two-year period were eligible to receive financial rewards—sometimes over $3,000 per teacher. School staff could decide to use the money for bonuses, for school resources, or for whatever else the staff agreed on. Schools that did not improve were required to develop an improvement plan. If a school's score declined by five points or fewer, the school was required to work with a "distinguished educator" assigned to them by the Department of Education. Such schools were also given more state funds. If a school's score declined by more than five points, the school was designated a "school in crisis." All parents would be notified of the findings, all staff would be placed on probation, and the distinguished educator would have the power to recommend retention or transfer of staff. If declines continued for four years, members of the local school board and the superintendent could also be removed from their positions (Anderman, 1997; S. Lewis, personal communication, 1999).

As the system unfolded historically, however, this strategy of rewards and punishments was never completely played out as it was intended. During 1995 and 1996, the years when the rewards and sanctions would have been administered after two-year cycles had been completed, the legislature softened its stance a bit. The phrase "schools in crisis" was changed to "schools in decline," and schools in decline simply received more resources in the form of support from "distinguished educators." After five years in the public school reform business, the Kentucky legislature had learned that change in schools comes slowly, and that harsh and punitive measures were not likely to create the changes in Kentucky schools which the legislators wanted (S. Lewis, personal communication, 1999).

What sort of writing program did the Kentucky Writing Advisory Committee have in mind? First, the Department wanted to create opportunities for students to write across the curriculum. To this end, they required that students submit writings not just from their English classes, but from other subject areas as well. Second, the Department wanted to stimulate process-guided writing instruction (cf. Spalding & Cummins, 1998). Finally, the Writing Advisory Committee wanted to encourage teachers to ask their students to write across a broader spectrum of genres, for a broader range of purposes, than they had been doing. The committee believed that far too much student writing in Kentucky was aimed at the teacher-as-examiner—that essays and reports for the teacher made up the bulk of writing in classrooms where writing of any sort was taking place. The committee hoped to encourage more writing for audiences beyond the classroom, for audiences in the "real world" (S. Lewis, personal communication, 1999). As we will see, this notion of "real world" audience vs. teacher-as-examiner audience sits at the core of the portfolio's ideology.

What can we tell about the committee's construal of the term "process writing instruction"? The *Writing Portfolio Development Teacher's Handbook* (Kentucky Department of Education, 1999) contained a section entitled "Guidelines for the Generation of Student Work for Writing Portfolios" that succinctly explained the construct "writing process." This explanation was originally prepared by the first Writing Advisory Committee in the early 1990s and has stood the test of time with no substantive changes. According to Starr Lewis, current director of the Kentucky Writing Program, these Guidelines represent "one of the finest documents to come from the Advisory Committee" and go a long way toward establishing the validity of the portfolio system (S. Lewis, personal communication, 1999). These Guidelines were subdivided into two categories: "Part A: Philosophical Guidelines" and "Part B: Applied Guidelines."

The portfolio system's "Philosophical Guidelines" called for teachers to "provide students with the skills, knowledge, and confidence" they would need in order to become "independent thinkers and writers," to "promote each student's ability to communicate to a variety of audiences for a variety of purposes," and to "provide information upon which to base ongoing development of a curriculum that is responsive to student needs" (Kentucky Department of Education, 1999, p. 1). Above all, portfolios and the instruction they supported should socialize students into the norm of student ownership:

> Since students must have total ownership of their writing, any intervention from teachers, peers, and/or others should enhance rather than remove or diminish that ownership and should be offered in the spirit of helping students re-assess their own work. At no time should students' ideas, revisions, or editing be characterized as teacher-, peer-, or parent-authored. (Kentucky Department of Education, 1999, p. 1)

Later in the Handbook in a section entitled "Marking Student Papers" teachers got more information about ownership:

> The Code of Ethics specifies that teachers may "indicate the position of errors," but they "shall not at any time make direct corrections or revisions on a student's work." This means that teachers may point out the location of errors using a variety of ethical methods (for example, circle spelling errors, underline letters that need to be capitalized, put check marks in the margins of lines , [etc.] . . .). . . . *These ethical guidelines apply to writing which might be placed in a student's assessment portfolio* [emphasis in original] (Kentucky Department of Education, 1999, p. 9)

"Applied Guidelines—The Writing Process" explained that writing was to be taught as a process involving six stages, including prewriting, drafting, conference, revision, editing, and publishing. During prewriting, "a writer determines a purpose for writing, selects ideas that communicate this purpose and address the needs of an audience, and organizes these ideas" (Kentucky Department of Education, 1999, p. 1). The Guidelines provided teachers with a number of suggested instructional activities for prewriting, including "creating opportunities . . . for students to think critically as they investigate topics," "providing . . . instruction in analyzing writers' forms, purposes, audience awareness, idea development, and organizational strategies," and "providing writing opportunities which allow for some choice and do not deprive students of . . . ownership of their writing" (Kentucky Department of Education, 1999, pp. 1–2).

The next three stages—drafting, conferencing, and revision—explained that writers focus more on thinking and ideas than on conventions and grammar as they develop a piece. When writers draft, they create sentences and "connect . . . one thought to another"; such work "usually require[s] a deeper level of thinking than do prewriting activities." When they confer, they "interact with teachers, peers, and/or others" who serve as responders who "question rather than dictate, critique rather than criticize, suggest rather than impose." When they revise, they "rethink . . . or 're-vision' . . . ideas" and "make decisions about what to add, delete, or change." An important task for the teacher was to "teach students how to review their writing with each other and to talk about possible changes"; this work meant that teachers "should provide class time during which this exchange can take place" (Kentucky Department of Education, 1999, p. 3).

The final stages—editing and publishing—explained that writers at some point turn their attention to conventions and mechanical soundness as they prepare their pieces for presentation to an audience. Noting that "not all pieces of writing will reach the publishing stage," the Guidelines required that "fourth grade students will publish four pieces and seventh and twelfth grade students will publish five pieces from their classroom folders when they choose to include them in their writing assessment portfolios."

Students were encouraged to use "dictionaries, thesauri (print and electric), spell checkers, or computer writing programs," and they could submit "many forms of publishing . . . (bound books, pamphlets, brochures, illustrated works, regular manuscripts" so long as the work is of "a size that will fit the standard writing assessment portfolio" (Kentucky Department of Education, 1999, pp. 4–5). Later in the Handbook in a section apart from the Guidelines, teachers were encouraged to bring technology into their writing classrooms: "The appropriate use of technology as part of the writing process is a valuable strategy. However, employing . . . word processors . . . only after pieces are completed is not an effective use of technology . . . . Students should be encouraged to use computers . . . during all phases of the writing process" (Kentucky Department of Education, 1999, p. 9).

Beyond the actual stages of the writing process, the Handbook urged teachers to support student growth as writers by way of reflective analysis. One of the required elements of the portfolio, the Letter to the Reviewer, asked students to write a description of himself/herself as a writer and an explanation of how the portfolio pieces were written and why they were selected. In the following language the Writing Advisory Committee sought to promote reflective analysis across the school year, not just during the time when portfolios were built:

> Teachers should have students reflect regularly upon their learning, thinking, and reading in various ways. . . . When students reflect upon their work, they learn about their strengths and weaknesses and can begin to improve themselves as thinkers and writers. . . . Students [whose teachers teach them to reflect] will more likely develop skills which will be important for composing the Letter to the Reviewer for their writing portfolios. (Kentucky Department of Education, 1999, p. 8)

The holistic scoring rubric used to score student writing portfolios may have undermined the view of the Writing Advisory Committee that teachers ought to teach writers, not writing. Although there was some initial indecision about whether to use a five-point or a four-point rubric (Callahan, 1997; Lewis, personal communication, 1999), the Department of Education decided to use a four-point rubric with the following category labels to describe achievement levels: novice, apprentice, proficient, and distinguished. Product-oriented by design, the scoring rubric aligned with the qualities of good writing designated by Paul Diederich (1974): ideas, mechanics, organization, wording, and flavor. The Guidelines urged teachers to employ process-guided instruction, but the bottom line as far as the state-sanctioned assessment system went was this: What was the quality of the product students submitted? Was the product focused and organized? Did it elaborate with details? Did it abide by the conventions?

System Design

The Kentucky writing portfolio system was designed for two purposes: 1) to provide a small portion of the data that would be used in the Accountability Index, and 2) to impact writing instruction in Kentucky schools. Originally designed in the early 1990s under the direction of Tish Wilson, then head of the Kentucky Writing Program (E. Lewis, personal communication, 1999), the design of the system has changed little over the decade. An important purpose of the founding Writing Advisory Committee was to broaden the types of writing students experienced in classrooms beyond the traditional essay, report, or research paper written for teachers as an examiner audience. To achieve this purpose, the system's design specified the submission of pieces of writing representing what the designers perceived to be a broad range of genres. These pieces were to be scored on the basis of equally broad features of good writing. The official names assigned to these genres and the number of pieces required have changed, but the basic design principle has not, nor have the values of the scoring rubric changed (S. Lewis, personal communication, 1999).

Collection

The *Kentucky Writing Portfolio Teacher's Handbook* (Kentucky Department of Education, 1992) permitted students to collect pieces from any subject area, not just from English/Language Arts. But the Handbook specified that at least one of the pieces submitted in the accountability portfolio was required to come from other than English/Language Arts classes for the elementary and middle grades; two content-area pieces were required for secondary portfolios. The Handbook suggested ways of compiling and storing working folders at various grade levels, but in keeping with its intention to foster local ownership of the system, it mandated no one method. A writing program consultant from Kentucky (M. Sallee, personal communication, 1999) explained her experience with the collection process as follows:

> Each district or school has its own collection procedure, . . . [and] KDE consultants (if asked) assist teachers in establishing a system that is feasible for each school. For instance, at my school each Language Arts classroom became the storage room for working folders. The students and/or teachers brought papers to these folders if they felt they might be chosen for the portfolio, then the folder was sent to the next grade level as the student progressed. At the accountability grade levels, the student should have many pieces from which to choose.

Sallee also described schools in which a writing resource teacher kept the working folders in a central location accessible to students and teachers.

What work was worth collecting?

The portfolio system designated certain kinds of writing as more worthwhile than others in keeping with the original intention to have a "showcase" portfolio system that would broaden opportunities to write beyond the traditional essay (S. Lewis, personal communication, 1999). For example, students at grade 12 during the implementation year were asked to collect pieces that could be classified in the following categories: personal narratives and short stories, poems, or plays/scripts. In addition, students were asked to collect pieces of writing done "to achieve any one or more of the following purposes: a) predict an outcome; b) defend a position; c) solve a problem; d) analyze or evaluate a situation, person, place, or thing; e) explain a process or concept; f) draw a conclusion; or g) create a model" (Callahan, 1997).

This menu broadened between 1991 and 1999 to permit even wider variation in student submissions. According to the 1999 Handbook, students at grades four, seven, and twelve were required to collect pieces in three categories: personal expressive writing, literary writing, and transactive writing. Personal expressive writing included personal narratives (works that recount a single incident in the student's life), memoirs (works focused on the significance of the relationship between the student and another person), and personal essays (an essay that focuses on a central idea about the writer or the writer's life). Literary writing included poems (compositions in verse), short stories (plot, setting, character, theme, point of view), and scripts/plays. Transactive writing included "... writing written from the perspective of an informed writer to a less informed reader . . . ; writing [that] is produced to get something done" (p. 14).

The range of submissions gradually took on an identifiable shape. E. Lewis (personal communication, 1999) described a recent contribution to professional development from the Kentucky Writing Program called *Kentucky Marker Papers* as follows:

> This document has samples of student writing showing a steady continuum of progress from beginning primary writers. The Marker Papers include continua for the following types of writing: personal narrative, memoir, short story, poem, feature article, letter, and editorial. These are the types of writing most often selected for the state writing portfolio.

The presence of this variety of writing in the Marker Papers document suggests that the Kentucky Writing Program may well have had a considerable impact on classroom writing instruction in the direction originally intended, that is, a movement away from the traditional essay, report, and library research paper.

Who had access to and owned the collections?

In both its early and late versions, the Handbook insisted that students were to have complete ownership of their portfolios. According to the original "Philosophical Guidelines," teachers were expected to observe the following: "The KIRIS Writing Portfolio Assessment acknowledges the student as sole creators, authors, and owners of their work. Teachers serve as colleagues, coaches, mentors, and critics." But on the basis of statements published in "Sharpen Your Child's Writing Skills," a pamphlet for Kentucky parents (Kentucky Department of Education, 1998), students—and their parents—may not have perceived themselves as having total ownership of the portfolio. A question in this pamphlet reads: "Will I get a copy of my child's portfolio?" The question is answered as follows: "Your child's original portfolio must be kept at the school. However, you may request a copy of it" (p. 18). This pamphlet also assured parents that besides the teacher "the primary intended audience of individual pieces, portfolio scorers, and any other person with whom the child chooses to share" constituted the entire class of people who had access to the portfolios.

A Kentucky Writing Program consultant with many years of portfolio experience in Kentucky described access and ownership to working folders and to portfolios as follows:

These working folders get a little full, so at the beginning of each school year students are asked to clean them out. Students toss what they feel is no longer appropriate or needed if other pieces can take their place. Students do, however, keep many pieces in their folders even if they know they will never use them in their portfolios for assessment simply because they like the pieces or they may have sentimental value. These working folders are given to the students at the end of their senior year, and many have used much of the work for freshman comp classes in college. Keep in mind, these folders belong to the student and he can take his folder any time he wants, but he is encouraged to keep it at school for many obvious reasons. (M. Sallee, personal communication, 1999)

A chart of portfolio contents is provided in Figure 7.1, and the portfolio collection process is graphically depicted in Figure 7.2.

Selection

According to the ethical guidelines established by the Writing Advisory Committee for the portfolio system, students were to be completely responsible for choosing pieces to submit in their portfolios. If anyone other than the student chose a piece, the act would be considered unethical. The following list of items was included under the heading "Not OK" in the "Code of Ethics for Writing Portfolios" published in the 1999 Handbook:

1. Assistance or intervention from teachers, peers, or others encouraging student choices that diminish personal ownership of the portfolio
2. Making selection of any portfolio entry for the student
3. Altering documentation attesting that portfolio contents were produced by the student (Kentucky Department of Education, 1999, p. 6)

When did selection take place?

Schools determined the timing of selection activities in light of a general time line established by the Department of Education, which set deadlines such that scores could be collected in the spring, the state could perform its audit, and reports to schools could be created by the following fall. The teachers in Callahan's (1997) study began selection processes in February. Sallee explained the selection process as follows:

Each year, if the school or district has a policy for a working portfolio at all grades, the kids usually make choices beginning in January so that revisions can be made. My students were still choosing in March right up to the last day. I encouraged this because I wanted the kids to value all their pieces and not feel locked in to a choice they had made at an earlier time. Teachers need to allow changes in choices up to the deadline. (M. Sallee, personal communication, 1999)

Figure 7.1

Types of Written Responses for Kentucky's Assessment

	OPEN-RESPONSE QUESTIONS	ON-DEMAND WRITING PROMPT	WRITING PORTFOLIO SELECTIONS
TIME NEEDED OR ALLOWED	10–15 minutes	90 minutes	Developed over time (during the school year)
Scoring Criteria	Individualized scoring guide tailored to each question—focus on content	KY Holistic Scoring Guide for Writing • audience/purpose • idea development, support • organization • sentences • language • correctness	KY Holistic Scoring Guide for Writing • audience/purpose • idea development, support • organization • sentences • language • correctness
Writer's Purpose	To show what student knows and can apply	Stated in prompt • narrate • persuade • respond	Student choice (e.g., to persuade, to entertain, to inform)
Writer's Audience	Teacher/test scorer	Stated in prompt	Student choice
	Short answer and/or mathematical representation	Stated in prompt • Gr 4: letter or article • Gr 7: letter, article • Gr 12: letter, article, editorial, or speech	Must include a Letter to the Reviewer and samples of personal, literary and transactive writing
Conferencing with others	No	No	Yes
Students Should	Look for specific questions asked, underline key words and phrases, identify how many parts need to be answered, then answer only what is asked for	Look for the audience, purpose and form stated in the prompt	Select pieces of their real-world writing which showcase their writing to a variety of audiences for a variety of purposes, using a variety of forms
Students Concentrate on	Writing brief answers with specific content information	Engaging the specific audience and accomplishing the purpose by developing ideas with specific support	Using the writing process to develop a number of different real-world pieces from which they make portfolio selections

Kentucky Department of Education, Portfolio Initiatives, 2/97 & 10/98—updated January 1999. (Reprinted with permission of the Kentucky State Department of Education, Frankfort, Kentucky, 40601.)

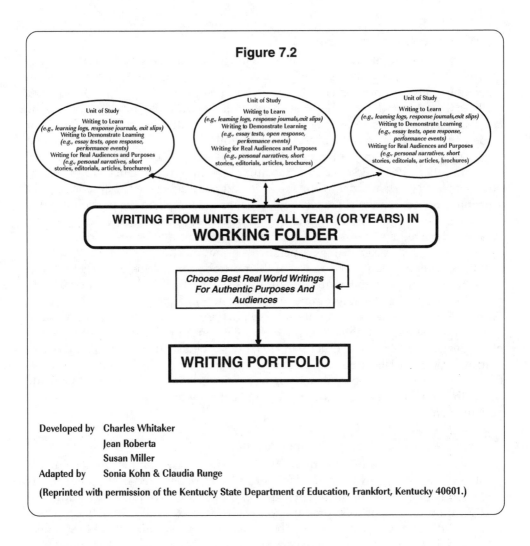

Figure 7.2

Developed by   Charles Whitaker
                     Jean Roberta
                     Susan Miller
Adapted by   Sonia Kohn & Claudia Runge
(Reprinted with permission of the Kentucky State Department of Education, Frankfort, Kentucky 40601.)

Who selected artifacts for presentation?

As we have seen, the "Code of Ethics" emphasized the need for students to feel total ownership of their portfolios. Of interest is the fact that the "Applied Guidelines" in the Handbook directed teachers to view the selection and submission process as "publishing." But many opportunities for external influence on students' choices existed in the system. For example, students selected or rejected pieces of writing on the basis of rubric values—not on the basis of their "own" categories and values. So the system's design provided little opportunity for students to come to understand their own set of values about writing as they could do in systems that provided for negotiated criteria (e.g., Howard, 1993). Further, because the system did not prohibit teachers from grading individual pieces of work (M. Sallee, personal communication, 1999), teachers expressed value judgments about work by way of grades before students engaged in the selection process. Whether students can be said to have "chosen" to include particular pieces within such a design is a matter for debate.

What was the purpose for selection?

The purpose for selection was to create a portfolio that could be evaluated under the rules of the system, and as near as we can tell, students' immediate purpose in "choosing" one or another piece of writing was compliance. Under the Guidelines teachers were directed to call this phase of portfolio work "publishing." Of note is the fact that there appears to be little incentive built into the system design itself for students to invest effort in their portfolios, although some schools chose to embed the writing portfolios in graduation requirements and the like (S. Lewis, personal communication, 1999). Essentially, according to the design, students were asked to do a lot of hard work in order to win rewards for their teachers or to help them avoid sanctions. Indeed, students' names were not supposed to be on the portfolios when they were scored (M. Sallee, personal communication, 1999); and the design of the system did not require that students learn individual portfolio scores—a decision left up to local administrators (S. Lewis, personal communication, 1999). Nor were there purposes beyond school, such as use of the portfolio for college entrance or placement purposes or use of the portfolio in hiring decisions (Spalding & Cummins, 1998), though such uses had been recommended in the literature about Kentucky's system (Mincey, 1996). This lack of student-centered purpose characterized the entire KIRIS system, not just the portfolios, which were a small part of KIRIS. Perhaps this aspect of the design explains why Anderman (1997) described schools' widespread use of unrelated incentives like throwing pies at or sliming their principal, having free breakfasts, or afternoons at a movie theater, or swimming parties, or enjoying a limousine ride to the prom, in order to encourage student participation during state assessment periods (p. 323).

Who was the audience for the presentation?

The audience for the presentation of the portfolio was an examiner audience made up of local teachers. In addition, student portfolios were removed from some schools (120 schools in 1999) and rescored by external raters as part of the state's audit system. Features of the portfolio presentation were specified in the Guidelines, which changed little over the years. Beyond the actual writings, students were to submit a Table of Contents giving the title of each piece of writing, the content area in which the piece was written, and the page number of the portfolio on which the piece could be found. Additionally, students were asked to write and submit a Letter to the Reviewer, that is, a student-written letter examining the student him/herself as a writer and reflecting on the pieces in the portfolio. Students were aware that the audience of their portfolio presentation would consist of examiners who would judge the merit of their work by applying the criteria of the rubric.

Reflection

The Writing Advisory Committee understood how important reflective analysis is in learning to write and tried to encourage it from the beginning of the system. In the 1999 Handbook, one chapter was entitled "Crucial Issues," and a subheading in this chapter was "Ongoing Reflection." Here teachers were told that they "should have students reflect regularly upon their learning, thinking, reading, and writing in various ways" and that students "learn about their strengths and weaknesses and can begin to improve themselves as thinkers and writers" through reflective analysis

(Kentucky Department of Education, 1999, p. 8). The portfolio system required students to write a Letter to the Reviewer, and this letter was scored as a piece of writing. Of interest is Spalding and Cummins' (1998) finding that as of 1996 many Kentucky high school seniors were unaware that this Letter had any bearing on the outcome of their portfolio scores.

What opportunities for reflection did the system provide?

Students' capacity to engage in reflective analysis was emphasized by way of the Letter, and opportunities for reflection did occur within the design of the system. Certainly, reflective analysis played an important part in the selection process as students went about creating their accountability portfolios during the spring of each school year. The Letter to the Reviewer discussed above did provide students with a formal opportunity to look back over their work and to consider their own qualities as writers.

What kinds of artifacts of reflective activity went in the portfolio?

Kentucky Writing Program consultants have acknowledged that stimulating students to engage in reflective analysis has not been the system's strong suit (E. Lewis, S. Lewis, M. Sallee, personal communication, 1999). In fact, efforts are currently underway to strengthen this aspect of the portfolio system. Here is what a writing consultant had to say in this regard:

> Reflection has been a weak aspect thus far, but . . . teachers and consultants are closer to addressing this at this time. We, the consultants, developed and delivered a Cluster Leader Training for all regions on REFLECTION beyond and before the Letter to the Reviewer. We trained leaders who then went back to their own districts and trained others. We also have compiled a help list for teachers to understand that reflection is a valuable part of the learning process overall. Schools and teachers are beginning to see that the approach to reflection can and should differ, but the letter to the reviewer has a focus that must be met, and that is that the student must show that he can talk about himself as a writer and follow the criteria of the scoring guide. (Sallee, personal communication, 1999)

The Letter to the Reviewer is classified as "Reflective Writing" on the portfolio menu and is defined as a letter "written by the student to discuss his/her growth as a writer and to reflect on the pieces in the portfolio." In this letter students may give "a description of himself/herself as a writer," an explanation of how the pieces in the portfolio were composed and/or selected, and "any other comments the student wishes to make about this year of writing." The 1999 Handbook also included a list of things the Letter is *not*; this list was written by a Kentucky teacher, Dottie Wilson, who granted the state permission to publish it:

[The Letter is not]
1. An opportunity to praise or criticize KERA
2. A generic description of the stages in the writing process
3. A thank-you note to express gratitude to a reviewer for assessing the portfolio
4. An evaluation of the student's teacher
5. A list of unsupported claims about the student's improvement as a writer

6. An unrevised, unedited piece written on the portfolio due date
7. A persuasive essay to convince the teacher how much the student enjoys writing
8. A final attempt to convince the teacher to give a higher grade (Kentucky Department of Education, 1999, pp. 12–13)

Student Voices

We have selected two letters to the reviewer written by Kentucky students during recent school years to provide a sample of the kind of reflective analysis in which students are engaging as part of their portfolio work. The first letter was written by a fourth grader, the second by a twelfth grader. Because the Kentucky State Department of Education, which provided these letters to us, asks student writers for permission to publish their letters only anonymously, we are unable to divulge the identities of these students. The following letter was written by a fourth grade student:

Letter to Reviewer

Dear Reviewer,

I, a fourth grader, have been working very hard on my writing portfolio this year. Writing isn't my best subject. This year I have learned that writing is really complicated. You have to support details with every thing you write on your paper. You have to use appropriate language in your writing portfolio stories. You have to have proof that something did happened in your writing portfolio story. Writing is really frustrating for me.

In my writing portfolio I have five different stories. I have two expressive-personal stories, one literary story, and two transactive stories. In my opinion, I think that expressive-personal stories are the easiest stories that I have written. The reason I think they are the easiest is because you write about something that happened to yourself in your lifetime. For example, my story "Nosiness" was simple for me to write because it was something that happened constantly every three hundred sixty five days, eight thousand seven hundred sixty hours, five hundred twenty five thousand six hundred, five hundred twenty five thousand six hundred [sic] seconds. Naturally, this would be the easiest to write because I know so much about it.

Before I ever begin writing I have to make a cheat sheet. A cheat sheet is a paper that shows your ideas about what you are going to write about. If you lose your cheat sheet you would have to make another. You have to have a cheat sheet or you can't write a story. A cheat sheet is important because if you don't have one or have lost one you might get off the subject.

While I have been working on my portfolio I have learned that I am expected to work independently and not need help every time I have an assignment of math, writing, homework, or social studies. Since I've learned to work independently on my writing I can work much more independently on my other work too. I have also learned a couple of new words: aggravating, information, desperately, incurable, frustrating, constantly, transactive, literary, and expressive-personal. These words have been used in my writing portfolio and also ways that I have felt while working on my portfolio.

The hardest part of writing my portfolio was when I had to revise my stories. I had to make the stories be better than the stories already were. I had to read my story. Then I had to decide where to put supporting details to make my story better and longer. I had to do this constantly until I had made my story longer and better. It was hard because I had to edit and revise even after I had added so much detail.

In conclusion, I have learned many things during my fourth grade year. I have learned there are different types of writing. I have also learned to work independently and not depend on any one else but myself to do my work. I have worked very hard on my writing portfolio this year. I have learned to write expressive-personal, literary, and transactive stories. I have learned a lot from writing this writing portfolio. My goal as a writer coming into inter-mediate was to become a proficient writer. I don't know whether or not I met this goal but I do know that I have improved a lot since primary. Hopefully, I will improve as the years go by. If I make as much progress as I have this year I know I'll keep getting better and better.

Sincerely,
A Kentucky Fourth Grader

This writer will likely at some point find himself/herself in the position of hav-ing to compile a twelfth grade KIRIS portfolio and, barring any major changes in the system as it is currently developed, will be able to make good use of the new vocabu-lary items learned during fourth grade. Here is a letter from a twelfth grade student:

Dear Considerate Reviewer,

When I first began writing, at the age of nine, I was extremely immature in my style, expression, and voice. I had virtually no idea how to develop a piece and create a mature work for my audience. At this stage of my aca-demic career, I feel I have improved significantly. I have learned to take an idea and develop it completely. My writings have become enhanced with relevant ideas, details, and transitions to make my creations flowing, such as when an artist adds color to his painting.

As I review the pieces that make up my portfolio, I realize that the memoir is one of my best. This sample is one which I feel shows my real emotions. It tells of a journey I embarked on with people I love, and also one I completed successfully. My voice is revealed as I tell my audience of pain, happiness, and sadness felt.

One piece of writing that I feel very undecided about is the commentary paper over cloning. I have struggled with this issue many times in my mind, and yet haven't come to a clear conclusion. Therefore, as I wrote this piece, choosing a side to represent was difficult. I tried, as I investigated my position deeply, to represent my choice well. Although it was written for a particular stand, I conveyed both sides, to give my reader a chance to make a personal choice.

In "Taking Away Individuality," I am speaking to those who want to strip high school curriculum of the arts. As a four year art student, I deeply expressed my views on how the issue should be handled. I felt that this work helped me not to be overly expressive. Without coming across too strong, I was able to state my opinion openly.

As I have slowly added the paint to my once bare canvas, I can see clearly the progress made. My portfolio has developed into a work I am proud to put my signature on. When the day comes that I am handed a new project, I am positive that I have the experience needed to produce an invaluable work of art. The past nine years have taught me lessons which I could never possibly forget. My English teachers have prepared me for real world assignments. I can express, compose, revise, reflect, and even (sometimes!) compromise. These gifts are ones that can be reopened again and again.

As you review my finale to four years of dedication, I hope you will keep an open mind. These pieces simply represent me. They show my emotions, they convey my thoughts, and most importantly, they have been put together with hard work. I hope the completion to my painting is pleasing to the eye, as well as the mind.

　　　　　　　　Sincerely,
　　　　　　　　A Kentucky Twelfth Grade Student

(Both of these Letters to the Reviewer were provided by Starr Lewis, who is currently in charge of the portfolio system for the Kentucky State Department of Education. They are reprinted here with the permission of the Kentucky State Department of Education.)

Evaluation

Evaluation seemed to lie behind all aspects of Kentucky's writing portfolios and was articulated by way of two scoring guides, a "holistic scoring guide" and an "analytic annotation guide." In 1999 fourth and seventh grade students were required to submit four pieces in their portfolios, twelfth grade students five pieces, and local teachers trained in the state's scoring protocol would score these portfolios using the four-point holistic rubric and the related analytic guide. The score points on this rubric were labeled "Novice, Apprentice, Proficient, and Distinguished," and characteristics of each developmental level were spelled out along each of six traits of writing: purpose/approach, idea development/support, organization, sentences, wording, and surface features.

What was the role of evaluation in the system?

The Kentucky Writing Portfolio system was focused on evaluation of written products from its beginning, and this focus did not change. The primary intention of the system was to contribute data with respect to student performance at each of four levels of development as discussed above and to ". . . provide specific information to teachers about an individual student's writing strengths" (Kentucky Department of Education, 1999, p. 9). These data were intended to "assist teachers in recognizing general areas of instructional need for the school" (p. 9). Additionally, these data were entered into the Accountability Index formula and weighted never more than 14 and never less than 10 percent.

How did the system ensure validity and fairness?

The Writing Advisory Committee believed that its claim to validity lay in its document entitled "Philosophical Guidelines" and "Applied Guidelines" (S. Lewis, personal communication, 1999). Although there was never any intention of doing away with writing-for-self and writing-for-teachers, the system was intended to legitimize writing intended to go beyond the classroom. The Handbook (Kentucky Department of Education, 1999) included language that reinforced the significance of "real" writing:

> While teacher-generated prompts may be appropriate for writing-to-learn and writing-to-demonstrate-learning exercises in the classroom, they often do not lead to the best portfolio entries. . . . If students select purposes and topics that are meaningful to them, they will have more investment in the process, and their writing is likely to be more successful. . . . Students [ought to have opportunities] to identify topics of interest, authentic audiences, and real purposes for their writing. . . . (p. 8)

Such a claim to validity goes well beyond the claims we've heard over the past few decades arguing for the validity of on-demand direct writing assessment strategies simply because students are writing and not filling in bubbles on a Scantron" sheet.

What about fairness? This area was quite contentious over the decade. For one thing, comparisons of schools were based on cross-sectional rather than cohort data. In other words, data describing the achievement of particular fourth grade students during one school year were stacked up against data describing a completely different population of fourth grade students during a completely different school year. To be sure, this flaw is present in virtually every state, but given all of the complex factors that can interact to change the nature of school populations from year to year, it can hardly be deemed fair, especially when sanctions are attached.

Darling-Hammond (1997) reported findings from several studies that showed an alarming instability in the Accountability Index attributable to this use of cross-sectional rather than cohort data. For example, one middle school of 200 students had been placed on the "merit" list during one particular year. The following year, after experiencing a change in enrollment patterns, the same school was placed on the "deficient" list. Furthermore, five of nine schools on the "sanctions" list in 1996 had been "in rewards" two years earlier. Such instances did nothing to inspire confidence, according to Darling-Hammond: "Educators in many schools, particularly small schools and those with large numbers of disadvantaged students or high turn-over rates, fe[lt] victimized by the accountability system because it d[id] not measure the actual progress of their students." (pp. 242–243)

What about reliability? Kentucky's system was built on traditional assumptions of interrater reliability, that is, that reliable scores can be warranted when two or more independent raters agree on the same score for a portfolio. To ensure reliability, the state trained local scorers using traditional calibration techniques and then hired a commercial test company to rescore some portfolios so that it could examine independent judgments for consistency or discrepancy. To guard against inflated scores, this commercial test company was asked to adjust local scores if they disagreed with audit data. This is precisely what happened in 1993, the year of the first audit. The test company adjusted school scores downward, and the department of education reported those adjusted scores to teachers with no explanation about the audit and its effect on scores. This event created an uproar among the state's teachers—teachers told the Writing Advisory Committee in no uncertain terms that they needed feedback on scoring if they were going to be audited—and the end of state auditing until 1996 (S. Lewis, personal communication, 1999).

By the time the audit system began again in 1996, the Kentucky Writing Program had been able to offer multiple professional development opportunities for teachers to internalize the values of the rubric (see Figure 7.3 on pages 200–201). Of interest is the fact that during the 1996 audit the Department of Education set up a system of triple checks by having "a select group of Kentucky teachers . . . independently score . . . 20 percent of the audited portfolios [for] quality control." When the 1996 audit was concluded, the department declared that Kentucky's teachers had grown "more comfortable" with the scoring system and had become "more accurate" raters of the Commonwealth's portfolios (Press Release No. 97-055).

The 1993 audit had indicated "inflated scores," that is, Kentucky's local scorers/ practitioners on balance gave student portfolios higher marks than commercial, external scorers gave them. The 1996 audit told a different story, however, as the gap between the professional and hired raters grew smaller. At the same time, a number of scholars questioned the reliability of Kentucky scores in light of a less impressive trend in scores on the National Assessment of Educational Progress (Lawton, 1996).

Suffice it to say here that traditional evidence of reliability has been a problem throughout the first decade of the Kentucky Writing Portfolio Assessment System. Every time the legislature met for its biennium sessions, the subject of the writing portfolios came up, and someone inevitably recommended either that the portfolios be eliminated or that they be dropped from the Accountability Index—usually argued on the grounds of unreliability. The Kentucky Writing Advisory Committee voted unanimously in 1997 to advise the state board that the portfolio system must remain a part of the Accountability Index. Because of this inclusion, the portfolio system had been taken seriously, the committee argued, and teachers had been given a voice in their own evaluation (S. Lewis, personal communication, 1999). Although the system contributed a small portion of data to the accountability formula, the contribution was enough to make it count: "Portfolios . . . are the only portion of the Commonwealth Accountability Testing System developed under the direction of, and evaluated by, the classroom teacher" (Kentucky Department of Education, 1999, p. 6).

Issues of Impact

Kentucky's writing portfolio assessment system maintained its political viability throughout the decade of the 1990s despite the fact that alternative assessment systems across the country crumbled under the weight of public pressure. This continuous presence is in itself a testament to its impact. How did it survive?

First, a number of right decisions were made early on. Professional development opportunities were a cornerstone of the system as evidenced by the Kentucky Writing Program's support of eight National Writing Project affiliates and its many other projects. During the early years of the system, teachers complained that the portfolios and their attendant changes were happening too fast, and there were many examples of miscommunication and misunderstanding (Callahan, 1997). But the Kentucky Writing Program developed a wide ranging and sustained approach to professional development, including regional writing consultants, writing project summer institutes, grants to schools, and a long list of televised professional development programs on topics like writing in the science classroom, poetry, and high school journalism (Kentucky Department of Education, 1999, p. 25). The KWP has been allocated a professional development budget of $2 million for a number of years (S. Lewis, personal communication, 1999).

Second, the professional development that did take place throughout the decade was grounded in local discussions and examinations of student work. "Before the portfolio system," said Starr Lewis during a telephone interview, teachers' talk about writing would focus on questions like 'Kids can't spell. Why not? Or why do they say "ain't"?" After the initial period of turmoil when the system was first implemented, at least three waves of change took place in discussions across the state. The first wave was about voice. Teachers were asking questions like these: What is voice? How do you know it? How do you teach it? Is it more important in some kinds of writing than in others? The second wave was about focus and purposes. Teachers wanted to know how having a focused purpose differed from determining a topic. The third wave was about idea development and its relationship to audience and purpose, particularly with respect to technical writing as distinguished from personal narrative (S. Lewis, personal communication, 1999).

Third, the state government and the public university system collaborated from the beginning to examine the consequences of reform. Although this examination produced mixed findings as we will see, it bespoke a seriousness and a willingness to learn that we don't see enough of in state assessment schemes. In the end, a classroom writing portfolio system rooted in values like student ownership and engagement, reflective analysis, and audience awareness resonated with current composition pedagogy. Although there were problems in each of these areas, efforts to make these pedagogical values manifest in classrooms have been sustained for a remarkably long period.

Impact on Learning and Teaching

Did student achievement in writing improve? According to data from the Kentucky Department of Education, improvement in writing achievement was continuous across the decade. On a scale of 140 points with 40 the cutting score for the "apprentice" level, state averages rose from 21.6 in 1993 to 33.1 in 1996, 39.0 in 1997, and 40.24 in 1998. Simultaneously, average audit score corrections to original school scores dropped from 39.5 in 1993 to 7.0 (P. Ladd, personal communication, 1999). Moreover, the Handbook (Kentucky Department of Education, 1999) opened with quite an optimistic statement that kept the focus on professional development and student growth:

> The quality of writing as measured by student performance has continued to improve across the state of Kentucky. As you assist your students with portfolio development, we encourage you to use this handbook and the addi-

Figure 7.3
KIRIS Portfolio Scoring Rubric
Kentucky Writing Assessment
Holistic Scoring Guide

NOVICE	APPRENTICE	PROFICIENT	DISTINGUISHED
• Limited awareness of audience and/or purpose • Minimal idea development; limited and/or unrelated details • Random and/or weak organization • Incorrect and/or ineffective sentence structure • Incorrect and/or ineffective language • Errors in spelling, punctuation, and capitalization are disproportionate to length and complexity	• Some evidence of communicating with an audience for a specific purpose; some lapses in focus • Unelaborated idea development; unelaborated and/or repetitious details • Lapses in organization and/or coherence • Simplistic and/or awkward sentence structure • Simplistic and/or imprecise language • Some errors in spelling, punctuation, and capitalization that do not interfere with communication	• Focused on a purpose; communicates with an audience; evidence of voice and/or suitable tone • Depth of idea development supported by elaborated, relevant details • Logical, coherent organization • Controlled and varied sentence structure • Acceptable, effective language • Few errors in spelling, punctuation, and capitalization relative to length and complexity	• Establishes a purpose and maintains clear focus; strong awareness of audience; evidence of distinctive voice and/or appropriate tone • Depth and complexity of ideas supported by rich, engaging, and/or pertinent details; evidence of analysis, reflection, insight • Careful and/or subtle organization • Variety in sentence structure and length enhances effect • Precise and/or rich language • Control of spelling, punctuation, and capitalization

SCORING CRITERIA		INSTRUCTIONAL ANALYSIS	COMPLETE/INCOMPLETE PORTFOLIOS
		Examining instructional strengths can assist in improving writing and learning in your school. Student portfolios can provide evidence of instructional practices. This section of the Holistic	A portfolio *is incomplete* if any of the following apply: • Table of Contents does not contain required information. • Table of Contents does not note

CRITERIA	OVERVIEW		
PURPOSE/AUDIENCE	The degree to which the writer • establishes and maintains a purpose • communicates with the audience • employs a suitable voice and/or tone		

(Reprinted with permission of the Kentucky State Department of Education, Frankfort, Kentucky, 40601.)

Figure 7.3 (cont.)

		Scoring Guide is provided to assist teachers in identifying sustained evidence of instructional practices through examination of student products. When scoring a student portfolio, scorers may identify *any number* of the instructional strengths listed below. The sustained performance in this portfolio demonstrates that the student has applied instruction in the following areas: • Establishing focused, authentic **Purposes** • Writing for authentic **Audiences**, situations • Employing a suitable **Voice and/or Tone** • **Developing Ideas** relevant to the purpose • **Supporting** ideas with elaborated, relevant **Details** • **Organizing** ideas logically • Using effective **Transitions** • Constructing effective and/or correct **Sentences** • Using **Language** effectively and/or correctly • **Editing** for correctness	study areas information (including the letter to the Reviewer) • There are fewer than 7 different entries, including Table of Contents and the Letter to the Reviewer. • One or more entries are plagiarized (must be proven) • One or more entries are different than those listed in the Table of Contents • One or more entries are written in a language other than English • One or more entires demonstrate only computational skills, or consist of only diagrams or drawings • Portfolio contains a group entry • Entries are out of order without clear descriptors on the Table of Contents *A portfolio is complete and will be scored according to how well it fulfils the criteria* of the Holistic Scoring Guide if one or more entries are: • out of order with clear descriptors on the Table of Contents • questionable concerning fulfillment of the purpose for which it is intended • questionable concerning plagiarism, but the plagiarism cannot be proven
IDEA DEVELOPMENT/SUPPORT	The degree to which the writer provides thoughtful, detailed support to develop main idea(s)		
ORGANIZATION	The degree to which the writer demonstrates • logical order • coherence • transitions/organizational signals		
SENTENCES	The degree to which the writer includes sentences that are • varied in structure and length • constructed effectively • complete and correct		
LANGUAGE	The degree to which the writer exhibits correct and effective • word choice • usage		
CORRECTNESS	The degree to which the writer demonstrates correct • spelling • punctuation • capitalization		

tional resources referenced here to support your own professional growth and the growth of your students as writers. (p. iv)

Has student achievement improved generally in Kentucky? Despite the presence of two independent research agencies, evidence to answer this question is inconclusive. According to the executive summary of the *1996 Review of Research on KERA* written by Pankratz, Lindle, and Petrosko (1999) and published on the University of Kentucky's Institute's webpage, improvement has been uneven:

> Six years into the implementation of policies specifically designed to improve schooling in Kentucky, the question at the top of all lists remains, "Is KERA working?" A common response of researchers is, "that depends on whom, when, and where you ask the question." Opinions fill the spectrum from success beyond all expectation to dismal failure of an experiment in education. Researchers . . . will tell you that progress toward the goals of reform is very uneven across schools, within schools, and across programs and practices, especially those that challenge tradition. There are real-life examples to support all of the differing opinions about the relative success of school reform in Kentucky. (p. 1)

What impact has the writing portfolio system had on writing instruction specifically? There is no simple answer to this question. One Kentucky writing consultant claimed that the impact on teachers has been positive: "The portfolio system has impacted our professional development tremendously. First, it motivated teachers to be interested in becoming better teachers of writing. Second, it focused teachers on real-world types of writing, rather than the cut-and-paste library reports and rehash of teachers' lectures we once saw as a steady diet in too many writing classrooms" (E. Lewis, personal communication, 1999).

Another writing consultant studied the relationship between portfolios and instruction in 1991–92 and again in 1994–95 and wrote the following: "Fourth grade student writing portfolios from Muhlenberg County show significant gains in students' writing skills and the instruction they are receiving in their classrooms. The 1994-95 portfolios provide evidence of the impact professional development, policy, instructional process, and curricular changes have made. . . . [Anyone] . . . who examine[s] this student writing can see the achievements" (Ladd & Hatton, 1995).

These consultants also pointed out professional development needs which future work ought to address:

> One of the big problems I see in the teaching of writing is that some teachers are really just tellers or assigners. They don't teach. They may read a model of the genre of writing they are assigning and talk about it. They then assign the piece of writing, the students do a pretty poor job of it, and the teacher then tries to fix all the problems through individual conferences and/or marginal notes. More teachers are learning through professional development how to create focused, intentional lessons which teach students the skills and strategies necessary to become successful writers of a variety of genres. (E. Lewis, personal communication, 1999)

In a survey study of the effects of the Kentucky system on first-year college students at the University of Kentucky who graduated from high school under the portfolio system, Spalding and Cummins (1998) reported a mixed set of conclusions. Although their study found that students had some positive remarks about the portfolio system, their strongest finding was disturbing: Almost two-thirds of the students believed that putting together their portfolios was not a useful activity with respect to preparing them for college. Spalding and Cummins (1998) also reported several excerpts from student-written comments on their survey representing what they described as student "frustration, cynicism, and confusion" (p. 182). We quote one of these excerpts here:

> It wasn't useful because . . . . My teacher made me write it her way, not the way I had. I had a piece of fiction that everyone liked—all my teachers, everyone. And my English teacher (12th grade) butchered it and made me rewrite it until it was how she would write fiction. (Spalding & Cummins, 1998, p. 182)

How widespread this phenomenon was is difficult to say.

Mincey (1996), a professor at Morehead State University in Kentucky, also conducted a survey of first-year college students and writing professors at her university during the Fall of 1995 with results that differed from those reported by Spalding and Cummins (1998). Interpreting and summarizing an array of survey data, Mincey (1996) concluded that freshman portfolio writers in the main "wrote more in high school than nonportfolio writers [which] has paid off [by making students] more comfortable with writing, . . . better writers, and [better prepared] for college" (p. 76). Mincey (1996) concluded that writing professors in the main believed that students had at least held their own with respect to basic skills since the start of the portfolio system and that "first-year college writers [were] demonstrating significant improvement in understanding the writing process" (p. 85). It is possible to argue that findings from the Mincey study differed from findings of the Spalding and Cummins study on the basis of differences in their respective university writing instructional programs. In other words, the portfolio system may have prepared students to feel more comfortable at Morehead because the writing curriculum at Morehead more closely resembled that promoted by the portfolio system (S. Lewis, personal communication, 1999). Beyond this point, however, remains the disturbing qualitative data about instructional coercion reported by Spalding and Cummins and echoed elsewhere (Callahan, 1997).

Koretz, Barron, Mitchell, and Stecher (1996) developed a report based on a study of participants in Kentucky's statewide assessment system generally and found the same sort of mixed effects that others have reported. Almost everyone involved in the system had positive and negative things to say. However, with respect to the issue of coercion, Koretz et al. (1996) summarized their data as follows:

> Teachers . . . reported that KIRIS has caused high stress. Most teachers strongly agreed that KIRIS has put teachers under "undue" pressure. Most teachers reported that teacher morale in their schools is low and has been harmed by KIRIS, and about half reported that KIRIS has reduced their own job satisfaction. A sizable minority reported that KIRIS has also decreased the morale of their students. (p. 51)

Of course, these findings refer to the entire range of accountability assessments in use in Kentucky at the time, not just to the writing portfolio system.

Almost everyone we read or consulted about Kentucky's writing portfolio system agreed that students in Kentucky have had many more opportunities to write since the portfolio system was implemented than they had in previous years. Similarly, almost everyone agreed that teachers have focused more intently on the teaching of writing as a consequence of the writing portfolio system. Moreover, there is some evidence that the quality of student writing improved over the decade. The most significant negative theme we found during our examination of the Kentucky story is this: Teachers and students alike may have felt controlled and manipulated by the portfolio system in ways that undermined the intent of the system, that is, to engage students in real writing for authentic purposes. The long-term consequences on students' attitudes toward writing, willingness to persist when the writing gets difficult, and capacity for independent intellectual work are unknown.

Problems and Potential Solutions

There is a long list of incongruities in the design of the Kentucky writing portfolio system which deserve mention. On one hand, the system was designed to encourage students to feel ownership of their work. On the other, students were not permitted to take their portfolios home; when work left the classroom to be scored, raters and students alike were anonymous figures; and some students got little or no feedback about their work.

On one hand, the system was designed as a way to bring local teachers into the evaluation process, to honor teachers as professionals by trusting their judgment. On the other, the system depended upon external audits coordinated by distant individuals with the power to adjust local scores, thereby diminishing whatever degree of trust in teachers had been communicated. Moreover, far too many teachers reported to researchers that their level of job satisfaction had decreased since KIRIS had been implemented. On one hand, the system was grounded in a philosophy of literacy learning which situates process and reflective analysis as essential instructional elements. On the other, the system asked for no evidence of process in the portfolios and emphasized reflective analysis in a letter that students wrote to an unknown examiner audience.

The design of the system made audience an ambiguous notion at best. The Handbook (Kentucky Department of Education, 1999) urged teachers to focus students' attention on their primary intended audience, that is, on the group of readers whom the student was actually addressing, and evidence of having this sense of audience was highly valued in the scoring rubric. But the audience for the Kentucky portfolio presentation was not the same audience as the audience for whom student writers had composed their pieces. However, this was the audience that held institutional power. Moreover, the Handbook (Kentucky Department of Education, 1999) explicitly rejected submission of "self-as-audience" or "teacher-as-audience" pieces. Kentucky's use of the term "real world" or "authentic" highlights the inherent problems we face when we invoke this notion in discussions about audience. The assessor's interest in students' messages, benevolent or otherwise, was hardly "authentic" and, therefore, could not be considered a "real world" audience.

This cluster of factors around the notion of "audience" in Kentucky probably shaped daily writing events in both subtle and profound ways, and we would encourage researchers to explore this question. To be sure, when students wrote their work, they may well have had a real audience in mind, but the impact of knowing that the examiner audience also existed lurking in the background surely came to problematize "audience" for students. M. Sallee (personal communication, 1999) indicated that teachers often worked hard to teach students to write for an authentic audience, that is, for an audience with a genuine interest in the writing. However, teachers also made clear to their students who the audience for the portfolio presentation really was. Across Kentucky there was no mistaking this audience.

Callahan (1997) provided examples that illustrate this problem. The requirement of two pieces from content areas forced some high school students to "fake" assignments—to create pieces either because they hadn't had the opportunity to write them in other classes or because they couldn't recognize a match between what they had done and what they believed the portfolio examiners wanted. Callahan also described a student who decided against submitting a piece written on the significance of Christmas. The piece expressed the student's feelings; although she wanted to "choose" it, the student decided not to because she couldn't make it fit neatly into any of the official genres.

These examples occurred during the implementation phase of the portfolio system and may represent less of a problem currently (S. Lewis, personal communication, 1999). But from our perspective, they represent incidents that are likely to reoccur in menu-driven designs with a product emphasis. This problem becomes exacerbated to the degree that stakes are attached to the portfolios. What do students do when they don't have opportunity to write in a given category either because of their school writing program or because they choose not to do so—or when that opportunity results in text that doesn't fit the menu well? The student who wrote the Christmas reflection would have had a quite different experience if she had perceived that the system could value and accommodate her work as a serious, worthwhile accomplishment. Perhaps the fault rested with her teacher, who did not help her see how her piece could fit within one of the broad menu categories. It seems equally likely that the fault may rest with the menu-driven nature of the system itself.

These problems will not be easily solved. The Writing Advisory Committee is well aware that portfolio scores must continue to win the trust of the public and policymakers by way of high levels of interrater agreements during audits, and the cost of reliability tends to be standardization and control. Standardization and control undermine local ownership. But the system could be redesigned to replace its menu of categories and its product-oriented rubric with a dimensional system. Instead of submitting particular types of writing, students could be asked to submit work that shows their range and versatility, their style and technical prowess, and the like. The effect of this change would be to broaden the kinds of writing that students could potentially submit.

Another change might be made in the way the portfolios are scored. Instead of basing judgments of quality strictly on features of written products as the rubric currently does, the scoring guide could place value on actual evidence of ownership and process. For example, rather than simply asking students to talk about process in the Letter to the Reviewer, the system could ask students to submit artifacts from their writing processes actually showing how they made decisions during revision. The Applied Guidelines call for teachers to ask students to explain their rationale for revisions; these rationales could be submitted as part of the portfolio and scored.

We believe that Kentucky's use of extrinsic incentives is faulty in a number of respects. First, if the idea is to improve student writing, then the incentives should be directed toward the student, not the teacher. Second, the use of extrinsic rewards in itself is questionable. Anderman (1997), a professor at the University of Kentucky, has argued that reformers in Kentucky, like reformers everywhere, have largely ignored the research on human motivation by ignoring the well-documented notion that extrinsic incentives undermine intrinsic motivation. No one in Kentucky knows whether this effect is occurring among Kentucky teachers as a consequence of KIRIS. What is known, however, according to Anderman, is that studies of non-rewarded schools report that teachers have lower levels of a sense of self-efficacy and higher levels of cynicism in the form of beliefs that schools which *did* receive rewards cheated. Finally, according to Anderman, research has taught us that high-stakes testing can result in lower levels of learning and motivation as well as higher levels of anxiety among students.

Though Kentucky has left unexamined its decision to rely on extrinsic incentives as the pivot point for school reform, it has examined what might be called the "push out-tune out-drop out" effect that researchers have identified as a consequence of some high-pressure, high-stakes testing strategies. Darling-Hammond (1997) explained this effect as follows:

> More than a decade's worth of evidence shows that simply setting test score goals and attaching sanctions to them does not result in greater learning—and sometimes produces destructive side effects. . . . In many states and school districts test-based sanctions have created incentives for schools to keep out or push out the most educationally needy students. Large numbers of students have been retained in grade so that their scores look better, placed in special education so that their scores will not count, denied admission, or pushed out of schools in order to keep average scores up. . . . Schools that take students who have been pushed out elsewhere and keep low-achieving students from dropping out are actually penalized in the accountability game. (p. 240)

Kentucky has acknowledged this problem and has made a good-faith effort to avoid some of the specific effects that Darling-Hammond mentioned. All Kentucky students are included in the school's accountability index, including special education students whose portfolio scores and core content test scores count. Schools are also assessed on their retention rates and drop-out rates. These two factors, as well as attendance rate and transition to school/work (for graduates), count as a part of each school's accountability index. Students who are sent to alternative schools for behavior problems or other problems are still counted in the index of the regular school from which they were sent. No matter how much a school's accountability index has risen, a school cannot receive rewards if it has not reduced its percentage of novice students by 10 percent from the previous biennium. A number of disincentives have been put in place to keep a school from pushing students out, retaining students in non-accountability grades, placing students in alternative programs, and teaching only the top students at the expense of low-achieving students (E. Lewis, personal communication, 1999).

One other problem, as Anderman (1997) pointed out, is that the Kentucky assessment system was designed to produce data describing student performance. It was not designed to produce data describing changes in instructional practices, an unusual state of affairs given that the purpose of KIRIS was to stimulate instructional change. This failure to assess instructional practice seems odd. If the assessment system did produce data describing students' opportunity to learn, then some of the less attractive aspects could be avoided (e.g., teachers who coerce students into making unwanted changes in their writing as per Spalding & Cummins, 1998). Anderman (1997) reported results of a survey showing that a majority of the public wanted changes in the assessment system so that such data could be generated. Further, according to Anderman (1997), a survey done by the Kentucky Institute for Education Research found that less than half of the principals, teachers, site-council members, and general public believed that KIRIS was working well. Teachers and principals claimed that they needed more concrete feedback about KIRIS results and student performance levels.

This problem could be addressed partly by modifying scoring procedures. Scorers could examine student portfolios in an effort to describe what must have gone on in classrooms in order for particular student work to have been done. But even more important would be the system's building in qualitative methods for examining opportunities to learn. Such an approach would emphasize instructional change as the centerpiece of reform and would contribute to change by giving schools useful feedback.

The on-going problem of interrater reliability and score inflation in Kentucky derives from what we believe to be an unnecessarily narrow view of reliability. A number of theorists have argued for a more comprehensive set of criteria for warranting the dependability of data than the traditional practice of independent interrater agreement used in Kentucky (see Underwood & Murphy, 1998, for a review). If Kentucky removed the threat of sanctions and replaced it with a system for performing qualitative "audits" along the lines recommended by Guba and Lincoln (1989), both dependability and the need for feedback could be addressed. But reliability is not the only issue. As Brian Huot wrote, "... in writing assessment interrater reliability means consistency among scorers and nothing else.... Translating reliability into fairness is not only inaccurate, it is dangerous because it equates statistical consistency with value about the nature of the judgments being made" (Huot, 1996, p. 557).

It remains unclear, however, whether these and other changes to the system would make much of a difference unless the threats to both student and teacher ownership and motivation as a consequence of the public accountability strategy are addressed. But this problem is independent of the use of portfolios and should not be laid at the feet of the portfolio system designers. If it is true that teachers decide to become teachers because they are intrinsically motivated to nurture and support young people, the extrinsic reward strategy could be the most serious problem of this system, especially if extrinsic incentives really do diminish intrinsic motivation. The solution here, of course, lies in the realm of politics. It may be time for policymakers to begin to explore portfolio assessment strategies that have the effect of supporting and enhancing teachers' intrinsic motivation to teach. (Material from the Kentucky Writing Portfolio: Writing Portfolio Development Teachers' Handbook is used with the permission of the Kentucky State Department of Education, Frankfort, Kentucky 40601.)

Opportunities for Discussion and Inquiry

1. The Kentucky system asks students to write for real-world audiences during their classroom instruction while simultaneously asking students to write for an examiner audience, that is, for the individuals who review and score portfolios. What influence might this complex relationship have on students' writing processes?

2. The Kentucky portfolio system illustrates the potential power of portfolios to create change in instructional practices. There is no question but that students wrote more after the system than they wrote before. Is the goal of stimulating more writing sufficient justification for the use of a writing assessment system? Why or why not?

3. Kentucky's system was developed under the assumption that instruction would not change unless teachers were given financial incentives. Do you believe that this assumption is true? What other strategies can you think of to promote change among teachers?

Acknowledgments

We want to thank Starr Lewis, director of the Kentucky Writing Program; Ellen Lewis, former director of the Kentucky Writing Program; Pam Ladd, writing consultant for the Kentucky Writing Program; and Modena Sallee, writing consultant for the Kentucky Writing Program, for their generous and gracious help in the development of this chapter. We could not have completed this chapter without their input and feedback.

References

Airasian, P. (1987). State mandated testing and educational reform: Context and consequences. *American Journal of Education*, May, 393–412.

Anderman, E. (1997). Motivation and school reform. In M. Maehr & P. Pintrich (Eds.), *Advances in Motivation and Achievement*. (Volume 10, pp. 303–337). Greenwich, CT: JAI Press, Inc.

Applebee, A. (1980). *A study of writing in the secondary school.* Urbana, IL: National Council of Teachers of English.

Aschbacher, P. R. (1991). *Performance assessment: State activity, interest, and concerns.* Los Angeles, CA: Center for Research on Evaluation, Standards, and Student Testing, University of California, Los Angeles.

Brewer, W. R. (1992). Can performance assessment survive success? *Education Week on the Web*, April 15, (http://www.edweek.org/htbin).

Callahan, S. (1997). Tests worth taking?: Using portfolios for accountability in Kentucky. *Research in the Teaching of English*, 31 (3), 1997.

Darling-Hammond, L. (1997). Right to Learn: A blueprint for creating schools that work. San Francisco, CA: Jossey-Bass Publishers.

Diederich, P. (1974). *Measuring growth in English.* Urbana, IL: National Council of Teachers of English.

Foster, J. D. (1991). The role of accountability in Kentucky's education reform act of 1990. *Educational Leadership*, 48 (5), 34–36.

Goodlad, J. (1984). *A place called school.* New York: McGraw-Hill.

Guba, E., & Lincoln, Y. (1989). *Fourth generation evaluation*. Newberry Park, CA: Sage Publications.

Honig, B. (1987). How assessment can best serve teaching and learning. *Assessment in the service of learning*, (pp. 1–9). Princeton, N.J.: Educational Testing Service.

Howard, K. (1993). Portfolio culture in Pittsburgh. In R. Jennings (Ed.), *Fire in the eyes of youth*, (pp. 89–102). St. Paul: Occasional Press.

Huot, B. (1996). Toward a new theory of writing assessment. *College Composition and Communication, 47* (5), 549–566.

Huot, B., & Williamson, M. (1997). Rethinking portfolios for evaluating writing: Issues of assessment and power. In K. Yancey and I. Weiser (Eds.). *Situating portfolios: Four perspectives*, (pp. 43–56). Logan, UT: Utah State University Press.

Jacobs, L. (1997, September 28). Dispute over Kentucky test section sparks broader debate. *Education Week on the Web*. (http://www.edweek.org/ew/vol-16/35ky.h16).

Kentucky Department of Education (1992). *Kentucky writing portfolio teacher's handbook*. Frankfurt, KY: Author.

Kentucky Department of Education (1998). *Sharpen your child's writing skills: A guidebook for Kentucky parents*. Frankfurt, KY: Author.

Kentucky Department of Education (1999). *Kentucky writing portfolio: Writing portfolio development teacher's handbook*. Frankfurt, KY: Author.

Koretz, D., Barron, S., Mitchell, K., & Stecher, B. (1996). *Received effects of the Kentucky instructional results information system (KIRIS)*. Santa Monica, CA: RAND. (RAND URL: http://www.rand.org).

Ladd, P., & Hatton S. (1995). *One district's approach to improving student writing: A study of fourth grade 1991–92 and 1994–95 Kentucky writing portfolios*. Unpublished manuscript.

Lawton, M. (1996). State test questions focus of renewed scrutiny. *Education Week on the Web. (http://www.edweek.org/ew/vol-15/19assess.h15)*.

Lewis, S. (1993). Kentucky writing portfolios: A history. *Kentucky English Bulletin, 43* (1), 9–11.

Madaus, G., & Kellaghan, T. (1993). Testing as a mechanism of public policy: A brief history and description. *Measurement and Evaluation in Counseling and Development 26*, (6), 10.

McDonnell, L. M. (1994). Assessment policy as persuasion and regulation. *American Journal of Education, 102*, 394–420.

Mincey, K. (1996). The impact of KERA writing portfolios on first-year college writers. *Kentucky English Bulletin, 68–85*.

Pankratz, R., Lindle, J., & Petrosko, J. (1999). Executive summary of research on KERA. (http://www.uky.edu/Education/IER/execsum1.html).

Russell, D., Lewis, S., & Riggs, A. (1996, May). Growing together: Curricular and professional development through collaborative portfolio assessment. *English Leadership Quarterly*, 13–19.

Sarason, S. (1990). *The predictable failure of educational reform*. New York: Athenum Press.

Sizer, T. (1984). *Horace's compromise: The dilemma of the American high school*. Boston: Houghton Mifflin.

Spalding, L., & Cummins, G. (1998). It was the best of times. It was a waste of time: University of Kentucky students' view of writing under KERA. *Assessing Writing, 5* (2), 167–200.

Steffy, B. (1993, September). Top-down—bottom-up: Systemic change in Kentucky. *Educational Leadership*, 42–44.

Underwood, T., & Murphy, S. (1998). Interrater reliability in a California middle school English/language arts portfolio assessment program. *Assessing Writing, 5* (2), 201–230.

Van Slyke, D., Tan, A., & Orland, M. (1994). *U.S. school finance litigation: A review of key cases.* The Finance Project. (http://www.financeproject.org/litigation.html).

Wiggins, G. (1992). Creating tests worth taking. *Educational Leadership, 49*(8), 2.

8 Vermont's Writing Portfolios: A Worthwhile Burden

Vermont's writing portfolio system began to grow in the thinking of Vermont's education commissioner and his colleagues sometime around 1988. Two years later, after establishing a development team comprised of volunteer teachers (Hewitt, 1995), Vermont's state department of education was prepared to pilot both a writing and mathematics portfolio system during the 1990–1991 school year—the first statewide portfolio project in the United States. Of great interest is the fact that the seeds of large-scale portfolio assessment were first sown in a state where the schools "retain[ed] a great deal of local autonomy" (Koretz, Stecher, Klein, & McCaffrey, 1994b, p. 5) and the education commissioner worried about "alienat[ing] teachers" (Mills as cited in Darling-Hammond, 1997, p. 244).

There seems to have been plenty of enthusiasm for the idea of portfolios among Vermont teachers, who ultimately came to find portfolios to be what Daniel Koretz, senior social scientist for the RAND Institute on Education and Training, called "a worthwhile burden" (Viadero, 1995). The state originally "[invited] students and teachers from 46 Vermont schools . . . to participate" and "98 [more] schools . . . asked to participate . . . [as] 'volunteers'" (Vermont Department of Education, 1991, p. 1). This norm of volunteerism distinguished Vermont from many other alternative assessment systems under development at the time in which state departments of education typically hired either teacher consultants or commercial test development companies to create their assessment systems (Koretz, et al., 1993) and then cajoled schools into "piloting" various designs. Of note is the fact that the writing portfolio assessment system has never been mandated by the Vermont legislature.

Despite the early outpouring of volunteer teachers and schools, Vermont did not make the mistake of trying to build its portfolio system on a shoestring. Policymakers took seriously the intention to use portfolios as a means of assessing their schools and showed it through funding the development process, including a year of "pilot" work to try out a design. The pilot year was never intended to yield scores for any public purpose, but the plan was to make scores public thereafter, preferably for individual schools, once everyone was comfortable with the system. Even so, as then-Education Commissioner Richard Mills was quoted as saying, the true mission was to discover promising practices: "We'll be able to point to schools that have been able to deliver and say, 'They're using these kinds of strategies.' Schools that aren't delivering can learn from the ones that are" (DeWitt, 1991).

This focus on creating a clearinghouse for practices offering promise to sister schools differed from the "sledge-hammer" approach to accountability (Darling-

Hammond, 1997) other states have taken, relying on public humiliation and embarrassment—or its counterpart, boasting rights—or on school reconstitution as remedies. The roots of the Vermont system grew in the innocence and idealism of a small state with just 100,000 students in its schools (Hewitt, 1995), a state with so many small schools that statisticians can't take statistically sound samples from schools (Koretz, et al.) and "matrix sampling" techniques are impossible (FairTest, 1999). The scale of assessment in Vermont together with its autonomous tradition perhaps allowed a kinder and gentler sort of assessment to emerge.

Nevertheless, Vermont managed to implement a writing portfolio assessment system that is of enormous importance to educators in every state regardless of the size of its schools and the scope of its problems. Of particular note is the fact that an advocacy group which studies state testing systems on the basis of criteria such as fairness, impact on teaching, and system coherence, recently rated Vermont's system as a "model" system—the only system in the country to have received the highest rating of "level five" (FairTest, 1999). The biggest change in the writing portfolio system since its inauguration has come in its scoring system, which was changed in the late-1990s to accommodate changing political and judicial circumstances. Nothing else really has changed in the foundations of the system.

Exemplar System

Vermont's writing portfolio system emerged in a state that had never had a statewide evaluation system of any sort prior to 1990, had no history of test-obsessed policymaking, and did not in fact adopt a statewide standardized test system until 1996 (Vermont Department of Education, 1996). During the late-1980s, however, Commissioner Richard Mills and his colleague Ross Brewer, then-director of policy and planning for the department, were facing mounting public pressure to "provide regular information on student performance" (Koretz, Stecher, Klein, & McCaffrey, 1994a, p. 1). According to Geof Hewitt (personal communication, 1999), this pressure came partly from the public's response to federal reports on education like *A Nation at Risk* (1983) which had painted a bleak portrait of American education. The public in Vermont had understandable questions about whether Vermont's public schools were working effectively during a time when the official discourse was proclaiming a crisis in schooling.

As a consequence, Commissioner Mills and his colleagues seized the opportunity to propose something innovative to the state board, a strategy like portfolio assessment, not as a way to force change in schools, but as a way to gather information. No one had suggested that the schools had reached a nadir and needed to be fixed. In fact, the Commissioner had explicitly rejected the suggestion that high stakes ought to be attached to the portfolios. According to Murnane and Levy (1996), Mills believed that such a use "would alienate teachers and jeopardize the most important goal, improving teaching in Vermont's public schools" (Murnane & Levy as cited in Darling-Hammond, 1997, p. 244). So the writing portfolio system emerged under the leadership of a commissioner who placed a premium on engaging teachers in collegial dialogue—and who had not been mandated to develop an evaluation system according to strict legislative criteria.

Context for the System

The national political climate in which Vermont's system emerged was favorable for portfolio assessment. At the time, the Bush Administration in Washington, D.C., was vigorously promoting the idea of a national test. However, there was also vigorous opposition to this idea on the grounds that a national test would likely be a standardized test which would reinforce the fragmented, low-level, skill-and-drill curriculum that researchers had identified as the major basis of the problem in the schools (Goodlad, 1984; Sizer, 1984). To diffuse this opposition, President Bush made clear through a Presidential advisory committee that he preferred a national testing program made up of diverse forms of testing, not exclusively standardized tests. For an example of a new and diverse assessment system, the advisory committee referred to new developments going on in Vermont (DeWitt, 1991).

With respect to the writing portfolio assessment system, the historic weight of this Presidential singling out of Vermont fell on the shoulders of a small committee of volunteer teachers led by Geof Hewitt, a poet and author, who served as the coordinator of the Vermont writing portfolio development team. According to his own account, if Vermont had been looking for an assessment expert to lead the way, Hewitt would probably not have been interested. He had been "writing and teaching writing residencies in schools and colleges [for the previous twenty years] . . . , always a little frustrated that [his] impact on a school seemed limited . . ." (Hewitt, 1995, p. 1). When the Vermont State Department of Education began its search for someone to organize the writing portfolio system, he was looking for something bigger to do, and the state seemed more interested in writing than measurement:

> So when I saw an ad in the local paper for a writing/secondary English consultant . . . , I interviewed for the position and bluffed my way through the question that asked about my experiences in writing assessment. I knew little about testing and had always been skeptical of the notion that one could devise a system that would fairly judge students' writing samples or measure the improvement of groups of students. Somehow, I wormed my way into the position. (Hewitt, 1995, p. 1)

As of this writing, Hewitt is still a writing consultant for the State Department in Vermont with an important role to play in the portfolio system.

In the spring of 1989 Hewitt invited seven Vermont teachers to meet with him and make recommendations to the state about how to set up a credible writing portfolio system. From the skepticism and enthusiasm of this small committee, and of teachers across the state who offered critique and feedback, came the seeds of a system which has endured throughout the decade (Vermont Department of Education, 1989)—though its rubric has changed significantly (Vermont Department of Education, 1999). As the complexity of portfolio assessment work made itself known after a few years of implementation, however, the enthusiasm among teachers wore off somewhat, and levels of skepticism rose. By the winter of 1993 teachers were complaining publicly about heavy demands on their time as the state continued to promote yet more innovations and reforms. Teachers also felt uncomfortable when schools were compared based on portfolio scores, scores that many deemed unreliable (Merina, 1993). Nonetheless, Daniel Koretz let the wider education community know through his public presentations that Vermont teachers considered this to be "a worthwhile burden" (Viadero, 1995).

Part of this discomfort began early on when psychometricians declared the portfolio system unreliable after its first official year of implementation: "In 1991–92, the quality of the data about student performance yielded by the portfolio program was so low that it severely restricted the appropriate uses of scores," wrote Koretz et al., (1993), in a summary of findings that had been reported to the Vermont Department of Education and to the state board (p. xxii). As a consequence of this report, the board decided that the portfolio data could be used at the level of state scores but could not be used to report scores back to individual schools. It is important to note that the researchers from the RAND Institute on Education and Training had relied on assumptions of the independent rater agreement model of reliability (cf. Underwood & Murphy, 1998). In this model, reliability is warranted when two or more raters agree independently in their judgments of performances. If these researchers were examining Vermont today, they might have chosen to broaden their assumptions to include qualitative lines of evidence as warrants for dependability (Moss, 1994a; 1994b) with perhaps different results. In any case, the early stigma of unreliability stayed with the system for a number of years with important influences on its history.

A number of historically important events began to take place in Vermont around 1994 which suggested that changes were coming in the writing portfolio assessment system. At a working session of the state board in February of 1994, the topic under discussion was the development of a comprehensive statewide assessment system complete with a set of standards. By February of 1995, the board had agreed on the assessment system's essential characteristics which spelled out the general and technical requirements for a statewide system. By January of 1996, the board had adopted Vermont's standards document considered by some to be a model document (FairTest, 1999) which provided a "fixed target" for the assessment system. At a meeting in November of 1996, Vermont's board agreed on a comprehensive statewide student assessment system that left room for local assessments, writing and mathematics portfolios, as well as standardized tests (Vermont Department of Education, 1996).

The board's decision in 1996 to mandate the use of standardized tests across the state represented the first time such a mandate had ever been placed on Vermont's schools. But this decision did not change Vermont's commitment to its portfolio system. "We are still committed to the portfolio," Sally Sugarman, the chairwoman of the state board, was reported to have said. "We [know] how effective portfolios have been in instruction, and teachers will want to continue to use them," she said. Doug Walker, manager of the state education department's school and instructional support team, explained that the use of standardized tests would lead to a shift in emphasis for the portfolio program: "We are trying to move away from using portfolio scores for comparing schools. Portfolios provide rich information about some very specific student skills and knowledge, but we were concerned about their use for accountability" (Manzo, 1996).

In 1996 the board also agreed to adopt *Vermont's Framework of Standards and Learning Opportunities*, a development with important implications for assessment in the state. Lawton (1996) explained that one reason for Vermont's interest in creating standards was that states like Arizona and California were setting a precedent by beginning to write their own standards for achievement. The federal government also played a part in bringing standards to Vermont. When the U.S. Congress reauthorized Title I in 1994, language in the bill required states to have "challenging" content and performance standards on the books by the 1997–98 school year. The document also required states to develop multiple-measure assessment systems aligned with their standards by the 2000–01 school year—or else forego Title I funds (Lawton, 1996). In 1994, two years before the publication of Vermont's standards document, educators began holding public forums and doing committee work across the state in preparation for writing what other states might call a "core curriculum" (Hewitt, personal communication, 1999). By 1996 a consensus document was ready to be implemented.

In February of 1997, Vermont's Supreme Court handed down a judgment which reverberated throughout the state. The justices declared that Vermont's system of funding its public schools violated the equal protection clause of the state constitution after hearing a suit originally filed by lawyers from the American Civil Liberties Union in March of 1995. The problem was that seventy percent of school funds were borne by local communities, a far greater proportion of local funding than that found in almost every other state, and some property-poor districts could not meet the standard as determined by the court despite the fact that their citizens were already being heavily taxed. Unlike the ruling in Kentucky in 1989 in which Supreme Court justices directed the legislature to make changes not just in its funding formula but also in the substance of schooling, the Vermont ruling did not stipulate a remedy but left one for the legislature to determine. Moreover, the Vermont ruling did not reach to the substance of schooling (Burge, 1997).

As a consequence of this court decision, Vermont's legislature passed the "Equal Educational Opportunity Act of 1997," otherwise known as Act 60, which set the amount of per pupil spending at $5,000 and imposed a uniform state property tax. In addition to its language with respect to educational finance, Act 60 also contained a section entitled "Educational Policy Provisions." This section required the state board and the state department to take action in a number of areas. For one thing, Act 60 required the board to continue in the direction it had been going for the past several years; that is, Act 60 required the board to develop standards for student performance and a means for assessing them and to provide schools with a clearinghouse for successful programs. There were additional requirements that were new; schools would now have to develop an Action Plan each year and prepare a report on the condition of the school for presentation to the local board (Vermont Department of Education, 1998).

Vermont educational leaders tried to accommodate both the spirit of the times and the letter of state and federal law by adopting a standardized test system and combining it with an already developed portfolio system. The standardized test would permit de-emphasizing portfolios as an accountability measure. At the same time, portfolios would provide a way to have a multiple-measures assessment system. The standardized test system would be mandatory, the portfolio system voluntary. To accomplish these objectives, Vermont turned to an old friend—the New Standards Project. NSP had developed an off-the-shelf standardized test system called the "NSP Reference Examinations." These examinations included on-demand writing prompts, passages to read followed by open-ended questions calling for written responses, and multiple-choice questions of the sort traditionally used to measure reading comprehension and editing. According to an NSP pamphlet (NSP, 1996), "What the Reference Exam does is to provide a snapshot of the kinds of work students can do in an on-demand situation. . . . It is designed to work in conjunction with a portfolio to provide additional information about student performance" (p. 1). Vermont ultimately revised its portfolio scoring system by adapting rubrics for scoring writing that NSP had developed between 1991 and 1996 when the New Standards Project created its national portfolio system. We will describe both the original and the new scoring systems in our examination of Vermont's writing portfolios.

Purposes for the System

As we have seen, an important purpose for the writing portfolio system was to create information about the effectiveness of public schooling to report to the citizens of Vermont who had been steeped in the national crisis discourse of the 1980s. But not just any school data would do. Of great historical importance is the fact that Vermont educators and policymakers alike were convinced from the beginning that standardized tests would not, indeed could not, produce the high quality of information that they wanted. Moreover, the well-documented negative impact that standardized tests have on curriculum and instruction (Madaus & Kellaghan, 1993), especially those of the multiple-choice variety, was of particular concern. The early decision against building a statewide assessment system around standardized tests was made largely because of the well-known problems associated with standardized tests, not because of a belief in the efficacy of portfolios. "This [use of portfolios] is a more difficult thing to do," Daniel Koretz was quoted as saying. "It's easy to buy a test from a contractor, spend three hours giving it, and send it off to be scored" (Rothman, 1989, p. 11).

Vermonters discussed the question of what a statewide assessment system might look like in public forums during the late 1980s just as they would later discuss the question of statewide standards in public forums beginning in 1994. From these public discussions, Vermont policymakers developed a clear understanding of the will of Vermont's teachers. Consider what Commissioner Mills had to say during the year prior to Vermont's pilot about the decision not to rely on off-the-shelf standardized tests:

> Teacher after teacher argued [that] standardized tests measure a narrow band of performance and trivialize the curriculum. . . . Others insisted there had to be a test . . . [to] show where the money goes. . . . To respond most appropriately to the concern over the lack of statewide assessment, we needed a way to combine the proven familiarity of standardized tests with something that would capture the full range of student performance. . . . We finally hit upon a unique approach, the centerpiece of which is an assessment of performance through a portfolio of student work. . . . (Mills, 1989, as cited in Tierney, Carter, & Desai, 1991, p. 158)

Unlike state legislatures in many of the 32 states that used statewide test systems at the time, the Vermont state legislature had not mandated that Commissioner Mills create a statewide testing system. As a consequence, Mills and his colleagues were not constrained by legislative language that could force them to make uneasy compromises. On the contrary, Mills had the luxury of developing his own proposal for a system and then asking the state board for its approval. "It is our responsibility to take on the issue before we are asked to," Mills was quoted as saying. "The legislature, the governor, and the public have been very generous, and have increased school funding by more than 40 percent over the past two years. We don't want to wait until the business community and legislature ask 'How well are we doing?'" (Rothman, 1989, p. 11). This freedom from legislative mandates permitted Mills and his colleagues to work closely with parents, teachers, and administrators in developing the proposal, a situation that likely goes a long way toward explaining the spirit of volunteerism among educators when the time came for the pilot.

From a scholarly perspective, Daniel Koretz and his colleagues (1994a) gave background on Vermont's early development from firsthand experience, having consulted with the department since August, 1988. According to Koretz and his colleagues, several core purposes for the portfolio system reappeared again and again in the lengthy deliberations that took place among educators and policymakers between 1988 and 1990. The following list of purposes shows the multidimensional nature of the design during this time:

1. Avoid the distortions of educational practice that conventional test-based accountability appeared to have created in some other states

2. Encourage good practice and be integrally related to the professional development of educators

3. Reflect the Vermont tradition of local autonomy, "encourage local inventiveness, [and] preserve local variations in curriculum and approach to teaching" (Mills & Brewer, 1988, pp. 3, 5)

4. Provide "a high common standard of achievement for all students" (Mills & Brewer, 1988, p. 3)

5. Encourage greater equity in educational opportunity (Koretz, et al., 1994a, p. 2)

These themes clearly place a premium on what has been called consequential validity, that is, the degree to which any measurement system enhances rather than diminishes each individual's opportunities to be a satisfied and productive human being (cf. Moss, 1994a; 1994b). System-induced problems in schooling were to be avoided while system-induced instructional enhancements were to be encouraged—all within a context of local autonomy. With few distortions and many enhancements, a high common standard might result with greater equity in opportunities to learn.

In an earlier report, Koretz and his colleagues (1993) went to some length to explain an inherent conflict in Vermont's system. According to these researchers, any system that sets out to improve instruction on the one hand while trying to measure student performance on the other faces a dilemma. If the goal is to measure student performance, the system must focus on the reliability of data, and in order to achieve reliability, the system must impose a scheme that will standardize the tasks asked of students. As a consequence, independent raters will be better able to note variations in the quality of performances with higher levels of agreement. The standardization of tasks required by this goal, however, tends to diminish the quality of teaching.

Koretz and his colleagues developed one concrete example to illustrate this point. To be fair and reliable, a standardized system must have a policy that requires teachers to give all students the same amount of help as they work on materials which might go into a portfolio. Though such a policy is very good for assessment, according to Koretz et al. (1993), it is very bad for instruction. Good instruction, in fact, requires that the teacher observe students in the act of working and then provide just the right amount of help at just the right moment of need—what we've come to call "scaffolding" in much educational literature. Here is what Koretz and his colleagues had to say about this dilemma in Vermont in 1993:

> For programs (such as Vermont's) that have both goals, success will depend on finding a working compromise between the two, deciding, for example, what

price in measurement quality is acceptable to gain additional leverage on instruction. The founders of the Vermont program, unlike many other reformers, openly confronted this dilemma at the outset, but experience is beginning to show how difficult it will be to resolve it. (Koretz et al., 1993, p. 97)

Indeed, Vermont continued to confront this dilemma head on as its system designers made changes in response to changing times.

The state department published a pamphlet entitled *"This Is My Best": Vermont's Writing Assessment Program 1990–91* which framed the "working compromise" as follows:

If writing portfolios are a good idea, an assessment program will be only one small part of what motivates their existence. Such a program will stay in place for its demonstrated value in encouraging dialogue, across the state, on what we value in writing. If that weren't so important, we could say the writing portfolio is "just a passing fad" and be done with it.

As of this writing, Vermont schools are required to participate in the state's standardized test system as a basis for developing their yearly action plans and their reports to local boards. These test scores are also factored into the state's decisions with respect to which schools need technical assistance. Although standardized scores are required, local schools have the option of using locally developed portfolio data, which the state board accepts just as readily as standardized test scores.

System Design

Vermont educators and policymakers have remained steadfast in their determination to make their writing portfolios serve teaching and learning, but judicial and political circumstances of the mid-1990s resulted in changes that tipped the balance between instructional and measurement purposes slightly. As we discuss elements of the design of the system, we will reference features of the original design and of the current design.

Collection

In the original design, guidelines for the collection of student work across time were developed by the Writing Assessment Leadership Committee, which met for the first time in the spring of 1989 (Vermont Department of Education, 1991). These guidelines remained in effect until the 1998–99 school year when the Vermont Department of Education published new requirements for a complete writing portfolio (Vermont Department of Education, 1999). As Koretz et al. (1993; 1994a; 1994b) repeatedly emphasized, Vermont's portfolios were originally "intended to permit continuing decentralized decision making and local variations in practice" (Koretz et al., 1994b, p. 5). In keeping with this intention, "teachers and students [had] nearly unconstrained choice in selecting tasks to be placed in the portfolios" given the "limited guidelines" governing what work was worth collecting established by committees made up largely of teachers (Koretz et al., 1994b, p. 6). By 1998, in keeping with the state board's adoption of Vermont's standards document in 1996 and the requirements of the Equal Opportunity Education Act of 1997, these limited guidelines and unconstrained choices had changed considerably as we will see, though the heart of the original design remained intact in the new system.

What work was worth collecting?

Beginning with the 1990–91 pilot year, students in Vermont were asked to collect writings that could demonstrate how well they "establish and maintain a clear purpose; demonstrate an awareness of audience and task; and exhibit clarity of ideas." They needed to collect pieces that showed how well they could achieve "unity and coherence" and select "details appropriate for the writer's purpose." They were asked to collect pieces that showed "personal investment and expression" and that showed a "tone . . . appropriate to the writer's purpose." Finally, they needed to collect pieces to illustrate their application of correct "usage (tense formation, agreement, word choice); mechanics (spelling, capitalization, punctuation); grammar; and sentences— as appropriate to the piece and grade level" (Vermont Department of Education, 1991).

For students in fourth grade, this collection could have included "poems, short stories, plays, or personal narrations; personal responses to a cultural, media, or sports exhibit or event; or to a book, current issue, math problem, or scientific phenomenon; and a prose piece from any curriculum area that [was] not English or Language Arts" (Vermont Department of Education, 1991, p. 7). For students in eighth grade, all of the above kinds of writing could become part of their collections, but these students were required to collect at least three prose pieces from content areas other than English. In addition to these pieces, each student was asked to select his/her one "best piece" for the year of any sort of writing and to write a letter explaining why this piece was selected. So it behooved students to maintain collections of their "best pieces" until the time for selection rolled around.

What was worth collecting changed for the 1998–99 school year to bring the writing portfolio system into alignment with Vermont's standards document. Students across the grades were asked to collect the following: a response to literature; a report; a narrative; a procedure; a persuasive piece; and a personal essay (Vermont Department of Education, 1999). Each of these types of writing had been defined in the standards under the subheading "Communication Standards."

A "response to literature" was a piece of writing in which students "show understanding of reading; connect what has been read to the broader world of ideas, concepts, and issues; and make judgments about the text" (Standard 1.7). A "report" was a piece in which students "organize and convey information and ideas accurately and effectively" (Standard 1.8). "Narratives" were defined as pieces in which students "organize and relate a series of events, fictional or actual, in a coherent whole" (Standard 1.9). "Procedures," according to a Memorandum from the Vermont Department of Education dated May 27, 1999, in which Standard 1.10 had been revised, were defined as pieces in which "students relate a series of steps that a reader can follow." A "persuasive piece" was a kind of writing in which students "judge, propose, and persuade" (Standard 1.11). While a "personal essay," again according to a department Memorandum which communicated a revision to the originally published document, was defined as a piece in which "students make connections between experience and ideas."

Who had access to and owned the collections?

The original design of the writing portfolio system seemed to leave issues of access and ownership up to local decision makers. The Writing Leadership Committee did recommend that "all students in a school should be required to keep a permanent portfolio" beginning in kindergarten and ending in twelfth grade. Along with this recommendation came the advice that students should keep "current year folders" from which work is "transferred to the permanent portfolio." Furthermore, the committee believed that "informal portfolio checks should be conducted at least once a year by the school's administrators" with "formal portfolio checks" done "by Vermont teachers . . . who will visit the school in teams of two or three reviewers" (Writing Leadership Committee, 1989). These recommendations suggested a system heavily weighted toward ownership of the portfolios by teachers and schools, but we have found no evidence that they were ever implemented.

Hewitt (1995) shed some light on ownership in Vermont in his own writing about portfolios and how best to use them. "The number one principle of managing portfolios is that the portfolio belongs to the student," Hewitt wrote. "[W]hen teachers use portfolios as if they were the assignment ('Now let's all write a piece for the portfolio!'), they place the burden of judgment before the act of creation, a pressured situation not unlike a writing test" (Hewitt, 1995, p. 67). Patricia McGonegal, a Vermont writing resource consultant involved in the development of the system from its start, also emphasized the centrality of student ownership of their work: "A portfolio will be rich to the very degree that it contains artifacts a student cares deeply about" (McGonegal as cited in Hewitt, 1995, p. 80). It will be of interest to watch developments with respect to ownership in Vermont over the next several years as students and teachers internalize the new type-specific rubrics.

Selection

Vermont's Department of Education developed a yearly calendar of events each year and circulated information to teachers through Vermont Writing Portfolio network meetings. Held several times throughout the year, network meetings offered state department personnel and local educators the opportunity to exchange information and to learn from one another. Ultimately, the selection process that led to the submission of portfolios was carried out under local control in order to meet the constraints of the state department's calendar.

Who selected artifacts for presentation?

There were no hard and fast rules governing who selected work for the portfolios. In various documents the recommendation is made that students and teachers ought to negotiate the selection of artifacts (Writing Leadership Committee, 1989; Hewitt, 1995). In other documents, evidence is presented suggesting that teachers sometimes played a big part in the selection process (Kay, Fitzgerald, Daniels, & Mellencamp, 1993). In keeping with the norm of local autonomy, from what we can tell the selection process varied across schools and grade levels.

What was the purpose for selection?

Vermont's teachers have never taught under legislation that obligated them to assign all of their students the task of creating writing portfolios that could be scored externally in a state audit, though Act 60 imposed the requirement that schools put forward a *sample* of mathematics and writing portfolios for state-level scoring. Moreover, the power of the state to reward and sanction teachers or schools for particular levels of performance on portfolios has never been invoked. In light of these noncoercive circumstances and the voluntary nature of the system, it seems plausible to argue that the purpose for selection was to discover how well students were writing.

What did students think about the purpose for selection? Kay, et al. (1993) interviewed students and parents to find out. One fourth grade boy responded as follows: "They're sent away to the state and it's for the state to see how well you explain things and how you come up with things, even if you got the wrong answer. It's to see if you have a neat thought process, to see if you have original ideas." An eighth grade boy came to a bit different conclusion: "I think they want a different way to test us rather than the regular format of the A, B, C, or D. You know how they're always saying about Japanese kids being smarter. I think they actually want to tell us how good we are."

Who was the audience for the presentation?

Early design documents recommended that local teachers make use of writing portfolios during conferences with both students and parents (Writing Leadership Committee, 1989; Vermont Department of Education, 1991). This recommendation seemed to reinforce the theme of local ownership and autonomy that permeated the design. However, it was also clear that external reviewers would examine at least a sample of portfolios from any given school. The idea was that through this process Vermont teachers would gradually internalize a common set of values with respect to what constitutes good writing. From what we can tell, the primary audience for the portfolios was Vermont teachers, many of whom volunteered for the work in order to promote improved writing instruction across the state.

Reflection

Vermont's Writing Leadership Committee took the position early on that encouraging students to reflect on their writing processes and products would be a key to the ultimate effectiveness of the portfolio system as a factor in instructional improvement. "Every mode of writing instruction comes down to the confrontation between the student and the blank page," the committee wrote in its first design pamphlet. "The writing process addresses that gap with a repertoire of strategies for each of the stages that writers go through. . . ." (Writing Leadership Committee, 1989, p. 5). In order for students to learn to control their own individual processes, teachers would need to help them become aware of themselves as writers during the composition of individual pieces and across a span of composition events.

Teachers, too, would need to practice reflective analysis in order to benefit from the portfolios. Indeed, the original criteria for school-level portfolio review teams included references to the nature of student writing over time in areas that portfolios are uniquely suited to examine: "Is there progress from earliest dated to most recently dated work?" "Is there evidence of sufficient variety to challenge all students and to allow each student an opportunity for success?" "How much evidence is there of teacher/peer responses to the student's drafts and opportunities for revision by the student?" (Tierney, et al., 1991, p. 161).

Hewitt (personal communication, 1999) acknowledged that the adoption of type-specific, holistic scoring rubrics subsequent to the development of state standards altered the balance between process/reflection and product in the system: "It is true that the analytic rubric [the old rubric], because of its generic nature, was more oriented toward writing process than the new rubrics, which focus, more specifically, on the necessary elements of each type of writing," Hewitt wrote in an email. In a 1998 letter to "Vermont Educators," however, Hewitt indicated that the state department planned to take steps to help teachers translate data from the new type-specific rubrics to the old analytical method: "November's writing network meetings will feature a discussion of the new Vermont writing rubrics. How do we apply a holistic scale to student writing while keeping a focus on [the original five dimensions of good writing as the founding committee determined them]?"

What opportunities for reflection did the system provide?

A primary opportunity for reflection was the "best piece" element of the original design. Each student was to select his/her "best piece" of writing for the year. This piece could have been written in any class; in fact, the piece did not have to address an academic subject at all. The Writing Leadership Committee decided to include this element in the design "in the expectation that it would help depict what students value in their own writing, that the process of its choosing would encourage students to reflect on their work, and that the evaluation of this piece would be especially helpful to the student writer" (Vermont Department of Education, 1991). The "best piece" was to be accompanied by a letter to the reviewer explaining the reasons for the choice and the process of its composition. Of interest was the fact that the best piece was assessed separately from the portfolio, though the five dimensions of the portfolio rubric were applied to these pieces.

Teaching students to "value" their writing had been on the minds of committee members for some time. In October of 1990, several members took a trip to Durham, New Hampshire, and talked with Donald Graves about his work with students in the area of "valuing" as a crucial aspect of writing. Committee members also talked with Graves about his related notion of "nudging" writers. Graves (1983) had written extensively about "valuing" as a skill foundational to effectiveness during revision: If students can't place a value on information in their writings, they have no way of making decisions about what to keep and what to cut. Moreover, the notion of "nudging" was important instructionally because it was through this technique that teachers could help students learn to develop skill in "valuing."

Donald Graves gave these members advice that made its way back to Vermont's design. He told them that students often were unable to explain why they selected certain pieces from their folders because they got little practice in doing so; the norm was for someone else to tell them whether their writing was good or bad. Clearly, the answer lay in changing this norm through a strategy like "best piece." Graves also told the committee members that teachers had an important role to play in moving students into new areas of writing through "nudges":

> A nudge is a request to experiment. Students ought to be trying new approaches to writing. Nudging helps students to keep their writing fresh and demonstrate a better range of genres and approaches to writing. . . . Here are some examples of nudges: "Take five minutes and underline the verbs in this first paragraph. Okay, then make three of them a little more precise." [Or] "In this piece you have introduced some characters, but I'm curious about what they look like. Take this scrap of paper and choose one of the characters. Write for five minutes showing your character." (Donald Graves as cited in Hewitt, 1995, p. 152–153)

In a larger sense, one might characterize the Vermont writing portfolio system itself as a giant "nudge" for teachers in the state, a request—or an invitation—to experiment that was widely accepted, carefully monitored, and thoughtfully debated.

Student Voices

Vermont's system design, as we have seen, originated as an effort not just to accommodate, but to promote student reflective analysis on both writing processes and products. As Hewitt (1995) wrote, "More than anything, the teacher is fostering an attitude: My work does matter. I'll save it and think about it, making decisions about the future of each piece of my writing. . . . I recognize that the purposes for writing extend way beyond the system" (p. 72). In the spirit of fostering such an attitude, Steven Borck's teacher, Mrs. Houston, who taught fourth grade at Wolcott Elementary, asked Steven and his peers at the end of each marking period to reflect on where they had been, where they were, and where they wanted to go as writers. Here are Steven's responses to one of those opportunities for reflection:

Third Marking Period

Steven Borck
4–27–93

1. How have you changed as a writer since fourth grade started? I have changed as a writer since fourth grade started because I now use more voice and tone, humor, and descriptive words.
2. What type of writing do you most enjoy? Why? I enjoy journaling the most because it's a good way to exprees your thoughts and emotions.
3. We've published our writing several ways. What was your favorite way? My favorite way of publishing my writing was when we gave it someone as a gift.
4. A third grader has asked you about writing in Mrs. Houston's room. What will you tell him? I would tell him that you get to use your imagination a lot and you have to make your writing interesting.
5. Is there anything you would like to see changed in the way we do writing? No I don't think so. I think our writing process is very efficient.
6. If you had the chance to describe the "fun" part of writing, what would you say? I would say that the "fun" part would be when it's all done and I am proud of it.

Steven's newfound sense of voice, tone, and humor showed up in the selection he made for his "best piece." Below we reproduce this selection and follow it with Steven's reflections as to why he selected the piece, how it was composed, and how the piece works.

Me

Yours truly came out of his mother on June tenth, nineteen eighty three in Connecticut. I went camping in Virginia when I was one, I repeat ONE YEAR OLD! Steven Peter Borck moved to Vermont when he was only four!

I think this family is really hung up on the number four, I mean we have *four* people in the house, *four* pets and I moved to Vermont when I was *four*! I have a mother, a father, and a brother, but, thank God, no sisters! My brother is okay, but sometimes he's so incredibly stupid I wonder why he has enough smarts to even talk!

There are only three words to describe school boring, boring, boring! That's what school's like for me. My favorite subject in school is art.

When I get out of college, I will be a scientist. I will invent a time machine! I will also invent a way to keep from aging and a way to clean up all the pollution on earth. Well, I hope you enjoyed my story.

By Steven P. Borck

Although we have no information to report about Steven Borck's subsequent growth as a writer and can say nothing about his progress with respect to solving the problems of aging and pollution, we can provide insight into his self-perceptions at the time he wrote the essay titled "Me." The following is a letter he wrote to his portfolio reviewer at the time:

Wollcott Elementary School
Wollcott, Vermont
April 28, 1993

Dear Reader,

I picked "Me" as my best piece because it has a lot of humor, (at least the second grade thought so!) voice and tone, and it explains my life and possibly the future of my life. It also introduces my life before it introduces my writing. I started "Me" with a couple of clusters on snowflakes for each paragraph. Then he grew into a couple of pages referred to as a rough draft. We gave him a sheild. I don't know why though. Then he evolved into a more formal form known as a second draft. Finally, he grew into a good-mannered, young final draft; but just for the heck of it we sharp pencil conferenced him to make him look good. I write with humor you see and my voice and tone are what you'd expect from a fourth grader who watches TV too much.

Sincerely,
Steven Borck

(Steven P. Borck's letter explaining why he picked "Me" and his "Third Marking Period Writing Reflections" are reprinted from *A Portfolio Primer: Teaching, Collecting, and Assessing Student Writing*, copyright (c) 1995 by Geof Hewitt, with permission from Geof Hewitt and Steven Borck.)

Evaluation

The original design of the scoring aspect of the system was what the Writing Leadership Committee called "an analytic scale" (see Figure 8.1). This scale consisted of five "dimensions" of good writing—purpose, organization, details, voice/tone, and a combination of usage, mechanics, and grammar—which were applied across all of the pieces in a portfolio such that five different dimensional scores could be reported. In this way, schools were expected to be able to use scoring data to help them refine their writing instructional programs by considering the percentages of their students who were rated as performing at certain levels within dimensions—and the portfolio system would then not have to specify particular writing assignments or tasks. For example, a school with a high percentage of students who did well in grammar and mechanics but a lesser percentage of students who did well in voice/tone might consider modifying instruction accordingly. The use of the five-dimension analytic rubric also furthered the intent of the Writing Advisory Committee to thwart attempts of journalists and others to rank schools easily in the media. From single portfolio scores, means could be easily computed, and schools could be ranked according to their mean scores. Having five separate scores meant comparing schools with five separate means, a messier picture indeed, one "less susceptible to a 'horse-race' interpretation of school differences." (Koretz et al., 1994b, p. 9)

From what we can tell, giving writing assignments and requiring that students craft "forms" (Lucas, 1988a; 1988b) were not respectable instructional tacks in Vermont, though they were prevalent. Of interest in this regard are the words of a Vermont teacher who was reflecting on what s/he had seen during the scoring of pilot year portfolios:

> A lot of very prescriptive assignments. I mean not only the assignment outlined, but the form, sentence by sentence, of the assignment outlined. Barf. I personally am never again going to assign something I don't feel like reading. (Vermont Department of Education, 1991, p. 13)

The analytic scoring guide would be applied to three separate sets of evidence: the portfolios themselves, the "best piece" in isolation from the portfolios, and an on-demand writing sample composed in response to a uniform prompt. Hewitt (1993) reported that there was some controversy about whether to apply the dimensional scoring rubric or a holistic rubric to the prompted, on-demand writings. Not surprisingly, teachers had been upset about the decision to collect a prompted writing sample at all: "How can I ask my students to write to an external prompt in a timed situation when all year I've been teaching them 'the writing process'?" many asked (Hewitt, 1993, p. 3).

Finally, things came to a head, and the teachers and administrators had a show down which foreshadowed a debate that would take place again several years in the future:

> In March, when the committee finally met to discuss the prompt, a two-hour debate erupted over [how the on-demand writing would be scored], a debate that raged between the committee [who argued for the dimensional scoring] and my supervisor ([who argued for] holistic—it won't cost as much as the complicated five-feature system). Here's one the committee won. . . . (Hewitt, 1993, p. 3)

After half a decade had passed, however, the subject came up again, and this time the supervisors won. As of this writing, Vermont is now using separate holistic scoring rubrics that are constructed according to writing types (see Figures 8.2, 8.3, and 8.4 for examples). It is too early to tell whether this scoring design will have a negative impact on writing instruction by promoting prescriptive assignments narrowly tailored to the values of the rubrics.

Figure 8.1
Vermont Writing Assessment
Analytic Assessment Guide

	Purpose	Organization	Details	Voice/Tone	Usage, Mechanics Grammer
In Assessing, Consider . . .	the degree to which the writer's response • establishes and maintains a clear purpose • demonstrates an awareness of audience and task • exibits clarity of ideas	the degree to which the writer's response illustrates • unity • coherence	the degree to which the writer's details are appropriate for the writer's purpose and support the main point(s) of the writer's response	the degree to which the writer's response reflects personal, investment and expression	the degree to which the writer's response exhibits correct • usage (e.g., tense formation, agreement, word choice) • mechanics—spelling, capitalization, punctuation • grammar • sentences as appropriate to the piece and grade level
Extensively	• Establishes and maintains clear purpose • Demonstrates a clear understanding of audience and task • Exhibits ideas that are developed in depth	• Organized from beginning to end • Logical progression of ideas • Clear focus • Fluent, cohesive	• Details are effective, vivid, explicit, and/or pertinent	• Distinctive voice evident • Tone enhances personal expression	• Few, if any, errors are evident relative to length and complexity
Frequently	• Establishes a purpose • Demonstrates an awareness of audience and task • Develops ideas, but they may be limited in depth	• Organized but may have minor lapses in unity or coherence	• Details are elaborated and appropriate	• Evidence of voice • Tone appropriate for writer's purpose	• Some errors are present

cont.

Figure 8.1 *cont.*

Sometimes	• Attempts to establish a purpose • Demonstrates some awareness of audience and task • Exhibits rudimentary development of ideas	• Inconsistencies in unity and/or coherence • Poor transitions • Shift in point of view	• Details lack elaboration or are repetitious	• Evidence of beginning sense of voice • Some evidence of appropriate tone	• Multiple errors and/or patterns of errors are evident
Rarely	• Does not establish a clear purpose • Demonstrates minimal awareness of audience and task • Lacks clarity of ideas	• Serious errors in organization • Thought patterns difficult, if not impossible, to follow • Lacks introduction and/or conclusion • Skeletal organization with brevity	• Details are random, inappropriate, or barely apparent	• Little or no voice evident • Tone absent or inappropriate for writer's purpose	• Errors are frequent and severe
Non-Scorable (NS)	• is illegible: i.e., includes so many undecipherable words that no sense can be made of the response. – or – • is incoherent: i.e., words are legible but syntax is so garbled that response makes no sense. – or – • is a blank paper.				

Reprinted with permission of the Vermont State Department of Education.

Figure 8.2
DRAFT VERMONT NEW STANDARDS RUBRIC FOR
Narrative Writing: Writing to Tell a Story
Standard 1.9 In written narratives, students organize and relate a series of events, fictional or actual, in a coherent whole

Criteria	Score Point 5 *Exceeds the Standard*	Score Point 4 *Accomplished Writing*	Score Point 3 *Intermediate Writing*	Score Point 2 *Basic Writing*	Score Point 1 *Limited Writing*	Score Point 0 *Unscorable*
CONTEXT, PURPOSE • Establishes situation, point of view, conflict, and plot, as necessary.	Score point 5 meets all the criteria in score point 4. In addition, a paper receiving this score renders a particularly dramatic recreation of events.	Establishes the situation by setting the action of the story within a clearly described time and place (Purpose).	Establishes adequate context	May give vague sense of context (Purpose).	Little or no context presented (Purpose).	There is no evidence of an attempt to write a narrative piece.
	Shows insight into the characters' motivation and the significance of events (Purpose).	Presents main characters effectively.	Presents characters in somewhat stereotypical fashion.	Identifies characters.	May list characters.	
		Maintains clear topic and focus (Purpose).	Establishes story line, with topic and focus.	Establishes story topic; attempts focus (Purpose).	Presents topic; no focus.	
		Narrator may reflect on the importance of events (Purpose).	Relies on a narrow range of strategies to develop story line.			
NARRATIVE STRATEGIES: VOICE/TONE AND ELABORATION (DETAILS) • showing the character in action • using dialogue to reveal character and advance action	Uses lively and concrete language; e.g., similes and metaphors (Details, Voice/ Tone).	Creates a believable world, real or fictional, developing action by dramatizing rather than telling what happens (Details).	Some strategies such as dialogue, used with effectiveness (Details).	May use some dialogue (Details). May have problems with pacing.	May list some generic details in a haphazard manner.	

cont.

(Reprinted with permission of the Vermont State Department of Education.)

Figure 8.2 cont.					
• dramatizing scenes • managing time through straightforward chronology, flashbacks, episodes and transition, foreshadowing • provides character motivation	Some language and images may invite readers to reflect on the significance of the events (Voice/Tone). Reveals a strongly individual voice. Uses a variety of sentence structures and length purposefully (Voice/Tone.)	Develops characters through effective use of dialogue, action, behavior, relationships with other characters (Details). Shows character growth or change or comments on significance of experience. Relevant, concrete details enable readers to imagine the world of the story or experience.	Some details may be generic, but they advance action and describe characters' personalities and actions.	Characters are often stereotypes, lacking motivation for actions (Details). May list rather than develop details.	May not describe characters (Details).
		Word choice is precise; uses a variety of sentence structures (Voice/Tone).	Generally uses predictable language Voice/Tone). May vary sentence length and type (Voice/Tone).	Some inappropriate word choices (Voice/Tone). Little variety of sentence structure or length (Voice/Tone).	Little attention to word choice (Voice/Tone). Usually short, simple sentences (Voice/Tone).
		Organized in a dramatically effective way.	Has a clear beginning, middle and end (Organization).	May lack effective beginning and/or ending or have an abrupt conclusion (Organization).	May have major gaps in coherence (Organization).
		Has an engaging beginning and moves through a series of events to a logical, satisfying ending (Organization).	Presents characters and events in such a way that readers can easily follow the story line (Organization).	May present characters and the sequence of events in a predictable way (Organization). Relies on straightforward "and then" chronology (Organization).	

Figure 8.3
DRAFT VERMONT NEW STANDARDS RUBRIC FOR
Report: Writing to Inform
Standard 1.8 In written reports, students organize and convey information and ideas accurately and effectively

Criteria	Score Point 5 *Exceeds the Standard*	Score Point 4 *Accomplished Writing*	Score Point 3 *Intermediate Writing*	Score Point 2 *Basic Writing*	Score Point 1 *Limited Writing*	Score Point 0 *Unscorable*
PURPOSE/STANCE, VOICE/TONE Topic/focus (Controlling idea) • Evidence of gathered information • Analysis of a situation followed by a suggested course of action • Prediction of possible outcomes of a situation • Appropriate stance • Anticipation of reader needs	Meets all the criteria listed in Score point 4 <u>and</u> uses strategies not always thought of for reporting information— e.g., personal anecdotes or dramatization impart information in an entertaining way.	A sense of Purpose, stated strongly or implied, unifies and focuses the report.	States controlling idea/focus but may not use it effectively to unify report.	Defines subject with a simple statement rather than controlling idea/focus.	May only state topic.	No evidence of an attempt to write a report.
		Shows a clear sense of direction appropriate to its <u>purpose</u>.	Shows evidence of having a general rather than a focused <u>purpose</u> in presenting information.	Conveys a lack of evident <u>purpose</u>.	Rarely conveys writer's intent.	
	Precise use of language conveys intent clearly and concisely.	Stance is that of a knowl-edgeable person presenting relevant information (<u>voice/tone</u>).	Stance is that of a person who has a desire to convey gathered information but sense of audience is vague (<u>voice/tone</u>).	Stance conveys less authority than seen in higher scoring paper. May be a monotone (<u>voice/tone</u>).	Stance is undeveloped. Monotone (<u>voice/tone</u>). Seems unaware of reader concerns or needs; no context.	
	The writer may reflect on the significance of the information.					
	Shows an exceptional awareness of readers' concerns and needs.	Context is clear throughout.	Establishes sufficient context.	May offer little context.		
ORGANIZATION AND COHERENCE • Appropriate patterns: chronological; historical; specific to general;	May demonstrate and unusual pattern or framework in which to embed information.	Organized in a pattern or framework suited to purpose, audience and context.	Generally uses predictable pattern.	Usually shows an organized plan but may have digressions.	Shows little or no evidence of purposeful <u>organization</u>.	

cont.

This rubric is adapted from materials created by the New Standards Project.
(Reprinted with permission of the Vermont State Department of Education.)

Figure 8.3 cont.						
general to specific; causal; sequential; other, appropriate for specific report • Overall coherence	May make useful connections between the information presented and other knowledge and experience.	Strong overall coherence and balance; uses transitions. Tight construction without extraneous material.	Has overall coherence; uses some transitions.	Has general coherence; stays on topic but may show weak transitions between paragraphs or sentences.	May lack coherence; no transitions.	
		Compelling opening, strong informative body, and satisfying conclusion (<u>organization</u>).	Clear beginning, middle, and end; may provide considerable information.	May have lengthy opening and abrupt closure; may present random bits of information.		
ELABORATION STRATEGIES, DETAILS • using specific concrete strategies • comparing, contrasting		Uses a variety of elaboration strategies effectively and appropriately; cites references as needed.	General information, not well-supported by concrete example (<u>details</u>).	Relies on general rather than specific <u>details</u>. May use irrelevant details, often presented in a list.	Random, disconnected, and/or unfocused opinions with some scattered facts.	
• naming, describing • reporting conversation • reviewing the history • explaining the possibilities • creating a scenario	The writer is extremely selective in presenting information, including relevant material and excluding that which would clutter the report.	Selects <u>details</u> relevant to the topic, purpose, and audience. Provides depth of information.	Some information may be irrelevant.	May rely on opinion rather than facts.	Presents very little information.	

Figure 8.4
DRAFT VERMONT NEW STANDARDS RUBRIC FOR **8th GRADE**
WRITING CONVENTIONS: GRAMMAR, USAGE, MECHANICS
Standard 1.6. Students' independent writing demonstrates command of appropriate English conventions, including grammar, usage, and mechanics.

Criteria	Score Point 5 Exceeds the Standard	Score Point 4 Accomplished Writing	Score Point 3 Intermediate Writing	Score Point 2 Basic Writing	Score Point 1 Limited Writing	Score Point 0 Unscorable
See grade-specific lists that enumerate 5th and 8th grade expectations, respectively, in: • sentence structure • formatting • capitalization • punctuation • spelling • grammar/usage Writing must be of sufficient length and complexity to demonstrate mastery.	Meets all the criteria listed for Score Point 4, <u>and</u> successfully handles conventions that are above grade level. There may be an occasional lapse resulting from the student's attempt to handle complexities in ideas or style or lapses appear intentional and effectively support the writer's purpose.	Writing generally shows control of the conventions of grammar, usage, mechanics and spelling. There may be some minor errors, but these errors do not divert the reader's attention or cause confusion about the writer's meaning. Lapses in grammar, usage, mechanics, and spelling appear to be intentional and support the writer's purpose	N/A Score point 3 is Not Applicable to this criterion.	Writing shows some control in the conventions of grammar, usage, mechanics, and spelling. Writing exhibits frequent errors which may be distracting to readers and may cause some confusion about the writer's meaning.	Writing shows little control of the conventions of grammar, usage, machanics, and spelling. Writing demonstrates serious and numerous problems which distract the reader and lead to confusion. Writing may be incoherent in places.	Score point 0 is not applicable to this criterion.

cont.

(Reprinted with permission of the Vermont State Department of Education)

Figure 8.4 cont.

8th GRADE EXPECTATIONS

Sentence structure
No unintentional fragments
No run-ons (Over-coordinated sentences are noted as a matter of rhetorical effectiveness)
No dangling participles/modifiers

Formatting
Poperly indented or blocked paragraphs
Properly placed hyphens when word is divided at the end of a line

Capitalization
Basic capitalization rules
Beginnings of sentences and quotes
Proper nouns

Punctuation
Internal and external punctuation involving quotation marks
Quotation marks around direct quotes
Commas after introductory clauses or phrases
Correct use of commas in dates, between city and state, and before conjunctions that join clauses
Commas before an aside with appositives, with two or more equally modifying adjectives, with transitional and parenthetical expressions, in direct address, and other standard comma rules

Commas or semi-colons for items in a series
Proper end punctuation
Apostrophes for contractions and possessives

Spelling
Correct spelling of high frequency words; plurals and word endings of grade-level words (check local curriculum); proper names and vocabulary unique to the topic; non-standard plurals; compound words; homonyms
No typographical errors

Grammar/Usage
Correct case of pronouns (subjective/objective)
No unclear pronoun antecedents or reference
Agreement of pronouns and antecedents
Agreement of subject and verb
Consistent verb tenses are in agreement
Correct use of common, non-standard verb forms
No word omissions resulting in grammatical errors
Correct use of homonyms
Correct use of commonly misused words

---

1. Awkward sentences, grammatically correct, are considered a matter of rhetorical effectiveness (see type-specific rubric).
2. Several complete ideas or facts connected by "and," if correctly punctuated, are likewise scored as part of the rhetorical effectiveness. Run-ons caused by missing end punctuation/ initial capitalization are noted as errors in GUM.
3. One sentence paragraphs, which have been properly indented or blocked, are not considered an error.
4. Typographical errors count as spelling errors. Students should correctly spell all grade-appropriate words *and any vocabulary or names that are unique to their topic.* Misspelled and misused homonyms count as GUM errors.

5. Word omission that results in a grammatical error is a GUM error.
   ERRORS IN *ITALICS* ARE NOT CONSIDERED SERIOUS AT THIS GRADE-LEVEL

   Faulty parallelism
   Misplaced hyphens in hyphenated words
   Comma after a short introductory phase is optional if meaning is clear
   Commas in non-restrictive phrases and clauses
   Incorrect plural possessives
   Failure to use subjunctive verb in hypothetical clauses
   Split infinitives
   Omission of possessive before a gerund

What was the role of evaluation in the system?

Hewitt (1993) described another early debate that took place around the question of whether the portfolios should be scored at all. The design would call for an on-demand, prompted piece of writing, a single "best piece" written in the classroom over time but scored apart from the portfolio, and the portfolio itself. "Assess a uniform, prompted writing sample, assess the best piece, but leave the writing portfolio for instruction purposes only," Hewitt reported as the dominant line of thinking coming from the development committee. "At the time, I was swayed by the persuasive skills of my fellow committee members," he continued, "but two years later the enormous value of assessing the portfolios became clear: students and teachers quickly internalize criteria when they consistently view their own and each other's writing through a common lens. And because of the assessment, teachers have the opportunity to glimpse what is happening in others' classrooms" (p. 2). It is important to note that Vermont portfolios have always been scored by Vermont classroom teachers, and the scoring sessions themselves have become part of a culture of staff development in the state (Hewitt, personal communication, 1999).

Other observers, however, found that teachers were not so quick to internalize the scoring criteria. During a scoring session in which teachers were rating essays written in response to the uniform prompt, a kind of scoring that offered much less challenge than that offered by whole collections of writings, Daniel Koretz and his colleagues (1994b) noted that raters demonstrated "considerable confusion . . . about the interpretation and application of the rubrics," and they "sometimes disagreed about which scoring dimension was germane to a specific attribute of a given piece." These RAND researchers concluded that the problem arose not just from the language of the rubrics, but also from "Vermont's unconventional and ambiguous delineation of genres" (Koretz et al., 1994b, p. 12).

On the other hand, Koretz and his colleagues (1994b) emphasized that efforts to homogenize and standardized elements of the portfolio system could

isolate assessment tasks from ongoing instruction, lessen the role of classroom teachers, focus attention on limited assessment tasks rather than on the continuing record of student work, and preclude the use of the assessment as a direct window on instruction. *Perhaps most important, it would lessen (or at least make more indirect) teachers' incentives to reform instruction on a daily basis* [emphasis added]. (p. 14)

Thus, although evaluation was important in the system, it was not important enough to risk isolating and fragmenting the work of teachers in classrooms.

It is wrong, however, to conclude that evaluation had no importance in Vermont. Its importance was embedded in the culture and history of public schooling in the state from the mid-1980s forward. Recall that Vermont's education commissioner had explicitly rejected the idea of attaching stakes to the portfolio system. However, he had insisted that the portfolios had value: "[T]he assessments do count," he was quoted as saying; "[T]hey are important because they are credible to teachers, parents, and community members, who believe they measure important abilities in authentic ways. The state's involvement of large numbers of teachers and community members in designing and discussing the assessments and its widespread reporting of results produce a medium-stakes environment for the assessment that has proved productive" (Richard Mills as cited in Darling-Hammond, 1997, pp. 244–245).

As the 1990s drew to a close, Vermont faced growing pressure to find ways to ensure that its public schools were providing equitable and effective opportunities for students to learn and grow. As we have seen, the changing political context brought about a change in how writings done by Vermont children were to be valued. In a system concerned in its formative discussions with the role of valuing as an act of student self-assessment, such a change in values is non-trivial. Moreover, recent functional discourse (letters, pamphlets, and the like) involving department leaders and teachers seems to have become peppered with more occurrences of words like "required contents" and "must be available when requested by the department" and "not acceptable." On the other hand, amidst a cluster of "writing portfolio teacher tips 1998–99" was this statement: "Poetry is invited as an 'Other.' Although it will not be scored, its inclusion now will help us develop an assessment process." It is comforting to know that at least somewhere in the current measurement and accountability frenzy, someone still has plans to teach and assess poetry.

NOTE: In the margins of a near final draft of this chapter, Geof Hewitt told us that as of May 27, 1999, teachers in Vermont were expected to teach students to write poetry. Standard 1.23 was drafted and added as a revision to Vermont's standards document as follows: "In writing poetry, students use a variety of forms." The standards document continued thusly:

This is evident when students:

Evidence preK–4	*Evidence preK–4 applies plus—*	*Evidence pre K–8 applies plus—*
1. Write poems with a purpose and an awareness of audience 2. Use words for their sounds and texture, as well as their meaning	3. Write poems in a variety of voices for a variety of audiences 4. Use figurative language and descriptive words and phrases in their poems 4. Write poems using dialogue, character setting, and plot; and 5. Write poems that express mood, thought or feeling.	6. Write poems that include the observance and intentional nonobservance of conventions

Scholars will watch with interest as interrater reliability data are collected with respect to this particular standard.

How did the system ensure validity and fairness?

Reliability has long been the bane of the Vermont portfolio assessment system. After reporting a number of positive consequences for instruction attributable to the portfolio system, Koretz et al. (1994b) summarized their findings with respect to reliability in two telling sentences: "Rater reliability was very low in both subjects [mathematics and writing] in the first year of statewide implementation. It improved appreciably in 1993 in mathematics but not in writing" (p. 7)—indeed, reliability in mathematics had nowhere to go but up. Here we report a summary of a lengthy and complex set of findings (Koretz et al., 1994a; 1994b):

1. On individual pieces scored on single dimensions in 1992 and 1993, Spearman rank-order correlations between independent raters clustered at .40.
2. Dimension-level scores which combined scores for all of the pieces in a portfolio across a single dimension were not any better.
3. Portfolio-level scores which combined data across all pieces and dimensions resulted in correlations around .60.

Demonstrating reliability with warrants in traditional psychometric assumptions has continued to be a worry for Vermont, but the department has not used portfolio scores to make decisions about individual students nor to reward and sanction teachers or schools, rather to focus professional development and bring coherence to writing instructional programs. Perhaps Vermont has been worrying with little reason.

What about validity? When Koretz, et al. (1994b) tried to establish the validity of Vermont's writing portfolio system, they ran into a number of problems. First, rater reliability was so poor that student-level scores could not be given with any confidence. Operating on the assumption that where reliability is poor validity cannot be good, Koretz and his colleagues were reluctant to even talk about validity in Vermont's portfolios (but see Moss, 1994a, 1994b, for an opposing perspective on this assumption). Second, though some schools gave locally determined standardized tests, there were no uniform statewide standardized test data available in Vermont to use as statistical anchors in an effort to establish "convergent" and "divergent" validity, that is, the extent of agreement between the instrument in question and other instruments commonly accepted as valid measures of a construct (convergent) and the extent of disagreement between the instrument and other instruments which have been validated for different constructs (divergent). Third, grading practices varied widely even within schools, not to mention between schools, rendering any analysis based on classroom grades highly suspect.

Koretz and his colleagues had two remaining options for establishing the convergent validity of the portfolio system. First, they could examine the relationship between the best piece scores and scores on the rest of the portfolio. In fact, the correlation coefficients between the best piece and the rest were quite high after disattenuation for unreliability, ranging from .77 in fourth grade to .89 in eighth grade (Koretz, et al., 1993, p. 39). These statistics appeared to suggest that there was some validity to the portfolios. However, because rater reliability for both the best piece scores and the rest scores was so poor, the researchers chose not to trust them and instead to examine the relationship between scores on the state's on-demand essay written in response to a uniform prompt and scores on the portfolios (rater reliability on the uniform writing prompt was high, ranging from .82 to .87 [p. 51]). What they found suggested that the system had at least some validity: "After disattenuating for rater unreliability, . . . the correlations on the portfolio and Uniform Test were moderate, ranging from .47 to .59" (p. 83).

Koretz and his colleagues decided to examine the relationship between scores on the writing portfolios and scores on the mathematics Uniform Test, a mixed-format test combining multiple-choice and open-ended items designed and scored by a commercial testing company, for evidence of divergent validity. Presumably, scores on this mathematics test and scores on the writing portfolios should not correlate well, since each assessment was intended to measure a different construct. However, even though the researchers "considered only scores from multiple-choice items and ignored [mathematics] items that required writing," writing portfolio scores correlated more highly with the mathematics uniform test than they did with the uniform writing test (p. 84) with respect to the fourth grade data. The reverse was true for eighth grade. Consequently, some evidence suggested that the writing portfolio system was valid while other evidence told the opposite story.

Scoring of collections of work reliably is ordinarily considered more difficult than the scoring of individual student responses to a fixed, uniform task as in a prompt, especially if the collections differ in genres and levels of task difficulty (Moss, 1994a; Nystrand, Cohen & Dowling, 1993). Evaluators of the Vermont portfolio assessment program cited "the tremendous diversity (lack of standardization) of tasks across portfolios" as an explanation for low rater reliability and for low score reliability (how dependably student scores generalize to other writing tasks) (Koretz, et al., 1994a, p. 43). Despite expert advice on how to standardize the design and improve rater reliability, however, the Vermont system did not change its open-ended design—until 1998. Time will tell whether Vermont is successful in translating its original analytic scoring system, which down played the role of uniform tasks in assessment and instruction, to a type-specific holistic scoring system with more specification of task.

Issues of Impact

The story of the impact of the Vermont writing portfolio system on schooling in the state is fraught with ironies. First, the system has survived for almost a decade with the sustained support of teachers, administrators, state department personnel, education commissioners, and state board members, but it has never carried much political and economic weight in the way that SAT scores, standardized test scores, and the like, do. Under ordinary circumstances one might expect most stakeholders to ignore such politically uncharged data, but not in Vermont. Second, the portfolio system emerged from the bottom up and grew in a direction that opposed the prevailing winds of top-down, bureaucratic accountability (Darling-Hammond, 1989), and only now after it has stood the test of time has the scoring system been changed in a way that could better support a bureaucratic accountability model. Regardless of this change, it seems unlikely that the tradition of local autonomy in Vermont, as the product of its very geography and history, will permit the kind of technical, mechanistic, routinized instruction found in larger states that have turned the clock back to a factory model, to take hold in its little patch of New England.

Impact on Learning and Teaching

Koretz and his colleagues (1993; 1994a; 1994b) reported extensively on the impact of the Vermont portfolio systems on learning and teaching in the schools. Unfortunately for our purposes, their focus was on the mathematics portfolio system. A full chapter in the 1993 report and two chapters in the 1994a report are devoted to such questions as—"How much change in class time devoted to certain topics is attributable to portfolios?" and "What about the amount of time students worked in small groups and pairs? Did it increase?"—but all of these data speak to the mathematics portfolio.

In the writing of Geof Hewitt and in the publications of the department of education we can glean some insight into the impact. For example, Hewitt reported that in the early 1990s the design committee collected 1,400 portfolios at random from across the state in order to identify "benchmark" pieces that would illustrate each of the four levels of accomplishment along each of the five original dimensions. These benchmarks would be used to calibrate teachers at a centralized scoring session where teachers would exchange portfolios, score their colleagues' portfolios on the basis of the benchmarks, and then go home to score their own portfolios and compare their scores with those issued by other teachers. Hewitt (1993) reported on findings from this benchmarking session and the impact the system had on teachers:

> What did we see when we collected 1,400 writing portfolios for random perusal . . . ? [W]e saw the whole imaginable range of fourth and eighth grade writing. In classrooms where the program had clearly not been welcomed by the teacher, . . . we found . . . a sheaf of worksheets and short-answer quizzes photocopied from workbooks. . . . [I]n the following year's review of portfolios, we observed a dramatic decrease (to close to zero) in the number of worksheets and short-answer quizzes. (pp. 4–5)

The fact that Vermont became affiliated with the National Writing Project in 1995–96 has been cited as evidence of the impact of the writing portfolio assessment system on the teaching and learning of writing (Hewitt, personal communication, 1999). During that year, Tish McGonegal, a portfolio writing-network leader "observed [to Geof Hewitt] that the state was giving so much attention to assessment that some teachers were losing sight of their own strategies for inspiring themselves, and their students, to write with investment" (Hewitt, personal communication, 1999). In order to help refocus instruction, she and Hewitt convinced the University of Vermont to be their site for a National Writing Project affiliate and developed the necessary resources to supply the matching and in-kind requirements of the application. Hewitt continued:

> This was a lot trickier than you might imagine, and we owe extraordinary thanks to then-Chair of the English Department, Alan Broughton, who knocked on doors $1000 at a time to raise the cash match, even talking the President of the University out of his final discretionary funds ($2500) remaining in that year's budget. The university was on a strict fiscal diet in 95–96, so Alan's feat is all the more heroic. We also have Paul Eschholz, of the University, to thank. Paul, who co-founded the VT Writing Project in the late 70s (with NEH support it lasted three or four years and involved more than 300 VT teachers), encouraged us to go through with the application and offered to serve as Co-director. He has been our liaison with UVM ever since. (Hewitt, personal communication, 1999)

It seems clear that Vermont was able to create a writing portfolio system that reached deeply into the local culture of schooling and had an important influence within the institution. Developments in Vermont over the coming years will indeed be interesting to watch.

Problems and Potential Solutions

Because Vermont never intended its system to produce scores of any consequence and thereby sidestepped the major problems faced by those who did intend to make consequential decisions based on portfolio scores, it is hard to isolate problems in its design. Some theoreticians might argue that Vermont's open-ended collection strategy was a problem in that it led to a range of other problems related to reliability. But the open-ended design supported the central purpose for the portfolios, which was, to serve teachers as a tool to make their writing instruction better.

All of the evidence we have reviewed suggests that the original purpose of Vermont's writing portfolio system was to improve writing instruction in the schools, not to hold schools accountable for achieving a particular measurable goal. Whenever there was an opportunity to compromise what the teachers considered the instructional integrity of the system, it seems that the decision went in favor of instruction and against measurement. Indeed, in 1991, there was even talk about reporting portfolio data to the public using descriptive words and phrases rather than numbers explicitly to "prevent newspapers' ranking schools on the basis of numerical averages" (Hewitt, 1993, p. 3). Vermont's Commissioner Mills had ruled out any use of high stakes in association with the portfolios.

Perhaps Vermont's system could have diminished the effects of the stigma of unreliability if Daniel Koretz and his colleagues (1993) at the RAND Institute had chosen to design their evaluation of the writing portfolio system with a greater emphasis on the collection of qualitative data to answer questions about changes in instructional practices and a lesser emphasis on the collection of quantitative data to answer questions about interrater reliability. CSE Technical Report 371 (Koretz et al., 1993), for example, one of the earliest scholarly documents about Vermont to be published, explained that the researchers consciously chose to study the implementation of the mathematics portfolio system, but not the writing portfolio system, by looking at its impact on instruction:

> Our initial efforts focused primarily on the mathematics portfolio program. The mathematics program represented more of a qualitative break with past instructional practice than did the writing program. In addition, large-scale direct assessments of writing are quite common, even if large-scale portfolio assessments are not, and there is research literature spanning decades about the characteristics of such assessments. In contrast, those building the Vermont mathematics assessment were largely plowing new ground, and their experiences could have important implications for the nationwide effort to develop direct assessments in mathematics. Accordingly, many of the results reported here pertain specifically to the mathematics program, while others pertain to both subjects. (pp. 7–8)

As a consequence of this decision, data are reported that give one a sense of how teachers were using the mathematics portfolios in their classrooms. For example, in their report on the mathematics portfolios, Koretz et al. (1993) found that "teachers and students remained confused at times about the use of mathematics portfolios," "many teachers had difficulty finding appropriate mathematics tasks," and "poor communication, insufficient information, and the rapid pace of implementation posed problems for many teachers in both writing and math" (pp. 16–17). In contrast, when data about the writing portfolio system were reported, these researchers devoted an entire chapter to issues of rater reliability in scoring with the following conclusion:

> [H]igh agreement rates can only be obtained when all students respond to the same or similar prompts or when they all produce works that fall within certain well-defined genres, for instance, each portfolio contains one poem, one short story, etc. That did not happen in Vermont in 1992. As a result, portfolio raters were asked to assess whether one student's response to one task was better than another student's response to a totally different task. This job would challenge even the most conscientious and skilled gradee, and given the results discussed above [i.e., dismal interrater agreement rates], we now have begun to question whether it can be done with an adequate level of consistency in an operational program. (pp. 50–51)

Our concern here is not with the evidence that rater agreement was hard to see. Instead, our concern is with the nature of the question. Given that the system was designed to generate data about whole writing programs rather than individual student writers, given that consequential decisions immediately affecting the life chances of individual students were not being made on the basis of the portfolio data, we find it hard to understand this focus on rater reliability. In the long run, a focus on the kinds of qualitative data about opportunities to write, impact on teachers, etc., discussed by Hewitt (1993) and others could have given Vermont more insight into how well the system was fulfilling its primary mission, which was to enhance instruction. The lesson for us is this: System evaluators need to be sure to investigate questions at the heart of the system rather than questions of theoretical interest.

We are not alone in our concern that traditional psychometric principles and the questions that they imply may be inappropriate for application in the domain of portfolios. Wile and Tierney (1996), for example, wrote the following:

> We find ourselves perplexed with the positivistic leanings of psychometricians perseverating on reliability, consistency, and generalizability as key qualities when trustworthiness, interpretability, situation specificity and empowerment seem more appropriate. With assessment intimately linked to elements grounded in an individual's experiences, constructivist analytic approaches offer stakeholders a level of trustworthiness rare among [positivistic] techniques. (p. 215)

Perhaps the biggest problem in Vermont was the contradiction inherent in designing a naturalistic, constructivist portfolio system—and then subjecting the design to the principles, assumptions, and criteria of traditional positivist psychometry.

Opportunities for Discussion and Inquiry

1. Vermont's system was originally designed to provide information that would be useful to teachers as they created school writing instructional programs. Toward this end the system included an "analytic rubric," that is, a rubric with different dimensions that could give targeted feedback. In 1998 the system stopped using this analytical rubric and replaced it with holistic rubrics, each geared toward a particular genre of writing. Which kind of scoring system—analytic or holistic—do you think would be more useful for teachers?

2. Through its history the Vermont portfolio system has privileged teachers in its design—as instructional and assessment leaders, as system designers, and as scorers. Moreover, a fundamental goal of the system from its beginnings has been to invite teachers to collaborate together in networks. How can system designers working with much larger state school systems ensure this sort of commitment to teachers? Is it an essential element in portfolio design?

3. Vermont's portfolio system is now embedded in an assessment system that includes standards for measuring the degree to which students have opportunities to learn. Do you agree that state governments ought to measure opportunity to learn? Why or why not? How might a portfolio system be used for this purpose?

Acknowledgments

We want to thank Geof Hewitt, writing consultant for the Vermont State Department of Education, for his input and feedback as this chapter was prepared. Without his help we would not have been able to complete this work.

References

Burge, K. (1997). Vermont ordered to alter funding of schools. *Education News* (2/06/97). *(http://www/state.vt.us/educ/scdecion.htm)*.

Darling-Hammond, L. (1989). Accountability for professional practice. *Teachers College Record, 91*(1), 60–80.

Darling-Hammond, L. (1997). *Right to learn: A blueprint for creating schools that work*. San Francisco, CA: Jossey-Bass Publishers.

DeWitt, K. (1991, April 24). Vermont gauges learning by what's in portfolio. *The New York Times*. (Education Section B, Wednesday) p. B7.

FairTest (1999). Testing our children: A report card on state assessment systems. *(http://www.fairtest.org/states/survey.htm)*.

Goodlad, J. (1984). *A place called school*. New York: McGraw-Hill.

Graves, D. (1983). *Writing: Teachers and children at work*. Portsmouth, NH: Heinemann.

Hewitt, G. (1993). Vermont's portfolio-based writing assessment program: A brief history. *Teachers & Writers 24* (5), 1–6.

Hewitt, G. (1995). *A portfolio primer: teaching, collecting, and assessing student writing*. Portsmouth, NH: Heinemann.

Kay, P., Fitzgerald, M., Daniels, P., & Mellencamp, A. (1993). *Voices from the hills: Parent, teacher, and student perspectives on school reform*. Paper presented at the meeting of the National Rural Education Association, October 14, 1993, Burlington, VT. Authors can be contacted at the University of Vermont.

Koretz, D., Stecher, B., Klein, S., McCaffrey, D., & Deibert, E. (1993). *Can portfolios assess student performance and influence instruction? The 1991–92 Vermont experience* (CSE Technical Report 371). Los Angeles: University of California, National Center for Research on Evaluation, Standards, and Student Testing.

Koretz, D., Stecher, B., Klein, S., & McCaffrey, D. (1994a). *The evolution of a portfolio program: The impact and quality of the Vermont program in its second year (1992–93)*. (CSE Technical Report 385). Los Angeles: University of California, National Center for Research on Evaluation, Standards, and Student Testing.

Koretz, D., Stecher, B., Klein, S., & McCaffrey, D. (1994b). The Vermont portfolio assessment program: Findings and implications. *Educational Measurement: Issues and Practice 13* (3), 5–16.

Lawton, M. (1996). State test questions focus of renewed scrutiny. *Education Week on the Web. (http://www.edweek.org/ew/vol–15/19assess.h15).*

Lucas, C. (1988a). Toward ecological evaluation: Part I. *The Quarterly of the National Writing Project and the Center for the Study of Writing, 10* (1), 1–3, 12–16.

Lucas, C. (1988b). Toward ecological evaluation: Part II. *The Quarterly of the National Writing Project and the Center for the Study of Writing, 10* (2), 4–10.

Madaus, G. & Kellaghan, T. (1993). Testing as a mechanism of public policy: A brief history and description. *Measurment and Evaluation in Counseling and Development 26*, 6–10.

Manzo, K. (1996, December 4). Vermont to combine standardized tests with portfolios. *Education week on the web, (http://www.edweek.org.ew.vol-16.14vt.h16).*

Merina, A. (1993, October). When bad things happen to good ideas. *NEA Today*, p. 4–5.

Moss, P. (1994a). Validity in high stakes writing assessment: Problems and possibilities. *Assessing writing, 1* (1), 109–128.

Moss, P. (1994b). Can there be validity without reliability? *Educational research, 23* (2), 5–12.

New Standards Project (1996). *1995 English language arts released task—middle school.* Harcourt and Brace Educational Measurement.

Nystrand, M., Cohen, A., & Dowling, N. (1993). Addressing reliability problems in the portfolio assessment of college writing. *Educational Assessment, 1* (1), 53–70.

Rothman, R. (1989). Vermont plans to pioneer with work portfolios: Assessment to include "best" pupil materials. *Education week.* Not dated, p. 11.

Sizer, T. (1984). *Horace's compromise: The dilemma of the American high school.* Boston: Houghton Mifflin.

Tierney, R., Carter, M. & Desai, L. (1991). *Portfolio assessment in the reading-writing classroom.* Norwood, MA: Christopher-Gordon Publishers.

Underwood, T. & Murphy, S. (1998). Interrater reliability in a California middle school English/language arts portfolio assessment program. *Assessing Writing, 5* (2), 201–230.

Vermont Department of Education (1989). *Vermont writing assessment: The portfolio* (a draft copy).

Vermont Department of Education (1991). *"This is my best": Vermont's writing assessment program pilot year 1990–91.*

Vermont Department of Education (1996). Developing a comprehensive assessment system: Milestones along the way. *(http://www.state.vt.us/educ/assmnt4.htm).*

Vermont Department of Education (1998, January 18). Vermont education matters: Memos, reports, and studies. *(http://www.state.vt.us/educ/memos.htm).*

Vermont Department of Education (1999). *1998–99 writing benchmarks: 5th grade.*

Viadero, D. (1995). Even as popularity soars, portfolios encounter roadblocks. *Education Week on the Web. (http://www.edweek.org/ew/vol-14/28portfo.h14).*

Wile, J. & Tierney, R. (1996). Tensions in assessment: The battle over portfolios, curriculum, and control. In R. Calfee & P. Perfumo (Eds.). *Writing portfolios in the classroom: Policy and practice, promise and peril* (pp. 203–215). Mahwah, NJ: Lawrence Erlbaum Associates.

Writing Leadership Committee (1989). Vermont writing assessment: The portfolio (A draft copy). This document is a handwritten draft copy of tentative design decisions made by the committee circulated to Vermont teachers for feedback.

9 The New Standards Project: Assessment for Standards-Based Reform

In the late 1980s and early 1990s there was serious concern about excellence in American schooling from a variety of sources. The New Standards Project was an attempt to address these serious concerns about limitations of the educational system in the United States and its ability to prepare America's youth—and America—to be competitive in a vastly changed world economy. Current assessment systems were under attack. As Lauren Resnick, the director of the Learning Research and Development Center at the University of Pittsburgh and co-director of the New Standards Project explained, "Standardized tests are outdated. They don't reflect the real-world problems that today's students will face when they leave school" (New Standards Project, 1991).

In preceding decades, the growth of technology had generated a need for workers—the scholars said—who could understand technical systems, as well as use them, and who could "participate in dispersed management systems requiring judgment and decision making" (Learning Research and Development Center, 1990). The minimal skills required for routine, repetitive tasks assessed by most tests were viewed as inadequate for the challenges that would be faced by students entering the workforce. Agreement was widespread that what was needed was an educational system designed to prepare people for "adaptive functioning in a technically complex environment," a system that would at the same time, set reasoning and thinking as goals for all students, not just society's elite (Language Research and Development Center, 1990).

At the time, many believed the existing educational system was incapable of promoting such a goal. And in fact, the vast majority of the workforce that the existing educational system was producing had only eighth grade skills (Language Research and Development Center, 1990). What was needed was an educational system that would prepare students to organize their thoughts, conduct analyses, and mount arguments—and an assessment system that would gauge how well they could *use* the facts they had learned (Cheney, 1991).

The assessment system in place, however, appeared to work against the new vision of education. Although school achievement tests were on the whole only weakly coupled to what might actually be taught in the classroom, they appeared to have a pervasive and negative effect on the curriculum. Studies had shown that teachers and districts shaped instruction to match the content and form of tests, especially when high stakes were attached (Corbett & Wilson, 1991; Door-Bremme & Herman, 1986; Haney, 1991; Madaus, 1988; Mathison, 1989; Smith, 1991). The impact appeared to be even greater for low-income students, because teachers of low-income students felt they were more accountable to tests (Dorr-Bremme & Herman, 1986; Rothman, 1992).

While this might not be seen as a problem if the tests had been worth teaching to, a number of scholars had argued that narrowing and fragmentation of the curriculum occurs when teachers rely on multiple-choice tests (Corbett & Wilson, 1991; Haertel & Calfee, 1983; Resnick & Klopfer, 1989; Wells, 1991). In an early article on the subject, Norman Frederiksen (1984) called the influence of multiple-choice tests on instruction—not discrimination against minorities or women—"the real test bias." Frederiksen noted the potential of such tests to focus too much attention on the basic skills:

> Improvement in basic skills is of course much to be desired, and the use of tests to achieve that outcome is not to be condemned. My concern, however, is that reliance on objective tests to provide evidence of improvement may have contributed to a bias in education that decreases effort to teach other important abilities that are difficult to measure with multiple-choice tests. . . . (p. 95)

Educators and policy makers alike were becoming aware that the existing assessment systems did not promote the kinds of curricula that would prepare people to function in a technically complex environment, nor to know how to adapt as that environment changed. Critics charged that standardized tests focused attention on low-level skills, to the detriment of higher-level concerns in education, such as the ability to articulate, investigate, and solve complex problems.

Moreover, although achievement testing was widespread in American schools, according to Cheney (1991), it was largely a "patchwork affair," with some students taking one examination and others another. This lack of uniformity prevented comparisons of a student's or school's performance with other students and schools across the nation. In addition, many of the examinations rated students' performance against the performance of students who had taken the tests previously, instead of the students' contemporaries or fixed standards. As Lynne Cheney points out, this approach to rating—comparing the performance of students today against the performance of students who took the test in the past—invites the "Lake Wobegon" effect, identified by J. J. Cannell (1987) and named after Garrison Keillor's fictional town, where "all the women are strong, all the men are good-looking, and all the children are above average." As a result, these kinds of tests are not particularly useful for evaluating teaching and learning (Cheney, 1991).

The antidote to these problems, many believed, would be the implementation of new high standards for student performance and assessments designed to measure students' progress toward achieving them. In other words, instead of comparing students with each other, students would be "judged against a known standard of achievement, a standard toward which they can work systematically and cumulatively" (Resnick, Nolan, & Resnick, 1995, p. 440). In tandem with new curricula and incentives for teachers and schools, policymakers believed that new standards and assessments could turn the ailing American educational system around.

The new curriculum that was proposed stemmed from work in the field of cognitive psychology. Research in this field had transformed understanding of how children learn. Instead of viewing learning as the "transmission" of knowledge from teachers to students, educators were coming to understand that children actively construct knowledge based on what they already know. Moreover, educators were coming to understand that children learned by interacting with others in their environment. And, instead of viewing knowledge as something that could be broken down into components so that students could learn each component sequentially, educators were beginning to understand that even the most "basic" tasks—such as reading—involve complex thinking and reasoning. Further, educators were coming to understand that children learned best when they were engaged in authentic tasks. What was needed, scholars proposed, was a "thinking curriculum" (Resnick & Klopfer, 1989).

The proposal that led to the formation of the New Standards Project outlined what would be needed to jump-start the new curriculum:

> What is needed is an assessment system that measures the acquisition of 'thinking' skills, that is tied to a curriculum designed to produce 'thinking' skills and that rewards effort in school. Such a system would reward student effort to master a thinking curriculum by providing access to college and jobs to those who did so. The same system could be used to reward school professionals who help their students to succeed against the new standard. It could be used to inform parents and the public of the standards to which students would be held and the material they were expected to master. And it could be used as a vehicle through which colleges and employers could participate in the setting of standards for those who would enter their institutions. (Learning Research and Development Center, 1990)

The Learning Research and Development Center and the National Center on Education and the Economy joined forces to develop the system.

When these two institutions began their joint project to develop a new system of examinations, a number of education leaders had concluded that the United States should have some form of national achievement testing. The climate was right for such an effort. In 1989 the President and the governors of the 50 states established ambitious national goals. Shortly after, the National Educational Goals Panel and the National Commission on Education Standards and Testing were established. After negotiation involving two administrations (Bush and Clinton) the Goals 2000: Educate America act was passed, an act which called on states to "establish learning standards, align assessments to them, and begin to bring curriculum, teacher preparation, textbooks, and in-service professional development into accord" (Resnick, et al. 1995, p. 439). Beginning in 1991, the federal government was supporting development of content standards in several subject areas. And in 1990–91, the state of Vermont was already piloting portfolio assessment with about half of the state's fourth and eighth graders (National Council of Teachers of English, 1991). Functioning outside of the institutions of the federal government, the New Standards Project was formed to "respond to the need for high-demand assessments based on clear outcome standards" (Resnick, et al., 1995, p. 439).

During the first year of the project, the reform wave crested. *The Daily Standard: The Voice for Higher Expectations*, a daily newspaper with brief articles about events and activities in the participating states published by New Standards at assessment development conferences, was replete with reports of reform initiatives:

> Last year . . . Oregon's governor signed into law a piece of legislation that mandates changes in the way students will be educated. . . . (New Standards Project, 1992c, p. 3)

This spring, the State Board of Education adopted a reform agenda to improve Delaware public schools. . . . As part of this agenda content standards and student performance standards will be established. . . . (New Standards Project, 1992c, p. 4)

We [South Carolina] are in the process of reforming our curriculum by developing curriculum frameworks. . . . Twelve schools are working with each other and with the State Department of Education to develop instructional units and performance based assessments which support the curriculum reforms in progress. (New Standards Project, 1992c, p. 4)

Wisconsin legislation calls for revision in the state "Student Assessment System." (New Standards Project, 1992b, p. 3)

Ft. Worth educators are working with local businesses to connect the importance of school with real life. . . . (New Standards Project, 1992b, p. 8)

Education in the State of Kentucky is going through a great deal of reform from the creation of School Based Councils, to Portfolio Assessments at grades 4, 8, and 12. (New Standards Project, 1992b, p. 4)

Along with state and district partners, the New Standards Project also forged links with other institutions. Of critical importance was the liaison with the National Council of Teachers of English. An institution already engaged in the creation of standards, NCTE brought to the table the voices of thousands of teachers, and sent the message that teachers were to play a role in all phases of the assessment activities. The NCTE role was formalized in the formation of the Literacy Unit, housed at NCTE in Urbana, and guided by Miles Myers, then Executive Director, and P. David Pearson, then Dean of the College of Education at University of Illinois at Champaign-Urbana. The liaison with NCTE brought an important connection to America's English language arts teachers to the collaboration. As Elaine Wetterauer, a teacher at Nathan Hale High School in Seattle, Washington, said at one of the conferences conducted by New Standards, "'I was a little suspect; I didn't know anything about [the New Standards Project]," adding that colleagues had told her NSP wasn't a teacher-led reform effort. 'When I found out NCTE was involved,' she said, 'I was really relieved.'" (Flanagan, 1994, p.1).

As a multi-state and multi-institutional collaborative effort, the New Standards Project was clearly poised to take a leadership role in reform.

Exemplar System

Going far beyond the 'multiple guess' tests that had constituted the dominant methodology for decades, the plan was for the new examinations to measure performance by assessing "portfolios of students' actual work, projects they had produced, and their answers on a 'new generation' of tests" designed to "show the depth of their knowledge and ability to apply it" (New Standards Project, 1991). The Learning Research and Development Center and the National Center on Education and the Economy envisioned a ten year effort to develop a "national examination system," that would include three forms of examination—"performance examinations, portfolios, and projects":

Students would sit for timed performance examinations, which would ask them to demonstrate that they have mastered the curriculum on which the examinations are based. Though these examinations might include some multiple-choice questions, much of the examination would require self-generated and more elaborate responses. Portfolios would be assembled from work that a student did over a period of months or years, documenting the capacity to create a number of different work products and select the best of them. Projects would be used to give students an opportunity to demonstrate their capacity to apply what they know in the context of solving a complex problem over a period of time, often in association with others. All of these modes of assessment would stress the application of knowledge and skill in real life situations. . . . (Learning Research and Development Center, 1990 p. 4)

Rather then create these assessments themselves, what the proposal authors had in mind at the time was "creating a flexible system that is matched to the unique requirements of America, with its longstanding tradition of state and local district authority for the provision of education" (Learning Research and Development Center, 1990, p. 4). What they proposed was not a single examination, but "an examining *system*" that would accommodate local versions as long as they met national standards. Monitoring the standards of these local examinations would be a responsibility of a "National Education Standards Board." As the proposal authors explained, "Each state represented on the Board would constitute its own State Education Standards Board, making assessment policy for its own state and assuming responsibility for the administration of the examinations in its own jurisdiction" (Learning Research and Development Center, 1990, p. 5).

Their plans included attention to the buy-in that would be necessary by the states. LRDC and NCEE had an important resource to draw on in this regard. The National Alliance for Restructuring Education, an NCEE program that consisted of several states and cities, had just made a commitment to band together in an effort to create a rigorous standard, a standard that the proposal authors hoped the rest of the nation would embrace in time.

What would the states and other partners get from the project? Lauren Resnick explained:

We don't turnkey a test: they don't give us X dollars so that we'll deliver a completed test a year and a half later. We do, in effect, turnkey a *process*, though. By working with us, the partners will be developing their capacity to create and score tasks, to train other people to develop and score tasks, to develop scoring procedures, to develop instructional programs that go with these new kinds of assessments, and so on. All of this is linked to their own curriculum standards, and they will be participating in the processes of public engagement in standards setting. So, in fact, what they get and what they give are intimately connected. (O'Neil, 1993, p. 21)

The initial plan called for the creation of a National Education Standards Board to set standards and develop model exams. States and districts could use the model exams produced by New Standards, or they could develop their own, calibrated to the national standards. As Daniel Gursky explained, "Teachers, schools, and districts would be free to determine the appropriate curriculum and textbooks for their students," a characteristic of NSP that distinguished its assessment plan from most others under discussion at the national level (Gursky, 1991, p. 55).

Assessment development in the English language arts unit of New Standards, according to Miles Myers and P. David Pearson, heads of New Standard's Literacy Unit, proceeded in three stages. In the first stage, teachers were brought together to develop on-demand language arts tasks of three to five days duration in which students "read one or more texts, responded to several open-ended reading prompts, and worked in small groups in one or more phases of the reading or writing activities" (Myers & Pearson, 1996, p. 6). During this stage New Standards also experimented with scoring student responses to the tasks. In the second stage, "hundreds of teachers were brought together from across the country to expand and refine the on-demand performance tasks and to experiment with various ways of scoring tasks and reporting results" (Myers & Pearson, 1996, p.7). During this stage New Standards also began to draft the performance standards for English language arts. In the third stage, New Standards began the portfolio development process. Student handbooks were produced and tentative portfolio designs piloted in field trials involving thousands of teachers and students around the country (Myers & Pearson, 1996).

A major part of the development work involved teachers and other subject-matter experts in the development of assessment tasks that were later piloted in many of the same teachers' classrooms. An early effort in this direction was a meeting at Snowmass, Colorado, attended by 450 "teachers, policymakers, business representatives, child advocates, and others." While the policymakers, business representatives discussed the contentious issues surrounding the creation of an examination system planned to be national in scope, the teachers and other subject-matter experts developed performance tasks for elementary, middle school and high school students in mathematics, reading, and writing (New Standards Press Release, August 5, 1991).

Experts also contributed to the process. Appropriate tasks, said members of the English-Language Arts Advisory Group:

- Are instructionally responsible
- Make presuppositions of task clear
- Should not reflect an arbitrariness in what is required of students
- Ask for, rather than command a response
- Give clear directions
- Involve students in thinking about social issues
- Allow for developmental levels
- Ask students to describe the sources of their information
- Involve translations across multiple ways of representing information
- Recognize that writing is idiosyncratic
- Are well integrated, purposeful
- Allow for some student choice
- Allow students to "harvest" prior learning and learn from the task itself
- Avoid activities that lead to "silly coaching"
- Integrate reading, writing, listening, speaking, and perhaps viewing
- Involve other content areas
- Employ sustained, purposeful communication
- Tap creativity, humor, playfulness
- Find out what kids can do, not what they cannot do

- Are sensitive to the resources available to less privileged schools
- Recognize social aspects of language use
- Contribute to a sense of community and caring in the classroom
- Allow students to reflect on the tasks, and give them adequate feedback about their performance (Resnick & Kapinus, 1992. Reprinted by permission of New Standards)

An initial plan following the Snowmass meeting called for the following next steps in the task development process:

- A summer task development workshop in 1992
- Local tryouts of tasks during September and October 1992
- Regional task refinement meetings to prepare tasks for "pre-piloting" in November 1992
- Regional pre-piloting in January 1993
- Selection of pilot tasks in February 1993
- Preparation of tasks for National piloting in March 1993
- National piloting in April 1993
- Regional scoring meetings in June 1993 (New Standards Project, 1992d)

At a later task development workshop in Phoenix in 1992, teams of teachers were sent by each partner state and district to engage in task development activities, discussions about content and performance standards and the types of preparation that students would need to meet them. Over 600 people attended. During the conference, teams completed a "performance task proposal form" which included a description of the task, an estimate of its duration, a statement about the educational outcomes to be measured by the tasks, a suggested pre-assessment activity, a description of student responses that would be required, a description of materials needed, and general guidelines for students' work.

The Council Chronicle, the newspaper of the National Council of Teachers of English, published the following example of the kind of task that teachers at the conference developed:

Imagine that four of the characters from the literature you have read this year have gathered in one place. Work in groups of four. Each group will:

- Choose the four characters and the setting.
- Develop an interesting script that reflects the personality of the characters. The script will deviate from the plots of the works where the characters originally appeared.
- Prepare to perform this script in front of your classmates. Consider casting, staging, scenery, costuming, and props.
- Perform your scene for your class. (National Council of Teachers of English, 1991, p. 1)

This kind of curriculum-embedded, highly engaging task contrasted sharply with the typical items included in achievement tests at the time. Exams such as the SAT and the ACT avoid testing for factual knowledge that a student might have acquired in any particular classroom. And such tests certainly did now allow collaboration "in groups of four." Students taking such tests answered items such as the following:

Select the lettered pair that best expresses a relationship similar to that expressed in the original pair:

YAWN:BOREDOM::   (A) dream:sleep   (B) anger:madness

                  (C) smile:amusement   (D) face: expression

                  (E) impatience:rebellion (Cheney, 1991, p. 3)

As the example illustrates, high-stakes achievement examinations—with the exception of the Advanced Placement Exams—were far removed from the classroom. As Lynne Cheney explained, most achievement exams did "little to advance the notion that hard work in school matters."

The collaborative effort to develop new, challenging curriculum-embedded tasks was exhilarating to participants at the task development conferences who could share ideas with professionals from other states. In *The Daily Standard: The Voice for Higher Expectations*, a daily newspaper with brief articles about events and activities in the participating states published by conference organizers, one participant wrote: "New York City got off to a rousing start. We are well represented from the five boroughs. We're anxious to get started on developing tasks and assessments. It is great to know that we are not alone. Coming here to meet people with similar goals is a 'very positive thing'" (New Standards Project, 1992c, p. 3).

The task development conferences were followed by further refinement of the tasks at home districts and schools and at a later task refinement workshop. Part of the agenda there was to develop a systematic approach to training teachers in task development (Gilchrist, 1992). The purposes of the task development process, according to Jim Gilchrist, Director of Operations, were 1) to "generate a pool of tasks for . . . pilot examination; 2) contribute to the pool of tasks for future use; and 3) give teachers practical experience in writing appropriate tasks" (Gilchrist, 1992, p. 2).

Some of the tasks generated by teachers were ultimately used in pre-pilots and pilots of on-demand integrated language arts performance assessments that integrated reading, writing, speaking, and listening. Plans for one pilot indicated the assessment was to be conducted over three class periods, preferably on three successive days. On the first day students read and wrote a variety of responses (scored). On the second day they discussed (speaking and listening) and engaged in other pre-writing activities (not scored); and on the third day they wrote in response to prompts (Resnick & Kapinus, 1992).

In later conferences, attention turned to portfolios. Again, a series of meetings, both large and small, were held. In 1993, NSP gathered experts in assessment and representatives of various portfolio projects around the country in Minneapolis to debate and discuss issues surrounding portfolio purposes and designs (National Council of Teachers of English, 1993). Among the many issues discussed were the following:

- Whether to score portfolios, or to use some other approach to gather information about students from portfolios
- Which scoring method to use, and how to obtain reliable scores
- Whether to include evidence of the writing process
- Whether there should be guidelines for reflections on growth and whether those reflections, or other student annotations would be represented in scores

- Whether changes should be made to the curriculum first, and then changes to the mode of assessment
- Whether and how to engage teachers in the development process
- What teachers could learn from working with students' portfolios
- What kinds of professional/staff development would be needed to support effective uses of portfolios in the classroom
- Whether there would be a constraining effect on the curriculum
- Whether external assessment would negatively impact students' ownership of their work
- What the results of the assessment would be used for
- How to involve students in their own assessments
- How the portfolio should be designed, e.g., to show growth? to demonstrate accomplishment?

The discussion and debate continued at a later conference held in October 1993 in Danvers, Massachusetts. There, teams of teachers and consultants began designing guidelines for portfolio assessment and support materials for students, teachers, and parents (Myers & Pearson, 1996). Twenty-one teams of teachers were selected on the basis of their experience in keeping portfolios, their experience in using portfolios for decision-making, and their experience in working with diverse student populations. Those who attended agreed to participate for a year. In subsequent months many of these same teachers attended two other conferences, one in San Francisco in February 1994 and one in Albuquerque, New Mexico in May 1994.

One outcome of these discussions was general agreement that the New Standards Project would work toward developing an approach to large-scale assessment that would not be dependent on a single model. The portfolio would be built around a set of content standards and scored with a system that could accommodate different models yet allow reasonable judgments to be made about a student's level of performance in relation to national and international standards. In this respect, the portfolio plan was conforming to the Project's goal to maintain a high standard, but accommodate diversity in the ways schools and districts met the standards. In one of the early New Standards Project publications, authors of *The Daily Standard* explained:

> We are not advocating a national test but rather a system in which assessments developed by many states and others can be compared to a high performance standard set for the nation. Such an approach would accommodate the rich variation in views and values in this country, while still enjoying the advantages of national—not federal—standards. (New Standards Project, 1992a, p. 2)

In addition to serving as a forum for discussion and debate about assessment issues, the conferences provided professional development for teachers. "A crucial goal" of a conference held at Indian Wells, California in July 1994 "was to get teachers well-versed in using portfolios and in some cases, help teachers who are already using portfolios to fit New Standards portfolios into their classrooms" (New Standards, 1994b, p. 1). Over 900 teachers attended the Indian Wells conference. As Cheryl Tibbals, New Standards Director of Assessment Administration explained, "We wanted to help teachers figure out how to put the New Standards' portfolio system under the hood of their own systems" (New Standards, 1994b, p. 1). The conference was also aimed at preparing teachers for field trials that began in the fall of 1994 and ultimately involved approximately 50,000 students from partner states and districts around the country (New Standards, 1994b).

Teachers were enthusiastic about the potential, but the process did not always run smoothly. For some teachers the tune changed by mid year. The writing portfolio design, which had been based on broadly defined dimensions of performance, was abruptly revised by NSP. Requirements for particular types of writing were added. In California, the reaction was volatile. At a mid-year meeting, teachers who reviewed the new portfolio "framework," particularly the secondary teachers, were unhappy. Some of them thought that the framework reflected a real change in philosophy, because the imposition of required types of writing implied a less flexible framework for students (and teachers and local districts) to use in putting together their portfolios. They objected to a dimension of performance that had been newly introduced—conventions—because they thought "conventions" should be embedded as a part of an earlier, and broader dimension "technical control and competence" that had been part of the earlier design. In the new portfolio design, students were asked to include a piece that demonstrated that they had explored a piece of literature in depth, a piece that dealt with public discourse (pieces that had not been "required" before), and five out of six types of writing. California teachers objected to the "one of this, one of that, and five out of six of those" approach.

In sum, the "old-timers" to portfolio practice in California were disturbed by the change in plans. They worried that they would be asked to assess their students with a rubric that they had not been warned about in advance. They didn't want to be put in the position of assessing "apples" with a rubric designed for "oranges." This episode speaks to the importance of keeping stakeholders informed of changes in plans and of being sensitive to teacher's concerns that they have adequate time to prepare and provide the curriculum that would allow their students a fair chance to perform well. These are concerns for those involved in the implementation of an assessment.

It is important to point out, however, that this was "development" work, not "real" assessment. In "real" assessment, scores would have been assigned to portfolios with consequences attached. And in fact, NSP had a compact signed by the original partners, which committed "all NSP personnel to the principle that no individual scores will be reported by NSP until all users of NSP materials have provided full and complete support (that is, a challenging curriculum and adequate material resources) for individual students attempting to attain a passing score" (Myers & Pearson, 1996, p.9).

Context for the System

The New Standards Project was a joint program of the Learning Research and Development Center at the University of Pittsburgh and the National Center on Education and the Economy. The John D. and Catherine MacArthur Foundation and the PEW Charitable Trusts funded the Project. Participating states and districts also contributed funds to the efforts. Numbers of participating states and districts varied across the years the project was in existence, depending upon local politics and availability of resources. In 1991, 16 states and 6 school districts participated. The 16 states were Arizona, Arkansas, California, Colorado, Connecticut, Delaware, Iowa, Kentucky, Maine, New York, Oregon, South Carolina, Texas, Vermont, Virginia, and Washington. The six districts were the Fort Worth Independent School District, New York City Public Schools, Pittsburgh Public Schools, Rochester Public Schools, San Diego Unified School District, and White Plains Public Schools. In later years, some states dropped out, and others joined. In some years, more than twenty states participated.

Purposes for the System

The aim of the New Standards Project was to ensure that thinking, problem solving, and reasoning were included in everyone's curriculum (Language Research and Development Center, 1990). An important difference between the examination system planned by New Standards and existing examination systems in the United States and other countries was that the New Standards system was aimed at *all* students, not just those who aspired to college (Cheney, 1991). In other words, equity was on the New Standards agenda. Everyone should benefit, the reasoning was, from the high expectations that achievement tests promote and the incentives they provide. As Lynne Cheney put the issue, "Many educators in the United States are coming to believe that it is a great mistake to limit achievement testing to a small group. A system that now benefits a few of our students should be put to work for all" (Cheney, 1991, p. 6).

Part of the equity agenda involved setting a high standard for all students. The National Center on Education and the Economy framed the issue like this:

> More than any other country in the world, the United States believes that natural ability rather than effort, explains achievement. The tragedy is that we communicate to millions of students every year, especially to low-income and minority students, that we do not believe that they have what it takes to learn. They then live up to our expectations, despite the evidence that they can meet very high performance standards under the right conditions. (National Center on Education and the Economy, 1990, p. 4)

Setting a high standard, NCEE argued, would move us a step forward toward producing a highly qualified workforce. "No nation has produced a highly qualified technical workforce," NCEE said, "without first providing its workers with a strong general education" (National Center on Education and the Economy, 1990, p. 3). Setting high standards and measuring *all* students' progress toward meeting those standards with achievement examinations were steps toward ensuring that students acquired that strong general education.

Another major difference between the examination system planned by New Standards and most existing achievement examinations in the United States was the explicit emphasis on curricula—on assessing what students had actually learned. Traditionally, achievement tests in America were only weakly linked to curricula. Achievement tests such as the SAT and the ACT, for example, avoid testing for factual knowledge that a student might have learned in the classroom (Cheney, 1991). Nor do they assess students' abilities to engage in complex performances or their awareness of the processes and strategies they use while they were engaged in them (Camp, 1993). As a result, most American achievement tests did not convey the idea that what one learned in school was important. The New Standards Project, on the other hand, sought to design assessments that would show how well students had learned what had been taught in the classroom. This explicit connection to classroom curricula made the assessment system planned by NSP particularly well suited to educational reform.

Indeed, of the systems profiled in this book, the New Standards Project was the most explicitly focused on educational reform. Lauren Resnick, Director of the Project made this point clear in an interview published in *Educational Leadership* (O'Neil, 1993):

> We believe that the American educational system has to begin to deliver on its rhetoric and see to it that all students are educated to high standards. The development of standards and assessments is a critical piece of reforming the entire educational system so that it is much more coherent and driven by much higher standards. We are not simply a standards or testing undertaking; we want standards and assessments to help bring about better student outcomes—a different quality and higher level of student achievement.

The key was the reform of classroom curriculum and instruction.

Resnick explained why she thought creating more tests would have a powerful impact on curriculum and instruction: "Because the evidence is just incontrovertible that whatever kind of test matters in the system has a heavy influence on classroom practice" (O'Neil, 1993, p. 17). In another publication, Daniel and Lauren Resnick elaborated on the thinking behind the idea that tests could be used to drive the curriculum in a better direction. It aptly captures the rationale for using assessment to reform instruction:

1. *You get what you assess.* Educators will teach to tests if the tests matter in their own or their students' lives. . . .

2. *You do not get what you do not assess.* What does not appear on tests tends to disappear from classrooms in time. . . .

3. *Build assessments toward which you want educators to teach.* . . . Assessments must be designed so that when teachers do the natural thing—that is, prepare their students to perform well—they will exercise the kinds of abilities and develop the kinds of skills and knowledge that are the real goals of educational reform. . . . (Resnick & Resnick, 1992, p. 59)

The nature of the educational reform envisioned by the New Standards Project included changes in how students view themselves and their academic work. The tradition in testing had few opportunities for students to take an active role in the testing enterprise itself; instead, this enterprise was run at a distance and students simply showed up with sharpened pencils on the day of the exam. The New Standards Project, however, asked students to take an active role by figuring out ways that they themselves could show how well they measured up—and ways to learn from the process. For instance, the Handbook explained to students ". . . it's important that you have a thorough understanding of the standards your work needs to meet. You will find those standards clearly defined in this handbook. . . . The standards are high, and the work you choose to include in your portfolio must meet them" (New Standards Project, 1994a, p. 5). The tradition in testing was for students to do their work and then take a test to find out whether they had learned anything from doing the work—even then, many students never learned why particular judgments were made. New Standards asked students to understand what good work is *before* they took the test—and then to do it and learn from its evaluation.

System Design

The New Standards system focused on four areas of the curriculum: English-language arts, mathematics, science, and applied learning. Although not a discipline in itself, applied learning asks students to perform tasks for which they will need knowledge of subject matter. Academic performance standards accompanied by samples of student work formed the core of the system, putting the emphasis squarely on curriculum and making expectations for students in relation to the curriculum explicit. As explained above, in the early years, directors indicated that plans for the performance assessment system included three components—"a one time exam, portfolios of student work, and long-term projects" (Gursky, 1991). In an interview with Daniel Gursky, Mark Tucker elaborated, explaining that the system would feature "on-demand essays or other performances assessed by teacher-judges." Both the portfolios and the projects, on the other hand, would involve long-term work. For portfolios, students would "compile a collection of their best work, such as lab reports, term papers, and creative writing assignments. . . . projects, most likely done in groups, might involve building a model bridge, investigating an aspect of community life, or completing a complex laboratory experiment" (Gursky, 1991, p. 55).

Over the course of the project, descriptions of what the New Standards portfolio would contain varied. A later publication by Warren Simmons and Lauren Resnick (1993) indicated that the portfolios themselves would contain the exam responses and projects in addition to other forms of student work:

> The most authentic and reliable estimate of students' capabilities comes from the work they do over extended periods of time under the guidance of teachers. For this reason, the heart of the New Standards assessment system will be student portfolios. The NSP Portfolios will contain three kinds of work:
>
> - work chosen by the district, school, teacher, and/or student;
> - prescribed projects and other extended leaning activities; and
> - responses generated by NSP matrix examination tasks.

In fact, early versions of the portfolio design did require prescribed projects. For instance, a draft version of the student handbook for New Standards Project English Language Arts Portfolio shared as a starting point for discussions about portfolio design with conference participants in Danvers, Massachusetts in October 1993 indicated that portfolios would contain an "introductory letter from the student," three projects that are "completed over a period of time," that are "situated/functional . . . [and] consist of more than one piece of communication and draw from multiple text sources. . . ." and various "gap fillers" that is, "other work to fill in gaps in the balanced framework." The "balanced framework" for writing included writing done in different settings (e.g., informal, conversational) and for different kinds of audiences (e.g., close personal audiences and "distant" public audiences). Later versions of the portfolio design, however, were very different.

Collection

What work was worth collecting?

Although early published descriptions of the contents of NSP portfolios varied—some descriptions included the on-demand assessments in the portfolio itself—the

1994–95 New Standards high school field-trial guidelines for students asked for work completed in the classroom, not for responses to on-demand assessments. The guidelines put the emphasis on classroom work; they asked students to demonstrate their abilities and accomplishments in three areas: 1) reading, 2) writing, and 3) the combined area of speaking and listening. Within each of these areas, students were asked to provide evidence that they had met particular standards spelled out in the field trial version of the student handbook as outcomes. The standards described in the Student Portfolio Handbook for high school students (New Standards, 1994a, pp. 8–17) are outlined in Figure 9.1.

Figure 9.1
New Standards Field-Trial Portfolio Standards

	Reading	**Writing**	**Speaking and Listening**
Standards	*Technical competence and comprehension* (make sense of passages; interpret, analyze, discover, connect and explore ideas and themes; recognize stylistic choices)	*Technical competence and effectiveness* (use correct spelling, grammar, etc.; explain ideas clearly; organize; use a variety of strategies; connect ideas and interpretations)	*Technical competence and comprehension* (make effective oral presentations and understand those of others; engage in discussions to clarify and explore issues)
	Range (read a quantity of material from literature and public discourse; read in depth (e.g. one type of writing, one subject, one author)	*Range* (write for a variety of purposes; write for a range of audiences; write in a range of styles and formats)	*Range and Versatility* (speak to a variety of audiences and for different purposes; use language to express reasoning clearly and creatively; listen and interpret accurately)
	Evaluate own work (recognize strengths and weaknesses of own reading; assess own progress during the year and explain attempts to improve as a reader; set goals for improvement)	*Evaluate own work* (recognize strengths and weaknesses of own writing; assess own progress and set goals for improvement; explain strategies used to improve writing)	

From "The impact of large-scale portfolio assessment programs on classroom practice," by S. Murphy, J. Bergamini, & P. Rooney, 1997, *Educational Assessment, 4,* p. 303. Copyright © 1997 by Lawrence Erlbaum Associates, Inc. Reprinted with permission.

The guidelines for students at the elementary level were somewhat different. For example, elementary students were expected to demonstrate competence in relation to four standards in each of the three language arts areas (reading, writing, and speaking/listening) instead of three, as was the case in high school and middle school. The four standards were "making sense," "tools and strategies," "showing range," and "taking responsibility." For example, for Standard 2 in Reading, (tools and strategies), students were told "You want to show that you can:

- Reread, pronounce unfamiliar words and use what you already know to help you understand what you're reading.
- Change the way you read depending on your purpose for reading.
- Use different ways to read things that are difficult for you.
- Read out loud with ease and with expression, so a listener can build understanding, too. (New Standards 1994c, p. 5)

Suggested evidence included tapes of the student reading aloud with expression, a "running record," and/or an explanation of how the student figured out unfamiliar words and text. For the standard "taking responsibility" on the other hand, students were expected, among other things, to show that they could describe their "progress as a reader," choose their "own reading material," and "choose things to read that are challenging" (New Standards 1994c, p. 7). Possible evidence included student made lists of things they liked to read and reflections on their progress as readers.

At the high school level, students were told to select ten to twelve samples of their work to include in their portfolio. Because the standards were relatively open-ended, a student could use any appropriate, individual work sample to demonstrate more than one of the standards in more than one of the three areas. For example, an essay about reading might be used to demonstrate technical competence in both reading and writing. However, as mentioned above, for writing, New Standards imposed additional constraints—a menu of required pieces.

In high school students were told to submit 5 of the following 6 types of writing: 1) writing to propose or persuade (e.g., an argument or an opinion about a controversial issue); 2) gathering and reporting information (e.g., a report on a topic); 3) responding to literature (e.g., an essay about a novel, play, or short story; an analysis of a poem; 4) telling a story (e.g., a narrative either experienced or created from imagination); 5) writing as a guide to action (e.g., a process analysis or how-to guide); and 6) exploring and analyzing (e.g., a discussion of a theme or idea such as freedom) (New Standards, 1994a, pp.18–19). At the elementary level, students were told to submit their "best writing pieces, from three of the following four categories: Response to Literature, Telling a Story, Gathering and Reporting Information, and Writing Instructions or Directions (New Standards 1994c, p. 21).

Students at all three levels were also asked to fill out "entry slips" to introduce each of the work samples. The directions for entry slips at the high school level, for example, asked students to identify which standards each entry was supposed to address, and in which language arts area (checked off on a list), to explain how each entry showed evidence of the standards (open-ended response format) and to explain anything else they would like scorers to know about the entry (open-ended response format).

Who had access to and owned the collections?

Unlike many of the other projects profiled in this book, where there was a more or less coherent set of instructional practices associated with the portfolio that teachers had agreed upon in advance, in the case of the New Standards Project, practices were necessarily diverse—as diverse as the practices in the hundreds of classrooms in which they were being piloted. As a result, it is impossible to provide a single, much less a straightforward answer to this question. Because hundreds of teachers around the country piloted the portfolio, it is likely that practices around access to the portfolio varied widely. Some teachers may have allowed students to take portfolios home to work on, others not. Some teachers may have allowed access only at particular times, say, at the end of the quarter, while others may have embedded the portfolios in instruction in ways that demanded that students use their portfolios on a daily basis. As far as we know, New Standards did not collect information about how New Standards portfolios were used in instruction in any systematic way.

Selection

High school guidelines for entries in the speaking and listening area were experimental and flexible enough so that students could use materials they already had, or create reflective entries about their abilities when they were putting their portfolios together. For example, the Student Handbook indicated that one form of evidence to show that they had met the standard for technical competence and comprehension was a "paragraph of self-evaluation on your speaking and listening skills as part of the letter of introduction to your portfolio" (New Standards 1994a, p. 16). Alternatively, students could submit an audiotape or video table of a presentation and/or evaluations of their speaking and listening skills by their teachers or peers.

At the elementary and middle school levels, guidelines for speaking and listening were similarly flexible. For example, at the elementary level accomplished speakers and listeners were expected to be able to describe their growth as speakers, "share new ideas and new ways to present them," "speak confidently," and "participate in discussions about important issues with classmates and friends" (New Standards 1994c, p. 15). Open-ended, the guidelines at all three levels—elementary, middle, and high school—could accommodate a wide range of speaking and listening experiences that might occur in America's classrooms.

Similarly, the relatively open-ended requirements for reading could accommodate a variety of student interests and curricula. They were flexible enough that students could be involved in making decisions about some of the books they would read and about the evidence they would present in their portfolios to document their reading accomplishments. Possibilities for evidence at the high school level included "a reading log . . . an annotated bibliography, or a reading list that demonstrates" that the student had "read a wide range of material" (New Standards 1994a, p. 18). Students could also submit an essay in which they showed that they "understood and appreciated a novel, play or short story with attention to plot, characters, setting and theme" (New Standards 1994a, p. 18). At the middle school level, students could submit reading logs to demonstrate their "technical competence and comprehension." In the elementary grades, students were asked to submit evidence of reading accomplishment in two broad categories: response to literature and response to informational texts (New Standards 1995e, p. 9). Several kinds of work could be used to meet these requirements, including literature logs, book reviews and book maps in the case of literature, and journal responses, reports, and "I Search" papers in the case of informational text.

The guidelines for writing, however, were more constraining. Although content was left open, the guidelines provided detailed descriptions of required portfolio entries that in effect, defined particularities of the writing curriculum that would have to be in place if students were to have appropriate entries to submit. Unlike the more open-ended guidelines that allowed students to demonstrate that they had met the standards with a variety of different kinds of work, the entry slip guidelines for writing specified criteria for the *particular* kind of writing that would be required. An example of one of the high school entry requirements in writing can be seen in Figure 9.2 (New Standards Project, 1995b). Entry slip guidelines for elementary and middle school were similar.

Figure 9.2
Entry Slip Guidelines for A Response to Literature

Name_____ Date_____

Writing Exhibit_____ Entry Slip #1_____

A Response to Literature

Attach one piece of writing that demonstrates how well you can use interpretive, critical, and evaluative processes to respond to literature (fiction, nonfiction, poetry, drama). *Include assignment sheets if you have them.* This entry shows your ability to write a response to literature. People who read this entry will look for evidence that you can:

- Engage the reader by establishing a context, creating a persona, and using other techniques to create interest
- Make an analytic, evaluative, and reflective judgment
- Support a judgment through references to the text; references to other works, authors, or nonprint media; and/or references to your own knowledge or experience
- Demonstrate an understanding of the literary work by:
  - suggesting an interpretation
  - analyzing the author's craft
- making connections to bigger issues and ideas
- Anticipate and answer a reader's questions
- Recognize possible ambiguities, nuances, and complexities.

Describe the assignment that prompted this work (attach other pages if needed):

What makes this work a good piece of evidence for this entry?

The work in this entry was done (check all categories that apply):

_____in_____class   _____as homework   _____with teacher feedback

_____in a group   _____alone   _____with peer feedback

_____as a first draft only   _____with revision   _____other conditions (explain)

_____

Reprinted by permission of New Standards

In the second year of the field trial, at the high school level portfolio requirements for speaking and listening were revised to be slightly more specific; entries were required for "gathering and reporting information," and "influencing the opinions of others" (1995a, p. 5). Teacher certification that students met the standards in informal speaking and listening was also required. Portfolio requirements for reading were also revised. As before, students were asked to demonstrate that they had read "many different materials" and that they had read in depth, focusing some of their reading "on a particular author, genre, issue or topic" (1995a, Entry Slip # 1, p. 18). Students were required to read within three different categories of discourse instead of just two, but they were not required to read particular texts or types of texts. Thus, the revised guidelines for reading were slightly more specific than the 1994-95 field-trial requirements had been.

Portfolio requirements for writing at the high school level, on the other hand, were revised to be slightly more flexible. Students were no longer required to put five out of six different types of writing in their portfolios. Instead, they were required to submit at least one entry in each of two more broadly defined categories. The first category included: 1) a response to literature, 2) a demonstration of proficiency in a literary genre, and 3) a narrative account. The second category included 1) a report, 2) a narrative procedure, and 3) a persuasive essay. A third required entry for writing could be a "free pick."

At the elementary level, in contrast, more writing entries were required. Along with a "free choice," evidence of "writing craft" (revision) and writing conventions, students were told to submit a "response to literature," a "report," an "account" (a "story"), and a "procedure" (a piece that "explains how to do something") (New Standards, 1995e, p.11). At the middle grades level, required entries included the ones for elementary school above, and in addition, a literary genre (e.g., fiction, poetry, drama) and a persuasive essay (New Standards, 1995f, pp. 19–24).

When did selection take place?

Unlike the other projects profiled in this book, in the case of the New Standards Project, it is impossible to provide a single, much less a straightforward answer to this question. Like the issue of "access" above, because hundreds of teachers around the country piloted the portfolio, it is likely that practices varied in significant ways. No doubt, some teachers left selection to the last days of the year. Others, however, tried to incorporate the portfolios in instruction. For example, Jan Bergamini, one of the teachers who piloted the New Standards Field-Trial Portfolio, provided a series of "practice" activities during the year. In November, she asked students to organize their writing folders, to pick the two pieces they liked best at the time, and to choose one to work on further to "make it better," and at the end of the month, she asked them to write a self-evaluation essay. Later, in December, she introduced the New Standards Student Portfolio Handbook and put the standards on the board for discussion. Focusing on the standards in writing, she asked the students to review the work in their writing folders, choose two pieces, and answer the following questions: "What pieces would you select?" "How do they meet the standards for writing?" "What would you need to do to these pieces to make them ready for the final May portfolio?" In January, she repeated this activity, and gave the students practice in writing comments on entry slips.

In March, Ms. Bergamini had the students work in groups to put the standards—range, self-evaluation, and technical competence—in their own words. Each group created a four point scale—"really great," "O.K.," "just about there," and "having trouble"—for each of the NSP standards. For example, one group of students described a "really great" self-evaluator in writing as someone who "assesses own progress," "understands weak and strong points of his writing," "sets goals for improvement," and "proves with examples." A student "having trouble" was described as "lost, unclear, and doesn't know." Posted on the walls around the room, the lists provided a backdrop for further discussion about the New Standards Field-Trial Portfolio requirements at other times during the remainder of the year.

Who selected artifacts for presentation/inclusion in the portfolio?

There appeared to be some latitude in the initial New Standards Project plan with regard to who would be selecting entries for student portfolios. In early publications, for example, project directors indicated that portfolios would contain "work chosen by the district, school, teacher, and/or student" (Simmons & Resnick, 1993). Student guidelines for the New Standards Portfolio, however, specified that it would be the student who would select artifacts for his or her portfolio: "Since you are the one to decide what goes into your portfolio, you'll need to get used to judging your own work by measuring it against the standards described in this handbook" (New Standards 1994a, p. 5). Guidelines for the middle grades portfolio made the issue crystal clear in its definition of the portfolio for students: "A portfolio gives you the opportunity to make your own choices in order to show what you know and are able to do. It lets you make the most important statement of your school career—This is who I am and what I can do." (New Standards 1995f, p. 10).

At the elementary level, although exhibit directions are addressed to the student, general guidelines are addressed to the teacher, not the student, and they don't contain advice about the matter of student choice. However, a letter addressed to the student says, "Each time you make a portfolio exhibit, you'll be told what the exhibit should include and how we'll judge your work. Your goal is to do the best you can do. . . . A portfolio lets you show what you know and can do."

What was the purpose for selection?

As explained earlier, unlike some of the other portfolio assessment systems profiled in this book, the emphasis of the New Standards Portfolio was on assessment, not instruction. Although students were advised to "show us you can: . . . set goals for improvement" (New Standards1994a, p. 11) in reality the portfolio was summative, not formative. In other words, students were asked to *demonstrate* that they could set goals—not really set them and show evidence of having worked to achieve them. The agenda for the New Standards was to measure what students had learned against predetermined criteria. In a case study of the implementation of the portfolio, researchers found evidence to suggest that students were quite aware of that agenda. Their awareness was clearly reflected in the comment of the student who wrote "I followed the standards I had to meet" (Murphy, Bergamini, & Rooney, 1997, p. 325).

Who was the audience for the portfolio?

The New Standards Portfolios had multiple audiences. One, of course, was the student's teacher. The New Standards Student Portfolio Handbook for high school students advised them about the purpose of the teacher's reading: "Your teachers will use your portfolio not only to judge, or assess, your level of achievement, but to understand what specific kinds of instruction, guidance and support you may need in order to improve" (New Standards 1994a, pp. 4–5). Other audiences were recommended. For example, guidelines for the 1995 elementary English language arts portfolio include the following recommendation for teachers:

> We all know the value of having students write for a specific audience. Not surprisingly, English Language Arts teachers report that having students present their portfolios to an audience motivates them to really polish their work. A student presentation of his or her portfolio to family members during a parent-teacher conference is also an effective way to communicate with parents. Presenting to peers is an alternative. While the presentation of the portfolio isn't a requirement, it's a very good instructional strategy. (New Standards 1995e, p.6)

The behind-the-scenes audience, however, was always the assessor. Students knew that their portfolios would be read and evaluated by unknown educators far beyond their classroom walls. Because there has never been an actual NSP portfolio assessment scoring session with stakes attached to those scores, we cannot report on the impact of this examiner audience in such a context. However, it seems likely that the distant and anonymous audience of examiners would have an important invisible presence in the day to day work of many students.

Reflection

What opportunities for reflection did the system provide?

The importance of reflecting on one's work was evidenced by its inclusion as "Standard 3 in Writing" in the field-trial high school portfolio guidelines: "Evaluate Your Work." Students were advised to demonstrate that they could:

- Recognize the strengths and weaknesses of [their]own writing . . .
- Assess [their]progress and set goals for improvement . . .
- Explain the strategies [they] have used to make [their] writing better. (New Standards 1994a)

What kinds of artifacts of reflective activity went in the portfolio?

Suggestions for evidence to show that students had met the standard, "Evaluate Your Work," included some that invited reflection:

- A paragraph of self-evaluation as part of your letter of introduction to your portfolio
- A chart on which you list the writing skills we've discussed (in the NSP handbook) with examples of how you've strengthened them or how you plan to do so . . .
- A detailed explanation on your entry slip telling why a piece was included (New Standards 1994a, p. 15)

When the portfolio design was revised after piloting, new opportunities for reflection were incorporated. In the middle grades and in high school, students were asked to include a reflective essay on literacy, explaining the process the student went through to create the portfolio and how the portfolio represented the student as "a competent reader, writer, speaker, and listener" (1995a, p. 37).

At the elementary level, the portfolio handbook told teachers that after students have put together the six entries of their writing exhibit, they would need to write their readers a letter that would be placed at the front of the exhibit:

> In this letter they will explain what writing goals they've set for themselves and how they've worked towards them; they will describe how their writing has improved, and explain how they sometimes used writing to help them learn about new things. If true, they will also tell how they sometimes choose to write even when it's not an assignment. (New Standards 1995e, p. 12)

Student Voices

In the New Standards Project, reflection generally meant assessment of one's own work. There was less attention paid to reflection on processes or the use of resources for writing than seen in some of the other portfolio projects profiled in this book. For example, the following was published in *The New Standard* as an example of reflection:

> I have really grown as a writer this year in fourth grade.
>
> The thing I have really improved on is my surface features. I have really improved on spelling, periods, using quotes where they are needed and indenting paragraphs.
>
> Another thing I have really improved on is using wording. I don't use little short sentences.
>
> I use description in my sentences and I don't repeat the same thing over and over again.
>
> I use complete sentences. At the beginning of the year. I also learned how to combined sentences.
>
> The last thing I improved on is writing in voice. I have learned how to stay on the topic and not change to another. (New Standards Project, 1994d. Reprinted by permission of New Standards.)

In some cases, like the student below, students used the letter primarily to explain which entries fit particular requirements:

> Dear Reader:
>
> Hi, my name is Elana, a sophomore at Mt. Diablo High School. I think the hardest part of this portfolio was finding the papers. I don't know if the paper I choosed are of my best work, but I know that I did my best this year than the years before. I know that I have improved in many ways.
>
> The writing to propose or persuade and exploring and analyzing are the papers that show my opinion about a certain subject. The telling a story paper shows process of my work. I have 2 rough drafts and the final draft. My free picks are papers that are close to my heart. Hope you like.
>
> My strengths are the way I express myself. My weakness is I don't put a lot of

effort. My other weakness is that I'm not articulate!

As you read my writing, I hope you could see my range.

Thank you,
Elana

(From "The Impact of Large-Scale Portfolio Assessment Programs on Classroom Practice," by S. Murphy, J. Bergamini, and P. Rooney, 1997, *Educational Assessment, 4,* pp. 323–324. Copyright 1997 by Lawrence Erlbaum Associates, Inc. Reprinted with permission.)

Appropriating language from the Handbook (e.g., "the writing to propose or persuade," "telling a story," "my range," "shows process"), the student compared her work to a priori requirements.

Evaluation

What was the role of evaluation in the system?

The core of the New Standards Project's effort to frame a new system for assessment was its system of standards and benchmarks. The process of development included educators, scholars, policymakers, parents, the business community, and other interested parties who met over the summer in 1995 to review them. According to an article by Karen Diegmueller in *Across the Nation*, focus groups, including "parents, self-described conservative and liberal voters, and adults from a variety of ethnic groups, among others," were "most accepting of standards that emphasized the 'basics.'" (Diegmueller, 1995, p. 6). The emphasis on basic skills can be easily found in the English-language arts standards in the area of technical competence. Students are expected to use correct spelling, grammar, and so forth (see Figure 9.1 above). But the standards also emphasize reading and writing as processes for creating meaning that vary according to audience and purpose.

A fourth grade teacher had this to say about the role that standards could play in bridging teaching and evaluation:

As a teacher, what I like best about the standards is the fact that there are clear standards that help me figure out what I should be teaching and give me an idea of what to expect from my students. . . . If teachers can show students the standards and say, 'Look at how your work matches up to the standards, students can then determine whether their work is good enough. (cited in New Standards Project, 1995d, p. 3)

In tandem with examples of student work, the standards operate as "benchmarks" for student performance. Work samples illustrate the kinds of work that students might do to demonstrate their achievement of the standards and are used in published editions of the standards to illustrate particular criteria.

For example, New York City's version of the New Standards performance standards contains the following excerpt from a student's paper on "My Life as a Sea Horse."

Hello! I'm a female seahorse! I'm trying to make my way home around a school of fish but I'm not having very much progress! These newborn fish are feisty. Every second, one jumps out at me!

Well, I might as well stop trying and go with the flow. I'm not a strong swimmer. While I'm floating, I'll tell you a little about myself.

First of all, I am a slender fish with a head shaped like a . . . what do you call them? Oh! It's shaped like a horse's head! Also, I have a monkey's tail. (Board of Education of New York City, 1997, p. 40)

Annotations accompanying the excerpt point out that the student's "friendly, conversational tone and the use of a female persona develop reader interest" (I might as well stop trying and go with the flow; I'm not a strong swimmer). Further, her "organization, spelling, usage and sense of syntax demonstrate fluency with the conventions of the written language." Her use of introductory words (Well, . . .) and rhetorical questions (what do you call them?), and "her humorous tone" provide evidence that she can select "the structures and features of language appropriate to the purpose, audience, and context of the work" (Board of Education of New York City, 1997, p. 41).

In addition to making performance expectations explicit for students and teachers, standards operated as "benchmarks" for curriculum. For example, the standards documents contain sample lists of books for different levels of schooling. At the middle school level there are in the fiction category, among others, Ananya's *Bless Me Ultima* and London's *The Call of the Wild*. In the non-fiction category there are Soto's *Living Up the Street*, and Herriot's *All Creatures Great and Small*. On the list for high school students are Hemingway's *For Whom the Bell Tolls*, Covey's *Seven Habits of Highly Effective People*, and magazines like *Time* and *Newsweek*. Sally Hampton, Director, English Language Arts for NCEE, explained that it was necessary to cite particular titles to show the caliber of works that would satisfy the guidelines, but that member districts and/or states were expected to construct their own lists of books to be addressed in the curriculum (Diegmueller, 1995).

For example, in New York City's version of the New Standards' performance standards, attention is paid to the large population of Spanish-speaking students in the city. Sample reading lists at the middle school level include titles such as Olaizola's *El hijo del quincallero*, and Otero's *La tavesia*. High school lists include titles such as Allende's *Eva Luna*, and Azuela's *Los de abajo* (Board of Education of the City of New York, 1997).

Because many teachers throughout the United States in various ways have adapted the New Standards portfolio system, we have no information about the use of the standards in grading. However, one of the "five things" students were told "to remember about portfolios" in the New Standards *Student Portfolio Handbook* was that: "In the future, teachers may well be using portfolios as an assessment tool to determine all or some of your grades" (New Standards, 1994a, p. 5). Many of the same issues that arose during exploratory scoring sessions would apply as well to procedures for standards-based grading of portfolios.

How did the system ensure validity and fairness?

Typically details about reliability checks, second readings, validity studies, and the like might answer this question. At least one district, to our knowledge, is moving to implement the New Standards Field-Trial Portfolio for informational purposes, although the system has yet to be fully implemented for accountability purposes. Data from this district indicate that NSP portfolios can be scored reliably (Norene Adams, personal communication).

In Pittsburgh, the district collects portfolios from a 15 percent random, stratified sample of high school students. (The teachers receive a list of students whose portfolios will be scored about two weeks before the end of school.) In 1999, approximately 75 percent of those portfolios requested were each scored twice. The district used this 75 percent to determine interrater reliability. The other 25 percent were portfolios that were immediately identified as unscorable, either because they were empty (Pittsburgh has a 40 percent mobility rate), or because they were literacy folders and not portfolios. This is not to say, however, that none of the 75 percent that were used to determine interrater reliability were identified as unscorable. The district used a six point rubric, 0 to 5. Some of the portfolios were given a score of zero (the "score" for unscorable portfolios). In the final analysis, proficient was considered a score of 4 or 5 (Norene Adams, personal communication).

All of the people who scored the portfolios in 1999 were either secondary language arts teachers or supervisors. One person, Diane Hughes, led the training and calibration. Scoring took place from 8 a.m. until 3 p.m. for five days, Monday through Friday during a week in August. Training and calibration took place for most of the day on Monday, and then raters were re-calibrated every morning (Norene Adams, personal communication).

Each exhibit in a portfolio was scored. If the scores were adjacent (e.g., one person scored the writing 3 and the other 4) that was considered a match (and that student received a score of 3.5). Portfolios were arbitrated if scores were not adjacent (e.g., one person scored the portfolio 3 and the other scored the portfolio 5). Raters were charged with an arbitration if their score was the "incorrect one." That is if rater one gave the portfolio a 3 and rater two gave the portfolio a 5 and then rater three gave it a score of 2 or 3, then rater two would be charged with an arbitration, but not rater one. If rater three gave a score of 4 then neither rater would be charged with the arbitration and the student would be given the score of 4. The total number of portfolios that needed a third reading because of a disagreement in a score for each kind of exhibit was: Reading (24); Writing (21); and Speaking (13). The number of portfolios where a third rater's score resulted in one of the first two raters being charged with an arbitration was: Reading (16); Writing (13); and Speaking (9). The total number of portfolios double scored was 842. The total number of portfolios scored was 1122. The reliability rates in 1999 were, by exhibit: Reading (98%), Writing (98%), Speaking (99%) (Norene Adams, personal communication).

It is also worth noting that New Standards made important contributions toward the development of procedures for ensuring valid and fair assessment systems in general. One contribution was the development of a system of training to benchmarks (exemplars of student work) that made it "possible to maintain scoring reliability even when scoring was done at multiple, dispersed sites" (Resnick, 1996, p.9). Myers and Pearson (1996) elaborate:

> First, we learned that rubrics, anchor papers, and commentaries (careful explanations of how a particular anchor paper maps onto the rubric) form an inseparable triad, and that the absence of any one component weakens the scoring process. All three—rubrics, anchor papers, and commentaries—were necessary to anchor a score point when working with large numbers of teachers who were often training others. (p. 7)

New Standards also explored a system for certifying judges as scorers "to serve as scoring leaders in their own local schools and districts" (Myers & Pearson, 1996). During training, "candidate scorers" discussed each of several benchmark papers extensively, and candidates continued training until they could meet a criterion "of assigning scores identical to the benchmark score to 16 of 20 successive papers" that they had not seen before (Resnick, 1996). Individuals who could score consistently in relation to a standard were identified and "certified." According to Lauren Resnick, using a process of this kind, it is possible to "calibrate different groups of scorers to the same standard" (Resnick, 1996, p. 9).

During the portfolio development process, New Standards also explored several approaches to evaluating portfolios. As Lauren Resnick (1996) points out, scoring individual papers is very different from scoring a portfolio:

> All students will not have responded to the same question, so there will be no simple way to select a paper that exemplifies a certain level of response. The scorer's job will be not only to judge the quality of a particular piece of work but also to decide whether a collection of portfolio entries, considered as a whole, displays all of the capabilities that are valued. This is a much more sophisticated and demanding judgment task than scoring a single piece of work. (p. 9)

One approach asked scorers to create inventories and make comments along with scores. A concern here was the time-intensive demands of the method.

Another approach involved assigning multiple scores for the different categories of evidence in the New Standards portfolios (New Standards, 1996). Developed in the summer and piloted in the fall of 1996, it appeared to hold some promise for addressing difficulties faced in obtaining reliable scores for collections of work. In English language arts, the reading exhibit received four scores: one for the literature requirement, one for the informational reading requirement, a certification for reading aloud, and a score and certification for the quantity, range, and depth requirement. The writing exhibit received eight scores: one each for the five different required writing types; a holistic score across the exhibit as a whole for purpose, audience, use of writing strategies, and organization; one score for conventions; and one for the evidence of writing "craft." The student's teacher provided certifications.

The multiple score approach allowed scorers to pay attention to characteristic features of particular genre or domains of writing. The value of an approach of this kind is that the scoring guides (rubrics) explicitly describe features of texts that are designed to accomplish particular social purposes. Students need to learn that "how a text works is a function of what it is for" (Cope and Kalantzis, 1993, p. 7). Teachers can use rubrics that explicitly describe *how texts work* to help students learn how to achieve the purposes they intend.

The scoring procedures were designed to address problems that can arise when diverse kinds of evidence can be used to meet the same standard. Because students were allowed to choose from a number of different kinds of entries and within each kind of entry, from a wide range of possible topics, each student's New Standards portfolio was somewhat unique. Decisions made by scorers are more complicated with a portfolio of this kind because they are asked to agree on more than quality. For instance, before they can judge quality, they must first agree that appropriate evidence has been submitted for the requirements of a particular scoring category.

In this exploratory approach, scorers looked for entries that were appropriately identified and recorded their findings by checking—or not checking—a box labeled "submitted."

Scorers must also find the evidence to be readable. In this exploratory approach, if an item was identified as "submitted," then the scorer was asked to determine whether the piece was readable, that is, legible and understandable. If the item was identified as "readable," then scorers were asked to determine whether the evidence met the definition of the category for which it was submitted.

Some students, for example, mistakenly labeled entries as narrative procedures (a category which consisted of "how-to" guides to action) that were actually "narrative accounts" (narratives with characters, plots, conflicts, and settings). Other students labeled entries as "response to literature" (the student's analysis of a literary genre written by someone else) that were actually "literary genre" (a category which included a story, play, poem or other literary genre created by the student). Some entries, on the other hand, weren't labeled at all, in which case the scorer had to identify the category.

The fourth and final step for scorers in this exploratory approach was to make a judgement about the quality of the evidence presented. That is, scorers were asked to decide whether the entry met the criteria for the exhibit and entry instructions. For instance, among other criteria, students who submitted a literary genre were expected to use "organizational patterns, formats, language, and other conventions appropriate for the specific genre," and to control "the genre's techniques" (New Standards, 1996, p. 3). Students who submitted a "response to literature," were expected to make "an analytic, interpretive, evaluative, or reflective judgment," and support the judgement "with appropriate evidence" (New Standards, 1996, p. 3). In this particular pilot scoring system, the final judgment was a yes-no decision. Student work was not scored on a scale. It met the criteria or it did not.

The piloting of this scoring system brought to light several possible explanations for disagreements in portfolio scoring—apart from disagreements about the quality of the work. For example, scorers sometimes disagreed as to whether a particular kind of entry had been officially "submitted." Interviews with scorers about the reasons for these discrepancies revealed that they were employing different decision rules. Some scorers required an official New Standards entry slip as evidence of "submission." Others were more lenient, content to hunt through the portfolio contents and the titles of papers for evidence that a particular kind of entry was present in the portfolio.

Other disagreements arose about the definition of a particular kind of work. For instance, instead of employing the New Standards criteria, some scorers employed their own particular classroom criteria for similar kinds of work when they scored portfolio entries. For instance, one of the required entries was a "report." For some scorers a report might call for little more than a brief sample of informational writing; for others, it required something more along the lines of a research term paper, with all the accompanying citations of sources.

Still other disagreements arose when readers confused decisions about whether a piece fit the definition for a particular kind of entry with judgments about the quality of the piece. That is, when deciding whether a particular piece met the criteria for a particular kind of entry, some scorers based their judgments on the presence of particular elements associated with particular genres rather than the caliber of the elements that were present. Because the interviews with scorers during the first pilot brought reasons for discrepancies to light, they led the way to better formulated decision rules and training procedures. Research and development work of this kind may help to eliminate some of the scoring discrepancies that have so plagued portfolio systems.

There are other issues to consider, of course, in any discussion of validity and fairness. Lauren Resnick outlines several, including the problem of ensuring that judgments are based on an adequate sample of "representative work," ensuring that students are protected "from the arbitrary judgments of individual teachers," and establishing the construct validity of the portfolio. It is in this latter area that agreed upon standards for evaluating the knowledge and skills that students are expected to learn are especially important. Grant Wiggins (1991) puts the issue this way, ". . . authentic assessment achieves validity and reliability by standardizing the scoring *criteria* of the (varied) products where traditional testing standardizes every 'item' (and, hence, the one *right answer* for each).

Creating an agreed upon framework that "dimensionalizes the content standards and specifies which dimensions must and which may be included in the assessment" is, according to Resnick, an important step toward establishing the construct validity of assessment. (Resnick, 1996, p. 15). In 1996, New Standards was working on a process through which a portfolio of student work could be "mapped" to the dimensions of the framework "to show how the work taken as a whole demonstrates competence in all of the dimensions specified" (Resnick, 1996, p. 16). The benefit to an approach of this kind is that the "mapping" would ensure that principled judgments about students' competence could be made even though there might be many different "curricular" routes to the same standard.

Issues of Impact

By 1996, the New Standards Project had evolved in substantial ways and had dropped the "Project" in its name, becoming simply "New Standards." When the project started, it was supported solely by foundation grants. Later, states and districts paid membership dues. Its affiliation with the National Council of Teachers of English, begun early on, ended around the time the project began planning to "enter the market place"—to sell the products that had been developed. Harcourt Brace Educational Measurement began marketing, distributing, and scoring the New Standards reference exams, and published the final version of the standards (Paslov, 1996, p. 2). In the summer of 1997, the partnership between the National Center on Education and the Economy (NCEE) and the Learning Research and Development Center at the University of Pittsburgh officially ended. Work continues, however, under the auspices of NCEE. New Standards is now a component of NCEE's America's Choice Schools program, a program that involves professional training sessions on school reorganization with a grounding in the New Standards Performance Standards, and the development of core assignments for curriculum.

There has been no systematic collection of data about the impact of NSP, a circumstance that is unfortunate, because such data would be useful in gauging the effectiveness of the project's initial approach to reform. Information about the impact of the project is sketchy. Several districts (New York, Pittsburgh, Chicago, Fort Worth) and at least one state (Vermont) are using some component of the New Standards work (New Standards, 1997, p. 3). In addition, an NCEE publication reports that schools and districts in Philadelphia and New Jersey have been administering the New Standards Reference Exam (National Center on Education and the Economy, 1999).

At the secondary level, the Pittsburgh Public Schools replaced the Arts PROPEL portfolio design and phased in the New Standards Portfolio in the mid-1990s. Since then, the district has emphasized the cross-content responsibilities of teachers to prepare students to meet the portfolio requirements. All teachers, for example, are responsible for encouraging students to meet the "read 25 books a year" standard—not just English teachers. In 1996, both kinds of portfolios were scored by the district, but in later years only NSP portfolios were scored (Norene Adams, personal communication). As explained above, the district reports high rates of agreement. At the time this chapter was written, data were used for informational purposes only, although district personnel reported that there was interest within the district in making school by school data available to the public.

While the data from Pittsburgh suggest that it is possible to obtain high rates of agreement when NSP portfolios are scored, there is relatively little evidence to date of the impact the portfolio has had on curriculum and instruction in schools. One study conducted in the classrooms of expert teachers in two schools in California during the pilot year suggests the portfolio guidelines impacted the curriculum in both positive and less than positive ways (Murphy, et al., 1998). Although the New Standards Field-Trial Portfolio had little, if any impact on the speaking and listening curriculum at the two sites, it did appear to have a positive impact on the reading curriculum. Both of the teachers changed their reading curriculum to provide evidence for the New Standards Portfolio and valued the changes they made. One teacher added a reading inventory assignment and viewed it as a new way to monitor her students' individual reading interests and progress. The other teacher added a new independent reading program that greatly increased the breadth of material covered in her curriculum.

In this study, although the New Standards portfolio requirements appeared to promote reform goals in the area of reading, the impact was very different in the area of writing. When the students put together the New Standards portfolios, the highly structured evidence requirements in writing, along with the unfamiliar terminology of the standards, appeared to inhibit them from engaging in self-assessment and intentional learning. Although the open-ended standards allowed decision-making in other areas of the language arts (speaking and listening, and reading) the requirements for specific types of writing left students with few choices or judgments to make and few opportunities to compare the quality of one piece of work with another. Instead they were led into a search-sort-label exercise to find writing of particular types.

Moreover, in spite of the teachers' efforts to translate, for many students the criteria remained inaccessible. As a result, they were reduced to trying to explain how their work approximated a priori standards and characteristics that were not well understood.

Requiring that students put particular types of writing in their portfolios will no doubt accomplish some of the goals of reform. Students will spend more time writing actual texts. But instituting requirements for particular types of writing won't guarantee that other important goals of reform will be met. To the contrary, if the prescriptive requirements of external assessment systems make intentional learning the "null" curriculum, as happened in this study, they may ultimately undermine the goals of reform. Self-directed learners have learned how to set goals, monitor their work, and assess their progress, but students will not learn how to do these things if they do not have opportunities.

Problems and Potential Solutions

The initial proposal for the funding of the New Standards Project commented on what would be needed to accommodate local variations in curricula and assessments, a design feature considered crucial to its success:

> While the design requires consensus on the syllabus for each subject—a speci-fication of what students should know and be able to do—it does not require agreement on the curriculum, the texts to be used and the organization and presentation of the course of study. In fact, our design will encourage, even demand, the development of a wide range of curricula engaging students with very different learning styles from many different cultures and back-grounds, all intended to bring students by many different routes up to the standard of accomplishment required by the examinations. (Learning Re-search and Development Center and National Center on Education and the Economy, 1990)

Whether diversity in curricula is a realistic expectation in a system that specifies par-ticular types of writing is a question that assessment designers—and users of the NSP portfolio—need to consider. It is likely, perhaps even probable, that if such a system were in place, the teaching of writing might be confined to the types on the test. California learned that lesson when the CAP test was put in place. Although educators applauded the move beyond the five-paragraph theme, curricula in Cali-fornia were quickly adjusted to fit the new scheme. In most schools, the eight types of writing were the order of the day. While eight might be better than one, since it sug-gests breadth in the curriculum, the system may nevertheless be constraining.

The specification of curricula guarantees that "You get what you assess." The question is, then, is this what we want? Are the writing types promoted by the New Standards portfolio the ones that everyone should teach? In districts where the cur-riculum needs revision, more writing would likely be—if only to meet the require-ments of the portfolio—an outcome. A potential problem, however, is that many dis-tricts and schools throughout the nation have other challenging curricula in place. To create New Standards portfolios, revision of the curricula would be required. For some districts and schools, this would be valuable, for others an unnecessary disrup-tion—one more change to make in the wake of reform.

A point we would like to make here is that we need to know more about the impact of performance and portfolio assessment on curriculum and instruction. Its use as a means to drive educational reform is predicated on the assumption that teachers will change what is taught to conform to the requirements of the new assess-ments. Few studies, however, have investigated the actual effects on curriculum teach-ing and learning. An exception is the investigation done by Amalsi, Afflerbach, Guthrie and Schafer (1995) of the effects of the Maryland School Performance Assessment Program on classroom instructional practice in literacy. Another is the work done by

Koretz, Stecher, Klein, and McCaffrey (1994) in their investigation of the impact of the Vermont portfolio assessment program, though this work is limited to the effects of the mathematics portfolios. A third is the work done by Underwood (1998; 1999) on the consequences of an internally developed portfolio assessment system. More research of this kind needs to be done if claims are to be made about the positive impact of new forms of assessment in education.

In addition to considering the impact on curriculum, the impact on students— and students' motivation and ownership—needs investigation as well. Kansas City, Missouri, middle school teacher Julie Collins, after participating in one of the New Standards portfolio development conferences wondered whether it was possible to have a national portfolio system without taking "yet another cookie-cutter approach" to assessment:

> You have to watch out for the issue of standardization and prescribing what teachers and students do in their classrooms. . . . I understand where New Standards is coming from as far as wanting to have an instrument that has common ground in Missouri and other states [but] . . . I'm very much in favor of allowing student choice [in portfolios]. I think that's where students' voices come through and that's what makes writing stronger—when students discover their own unique talents. (quoted in Flanagan, 1994)

Everyone engaged in assessment development should share her concern.

Opportunities for Discussion and Inquiry

1. What are the implications of giving students no choice in the kinds of entries they submit in their portfolios? A narrow field of choice? A wide open field such as "best works" or "favorites"?

2. What roles can/should teachers play in assessment development at the national level? Locally?

3. What kinds of contradictions do you see in the revised New Standards/NCEE agenda? Are "core assignments" more likely to ensure high standards or formulaic teaching?

4. When New Standards agreed to work with Harcourt, Brace, and Javonovich, NSP made an alliance with a commercial standardized test development company. What relationships between such companies and other organizations interested in furthering portfolio assessment do you believe might be viable and productive?

Acknowledgments

We would like to express our appreciation to Sally Hampton, Director, English Language Arts for NCEE, Elizabeth Stage of the New Standards Project, and Norene Adams, of the Pittsburgh Public School District for the help they provided as we gathered information for this chapter. We would also like to acknowledge the work of all the other authors who have told parts of the New Standards Project story in the past. Their publications were enormously helpful to us as we reconstructed the Project's history.

References

Almasi, J., Afflerback, P., Guthrie, J., & Shafer, W. (1995). *Effects of a statewide performance assessment program on classroom instructional practice in literacy*, (Reading Research Report No. 32). College Park, MD: National Reading Research Center, University of Maryland.

Board of Education of the City of New York. (1997). *Performance standards: English language arts, English as a second language, Spanish language arts*. New York City, NY. Author.

Camp, R. (1993). The place of portfolios in our changing views of writing Assessment. In R. E. Bennett & W. C. Ward (Eds.), *Construction versus choice in cognitive measurement: Issues in constructed response, performance testing, and portfolio assessment* (pp.183–212). Hillsdale, NJ: Lawrence Erlbaum Associates.

Cannell, J. J. (1987). *Nationally normed elementary achievement testing in America's public schools: How all fifty states are above the national average*. Daniels, WV: Friends for Education.

Cheney, L. (1991). *National tests: What other countries expect their students to know*. Washington, DC: National Endowment for the Humanities.

Cope, B., & Kalantzis, M. (Eds.). (1993). *The powers of literacy: A genre approach to teaching writing*. Pittsburgh, PA: University of Pittsburgh Press.

Corbett, H. D., & Wilson, B. L. (1991). *Testing, reform, and rebellion*. Norwood, NJ: Ablex.

Diegmueller, K. (1995). 14-state reform project releases draft standards. *Across the Nation, 1,* 6.

Door-Bremme, D. & Herman, J. (1986). *Assessing student achievement: A profile of classroom practices*. Los Angeles, CA: Center for the Study of Evaluation.

Flanagan, A. (1994). ELA teachers engaged in massive portfolio project. *The Council Chronicle, 4* (1), 1, 4–5.

Frederiksen, N. (1984). The real test bias: Influences of testing on teaching and learning. *American Psychologist, 39* (1), 193–202.

Gilchrist, J. (September 4, 1992). Memo to site coordinators and attendees at the Phoenix conference re: Follow up on the conference and plans for the future. New Standards Project. University of Pittsburgh, Pittsburgh, PA: Learning Research and Development Center.

Gurskey, D. (1991, April). Ambitious measures. *Teacher Magazine*: 51–56.

Haertel, E. H., & Calfee, R. C. (1983). School achievement: Thinking about what to test. *Journal of Educational Measurement, 20,* 119–32.

Haney, W. (1991). We must take care: Fitting assessments to functions. In V. Perrone (Ed.), *Expanding student assessment*. Alexandria, VA: Association for Supervision and Curriculum Development.

Koretz, D., Stecher, B., Klein, S., & McCaffrey, D. (1994). *The evolution of a portfolio program: The impact and quality of the Vermont program in its second year (1992–93)* (CSE Tech. Rep. No. 385). Los Angeles: University of California, Center for Research on Evaluation, Standards, and Student Testing.

Learning Research and Development Center and National Center on Education and the Economy (1990). *Setting a new standard: Toward an examination system for the United States*. Unpublished proposal. University of Pittsburgh, Pittsburgh, PA, and Rochester, NY: Authors.

Madaus, G. F. (1988). The influence of testing on the curriculum. In L. Tanner (Ed.), *Critical issues in curriculum*, Eighty-seventh Yearbook of the National Society for Study of Education (pp. 83–121). Chicago: University of Chicago Press.

Mathison, S. (1989, April). *The perceived effects of standardized testing on teaching and curricula.* Paper presented at the Annual Meeting of the American Educational Research Association, San Francisco, CA.

Murphy, S., Bergamini, J., & Rooney, P. (1997). The impact of large-scale portfolio assessment programs on classroom practice: Case studies of the New Standards field-trial portfolio. *Educational Assessment, 4* (4), 297–333.

Myers, M., & Pearson, P. D. (1996). Performance assessment and the literacy unit of the New Standards Project. *Assessing Writing, 3* (1), 5–29.

National Center on Education and the Economy. (1990). *America's choice: High skills or low wages! The report of the commission on the skills of the American workforce.* Executive Summary. Washington, DC: Author.

National Center on Education and the Economy. (1999). Q & A. *Expecting More, 2* (3). Washington DC.: Author.

National Council of Teachers of English (1991). Educators look for new standards, assessments. *The Council Chronicle, 1* (2), 1. Urbana, IL: Author.

National Council of Teachers of English (1993). New Standards takes close look at portfolios. *The Council Chronicle, 3* (2), 1–2.

National Council of Teachers of English & International Reading Association. (1996). *Standards for the English language arts.* Urbana, IL: NCTE & Newark, DE: IRA.

New Standards Project (August, 1991). Press release. Washingtion, DC: Author.

New Standards Project (1992a). Framing the issue. *The daily standard, 2,* (1). Washington, DC: Author.

New Standards Project (1992b). Team updates. *The daily standard, 2,* (3). Washington, DC: Author

New Standards Project (1992c). Team updates. *The daily standard, 2,* (4). Washington, DC: Author

New Standards Project (1992d). Snowmass, CO, summer workshop handout. Washington, DC: Author.

New Standards Project (1993). *New Standards Project English language arts portfolio. A student handbook.* Portfolio Pilot Meeting, Danvers, MA. Washington, DC: Author.

New Standards (1994a). *Student portfolio handbook: High school English language arts.* Field trial version. Washington, DC: Author.

New Standards (1994b). Teachers draw inspiration, perspiration at summer meeting. *The New Standard, 2,* (4). Washington, DC: Author.

New Standards (1994c). *Student portfolio handbook: Elementary school English language arts.* Field trial version. Washington, DC: Author

New Standards (1994d). Reflection in the portfolio mirror. *The new standard, 2,* (7). Washington, DC: Author.

New Standards (1995a). *New Standards portfolio field trial: High school English language arts.* 1995–96 Workshop Edition. Washington, DC: National Center on Education and the Economy: Author.

New Standards (1995b). *New Standards 1995–96 high school English language arts portfolio.* Washington, DC: National Center on Education and the Economy: Author

New Standards (1995c). *Performance standards: English language arts, mathematics, science, applied learning, Volume 3, High School* . Consultation Draft. Washington, DC: National Center on Education and the Economy: Author

New Standards (1995d). Standards connect classrooms across the country. *The New Standard, 3*, (3). Washington, DC: National Center on Education and the Economy: Author.

New Standards (1995e) *New Standards 1995–96 Elementary English language arts portfolio*. Washington, DC: National Center on Education and the Economy: Author.

New Standards (1995f) *New Standards 1995–96 Middle grades English language arts portfolio*. Washington, DC: National Center on Education and the Economy: Author.

New Standards (1996). *ELA portfolio scoring conference handout*. Washington, DC: National Center on Education and the Economy: Author.

New Standards (1997). Standards: From good idea to reality. *The New Standard, 5*, (1). Washington, DC: National Center on Education and the Economy: Author.

O'Neil, J. (1993, February). On the New Standards Project: A conversation with Lauren Resnick and Warren Simmons. *Educational Leadership*, 17–21.

Paslov, E. (1996). Untitled letter addressed to Dear Colleagues. *The New Standard, 4*, (2). Washington, DC: New Standards.

Resnick, D., & Kapinus, B. (February 7, 1992). Letter to the English-Language Arts Advisory Group, New Standards Project.

Resnick, L. (1996). Performance puzzles: Issues in measuring capabilities and certifying accomplishments. (Center for the Study of Evaluation Technical Report No. 415). Los Angeles, CA: National Center for Research on Evaluation, Standards, and Student Testing, University of California, Los Angeles.

Resnick, L. B., & Klopfer, K. (1989). *Toward the thinking curriculum: Current cognitive research. 1989 Yearbook of the Association for Supervision and Curriculum Development*. Alexandria, VA: The Association for Supervision and Curriculum Development.

Resnick, L., & Resnick, D. (1992). Assessing the thinking curriculum: New tools for educational reform. In B. Gifford & M. C. O'Connor (Eds.), *Changing assessments: Alternative views of aptitude, achievement and instruction*. Boston: Kluwer Academic Publishers.

Resnick, L., Nolan, K., & Resnick, D. (1995). Benchmarking education standards. *Educational Evaluation and Policy Analysis, 17* (4):438–461.

Rothman, R. (1992). Auditors help Pittsburgh make sure its portfolio assessment measures up. *Education Week, 11* (40): 1–4.

Sheingold, K., Heller, J. I., & S. T. Paulukonis. (1994). *Actively seeking evidence: shifts in teacher's thinking and practice through assessment development*. (Tech. Rep. No. 94–04). Princeton New Jersey: Educational Testing Service.

Simmons, W., & Resnick, L. (1993, Febuary). Assessment as the catalyst of school reform. *Educational Leadership*, 11–15.

Smith, M. L. (1991). Put to the test: The effects of external testing on teachers. *Educational Researcher, 20* (5), 8–11.

Underwood, T. (1998). The consequences of portfolio assessment: A case study. *Educational Assessment 5* (3), 147–194.

Underwood, T. (1999). *The portfolio project: Assessment, instruction, and middle school reform*. Urbana, IL: National Council of Teachers of English.

Wells, P. (1991). Putting America to the test. *Agenda, 1*, 52–57.

Wiggins, G. (1991, August). *A brief argument for "authentic assessment."* Unpublished manuscript. (An essay prepared for the New Standards Project meeting at Snowmass, Colorado.)

10 Making Decisions about Assessment

In preceding chapters, we have profiled the designs of eight portfolio assessment systems developed and implemented during the late 1980s and early 1990s in response to enormous political, pedagogical, and popular interest in alternative, authentic assessment. Two of these systems—Vermont and Kentucky—have sustained themselves throughout the decade and appear to have become almost institutionalized in their settings for very different reasons. Four of them—Arts PROPEL, almost as widely studied as Kentucky; Chinle, a noble experiment in diversity; and Ruff and Mt. Diablo, two little-known school projects—have not fully sustained themselves in their original designs but have contributed important insights for future portfolio systems designers to consider. One system, the New Standards Project, frequently discussed in both scholarly and policy discourse, replaced Arts PROPEL in Pittsburgh and also influenced Vermont's redesign in the late 1990s of its scoring system component. Another system—the two-part system that was developed in Region 15 in Connecticut—appeared in full form late in the decade and gained a strong footing in local culture because of its grounding in a planned, long-term pattern of curriculum and staff development begun in 1980.

From our perspective, a striking lesson from all of these portfolio histories—perhaps the distinguishing feature that makes portfolios what they are—is the fact that portfolio assessment systems are inseparable from the people and situations in which they were made and used. We find an apt metaphor for portfolio assessment design theory in the organic architectural philosophy of Frank Lloyd Wright, who struggled his entire professional life within a culture of design that privileged "rational systems of mass production" (Blake & Sudler, 1996, n.p.). Wright, of course, sought ways to make his buildings serve people in situations and locations, whether designing for an urban or rural setting, a goal at odds with modularity and prefabrication.

Like Wright's buildings, the portfolio systems profiled here were not prefabricated. Indeed, they were intertwined with, and shaped by the social, ideological, cultural, and institutional aspects of the situations in which they emerged. The New Standards Project came about as a result of the national affiliation of politically defined educational units in an effort to create a systematic way to measure student achievement against national standards with enough flexibility to preserve local autonomy, enough sophistication to nudge teachers toward more promising practices, and enough reliability and validity to compete with standardized tests in arenas like admission-to-college formulas. Vermont and Kentucky came about because of statewide concerns that the children in those states may not have had fair and equitable opportunities to learn; their portfolio systems were designed to improve literacy instruction and to measure that improvement. Chinle came about because the schools there had not historically done well by the Navajo children; so the portfolio system was designed to privilege both local and mainstream cultural values equally. Region 15 came about because its leaders in the early 1980s set a course to promote self-regulated learning.

While the systems profiled here were shaped by the social, ideological, cultural, and institutional aspects of the situations in which they emerged, in some cases they were enervated by them as well. Assessment and curriculum specialists in Chinle sought to create a system that would serve the children of the region by valuing native Navajo culture on par with mainstream Arizona culture; a bi-cultural system called for bi-cultural standards and bi-cultural portfolios to demonstrate those standards. But standards-based reform at the state level spotlighted mainstream culture instead, making bi-cultural assessment a secondary concern. Specialists in Vermont planned to engage Vermont teachers in an extended conversation about what makes good writing and about how writing can be well taught. A system intended to construct assessment and pedagogical intersubjectivity within the profession across an entire state, even a small state, needed an open-ended design that promoted civil yet vigorous debate, risk-taking, and community. But pressure to obtain psychometric reliability led to a type-specific scoring system. Specialists in Kentucky, who did not want to have to create and implement their portfolio system as quickly as policymakers demanded, especially not in such volatile circumstances, were nevertheless obligated to help find a way to ensure equal protection to the state's children who in years past had attended schools with widely differing resources. As a consequence, the system in Kentucky was designed to serve two purposes: teacher accountability and the improvement of writing curriculum and instruction. That the portfolio system itself was created with a strong product focus while its creators counted on staff development to serve curriculum improvement purposes mirrors the political and legal circumstances in which those purposes emerged.

In the spirit of Fourth Generation Evaluation (Guba & Lincoln, 1989), each system perhaps ought to be measured against how well it served the people it was designed to serve in their particular situations and locations, rather than against arbitrary design principles or technical psychometric criteria. Indeed, we shall not suggest such criteria or rigid design principles here. Our purpose in profiling these systems was not to assert that any one system was or is inherently better than any other or to provide simplistic recipes for system designers in similar situations. Instead, we hoped to alert readers to major issues that need to be considered in the development, implementation, and sustenance of portfolio systems. Many of the issues we raise apply as well to assessment systems that employ other methods.

The set of issues we will introduce here is certainly not exhaustive, however, and we invite our readers to consider those that may be unique to their own situations as well. Neither can we pretend to know which portfolio design options might ultimately prove to be the best ones for a given situation, but we do suggest that the issues addressed here probably ought to be considered by system designers *before* they make any irrevocable decisions. As we have seen in all of these projects, early design decisions have an enormous impact, and once systems become part of an institution, they can be difficult to change. Thoughtful examination of contextual and design issues are important to long-term effectiveness.

In the sections that follow, we will compare and contrast the approaches taken by the projects we have profiled. We group issues under four headings: 1) aspirations for students, 2) perspectives on learning and curriculum, 3) approaches to reform and accountability, and 4) methods for establishing fairness, reliability, and validity. Our ordering of these issues is deliberate, because we think that debates over technique sidestep too often the more substantive and critical questions pertaining to how students learn and the best ways to teach them. As Wile and Tierney (1996) remind us, "Just as with instruction, assessment procedures divorced from theory, even though technically sound, are pedagogically and ethically bankrupt" (p. 205).

Accompanying each section, we will suggest questions for assessment designers to consider. To begin, assessment designers might ask themselves: What are our aspirations for students?

Aspirations for Students

None of the systems we examined in this book was designed to rank students in a normal distribution in the same way that standardized tests do. None of them yielded statistics like "national percentile rank" or "grade level equivalent" or "stanine"—all traditional standardized statistics designed to communicate where a particular student falls in relationship to his/her peers. Why not? None of these portfolio systems set out to answer the question "How do students compare with others in a normal distribution when we factor out what they actually did in their classrooms and schools?" Instead, these portfolio systems all asked, in one way or another, the following question: "How are these students doing as writers—sometimes as readers as well—when we look at what they *are* doing in their classrooms?" While standardized statistics may tell us whether Jane is doing "better" than Janet as a user of punctuation, for example, that is almost all they *do* tell us—they *don't* tell us whether either child is reaching her potential, whether either child is competent to do any particular task, or whether either child even *cares* about literacy work.

In a transparent and intuitively understandable way, all of the systems we have examined focused on what children actually did as writers, sometimes as readers, in regular classroom settings in the light of qualitative criteria. These systems were not designed to tell us the size of the gap between Jane and Tommy when we stack them up against their peers; these systems provided information about whether Jane is a novice or an apprentice writer; whether Tommy rarely or frequently makes wise revisions in his drafts; whether Jane is deeply engaged with her work consistently over time or seems to flit from task to task, always staying on the surface of things; whether most students make substantive revisions in drafts or simply recopy. This focus on actual work and on records of that work permits inquiry into product quality that can lead to ranking and decision making, to be sure, and in some portfolio systems such was the case. But the original and dominant intention of all of these systems was to look at classroom work processes and/or products against a backdrop of criteria, to try to help teachers see more clearly how to improve their instructional practices, and to help students learn to engage actively and responsibly in the kinds of literacy practices that might help them grow as people and as citizens.

In this context it is important to note that each of the systems we have profiled began with aspirations for students. Mt. Diablo wanted engaged, responsive learners. Vermont wanted competent writers with personal investment and voice in their work. Chinle wanted a system that would acknowledge and value the students' Navajo culture and create a bridge to the mainstream world at the same time. Charles Ruff wanted engaged readers who took on the identity of a reader and *lived* as a reader. Kentucky wanted student writers who could compose effectively across a variety of situations in the real world. Connecticut wanted competent, self-regulated learners. Arts PROPEL wanted planful, effortful, strategic, reflective learners who approach academic tasks with the disposition of an artist.

A reason for making aspirations for students the centerpiece for decisions about assessment is that it helps system designers to keep the focus on the needs and best interests of the student—where it should be—instead of peripheral concerns. That said, it is also important to acknowledge that the aspirations for students of each of these projects are different. Moreover, within the histories of each of the projects profiled here, there is evidence that competing visions of what is best for students are continually in play. All of these systems, it should be remembered, were created in response to a perceived need to change the status quo. And for several of the schools and districts and states discussed here, things have changed yet again in the years since these projects were begun.

As much as we might wish for consensus, not everyone shares the same vision about educational goals, or the appropriate approach to achieving them. For this reason it is important to make aspirations explicit. It is not typical for schools to do this; they seldom systematically consider what it is that they want for students, much less publicize those aspirations so that other stakeholders in the children's education can join in the dialogue and debate. But doing so, from our perspective, is critical, if only because it is fair to students to let them know "up front" what to expect so that they have a fair chance to succeed. Although everyone may not agree on all of the goals for students, everyone ought to know and understand their nature.

LeMahieu and Foss (1993) made visible the assumptions of "standards-based reform" for policymakers in a paper that has relevance here. According to these authors, Assumption #1 is as follows: "standards-based reform requires that considerations of what students should know, be able, and be disposed to do should be placed at the center of reform efforts" (p. 2). System designers who do not begin at this point yet intend to implement a portfolio system run the risk that "the winds of change will blow powerfully through the halls of . . . schools, but unfortunately not into any of the classrooms" (p. 2).

However, instead of the word "standards," we've deliberately chosen to use the word "aspirations", if only to make the points that not all "standards" are the same and that one can have "aspirations" (or apply standards) without prescribing curriculum in advance. Although all of the projects profiled here were developed in the context of educational reform, not all of the projects were examples of "standards-based reform" as it is typically described. To be sure, some of the schools did use a standards-based approach; that is, they developed fairly detailed expectations for "what students should know and be able to do" and then proceeded to develop new assessments to measure those expectations. The New Standards Project is an example of this approach to reform. Others schools and districts, such as Charles Ruff and Mount Diablo and Arts PROPEL, however, framed their aspirations for students in ways that did not spell out in advance a particular *body of knowledge or set of skills to be learned*. They emphasized instead the *kind of learner* they hoped would emerge from participation in schooling. Their assessments were designed to engage students in particular kinds of learning practices and to capture information about students' learning processes and development as well as their products.

Questions for reflection:
1. What kind of learner do we want our students to become?
2. What knowledge, skills, or attitudes do we want students to acquire?
3. Do our aspirations for students call for a standards-based approach or an educational context that is open-ended and divergent?
4. How will we make our expectations public?
5. What relationship will our portfolio system have with classroom grading practices? To what degree will grading practices be made transparent and public? How?

Views of Learning and Curriculum

Portfolio designs vary in the ways they represent content and in the ideas they promote about the purposes for education and the best ways to go about accomplishing those purposes. In fact, contrasting and sometimes conflicting, theoretical perspectives on learning and on the purposes and content of curricula provide the fuel for debates about portfolio practice. Transmission and acquisition are the metaphors behind the traditional model of teaching and learning, and standardized assessments are typically used to check to see whether bodies of information, or in the case of writing assessment, formulas for writing, have been received by passive students whose heads are seen, metaphorically, as containers. The social-constructivist model of teaching and learning, in contrast, emphasizes the learner's active role in the "construction" of knowledge and the socially situated nature of much of that learning (Gipps, 1999), invoking a metaphor that has been referred to as the participation metaphor (Sfard, 1998). Focusing on learners engaged in activities with others, social-constructivist theorists emphasize the social and dynamic nature of learning, describing learning and sometimes even knowledge itself in terms of social (co)participation (Lave and Wenger, 1991) and apprenticeship (Rogoff, 1990).

One way to see these contrasting perspectives is to look at the ways particular programs have framed answers to the questions students and teachers often ask about portfolios, questions which on the surface may seem purely pragmatic, but which in actuality have important theoretical implications. These theory-in-practice questions, "What goes in the portfolios?" and "Who decides?" reveal beliefs about how children learn, and how teachers should go about teaching them.

Collection

The systems we have profiled here relied largely on written texts as the "stuff" that went inside portfolios, though some systems had room for drawings and sketches, diagrams, photographs, audio and video recordings, and other kinds of artifacts. But the contents of portfolios of each of the different projects varied in other ways, as did the procedures for collecting them. Although the purpose of the portfolio certainly played a role, to some degree the variation we saw reflected contrasting perspectives on learning and curriculum. For example, although the New Standards Project portfolio contained a process entry, it was primarily a "showcase portfolio." The purpose of the process entry was to "showcase" the students' mastery of techniques of revision. The writing exhibit was designed to demonstrate mastery of particular types of writing and writing conventions. The guidelines for portfolio contents specified the types. In other words, the guidelines specified what kinds of writing children should know and be able to do. Analogous to a criterion-referenced test and echoing the assumptions of the theory of mastery learning, the New Standards Portfolios were designed to demonstrate that particular objectives of schooling had been met.

Standards-based models allow for the collection of a sample of student work that has taken an extended period of time to complete and for the collection of multiple samples of student work over time (Taylor, 1994). But the amount of growth accomplished during the period in which the work is gathered is not a concern. Similarly, the standards model allows for performances that include cycles of feedback and revision as well as collaboration, but the focus is on the outcomes of processes, not the processes themselves. *How* students went about doing their work—their level of engagement, use of technological and human resources and tools, and so on—is largely immaterial.

In contrast, other kinds of portfolios such as the Arts PROPEL "process-folios," were designed to show work at various stages of completion (and refinement) and evidence of the processes and tools used in their creation (e.g., note cards, outlines, list of references, early drafts, final drafts, written reflection on the process). Even the end-of-course portfolio design characterized the work as "in progress." As one of their entries, students were asked to select an "unsatisfying piece" and explain how they might change it. Portfolios of the Arts PROPEL design invited what Louise Wetherbee Phelps (1989) calls a "formative attitude," an attitude which asks students and teachers to think of the student's text as a piece "in the process of evolution" (p. 51). Process-folios gave Arts PROPEL teachers traces of the evolution of pieces of writing. Although the portfolios were ultimately used for a public accounting of school performance, their design highlighted learning and process and the student's responsibility in learning.

Like the portfolios in Arts PROPEL, portfolios in Connecticut's Pomperaug Regional School District 15 highlighted the student's responsibility in learning and invited a formative attitude. Students there engaged in writing exercises, considered elements of quality, assessed and evaluated completed work, and set new goals in a continual cycle of learning. The contents of students' portfolios were determined in part by the goals that students had set for themselves at the beginning of the year and in part by the progress they made toward them. When the students had identified areas of improvement and/or accomplishment, they selected three to five pieces of writing as evidence. While most portfolios profiled here asked "How well do you write?" portfolios in Arts PROPEL and Region 15 asked "To what degree are you becoming an independent learner?"

The Arts PROPEL and Region 15 portfolios reflect a social-constructivist view of learning and curriculum, a perspective in which knowledge is viewed not as information to be transmitted from an expert to a neophyte, but as a mental representation which must be constructed by the learner. Students learn by integrating new knowledge into their existing schemas, scripts, and models, and by reorganizing those knowledge structures when new information conflicts with old. Social-constructivists emphasize the socially-situated nature of that learning; that is, learning takes place through transactions between student and student, student and text, student and teacher. Viewed from a social-constructivist perspective like that exemplified in Pittsburgh and Connecticut, then, assessment procedures are inevitably a part of the dialectic of teaching and learning, part of the process which shapes what knowledge is, what is learned, and how students learn. Assessments which reflect this perspective provide a means for engaging students in self-reflection and for expanding their roles as collaborators in learning activities.

Selection

The approaches taken to the selection of portfolio contents in the projects profiled in this book varied widely. In Vermont, although project leaders recommended that teachers and students negotiate portfolio contents, there were no hard and fast rules. While the selection process varied across schools and grade levels, evidence suggests that teachers sometimes played a role in the process. In Chinle, although students were free to choose pieces of work for the "free choice" selection, teachers had the ultimate authority to decide when a particular task or assessment activity would be included to meet other portfolio requirements. In contrast, at Mt. Diablo, students made selections. But in the early years of the project their selection was constrained by a menu of required writing types. Over the years their autonomy grew as the design of the portfolio became more open-ended. Vermont began its system by giving students wide latitude in submitting whatever kind of writing they wanted to submit in the form of a "best piece," and although there were several "types" called for, the definition of types which was used initially was also broad. Lately, however, Vermont has designed a menu of types and has asked students to select writings which fall within the constraints of the menu, though one of those types is "poetry" broadly construed. At Charles Ruff Middle School, students selected pieces of work for their portfolios, but they did so only after having been given feedback from their peers, teachers, and parents. In New Standards' schools, student choices were constrained by the menu of required writing types. If students had only a single piece of writing that fit the criteria, they had no choice at all. And, at all schools students' selections were constrained because they were made from work that had been assigned by their teachers.

For many involved in portfolio practice, the selection process is the key to the learning potential of portfolios. In Kentucky, for example, the state handbook included a code of ethics governing the selection process in an effort to ensure students' ownership of their work. Recognizing the unique opportunities for learning that portfolios can provide, various groups and individuals involved in the development of portfolio programs argue that portfolios should emphasize choice and student authority to enhance the opportunities for learning in the experience of putting the portfolio together. For example, Roberta Camp (1990) described aspects of portfolios which teachers consider essential:

- Multiple samples of writing, preferably collected over a sustained period of time
- Evidence of the processes and strategies that students use in creating at least some of those pieces of writing
- Evidence of the extent to which students are aware of the processes and strategies they use in writing and of their development as writers (p. 10)

Of particular interest is the emphasis on the students' awareness of their *own* processes and strategies for writing and their *own* ability to articulate their development.

Similarly, several of the guidelines proposed by Paulson, Paulson & Meyer (1991) highlight the importance of the students' role in generating the contents of the portfolio and in deciding how their work will be represented to external audiences. According to Paulson, et al., students should have the opportunity to shape the information about themselves that the portfolios will convey. In other words, they should have the right to say what *won't* be included in the portfolio:

- Portfolios should provide opportunity for students to engage in self-reflection.
- Students should be involved in selecting the pieces included in the portfolio.
- The portfolio should convey a sense of the student's activities and intentions in generating it.
- The final portfolio should contain only material that the student is willing to make public. (p. 60)

All of this work highlights the importance of student "ownership" as well as the interchange that is possible in classrooms where assessment is integrated with instruction. In fact, much of the literature on portfolios suggests that portfolios should provide opportunities for students to exercise judgment about their own work, monitor their own progress, set goals for themselves, and present themselves and their work to others (see also Camp, 1990, 1992; Murphy & Smith, 1990, 1991, 1992; Tierney, Carter, & Desai, 1991; Wolf, 1989; Yancey, 1992).

Yet as the examples above illustrate, approaches to dealing with the issue of student authority can differ in significant ways in portfolio design. Standards-based systems set expectations for what educators believe to be the most important, established, and widely accepted facts, concepts, or skills. When these systems narrowly prescribe portfolio contents, they run the risk of being less effective in moving students beyond mere compliance toward the development of "agency," the "personal style, assurance, and self-control that allow [the individual] to act in both socially acceptable and personally meaningful ways" (Sizer, 1973, cited in Posner, 1992, p. 95.). Development of agency, a fundamental principle of an experiential perspective in curriculum studies, requires giving students a measure of control over their environment and education by yielding a degree of decision-making responsibility and power (Posner, 1992). To develop agency, students need to make choices. They need to be able to play a role in discussing and negotiating the terms and outcomes of assessment.

Allowing students to negotiate may seem a radical approach to assessment. Indeed, in traditional assessment, others—external assessors or the teacher—define the task and evaluate the student's production. Yet increasingly, and in the literature on portfolios in particular, there are calls for increasing student participation and voice in the assessment process. Even when their ultimate purpose is accountability to outside agencies, the argument goes, portfolios should not be mere repositories of work saved for others to evaluate; they should be process portfolios, easily accessible to students, and tools for learning, (D'Aoust, 1992; Jongsma, 1989; Tierney, et al., 1991).

Social and Cultural Aspects of Literacy

All of the portfolio projects we examined postponed dealing with a problem that will continue to plague us until literacy educators—and those policymakers who regulate public pedagogy—learn to focus as deeply on the social and cultural aspects of literacy practices as they do on the technical aspects of literacy and on textual products. Street (1984) and others have argued convincingly that literacy practices are in essence social practices which take on meaning only in particular cultural and historical contexts to serve situated purposes, a theme that was missing from many of the systems we examined. Three tacit assumptions ran through the design of the systems that ignored this theme: 1) that the social situations and cultural patterns surrounding students' lives need not be considered during assessment as having a significant shaping power over their literacy practices and products (literacy in a vacuum); 2) that mastering literacy in one place and time is tantamount to mastering a universal literacy for all places and times (literacy as a universal technology); and 3) that literacy products can be viewed as objects apart from the circumstances in which they were created *and* apart from the circumstances in which they are construed (literacy as a commodity).

For an obvious example of how these systems separated literacy from its social and cultural situations of practice, consider this: What was largely absent from the portfolios of projects we profiled (with the exception of the New Standards Portfolio system, which never really went beyond discussing it) was evidence of student talk—discussion, debate, presentation, conversation, and collaboration. Talk was left out partly for a practical reason: It is simply difficult to collect and transport artifacts of conversation. But there are two other reasons, we believe, that talk has typically been left out of portfolio assessment—reasons that grow from the academic culture of schools in America. First, as we have already pointed out, our schools have a long tradition of insisting that students "do their own work" and "don't cheat." The tradition demands that children find the answer for themselves, grasp the meaning on their own, and think their own thoughts. It demands that children not depend on others for help, for ideas—for answers. Indeed, collaborative student work is often not taken seriously, particularly not in assessment situations, because it does not represent an "alone-shipwrecked-on-a-desert-island" effort.

Second is the more contemporary—if more complex—issue of ownership, a valued aspect of portfolio practice, but an idea which may inadvertently support the notion that literacy exists or can be separated from the social and cultural context in which it occurs. Although the metaphor of student ownership is appealing because it implies student engagement and commitment and so on, it seems in conflict with the many voices and dialogues characteristic of both writing and reading. Moreover, the ownership metaphor can merge with the idea that students should "do their own work," so that students who read and write in social and cultural solitude are viewed as the only true "owners" of their work. Thus, the norms of "cheating" and the metaphor of "ownership" can reinforce one another's potency.

When we really begin to examine the role of the community in literacy learning, the separation of literacy from context becomes untenable. Consider, for example, the social and cultural basis for the writing of a memoir. On the surface it would appear as if a memoir, more so than perhaps any other kind of writing, *ought* to be owned by the author, *ought* to be the result of the individual mind. But the shape and look of texts in this genre hardly originate with the writer; all of us rent in a Bakhtinian sense and use knowledge of memoir learned through experience in our community as we make our writing work with and for our audiences. We make use of our knowledge that our audience expects to read a narrative of an unusual or thought-provoking personal event to move us along and to make decisions during composing processes. How much of this use of our knowledge of our audience as a tool during our writing is cheating? How much of the work do we own? How much do we rent?

Miller's (1984/1994) definition of genre as "a complex of formal and substantive features that create a particular effect in a given situation" (p. 25) and "typified rhetorical actions" that occur during "recurrent situations" (p. 24), underscores the significance of the social in writing. This view of genre combines content and form into a "complex," a term which suggests that the relationship between form and content may change as we consider different genres. For example, the index as a genre might well be defined almost exclusively by way of formal features—items organized alphabetically, page numbers following each item, placement at the end of a book, etc. The apology as a genre, however, might be better defined by way of substance—a confession or an admission of guilt followed by a plea for forgiveness followed by an explanation or a promise. But whether we are speaking about an index or an apology, the bottom line is that we are talking about socially organized knowledge which we can neither learn nor use in isolation—social knowledge that enables us to enact literacy practices for social purposes.

Further, Miller's (1984/1994) definition links content and form—"typified rhetorical actions"—with purpose and occasion—"recurrent situations"; we can't talk about a genre without talking about its use, that is, the motivations that give rise to it and the consequences of each instantiation. In fact, motivations and consequences may be critically important factors in planning for instruction, as Miller noted:

> What we learn when we learn a genre is not just a pattern of forms or even a method of achieving our own ends. We learn, more importantly, what ends we may have: we learn that we may eulogize, apologize, recommend one person to another, instruct customers on behalf of a manufacturer, take on an official role, account for progress in achieving goals. (pp. 38–39)

Indeed, the presence of a genre within a cultural pattern likely as not tells the student writer that s/he may have something to say—just as others have had things to say of a substance and shape like thus and so genre. The genre may beget the writing. How much of this use of genre knowledge learned by way of experience in a community is cheating? How much of a genre do we "own"?

Recent shifts in theorizing about genres are paralleled by what some scholars have characterized as nothing less than a paradigm shift in how we theorize about learning and knowledge (e.g., Lave, 1996; Salomon & Perkins, 1998; Sfard, 1998). Key to this shift is the question of whether learning leads to knowledge (static, a stored commodity) or to doing (an aspect of activity). If learning leads to knowledge, that is, to a mental structure or representation stored as a unit in an individual's memory, then the presence and quality of one's knowledge can be determined only when the individual is isolated from the group—no talking, no resources, no help. In this view knowledge is an individual possession which can be carried around and acted upon irrespective of social or cultural circumstances. On the other hand, if learning leads to doing, that is, to ". . . the production, sustenance, and transformation of participants' knowledgeable identities . . ." (Lave, 1996, p. 159), then its presence and qualities can be determined only when the individual is engaged in activity; in the case of literacy, which is by nature social, such activity would have to be done in a social context.

Sfard (1998) explained these competing theories of learning with reference to the "acquisition metaphor" (AM) and the "participation metaphor" (PM). The AM, which according to Sfard has dominated our thinking about learning for centuries, characterizes learning as "gaining possession over some commodity," and the learner is seen as a "lone entrepreneur" (p. 6). The PM, which has just lately appeared in our discourse about schooling and is challenging traditional AM notions, entails learning as "becoming a member of a certain community" and being able to "take part" in the usual activities of that community (p. 6). Although most proponents of the PM do not dispute the existence of internal mental structures, such knowledge is merely an "aspect of practice/discourse/activity," not a "property, possession, commodity" (p. 7). The PM suggests that learners should be viewed as persons ". . . interested in participating in certain kinds of activities rather than in accumulating private possessions . . .": "In the image of learning that emerges from this linguistic turn, the permanence of *having* gives way to the constant flux of *doing*," [and] "the identity of an individual . . . is a function of his or her being (or becoming) a part of a greater entity" (p. 6).

The PM perspective on learning together with social and culturally oriented theories of literacy have profound implications for portfolio assessment. On one level, they suggest that our assessments ought properly to focus on whether students are successfully using literacy practices during activities involving the communities into which they hope to become socialized. This focus, of course, carves out an important role for students' own intentions and goals as learners. It also makes problematic the use of menus of universal text types as the basis for portfolio construction. On another level, these perspectives require that we rethink some of the most basic notions of psychometrics, including distinctions between formative and summative assessment. According to Sfard (1998):

> While the concept of acquisition implies that there is a clear end point to the process of learning, the new terminology leaves no room for halting signals. Moreover, the ongoing learning activities are never considered separately from the context within which they take place. The context, in its turn, is rich and multifarious, and its importance is pronounced by talk about situatedness, contextuality, cultural embeddedness, and social mediation. (p. 6)

Collaboration vs. cheating

Of course, we don't want students to *cheat*—we want them to be intellectually honest. We *don't* want students to feel no stake in their work—we want them active, critical, reflective. But the answer lies not in discounting student work that has been done collaboratively, a pragmatic solution for the assessor, but one with serious implications for pedagogy. The answer instead lies in supporting students as they develop their inner system of intellectual ethics, a system of values that ought to be modeled in every classroom and school. One might counter—rightly—that this solution could be overly idealistic in a high-stakes context of reward and punishment. This issue is important and deserves both scholarly and political attention. It certainly deserves attention in the context of the design of a portfolio assessment system.

Reflection

Related to the effort to engage students in making choices about their work, is the effort to engage students in reflection. Although all of the projects profiled here paid some attention to reflection, the approaches they took varied widely, both in the prominence they gave to this aspect of portfolio practice and in the kind of reflection they encouraged. For example, reflection was the cornerstone of the Arts PROPEL approach to portfolios. It was embedded in the design of the end-of-year portfolio itself, which asked students to select pieces that were satisfying and unsatisfying and to reflect on what made them so. It was embedded in daily instruction in teacher-student "reflective interviews," in public occasions for reflection such as class critiques, in reflective writing exercises, and it included reflection on processes and development over time as well as self-assessment of products. Patterned in part after Arts PROPEL, the Charles Ruff portfolio system also gave reflection prominence both in its delineation of what ought to go into the portfolio and in its scoring rubric, a prominence that had a deep impact on classroom instruction.

In other projects, in contrast, reflection played less of a role. Although reflective analysis played a part in the selection process and in the required "Letter to the Reviewer," Kentucky Writing Program consultants acknowledged that reflection was "not the system's strong suit." Indeed, the Kentucky portfolio handbook did a better job of explaining to teachers what reflection is *not* than it did in explaining what reflection *is*. In Chinle, the role of reflection was similarly minimal. Student reflection was not embedded in, nor required as part of the portfolio system. Students were not as clearly or directly involved in the selection process, and asking students to reflect on their work was not a widespread practice among teachers, perhaps because of cultural considerations. In the New Standards Project, reflection was required, and its importance highlighted by the standard known as "Evaluation," a standard that required students to show they could recognize the strengths and weakness of their own work, assess their progress and set goals for improvement. But in a summative assessment, setting goals for improvement was moot. In Region 15, on the other hand, reflection looked both back and forward. Students set goals at the beginning of the year, and evaluated their progress toward those goals at the end. Key to both student and teacher portfolios, reflection was aimed at promoting the students'—and teachers'—skills of self-assessment and goal setting in a cycle of learning. Clearly, the diversity of practices suggests a need for a better understanding of the role that reflection can play in assessment systems and under what conditions.

Questions for Reflection

1 What perspective on learning and curriculum best fits with the aspirations we have for students?

2 What approach to collecting portfolio contents is most congruent with our perspective on learning and curriculum?

3 What guidelines for selection can we propose that complement our perspectives on learning and curriculum?

4 What kinds of reflection are appropriate given our purposes and the characteristics of our students?

5 How will we deal with the social aspect of literacy learning? What will constitute cheating? Will we allow students to collaborate on portfolio entries?

6 Will we include oral language in the design? If so, how?

Models of Reform, Assessment, and Accountability
Portfolio Purposes

In a conceptual article intended in part to define the term "learning entity" as part of a theory of social learning/distributed cognition, Salomon and Perkins (1998) conceived of a team of educators working collaboratively to improve a school as a social "learning system," defined as ". . . an information-processing system aimed at facilitating . . . [the] critical conditions [necessary] for learning . . ." (p. 3). Within such a system colleagues can scaffold one another's improvement by ". . . elaborat[ing] on individual attempts to solve something the individual could not do on his or her own" (p. 2). However, individual improvement is but one part of the picture, for a social learning system can acquire collective knowledge distributed among its members. Here are Salomon and Perkins' (1998) words:

> A sports team attains patterns of coordination among the individuals that might be useless for any of the team members functioning alone. A business organization develops internal procedures, based on commonly held tacit assumptions, that meet customer demands more efficiently and more quickly. In such cases, the agreements need not be stated, and the procedures are not executed (or perhaps not even overseen) by any one individual, but they advance the performance of the organization. (p. 5)

In short, social entities—including institutions like schools—can and must learn and improve just as individuals can learn and improve.

Some of the systems we have discussed recognized the need for institutional learning. In contrast to merit pay schemes designed to motivate individual teachers, for example, Kentucky developed an incentive scheme that rewarded, or sanctioned, *entire schools*. Such a policy assumes that improvement in schools comes about as a consequence of the collective improvement of a group or a team of educators, *not* as a consequence of improving the teaching skills of individual teachers. A recent report published by the National Research Council (1999), in fact, concluded that external accountability measures are doomed to fail unless schools as social entities develop what the report termed "internal accountability," which ". . . includes the norms by which teachers operate, the expectations they hold about student learning, and the processes they use to carry out their work" (p. 97). Schools with "weak internal accountability" are unlikely to respond to rewards or threats because such schools have a tendency to respond ". . . by summoning their own individual beliefs, rather than by consulting with colleagues and attempting to work collectively for improvement" (p. 97).

Every portfolio system discussed in this book was developed within the context of a reform effort designed to improve *entire schools*, not just to improve *individual teachers*. But each of the systems had its own purpose or cluster of purposes. The system at Charles Ruff Middle School was intended to bring coherence to the language arts instructional program, to change the power relationship between teachers and students, and to encourage students to accept ownership of and responsibility for their work as literacy learners. The Arts PROPEL system was intended to encourage a change in teachers' perspectives on what it takes instructionally to create good writers; to broaden and deepen student opportunities to become reflective learners; and to create a larger district culture that privileged student goal setting, reflective analysis, and self-assessment. The Region 15 system set out to create self-regulated learners who understood and could apply visible and stable criteria to their work among both their students and their teachers. From these examples it should be obvious that each system not only had specific objectives, but was clear about what they were.

As we looked across these exemplar systems, we noted that each system addressed at least three purposes in varying degrees: a student-centered purpose, a teacher-centered purpose, and an institution-centered purpose. The Mt. Diablo system and Region 15's collaborative teacher portfolios, for example, focused predominantly on a teacher-centered purpose, that is, on teacher inquiry into local instructional conditions. Both systems also focused somewhat on a student-centered purpose. In Region 15 the purpose was to stimulate self-regulated learning, while in Mt. Diablo the purpose was to create a culture in which student investment and engagement would flourish. Although Mt. Diablo's institutional purpose was less clear than other systems, there was nonetheless such a purpose: to provide institutional structures that support reflective practice and the construction of local knowledge. Region 15's institutional purpose was more easily discerned: to provide an alternative approach to teacher evaluation that would broaden and deepen teachers' opportunity to learn their craft.

Some of the systems, however, seemed to have established purposes in each of these three areas which may have worked against one another. For example, the Kentucky system was designed to promote ownership and reflective analysis among students as a student-centered purpose, but the decision to make the system serve the institutional purpose of disseminating rewards and sanctions complicated implementation such that the goal of student ownership might have been compromised in some schools. In the case of Kentucky, however, the priority purpose at least initially was the institutional purpose; system designers hoped to mitigate any negative effects this priority might have had on other purposes by way of staff development. The Vermont system was designed with the institutional purpose of creating data that could be used in public forums to satisfy the public's need to know how well Vermont schools were doing, but the teacher-centered purpose of preserving local autonomy led designers to open the aperture of the portfolios so wide that public confidence in the data was undermined. In the case of Vermont, however, the teacher-centered purpose was the priority purpose; publicly recognizing this priority could have made a difference in how the system played out historically. We have come to believe that there will be contradictory purposes in almost any system in any situation primarily because portfolio assessment systems by definition embrace a much wider array of purposes than any other traditional or alternative assessment strategies. The key here is not to eliminate all problems but to identify them before they appear and take steps to minimize their effects.

The systems we have studied that have addressed this inherent complexity most effectively appear to have been those with built-in institutional structures to support communication, analysis, and planning across all levels of the system. In Pittsburgh the system included conferences involving teachers, supervisors, and researchers who discussed problems and solutions in the context of examining student portfolios. In Region 15 the system included the option for teachers to submit their portfolios to their supervisor who would examine this work in light of what the teacher was trying to accomplish and then discuss the portfolio with the teacher. In Kentucky the

Department of Education funded a network of regional writing consultants who worked closely with local schools throughout the decade and managed to make an enormous positive change in the system's implementation. At Charles Ruff the system included a portfolio coordinator who was responsible for maintaining open lines of communication among all of the teachers such that misunderstandings could be minimized. All of the systems we have profiled have made use of existing institutional structures ranging from already existing departments and department meetings to already existing personnel in their current roles. But all of the systems have also required new structures, including new organizations and routines as well as new personnel with newly defined roles.

Models of Assessment

It should be clear by now that the design of any portfolio assessment system must begin with a consideration of local context and purposes. In a general sense, however, we perceive that at least two broad, often competing, models of assessment coexist within the current American culture of testing, and the features of both models are likely to show up simultaneously to one degree or another in almost every local context. Both of these models of assessment are currently embedded in educational reform initiatives as either regulators or "persuaders" (McDonnell, 1994). Both, also, have been used to promote reform along what Kohn (1999) has called "horizontal" and "vertical" dimensions. Reforms along the horizontal dimension are those which seek to change instruction in some way. Reforms along the vertical dimension are those which seek to increase student performance by manipulating standards for learning. To be sure, almost any reform initiative worth the name likely claims to seek an impact along both dimensions, but as we have seen at least with respect to portfolio assessment systems some systems (e.g., Mt. Diablo) emphasize the horizontal dimension while others (e.g., New Standards Project) emphasize the vertical dimension.

Besides differences in emphasis along these two dimensions, these two general models of assessment operating in the American culture of testing also take a different stance on how it is that assessment can be used to create changes along one or the other dimension. On one hand, there is an assessment model that privileges student standing, status, and rank above all else; this model involves "tough standards," objective tests, and extrinsic incentives. Although the stance taken by proponents of this model may include an argument for a particular kind of instruction, *how* students are taught tends to be much less important than *where* students land within the normal distribution when measured against a standard. On the other hand, there is an assessment model that privileges student engagement, reflectivity, and growth; this model involves negotiated standards, authentic tests, and intrinsic motivators. Although the stance taken by proponents of this model may include an understanding of the need to certify and place students at some point in their academic careers, *how* students are taught tends to be the predominant concern. When there is a public clash between proponents of these two models, the clash usually generates more heat than light, often because proponents of either model mistrust proponents of the other. It behooves system designers, therefore, to understand the assumptions and principles operating within each of these assessment models in order to fashion the best possible "working compromises" (Koretz, et al., 1994) to serve people in their situations and locations.

A framework that may be helpful to individuals engaged in the development of portfolio programs, who are concerned about the issues raised in this section, was developed by Roberta Camp and Drew Gitomer in 1990. Illustrated in Figure 10.1, it contrasts the characteristics of traditional and instruction-based assessment.

Figure 10.1
Assessment as a Vehicle for Improving Instruction

TRADITIONAL	INSTRUCTION-BASED
1. Quantitative	1. Qualitative
2. Unidimensional	2. Multi-dimensional
3. Norm-referenced	3. Individually referenced
4. Curriculum-independent	4. Direct connection to curriculum
5. Atheoretical	5. Based on theory of the student as learner
6. Summative	6. Formative
7. Inexpensive administration and scoring	7. Administration and scoring expensive if separtated from professional development
8. Refined psychometric methods	8. Methods of determining quality of information still under development
9. External assessor	9. Student self-assessment
10. One-time event	10. Extending or recurring over time
11. Teacher-proof	11. Teacher mediated

Camp, R. (1990, May). Paper presented at the Symposium on Literacy Assessment: Setting an Agenda for the 90s. Annual meeting of the International Reading Association, Atlanta, GA. Reprinted with permission of Roberta Camp and Drew Gitomer.

As further illustration of the assumptions and principles of these two competing models of assessment consider the assessment philosophies of two non-profit, nationally organized groups which have clear and public political agendas with respect to assessment: the Education Commission of the States (ECS) and the National Center for Fair & Open Testing (FairTest). Each organization has a website with a number of internal and external links which interested readers ought to visit in conjunction with reading this chapter.

ECS was formed in the mid-1960s after James Conant Bryant, then-president of Harvard University, wrote about the need for an "interstate planning commission for education" separate from the federal government. In 1966 a vote was taken at the National Governor's Conference which resulted in a unanimous agreement that a nationwide alliance of political leaders aimed at improvements in education ought to be formed with the active and personal participation of all of the governors. Among a cluster of functions including serving as a clearinghouse of information about education and assessment, the ECS (1999) has also taken on the responsibility of gathering together "the best thinking on educational accountability" and has developed a website called "Performance-Based Accountability" (http://www.granite.cc:/3009).

In its organization section called "Performance-Based Accountability," ECS provides the following list of the elements of accountability:

1. Standards
2. Performance data
3. Methods for judging performance
4. Rewards for high performance
5. Consequences for low performance
6. Reports
7. Building capacity
8. Information management systems

The bottom line for ECS with respect to developing a performance-based accountability system is as follows:

> As state leaders come to understand the importance of human capital in determining competitive advantage, the focus of educational accountability is [on] how well the educational system builds and develops skills and knowledge. [Thus we have] performance-based accountability systems in which teachers, schools, and districts are expected to meet specific outcomes in terms of student learning. . . . (ECS, 1999, at *www.granite.cc:/3009*)

To ensure improvement along this vertical dimension, ECS recommends that system designers begin with standards, that is, clarify expectations, and then develop mechanisms that provide incentives for learning to improve. Once standards are clarified, problems should be diminished because "students, parents, and teachers know what is expected of them and can then adjust their behavior accordingly." With both positive and negative incentives in place, the rationale is, problems should also begin to diminish, especially if the system injects competition into the mix by comparing the performance of system participants to one another.

FairTest was formed almost 20 years later than ECS, in 1985, in response to what was perceived to be increasing pressure to employ standardized tests across all levels of education. According to Bob Schaeffer, Public Education Director for FairTest (Schaeffer, personal communication, 1999), FairTest came about as a result of a conference attended by staff from the NAACP Legal Defense Fund, Lawyers Committee for Civil Rights Under Law, the Mexican American Legal Defense Fund, and other groups. Participants in that June 1985 event agreed that standardized exams were becoming the nation's gatekeeper for educational quality and social mobility, and that an organization dedicated to monitoring the testing enterprise and advocating for assessment reform should be created.

In contrast to ECS, which focuses on changes along the vertical dimension with tests as regulators and persuaders, FairTest (1999) as an advocacy organization states on its website that it "works to end the abuses, misuses, and flaws of standardized testing and to make certain that evaluation of students and workers is fair, open, accurate, accountable and educationally sound." The organization advocates the following basic principles:

- Tests should be fair and valid. Tests should provide equal opportunity, rather than favor individuals on the basis of race, ethnicity, gender or income level.
- Tests should be open. Independent researchers should have greater access to testing data, including evidence of test validity and reliability.
- Tests should be viewed in their proper perspective. Safeguards must be established to ensure that curricula are not driven by standardized testing and that test scores are not the sole criterion by which major educational and employment decisions are made.
- Alternative assessment instruments should be developed. New methods of evaluation that fairly and accurately diagnose the strengths and weaknesses of students, workers, and programs need to be designed and implemented.

To promote these principles, FairTest has become involved in a range of activities ranging from publication of reports, analyses, and other documents as well as provision of technical assistance to individuals and groups involved in testing-related issues. An important activity with implications here is FairTest's use of a system for evaluating the quality of state-wide assessment systems.

FairTest distinguishes between a "factory model of education," which this organization argues has had prominence in American education since the 1920s, and a reform model of American education begun in the 1990s that offers the promise of breaking the factory model's hold on schools. According to FairTest (1999), "the promise of school reform in the 1990s has been to break with that inadequate, often harmful model of schooling. As one part of reaching that goal, assessment must be fundamentally restructured to support high standards without standardization" (http:www.FairTest.org). FairTest (1999) developed a set of criteria against which any state's assessment can be measured:

Standard 1: Assessment supports important student learning.
1.1. Assessments are based on and aligned with standards.

1.2. Multiple-choice and very-short-answer (e.g., "gridded-in") items are a limited part of the assessments; and assessments employ multiple methods, including those that allow students to demonstrate understanding by applying knowledge and constructing responses.

1.3. Assessments designed to rank order, such as norm-referenced tests (NRT), are not used or are not a significant part of the assessment system.

1.4. The test burden is not too heavy in any one grade or across the system.

1.5. High stakes decisions, such as high school graduation for students or probation for schools, are not made on the basis of any single assessment.

1.6. Sampling is employed to gather program information.

1.7. The evaluation of work done over time, e.g., portfolios, is a major component of accountability and public reporting data.

1.8. Students are provided an opportunity to comment on or evaluate the instruction they receive and their own learning.

1.9. Appropriate contextual information is gathered and reported with assessment data.

Standard 2: Assessments are fair.

2.1. States have implemented comprehensive bias review procedures.

2.2. Assessment results should be reported both for all students together and with disaggregated data for sub-populations.

2.3. Adequate and appropriate accommodations and adaptations are provided for students with Individual Education Plans (IEP).

2.4. Adequate and appropriate accommodations and adaptations, including translations or developing assessments in languages other than English, are available for students with limited English proficiency (LEP).

2.5. Multiple methods of assessment are provided to students to meet needs based on different learning styles and cultural backgrounds.

2.6. Students are provided an adequate opportunity to learn about the assessment.

Standard 3: Professional development.

3.1. States have requirements for beginning teachers and administrators to be knowledgeable about assessment, including appropriate classroom practices.

3.2. States provide sufficient professional development in assessment, including in classroom assessment.

3.3. States survey educators about their professional development needs in assessment and evaluate their competence in assessment.

3.4. Teachers and other educators are involved in designing, writing, and scoring assessments.

Standard 4: Public education, reporting, and parents' rights.

4.1. Parents and community members are educated about the kinds of assessments used and the meaning and interpretation of assessment results.

4.2. The state surveys parents/public to determine information they want on assessments and whether assessment reports are understandable.

4.3. Reports should be available in languages other than English if a sizeable number or significant percentage of the student population come from homes where another language is commonly used.

4.5. Parents and/or students have the right to examine assessments, appeal assessment scores, or challenge flawed items.

Standard 5: System review and improvement.

5.1. The assessment system is regularly reviewed.

5.2. The review includes participation by various stakeholders and evaluation by independent experts.

5.3. The review studies how well the system actually is aligned to standards.

5.4. The review studies the impact of the assessment(s) on curriculum and instruction.

5.5. The review studies whether assessments assess critical thinking or the ability to engage in cognitively complex work within a subject.

5.6. Reviews for assessments at grade 3 or below study whether the assessments are developmentally appropriate.

5.7. Reviews study the impact of assessment programs on student progress and particularly the impact of any high stakes tests, such as high school exit exams, on graduation rates.

5.8.   Reviews study the technical quality of assessments.

5.9.   The state reviews local assessment practices.

5.10. Reviews help guide improvements in the assessment system that will bring the program more in line with the *Principles and Indicators*.

The full *Principles and Indicators* text is available from FairTest at 342 Broadway, Cambridge, MA 02139 for $10.00 and may be ordered from website http://www.fairtest.org.

The ECS model with its emphasis on rank order of student performance, rewards and sanctions for performance, and competition among the various participants in the system seems to provide a good working contrast to the FairTest model with its emphasis on client rights, truth in testing, and minimum intrusion. System designers would do well to discuss the similarities and differences between these two models in depth as a preliminary activity leading to local clarity of purpose and design options.

The FairTest perspective with its emphasis on client rights is similar to the position taken by Wile and Tierney (1996). These authors contrast constructivist views of curriculum, instruction, and assessment, which "suggest an educational context that is open-ended and divergent," with traditional positivist perspectives which, they claim, reflect a "production orientation," and a school climate in which the "teacher's role as analyst is reduced to managerial tasks: modeling prescribed experiences, devising rewards and punishments, and keeping accurate accounts."(pp. 206–207). Wile and Tierney argue that pressures to apply "positivistic theories of assessment to the constructivist theories of learning . . . can lead to a moral schizophrenia, ultimately compromising both innovative and traditional points of view of assessment." Their framework for analyzing assessment issues from the traditional and constructivist perspectives may be useful to those engaged in educational reform (see Figure 10.2).

Figure 10.2
Assessment Issues

Assessment Issue	Traditional View	Constructivist View
Orientation	Production	Client service
Values	Productivity	Customer satisfaction
Measurement focus	Efficiency/quantity	Effectiveness/quality
Theoretical frame	Positivistic	Constructivist
Conception of student	Student-as-product	Student-as-client
Assessment audience	Public constituencies	Individual students
Assessment aims	Broad view/simplistic	Narrow view/complex
Curricular goal	Uniformity	Diversity

Wile, J., & Tierney, R. J. (1996). Tensions in assessment: The battle over portfolios. In R. Calfee & P. Perfumo (Eds.), *Writing Portfolios in the classroom: Policy and practice, promise and peril.* Mahwah, NJ: Lawrence Erlbaum Associates, (p. 207). Copyright 1966 by Lawrence Erlbaum Associates. Reprinted with permission.

Models of Accountability

In traditional bureaucratic accountability systems, personnel who administer and oversee standardized test systems usually face pressures associated with scheduling test windows, ensuring codes of ethics, disseminating testing materials, and the like. But they are not called on the carpet to explain why achievement is low when it is— nor are they given awards for their work in raising achievement when it is high— because they are not seen as part of curriculum and instruction. In contrast, portfolio systems operators were perceived as partly responsible for curriculum because their boundaries for collection and the values in their rubrics impacted what teachers could and would teach and students could learn. These portfolio designers and operators were partly responsible for instruction because their systems often came complete with staff development packages intended specifically to prepare teachers to teach in the manner supported by the portfolio design.

Moreover, teachers were much more heavily involved in the design, operation, and implementation of these portfolio systems than they ever could have been in standardized test systems. On school days when students take standardized tests which teachers have no part in designing, teachers are held at arm's length from their students. Special "Do Not Disturb" signs are taped to classroom doors, and silence prevails as bubbles are filled in or short responses are penned. In contrast, during periods when portfolios are being assembled, teachers face a beehive of activity. Engagement levels run high, and much learning takes place as students make choices, reflect on those choices, and prepare their presentation for whatever audience the system has designed.

The bare facts of the systems we have profiled in this book suggest that portfolio systems have had serious political and implementation problems when they have been developed to serve a more or less bureaucratic model of accountability (Darling-Hammond, 1989). Bureaucracies can be effective when the work is routine, mechanistic, and highly predictable, but teaching and learning are not routine kinds of work. The work of teachers and students as literate human beings in a democracy is complex, situationally and culturally bound, and often unpredictable. Systems that wanted to change teachers from the outside and discounted this fact sometimes had the unintended consequence of marginalizing teachers and students and making them less enabled to respond to their own needs.

The degree to which a portfolio system serves a bureaucratic model of accountability seems almost proportional to increases in the number of participants in the system. Why would this be so? For one thing at a purely mechanical level, as the number of portfolios to be scored rises, the need for routine and predictability also appears to rise. At a middle school like Charles Ruff, a high school like Mt. Diablo, even a small state like Vermont, the stage is small enough that the actors and actresses can get acquainted with one another. But when the project involves a state like Kentucky or nineteen states in a consortium like the New Standards Project, policies rather than persons must keep the trains running on time.

The large-scale systems we analyzed also tended to be product-focused. In part, this focus may stem from the difficulties that are associated with making higher-order thinking skills such as self-reflection, the prewriting process, the editing process, and reading responses "visible." As Miles Myers (1996) explains:

The need for visible and stable data showing reading and writing processes has led to the invention of new genres of response: double-entry journals, two column contrasts (character's word in one column; character's thoughts in others), drawings of a situation and their explanations, Venn diagrams showing different and overlapping attitudes, organization charts (story trees, charts of family relationships), learning logs recording strategies and miscues in reading and writing, narratives about one's literacy development, value-scales, and meaning scales (semantic differential scales). (p. 162)

Data of this kind are more difficult to score reliably. Early versions of the New Standards Portfolios contained varying amounts of these kinds of evidence, but ultimately, collection guidelines emphasized products more than process. In the 1995/96 version of the New Standards Portfolio, for example, high school students were required to submit three pieces of writing as evidence of their reading accomplishment with different sorts of texts (one for literature, and two for informational, public, or functional). In writing, as explained earlier, specific types of writing were required, and writing process was demonstrated with a single entry in which students were expected to show they could "make substantive changes as appropriate both in the organizing structures of a piece and at the sentence level" (New Standards Project, 1995, Entry Slip #1: Use of Processes and Strategies for Writing).

Portfolio systems designed to accommodate the bureaucratic model tend to *prescribe* implicitly or explicitly not just which types of textual activity are valued, but how those types ought to be made (the "test worth teaching to"). Such prescriptions may represent the current universe of discourse quite comprehensively, but they perpetuate a view of writing as "crafting forms" as opposed to "authoring" in a real world sense (Lucas, 1988). Systems of this kind tend to *control* teaching and learning in ways that can work against what we know about the principles of academic achievement motivation (Anderman, 1997; Covington, 1992). Without doubt these systems have been conceived with the most benevolent of intentions; but from our perspective, prescription and control can inhibit thoughtful, reflective learning and teaching. Instead, they can lead to rote "delivery" of instruction, formulaic teaching, and the deskilling of teachers. As Darling-Hammond (1989) explains,

> In the bureaucratic conception of teaching, teachers do not need to be highly knowledgeable about learning theory and pedagogy, cognitive science and child development, curriculum and assessment; they do not need to be highly skilled, because they do not, presumably, make the major decisions about these matters. Curriculum planning is done by administrators and specialists. . . . Inspection of teachers work is conducted by hierarchical superiors, whose job is to make sure that the teacher is implementing the curriculum and procedures of the district. Teachers do not plan or evaluate their own work; they merely perform it. . . . The problem with the bureaucratic solution to the accountability dilemma in education is that effective teaching is not routine, students are not passive, and questions of practice are not simple, predictable, or standardized. (p. 64)

The alternatives to the bureaucratic model of accountability (and schooling) that Darling-Hammond offers are "client-oriented" and "professional" accountability. As Darling-Hammond (1989) explains, "[c]lient-oriented accountability requires that teachers primarily teach *students* rather than teaching *courses*, that they attend more to learning than to covering a curriculum" (p. 73). Anchored in a learner-centered view, client-oriented accountability demands new roles for teachers, including their participation in the evaluative and decision-making functions of schools, their collective review of teaching practices and policies and their collective investigation of problems (Darling-Hammond). In short, client-accountability demands professional accountability. As Darling-Hammond sees it, "[s]ocialization into [the] norms of inquiry and collaboration must be . . . part of the daily life of all teachers if they are to begin to permeate the profession" (p. 74). Instead of "enforcing standardization," a learner-centered view challenges us "to create accountability mechanisms that will support the nonstandardized, individually appropriate teaching strategies needed to produce success for diverse learners" (Darling-Hammond & Snyder, 1992, p. 12).

In some of the schools and districts we profiled, there was evidence that client-centered and professional accountability systems lived side-by-side with bureaucratic systems, and that some school systems actually supported alternatives to the bureaucratic model. In the Arts PROPEL project, for example, the portfolio design did not require standardized entries. It was a learner-centered model. Moreover, teachers in Arts PROPEL figured prominently in the design and evaluation of the portfolios. In the Mt. Diablo Project, teachers used student portfolios to engage in collective research into the effectiveness of their teaching practices. In Region 15 in Connecticut, teachers participated in a long-term change effort which involved investigating and developing new approaches to teaching. In addition, they were engaged in projects of inquiry and portfolio development as part of their own evaluation. In Charles Ruff Middle School, teachers themselves designed the portfolio experiment, taking action into their own hands to improve accountability at their school. In all of these examples, to use Darling-Hammond's (1989) terms, teachers assumed collective responsibility for accountability.

The "Working Compromise"

Koretz, Stecher, Klein, McCaffrey, and Deibert (1993) pointed out that portfolio assessment systems with the dual goals of accountability and improved instruction face a harsh dilemma and must establish a "working compromise" in order to function. For measurement purposes, some experts argue that portfolio systems require standardized tasks, rubric-driven or menu-driven collection and selection procedures, and uniform scoring protocols. The instructional problems associated with this kind of standardization, however, are legion. Standardized tasks require policies regulating how much help teachers can ethically provide, a major disadvantage for anyone coming to education from a Vygotskian perspective. Rubric- or menu-driven collection and selection procedures and the inflexible values they represent can marginalize students and diminish opportunities to learn. Indeed, standardized scoring protocols appear to have as much to do with political coercion as calibration (e.g., Elbow, 1994). And it is ironic to note that these systemic aspects of standardization tend to promote high levels of agreement between raters and therefore high levels of trust in resultant data.

For purposes of improved instruction, standardized classrooms are probably not the answer—if we give credence to the research into the complexities of judgment involved in teaching (Darling-Hammond, 1997). Indeed, Daniel Koretz and his colleagues (1994) acknowledged in Vermont that the amount of instructional support available to students *ought to vary* on the basis of the professional judgment of teachers, a stipulation that is anathema to measurement. But some assessment experts have all but conceded that portfolios without policies regulating instructional support (or statistical formulas that adjust for differentials in instructional support) are all but useless as measurement tools. Gearhart, Herman, Baker, and Whitaker (1993), for example, concluded that "the validity of inferences we can draw about student competence based solely on portfolio scores" is limited because "the quality of [student] work [is] a function of substantial and uncontrolled support" (p. 7).

What seem more likely to promote good teaching than standardizing tasks are strategies that help teachers better observe diverse students, analyze and interpret what they see, and act on their professional judgments in live classrooms. Whether the teacher is one of those from Vermont who volunteered to stop giving students so many worksheets and started asking for more writing as a consequence of his or her participation in the portfolio system, whether the teacher is one of those from Mt. Diablo who decided to voluntarily change her approach to the teaching of revision during the subsequent year or whether the teacher is one of those non-Native teachers from Chinle who learned to understand the Navajo way and thereby became better able to help students—wherever a teacher practices—observation, analysis, interpretation, and action are the foundation of support for students. It seems reasonable to argue that assessment has a place within this foundation, that assessment ought to be funded, and that assessment ought to be professional in nature.

This is not to say that portfolio systems that help teachers do these things need be disorganized, idiosyncratic, or incoherent. To the contrary, the systems that accomplished these goals that were profiled here were highly organized, public, and consistent. There may have been a "working compromise" that down played measurement for purposes of comparison and that highlighted instead improvement for purposes of learning, but the improvement systems *themselves* that we have examined have been planned and predictable, though not inflexible. Anyone who would design his or her own portfolio assessment system would do well to think long and hard about the kind of "working compromise" that he or she and colleagues are willing to make.

Questions for Reflection

1. What approaches to educational reform and accountability are congruent with our views of learning and curriculum and our aspirations for students?

2. To what extent will our portfolio system promote a bureaucratic or a professional model of accountability? What opportunities do we have to promote a professional model? How will we take advantage of these opportunities?

3. How will we address the "working compromise," that is, the trade-off between the need to measure performance and improve instruction? How much measurement is necessary for our purposes? How much can instruction tolerate?

Fairness, Reliability, and Validity

Fairness, reliability, and validity are bottom-line concerns across all assessment events, portfolio and otherwise, where power is represented and people's lives are at stake. When high-stakes decisions about resources or placement or admission are being made on the basis of assessment data, fairness of action and dependability of data are critical concerns. (This is not to suggest, however, that in our view current approaches to ensuring reliability and validity are optimum [cf., Guba, 1978; Guba & Lincoln, 1989; Moss, 1994a, 1994b].) But not all educational decisions that ought to be made in light of assessment data have immediate impact on an individual's chances in life; sometimes local knowledge is needed, for example, to improve school planning (Charles Ruff) or to promote common understandings (Arts PROPEL, Chinle, Vermont). To rate the effectiveness of all assessment strategies by strict tests of reliability when some strategies aim to serve the motivational, professional, or equity aspects of measurement is not only unnecessary, but potentially counterproductive. Teachers and other knowledge-based practitioners who decide how to handle complex issues in day-to-day work with people must be permitted their intuition and their access to experience—knowing they are sometimes wrong. Suggestive information about these low-stakes decisions is perhaps much more valuable to them than are impeccable summative data and high-stakes pressure to make all the right decisions all the time. Indeed, it would be unfair to students to devalue this less reliable but highly useful information just because it has less immediate impact on the lives of individuals.

Moreover, instructional decisions often involve a counter-intuitive perspective on fairness. For example, proponents of measurement for pedagogical purposes try to accommodate the Vygotskian concept that fairness may mean giving a capable student very little help while another struggling student gets a lot of help during work on the same or similar task. Of central importance in this scenario is the teacher's record of the knowledge that one student could do with little help what another could do only with a lot of help, for this record tells the teacher that one student needs a more challenging task while another needs more practice with the same task. This sort of assessment—deciding on a student's status as a novice, apprentice, or expert within the zone of proximal development with respect to a given level of difficulty of task—may be less reliably done, but it is much more useful instructionally, and it is the sort of assessment that can be promoted by portfolios.

It is perhaps fitting that a century dominated by standardized tests designed to rank children in columns for ease of sorting should end with an antithetical movement dominated by portfolios that seek to understand children in order to reach them and teach them. From our perspective, the answer to the tension created by these opposing ideas lies not in "balancing" our uses of standardized tests with our uses of portfolios or other kinds of performance assessments. Although it may be more expensive, it is just as possible to rank students using data from performance assessments as it is to rank them using data from standardized tests. Giving students a standardized test and combining these data with data from alternative assessment strategies may be "balanced" on a scale of Justice, but it isn't always thoughtful. Instead, the answer lies in clarifying when we need to rank students and when to understand them—and we need to find ways to value and institutionalize defensible systems—using multiple indicators to develop a well-rounded portrait of a pupil's achievement—that can serve each purpose when the need appears. As Eunice Greer, who worked with David Pearson and Miles Myers in the New Standards Project, has commented a number of times in her presentations, "We ought to stop trying to eat soup with a fork when we have plenty of spoons nearby and we know that forks are only going to make a big mess."

We also need to be highly sensitive to the impact of assessment on people and schools, in Samuel Messick's terms, a consideration of consequential validity. Unlike the alternative assessment systems profiled here, in the architecture of standardized tests, people and situation are assumed to be irrelevant, except that cheating is forbidden and demographic characteristics of the tested population ought to align with the characteristics of the population used to create the test's norms. The nature of the social, cultural, or institutional problem that calls forth a standardized test has little to do with the nature of the test itself. And, in psychometric terms the tools for determining the worth of the test—reliability and validity—have typically been defined separately from the particular situation in which the test is used. Indeed, standardized tests are supposed to be neutral, uniform, curriculum-independent, and static—the one-size-fits-all solution. In reality, however, many test-takers shape their lives around standardized tests—they have to study and learn the content of the test, or at least content within the domain of the test; master the kinds of cognitive routines called for by the test-maker; answer questions in a way that is acceptable to what is often a commercial company. That is to say, there are pedagogical aspects of measurement that need to be taken into account.

The pedagogical aspects of measurement involve consequences for teaching and learning. Whether students perceive themselves as pawns in a game being manipulated by more powerful others or as responsible agents with a voice in what happens to them is a pedagogical aspect of measurement: the motivational aspect. Whether teachers improve their confidence and capacity to teach current and future students as a result of participation in assessment or become demoralized, deskilled, and depressed is a pedagogical aspect of measurement: the professional aspect. Whether teachers create a "thinking curriculum" or narrow the curriculum to those skills that are most easily assessed is a pedagogical aspect of measurement—the curricular aspect. Whether schools enhance opportunities to learn for the children who attend them—or respond mechanically to the edicts of distant authorities—is a pedagogical aspect of educational measurement: the equity aspect. Reliability and validity are necessary but insufficient conditions if one's goal is to improve schools for children. The motivational, professional, curricular, and equity aspects of measurement may perhaps be more difficult to document than test-retest reliability or convergent and divergent evidence of validity, but they are equally, if not more important in establishing the value of any assessment system or test. And considerations such as these are of increasing interest to measurement specialists and scholars who are redefining validity to include the consequences of the assessment, in particular, the impact on curriculum and participants (Frederiksen & Collins, 1989; Linn, Baker, & Dunbar, 1990; Messick, 1989a, 1989b, 1994; Moss, 1992, 1994a, 1994b).

The Problem of Reliability

Scoring of collections of work reliably is generally perceived to be more difficult than the scoring of individual student responses to a fixed task, especially if the collections of work contain different assignments. For example, evaluators of the Vermont performance assessment program cited "the tremendous diversity (lack of standardization) of tasks across portfolios" as an explanation for the unacceptably low interrater correlations obtained by portfolio raters during the first years of the program's implementation, (Koretz, et al., 1994, p. 43). Moss (1994b) reported that where acceptable interrater reliability has not been achieved, field workers have usually tried greater levels of specification of portfolio contents, or a modification of scoring procedures such that work samples are rated one at a time, not as collections, in order to improve reliability in scoring (Nystrand, Cohen, & Dowling, 1993). However, because piece-by-piece scoring focuses attention on the characteristics of a single kind of task, this approach does not tap the unique information available in a *collection* of student work, in particular, information about the student's control of processes and use of resources for reading and writing or the student's ability to evaluate his or her own work (Murphy, 1999). Neither is this approach very useful for capturing information about the breadth of a student's abilities.

Calls to standardize the contents of portfolios are frequently based on a tacit assumption that psychometrics cannot change, and that portfolios therefore must be shaped to meet the demands of psychometrics. But as explained above, work is now being done to create new assessment theory (Frederiksen, Mislevy, & Bejar, 1993; Linn, et al., 1990) and new models for assessment (Camp, 1993; Frederiksen & Collins, 1989). What the new measurement theory implies is that an assessment should be compatible with the kind of learning it claims to measure. Rather than fit portfolios to the demands of old psychometric models, then, portfolios might well be seen as providing reasons for devising new methods for obtaining credible judgments about students which would enhance learning and contribute to the health of educational system as a whole (Murphy & Camp 1996).

Some proponents of assessment reform argue that when portfolios are personalized and conceptualized as more than just collections of student work, they encourage the pursuit of personal cognitive learning goals—what Bereiter and Scardamalia (1989) call "intentional learning." They prompt students to look back, to digest and debrief, and to review what happened so that they can set new goals and determine next steps (Camp, 1992; Johnston, 1983; Zessoules & Gardner, 1991). In fact, a common argument for using portfolios in both instruction and assessment is that they can provide students with opportunities to engage in reflection and formative self-evaluation. For this reason, in many portfolio classrooms the student's participation in reflecting on, and in making decisions about the contents of his or her portfolio, is considered of critical importance (Howard, 1990; Camp, 1992; Daiker, Black, Sommers & Stygall, 1996; Paulson, et al., 1991). Indeed, within portfolio systems, choice is thought to be central to the construct being assessed: "the ability to reflect on and evaluate one's own writing is seen as a critical component of one's development as a writer" (LeMahieu, Gitomer, & Eresh, 1995, p. 23).

However, the freedom portfolios can give students to choose how they will present themselves to others, may be perceived as a liability by those who have concerns about technical matters such as interrater agreement in large-scale assessment. Thus, the assets perceived by some participants are themselves sources of tension in portfolio design when perceived by others from another context (Murphy & Camp, 1996).

As explained above, one difficulty in creating a system that will accommodate the student's participation in making decisions about the contents of his or her portfolio is that the contents will vary widely from one portfolio to the next. This variability may make it more difficult for judges to obtain acceptable levels of agreement, particularly when the scoring system forbids interaction among judges as was the case in Pittsburgh. (Recall that in the Pittsburgh scheme, judges gave independent ratings and disagreements were moderated by a third "reader.") In such systems, judges are not allowed to negotiate disagreements. To obtain acceptable levels of rater reliability in this kind of system, judges must share the same standards and have finely tuned perceptions of how those standards are realized in student work. In other schemes, such as dissertation committees, there may be significant amounts of interaction and negotiation among assessors that provide opportunities for clarifying misunderstandings and reaching consensus, but in traditional, independent rating schemes of the kind employed in most assessments for educational accountability, negotiation is not allowed.

Pittsburgh overcame the difficulty associated with the independent rating scheme, that is, the possibility that idiosyncratic standards held by judges and the diversity of portfolio contents might inhibit agreement. Part of the explanation for their success may be that they used a smaller number of more highly trained scorers than has been the case in projects where the consistency of judgments has been more erratic. No doubt, the processes that guided the development of the assessment and the evaluative framework (rubric) also contributed to the reliability of the raters' judgments.

In the rubric development process, teachers were full partners. In an interview with one of the authors of this book, Jerry Halpern, a Pittsburgh teacher, described his participation in the assessment development process as "truly a study group, a staff development and a learning experience. The other partners honored what we teachers felt and thought about student engagement. It was a portfolio process in and of itself" (Halpern, personal communication). As LeMahieu and Foss (1993) explain, the rubric ". . . was derived from many teachers and administrators repeatedly examining student work and developing a vocabulary that people could use to discuss that work. . . . As this vocabulary evolved and carried a shared meaning among its users, a shorthand version of it was embodied in the rubric" (p. 18). In this way, the process of rubric development contributed to a shared set of meanings.

LeMahieu and Foss (1993) point out, and it is certainly worth reiterating here, that the sustained and recursive discussions of student work that occurred over several years in the district and in Arts PROPEL may have contributed to the projects' success in meeting the traditional psychometric criteria of reliability. They remind us that these kinds of focused discussions form the basis of alternative approaches for arriving at well-warranted conclusions. Pamela Moss (1994a) explains the applicability of a hermeneutic approach with respect to generalization across readers:

> A hermeneutic approach to assessment would involve holistic, integrative interpretations of collected performances that seek to understand the whole in the light of its parts, that privilege readers who are most knowledgeable about the context in which the assessment occurs, and that ground those interpretations not only in the textual and contextual evidence available, but also in a rational debate among the community of interpreters. Here, the interpretation might be warranted by criteria like a reader's extensive knowledge of the learning context; multiple and varied sources of evidence; an ethic of disciplined collaborative inquiry that encourages challenges and revisions to initial interpretations; and the transparency of the trail of evidence leading to the interpretations, which allows users to evaluate the conclusions for themselves. (p. 7)

Conditions in schools sometimes work against the development of a shared technical culture (Darling-Hammond, 1997; Lortie, 1975). Teachers often work in isolation, without the kind of highly evolved socialization processes that foster shared technical expertise, as do doctors, lawyers, or airline pilots. In other professions, opportunities to learn and personal assistance come from the structured interaction with co-workers. But the "cellular" organization of schools often constrains the amount and kind of interaction among teachers (Lortie, 1975). As Lortie explains it, using the analogy of the cell, isolation in the one-room school house simply multiplied into many isolated cells as school populations increased. Despite physical proximity to colleagues, teachers in modern schools still mostly work alone, separated for long intervals of time, surrounded by students, and inducted into the profession in a more or less "sink or swim" fashion (Darling-Hammond, 1997; Lortie, 1975; Sarason, 1990).

A major cost of isolation is the lack of a common language for talking about teaching and student work. Arts PROPEL and the Pittsburgh Public Schools, the Chinle District, Charles Ruff teachers, and others profiled in this book took a step toward solving that educational problem by engaging teachers in focused discussions of student work. Collaborative assessment of student work can lead to teacher reflection and change (Sheingold, Heller, & Paulukonis, 1994).

As Pamela Moss (1994) reminds us, a number of assessment specialists have advised against using the judgments of classroom teachers (Mehrens, 1992; Resnick & Resnick, 1992). Resnick and Resnick (1992), assert, for example, that teachers should not be involved in grading the performance of their own students:

> A principal requirement of accountability and program evaluation tests is that they permit detached and impartial judgments of students' performance, that is, judgments by individuals other than the students' own teachers, using assessment instruments not of the teachers' devising. . . .The public function of certification would not be met if teachers were to grade the performance of their own students. (pp. 48–50)

In the context of large-scale programs, some attempt to avoid having teachers score their own students seems warranted. As Moss (1994) explains, from a psychometric perspective, the call for "detached and impartial" high stakes assessment reflects a profound concern for fairness to individual students and protection of stakeholder's interest by providing accurate information" (p. 9).

However, removing teachers from the picture silences the voices of those who are most knowledgeable about the context, an important criteria for credible evidence from the hermeneutic perspective (Moss, 1994). Moreover, if teachers are prevented altogether from participating in assessments, they will fail to reap the professional development benefits that such participation can bring (Sheingold, et al., 1994). Thus, there is a systemic validity consequence to the decision to eliminate classroom teachers from the assessment process as well.

Many educators have raised concerns about the absence of teachers' voices in accountability schemes that affect them and their students (Darling-Hammond & Snyder, 1992; Lieberman, 1992; Lucas, 1988; Murphy 1997) and scholars have voiced concern about the potentially deleterious effects of assessment on the professional identities of teachers (Pearson & Valencia, 1987). If teachers are removed from the picture, there is little chance that the assessment system will promote the kinds of learning it purports to measure. As we have seen, it is possible to retain teachers' voices in assessment and still create reliable data. Portfolio assessment system designers would do well to think carefully about the roles that teachers will play in any system they may develop.

Questions for Reflection

1. How will we establish that the system is fair, valid and reliable? What approach will we take?
2. To what degree will we rely upon external raters to warrant the dependability of our data?
3. If the portfolios are scored, what role will teachers play in the scoring process?
4. If teachers score the portfolios, how will we build in staff development and other collaborative structures over time to enhance the dependability of judgments?
5. To what degree do stakeholders in our system (students, teachers, parents, school administrators) agree that our system is fair, reliable, and valid? How will we determine this?
6. How much evidence of interrater reliability is necessary in order for the system to serve its purposes? If high levels of interrater reliability are needed, what evidence is there that the system has positive consequences for teaching and learning?
7. What evidence can be gathered that shows that portfolio raters are knowledgeable about literacy products and processes as well as literacy instruction?
8. When high-stakes decisions are made on the basis of portfolios, what evidence can be gathered to show that students had equal access to materials, high-quality instruction, and responsive preparation for the portfolio assessment process?

An Afterword

Where does this analysis leave us? Although we have covered much ground, we know that we have omitted some significant dimensions of assessment development and portfolio practice. We have not, for example, dealt in any detail with many of the more technical aspects of assessment. While these aspects of assessment did not fit into our more "broad brush-stroke" analysis of the sample of portfolio projects reviewed here, they are nevertheless important for a thorough understanding of assessment and the uses of assessment in reform. Nor did we deal in any detail with the day-to-day realities of portfolio practice—the practical details of implementing and managing portfolios in classrooms—although we have provided a variety of assessment tools, rubrics, sample assignments, and the like. There are a good many resources for these additional topics in the literature on assessment and portfolios; many have been referenced in preceding chapters. Our intention instead was to look closely at particular portfolio practices to consider the theories and paradigms that underlie them as well as the issues the projects raise for program development. We hope that reflecting on the approaches taken by others will be helpful as you make decisions about your own assessment programs. Some of the issues raised here go far beyond the world of "portfolios." They speak to the larger issues of the kinds of aspirations we have for students, our views of the professionals responsible for them, and the nature of the institutions and education we provide for them.

Acknowledgments

We want to thank Bob Schaeffer, Public Education Director for FairTest, for his help in collecting information about the origins of the FairTest organization. And for her help in indexing sources and putting the entire manuscript together, we would like to extend a special thanks to Iola Threatt.

References

Anderman, E. (1997). Motivation and school reform. In Maehr, M., & Pintrich, P. (Eds.). *Advances in motivation and achievement, Volume 10*, (pp. 303–337). Greenwich, Connecticut: JAI Press, Inc.

Bereiter, C., & Scardamalia, M. (1989). Intentional learning as a goal of instruction. In L. B. Resnick (Ed.), *Knowing, learning, and instruction: Essays in honor of Robert Glaser* (pp. 361–392). Hillsdale, NJ: Erlbaum Lawrence/Associates.

Blake, P., & Sudler, L. (1996). *Frank Lloyd Wright: The man.* Grolier Multimedia Encyclopedia (http://www.adelaide.net.au).

Camp, R. (1990). Thinking together about portfolios. *The Quarterly of the National Writing Project and the Center for the Study of Writing, 12* (2), 8–14.

Camp, R. (1990, May). Setting an agenda for the 90s. Symposium on Literacy Assessment. Annual meeting of the International Reading Association, Atlanta, GA.

Camp, R. (1992) Portfolio reflections in middle and secondary school classrooms. In K. B. Yancey (Ed.), *Portfolios in the writing classroom* (pp. 61–79). Urbana, IL: National Council of Teachers of English.

Camp, R. (1993). Changing the model for the direct assessment of writing. In M. Williamson & B. Huot (Eds), *Validating holistic scoring for writing assessment: Theoretical and empirical foundations*, (pp. 45–79). Cresskill, NJ: Hampton Press, Inc.

Covington, M. (1992). *Making the grade: A self-worth perspective on motivation and school reform.* New York: Cambridge University Press.

Daiker, D., Black, L., Sommers, J., & Stygall, G. (1996). The pedagogical implications of a college writing portfolio. In E. White, W. Lutz, & S. Kamusikiri (Eds.), *The practice and politics of assessment in writing*, (pp. 257–270). New York: Modern Language Association.

D'Aoust, C. (1992). Portfolios: Process for students and teachers. In K. B. Yancey (Ed.), *Portfolios in the writing classroom.* (pp. 39–49). Urbana, IL: National Council of Teachers of English.

Darling-Hammond, L. (1989). Accountability for professional practice. *Teachers College Record, 91*, (1), 60–80.

Darling-Hammond, L. (1997). *Right to learn: A blueprint for creating schools that work.* San Francisco, CA: Jossey-Bass Publishers.

Darling-Hammond, L. & Snyder, J., (1992). Reframing accountability: Creating learner-centered schools. In A. Lieberman (Ed.). *The changing contexts of teaching*, 91st Yearbook of the National Society for the Study of Education. Chicago: University of Chicago Press.

Education Commission of the States (1999). *(http://www.granite.cc:/3009).*

Elbow, P. (1994). Will the virtues of portfolios blind us to their potential dangers? In L. Black, D. Daiker, J. Sommers, & G. Stygall (Eds.), *New directions in portfolio assessment: Reflective practice, critical theory, and large-scale scoring* (pp. 40–56). Portsmouth, NH: Boynton/Cook.

FairTest (1999). (http:www.FairTest.org).

Frederickson, J., & Collins, A. (1989). A systems approach to educational testing. *Educational Researcher, 18* (9), 27–32.

Frederiksen, N., Mislevy, R., & Bejar, I. (Eds.). (1993). *Test theory for a new generation of tests.* Hillsdale, NJ: Lawrence Erlbaum Associates.

Gearhart, M., Herman, J., Baker, E., & Whittaker, A. (1993). *Whose work is it? A question for the validity of large-scale portfolio assessment.* CSE Technical Report 363. Los Angeles: University of California, CRESST Institute on Education and Training.

Gipps, C. (1999). Socio-cultural aspects of assessment. In A. Iran-Nejad & P. D. Pearson (Eds.). Review of research in education. Washington, DC: American Educational Research Association.

Guba, E. (1978). *Toward a methodology of naturalistic inquiry in educational evaluation.* Center for the Study of Evaluation, UCLA Graduate School of Education, University of California, Los Angeles.

Guba, E. & Lincoln, Y. (1989). *Fourth generation evaluation.* Newberry Park, CA: Sage Publications.

Howard, K. (1990). Making the writing portfolio real. *The Quarterly of the National Writing Project and the Center for the Study of Writing, 12* (2), 4–7, 27.

Johnston, B. (1983). *Assessing English: Helping students to reflect on their work.* Philadelphia: Open Court Press.

Jongsma, K. S. (1989). Portfolio assessment. *The Reading Teacher, 43,* 264–265.

Kohn, A. (1999). Website on issues related to testing. *(http://www.alfiekohn.com).*

Koretz, D., Stecher, B., Klein, S., & McCaffrey, D. (1994). *The evolution of a portfolio program: The impact and quality of the Vermont program in its second year (1992–93).* (CSE Technical Report 385). Los Angeles: University of California, National Center for Research on Evaluation, Standards, and Student Testing.

Koretz, D., Stecher, B., Klein, S., McCaffrey, D., & Deibert, E. (1993). *Can portfolios assess student performance and influence instruction? The 1991–92 Vermont experience.* (CSE Technical Report 371). Los Angeles: University of California, National Center for Research on Evaluation, Standards, and Student Testing.

Lave, J. (1996). Teaching, as learning, in practice. *Mind, Culture, and Activity, 3* (3), 149–194.

Lave, J., & Wenger, E. (1991). *Situated learning: Legitimate peripheral participation.* Cambridge, England: Cambridge University Press.

LeMahieu, P., & Foss, H. (1993). Assumptions of standards-based reform and their implications for policy and practice. Unpublished manuscript.

LeMahieu, P., Gitomer, D., & Eresh, J. (1995). Portfolios beyond the classroom: Data quality and qualities. (Center for Performance Assessment Technical Report # 94–01). Princeton, NJ: Educational Testing Service.

Lieberman, A. (1992). The meaning of scholarly activity and the building of community. *Educational Researcher, 21* (6), 5–12.

Linn, R. L., Baker, E., & Dunbar, S. B. (1990). Performance-based assessment: Expectations and validation criteria. *Educational Researcher, 20* (8), 15–21.

Lortie, D. (1975). *School teacher: A sociological study.* Chicago: University of Chicago Press.

Lucas, C. (1988). Toward ecological evaluation: Part I. *The Quarterly of the National Writing Project and the Center for the Study of Writing, 10* (1), 1–3, 12–16.

McDonnell, L. M. (1994). Assessment policy as persuasion and regulation. *American journal of education, 102,* 394–420.

Mehrens, W. A. (1992). Using performance assessment for accountability purposes. *Educational measurement: Issues and Practice, 11* (1), 3–20.

Messick, S. (1989a). Meaning and values in test validation: The science and ethics of assessment. *Educational Researcher, 18* (2), 5–11.

Messick, S. (1989b). Validity. In R. L. Linn (Ed.), *Educational measurement* (3rd. ed., pp. 13–104). New York: American Council on Education and Macmillan.

Messick, S. (1994). The interplay of evidence and consequences in the validation of performance assessments. *Educational researcher, 23* (2), 13–23.

Miller, C. (1984/1994). Genre as social action. In A. Freedman & P. Medway (Eds.). *Genre and the new rhetoric* (pp. 23–42). Bristol, PA: Taylor & Francis Inc.

Moss, P. (1992). Shifting conceptions of validity in educational measurement: Implications for performance assessment. *Review of Educational Research, 62 (3),* 229–258.

Moss, P. (1994a). Validity in high stakes writing assessment: Problems and possibilities. *Assessing writing, 1* (1), 109–128.

Moss, P. (1994b). Can there be validity without reliability? *Educational Research, 23* (2), 5–12.

Murphy, S. (1997). Teachers and students: Reclaiming assessment. In K. Yancey & I. Weiser (Eds.), *Situating portfolios: Four perspectives* (pp. 72–89). Logan, UT: Utah State University Press.

Murphy, S. (1999). Assessing portfolios. In C. Cooper & L. Odell (Eds.), *Evaluating writing,* (2nd ed., pp.114–136). Urbana, IL: National Council of Teachers of English.

Murphy, S., & Camp, R. (1996). Toward systemic coherence: A discussion of conflicting perspectives on portfolio assessment. In R. Calfee & P. Perfumo (Eds.), *Writing portfolios in the classroom: Policy and practice, promise and peril* (pp. 103–147). Mahwah, NJ: Lawrence Erlbaum Associates.

Murphy, S., & Smith, M. A. (1990). Talking about portfolios. *The Quarterly of the National Writing Project and the Center for the Study of Writing, 12* (2), 1–3, 24–27.

Murphy, S., & Smith, M. A. (1991). *Writing portfolios: A bridge from teaching to assessment.* Markham, Ontario, CA: Pippin Publishing Ltd.

Murphy, S., & Smith, M. A. (1992). Looking into portfolios. In K. B. Yancey (Ed.), *Portfolios in the writing classroom* (pp. 49–61). Urbana, Il: National Council of Teachers of English.

Myers, M. (1996). Sailing ships: A framework for portfolios in formative and summative systems. In R. Calfee & P. Perfumo (Eds.), *Writing portfolios in the classroom: Policy and practice, promise and peril* (pp. 149–178). Mahwah, NJ: Lawrence Erlbaum, Associates.

National Research Council (1999). *Testing, teaching, and learning: A guide for states and school districts.* Washington, DC: National Academy Press.

National Center for Fair & Open Testing (1999). *(http://www.fairtest.com).*

New Standards (1995). *New Standards portfolio field trial: Middle grades English language arts.* 1995–96 Workshop Edition. Washington, DC: National Center on Education and the Economy. Author.

Nystrand, M., Cohen, A. S., & Dowling, N. M. (1993). Addressing reliability problems in the portfolio assessment of college writing. *Educational Assessment, 1* (1), 53–70.

Paulson, F. L., Paulson, P. P., & Meyer, C. A. (1991). What makes a portfolio a portfolio? *Educational Leadership, 48* (5), 60–63.

Pearson, P. D., & Valencia, S. (1987). Assessment, accountability, and professional prerogative. *Research in literacy: merging perspectives; Thirty-Sixth yearbook of the National Reading Conference.* Rochester, New York: National Reading Conference.

Phelps, L. W. (1989). Images of student writing: The deep structure of teacher response. In C. M. Anson (Ed.), *Writing and response: Theory, practice, and research.* (pp. 37–67). Urbana, IL: National Council of Teachers of English.

Posner, G. (1992). *Analyzing the curriculum.* New York: McGraw Hill.

Resnick, L. B., & Resnick, D. P. (1992). Assessing the thinking curriculum: New tools for educational reform. In B. R. Gifford & M. C. O'Connor (Eds.), *Changing assessments: Alternative views of aptitude, achievement and instruction.* Boston: Kluwer Academic Publishers.

Rogoff, B. (1990). *Apprenticeship in thinking: Cognitive development in social context.* Oxford, England: Oxford University Press.

Salomon, G. & Perkins, D. N. (1998). Individual and social aspects of learning. In P. D. Pearson & A. Iran-Nejad, *Review of Research in Education* (Vol. 23, pp. 1–24). Washington, DC: American Educational Research Association.

Sarason, S. (1990). *The predictable failure of educational reform.* New York: Athenum Press.

Sfard, A. (1998). On two metaphors for learning and the dangers of choosing just one. *Educational Researcher, 27* (2), 4–13.

Sheingold, K., Heller, J., & Paulukonis, S. (1995) *Actively seeking evidence: Teacher change through assessment development.* (Report #94-04). Princeton, NJ: Center for Performance Assessment, Educational Testing Service.

Sizer, T. (1973). *Places for learning, places for joy: Speculations on American school reform.* Cambridge, MA: Harvard University Press.

Street, B. (1984). *Literacy in theory and practice.* New York: Cambridge University Press.

Taylor, C. (1994, Summer). Assessment for measurement or standards: The peril and promise of large-scale assessment reform. *American Educational Research Journal, 31* (2): 231–262.

Tierney, R., Carter, M., & Desai, L. (1991). *Portfolio assessment in the reading-writing classroom.* Norwood, MA: Christopher-Gordon Publishers.

Wile, J., & Tierney, R. (1996). Tensions in assessment: The battle over portfolios, curriculum, and control. In R. Calfee & P. Perfumo (Eds.),. *Writing portfolios in the classroom: Policy and practice, promise and peril* (pp. 203–215). Mahwah, NJ: Lawrence Erlbaum Associates.

Wolf, D. P. (1989). Portfolio assessment: Sampling student work. *Educational Leadership, 46,* 35–39.

Yancey, K. B. (Ed.). (1992). Portfolios in the writing classroom. Urbana, Il: National Council of Teachers of English.

Zessoules, R., & Gardner, H. (1991). Authentic assessment: Beyond the buzzword and into the classroom. In V. Perrone (Ed.), *Expanding student assessment* (pp. 47–71). Alexandria, VA: Association of Supervision and Curriculum Development.

Author Index

Subject Index

About the Authors

Sandra Murphy is a Professor in the Division of Education at the University of California, Davis. She received her Ph.D. in Language and Literacy from the University of California, Berkeley. She teaches graduate-level courses on research on reading and writing and has taught high school English and freshman composition at the college level. She co-authored *Designing Writing Tasks for the Assessment of Writing* (with Leo Ruth) and *Writing Portfolios: A Bridge from Teaching to Assessment* (with Mary Ann Smith) and has written several articles on the acquisition of literacy and the assessment of writing. Areas of special interest include writing assessment, reading comprehension, critical perspectives on literacy, and oral and written language differences.

Terry Underwood is an assistant professor in the Language and Literacy program at California State University, Sacramento, where he teaches courses in secondary literacy, comprehension and composition instruction, and assessment. He has published several articles on the relationship between assessment and instruction in journals as well as a book titled The Portfolio Project: Assessment, Instruction, and Middle School Reform (NCTE).

He lives in Roseville, California, with his wife, Joanne, and their daughter, Karen.